# C# 6 and .NET Core 1.0

## Modern Cross-Platform Development

Create powerful cross-platform applications using C# 6, .NET Core 1.0, ASP.NET Core 1.0, and Visual Studio 2015

**Mark J. Price**

BIRMINGHAM - MUMBAI

# C# 6 and .NET Core 1.0

First published: March 2016

Production reference: 1180316

Published by Packt Publishing Ltd.
Livery Place
35 Livery Street
Birmingham B3 2PB, UK.

ISBN 978-1-78528-569-1

www.packtpub.com

# Credits

**Author**
Mark J. Price

**Reviewers**
Dustin Heffron

Liviu Ignat

Efraim Kyriakidis

**Commissioning Editor**
Edward Gordon

**Acquisition Editor**
Kirk D'Costa

**Content Development Editor**
Pooja Mhapsekar

**Technical Editor**
Vivek Pala

**Copy Editor**
Pranjali Chury

**Project Coordinator**
Francina Pinto

**Proofreader**
Safis Editing

**Indexer**
Tejal Soni

**Production Coordinator**
Aparna Bhagat

**Cover Work**
Aparna Bhagat

# About the Author

**Mark J. Price** is a Microsoft Certified Trainer (MCT) and Microsoft Specialist, Programming in C# and Architecting Microsoft Azure Solutions, with more than 20 years of educational and programming experience.

| **Microsoft** | **Microsoft** | **Microsoft** |
|---|---|---|
| **C E R T I F I E D** | Specialist | Specialist |
| Trainer | Programming in C# | Architecting Microsoft Azure Solutions |

Since 1993, Mark has passed more than 90 Microsoft programming exams and specializes in preparing others to pass them too. His students range from professionals with decades of experience to 16-year-old apprentices with no experience at all. He successfully guides all of them by combining educational skills with real-world experience, consulting on and developing systems for enterprises worldwide.

Between 2001 and 2003, Mark was employed full-time to write official courseware for Microsoft in Redmond, USA. His team wrote the first training courses for C# and .NET while they were still an early alpha version. While with Microsoft, he delivered "train-the-trainer" classes to get other MCTs up to speed in C# and .NET.

In 2010, Mark took a postgraduate certificate in education (PGCE). He taught GCSE and A-level mathematics in two secondary schools in London. Mark holds a Computer Science BSc (Hons) degree from the University of Bristol, UK.

I'd like to thank my parents, Pamela and Ian, for raising me to be polite, hardworking, and curious about the world. I'm grateful to my sisters, Emily and Juliet, for loving me despite being their awkward older brother. I'd also like to express my gratitude to my friends and colleagues who inspire me technically and creatively. Lastly, thanks to all the students I have taught over the years for making me strive to be a better teacher, especially Jared.

# About the Reviewers

**Dustin Heffron** is a software engineer by day and an independent game developer by night. He has over 10 years of experience programming in various languages and 7 years of experience working with C# and .NET.

Currently, Dustin works as a software engineer for Johnson Controls Inc. He is also the cofounder and CEO of SunFlake Studios, which was founded in late 2015. He released his first commercial game, *Squash Master*, in early 2016 and is planning to develop additional games in the coming months and years.

Dustin has a long history of reviewing for Packt Publishing, including the book *XNA 4.0 Game Development by Example: Beginner's Guide* and the video tutorial series *XNA 3D Programming by Example*. He also coauthored the video tutorial series *XNA 3D Toolkit* with Larry Louisiana.

**Liviu Ignat** is a full-stack developer and architect, technology geek, and entrepreneur, who has been writing commercial software since 2004. He started with VB6, soon moved to .NET Java, and then continued by moving to front-end web development. He has fun with everything that is a functional language, such as F#, Scala, Swift, JavaScript, and so on.

Currently, he is a senior software engineer at AppDirect (`http://appdirect.com`), Munich, and he is also the CTO of his own startup (`http://giftdoodle.com`). He has been involved in building distributed backend services, mostly with .NET and complex single-page web apps. He is a big fan of microservices with C#, NodeJS, Scala, and Docker, single-page apps, and native apps with Android and IOS.

When he is not coding, Liviu loves snowboarding during the winter, sailing to exotic places during the summer, or just traveling the world. You can find and contact him at `http://ignat.email/`.

**Efraim Kyriakidis** is a skilled software engineer with over 10 years of experience in developing and delivering software solutions for diverse customers and projects. He's well-versed in all stages of the software development lifecycle. His first acquaintance with computers and programming was a state of the art Commodore 64, back in the '80s as a kid. Since then, he has grown up and received his diploma as Electro technic engineer from Aristotle University Thessaloniki in Greece. Through out his career he has mainly worked with Microsoft technologies, using C# and .NET since .NET 1.0. He currently works for Siemens AG in Germany as a software developer.

# www.PacktPub.com

## eBooks, discount offers, and more

Did you know that Packt offers eBook versions of every book published, with PDF and ePub files available? You can upgrade to the eBook version at www.PacktPub.com and as a print book customer, you are entitled to a discount on the eBook copy. Get in touch with us at customercare@packtpub.com for more details.

At www.PacktPub.com, you can also read a collection of free technical articles, sign up for a range of free newsletters and receive exclusive discounts and offers on Packt books and eBooks.

https://www2.packtpub.com/books/subscription/packtlib

Do you need instant solutions to your IT questions? PacktLib is Packt's online digital book library. Here, you can search, access, and read Packt's entire library of books.

## Why subscribe?

- Fully searchable across every book published by Packt
- Copy and paste, print, and bookmark content
- On demand and accessible via a web browser

# Table of Contents

# Preface

There are many C# books, some, more than a thousand pages long, that aim to be comprehensive references to the C# programming language and the .NET Framework.

This book is different—it is concise and aims to be a fast-paced read that is packed with hands-on walkthroughs. I wrote this book to be the best step-by-step guide to modern cross-platform C# and .NET proven practices.

I will point out the cool corners and gotchas of C# so you can impress colleagues and employers and quickly get productive. Rather than slowing down and boring some of you by explaining every little thing, I assume that if a term I use is new to you, then you know how to Google it with a search engine such as DuckDuckGo.

At the end of each chapter, there is a section entitled *Practicing and Exploring*, which contains questions to test your knowledge, and usually a hands-on practical exercise, and you will explore topics in depth on your own with a little nudge in the right direction from me.

You can download solutions for the exercises from the GitHub repository at `https://github.com/markjprice/cs6dotnetcore`. I will provide instructions on how to do this using Visual Studio 2015 at the end of *Chapter 1, Hello C#!, Welcome .NET Core!*.

## What this book covers

*Chapter 1, Hello C#!, Welcome .NET Core!*, is about setting up your development environment and using various tools to create the simplest application possible with C#. You will learn how to compile C# code at the Command Prompt and how to write and compile code using Visual Studio. You will also learn about the different .NET platforms: .NET Framework, .NET Core, and .NET Native.

*Chapter 2, Speaking C#*, is about the C# language, the grammar and vocabulary that you will use every day to write the source code for your applications. In particular, you will learn how to declare and work with variables of different types.

*Chapter 3, Controlling the Flow, Converting Types, and Handling Exceptions*, is about writing code that makes decisions, repeats blocks of statements, converts between types, and handles errors. You will also learn the best places to look for help.

*Chapter 4, Using Common .NET Types*, is about how .NET types are related to C#. You will learn about .NET Framework, .NET Core, and their class library assemblies of types that allow your applications to connect together existing components to perform common practical tasks.

*Chapter 5, Using Specialized .NET Types*, is about .NET types used to diagnose problems, support multiple languages and cultures, and access features and applications outside of .NET.

*Chapter 6, Building Your Own Types with Object-Oriented Programming*, is about all the different categories of members that a type can have, including fields for storing data and methods for performing actions. You will use OOP concepts such as aggregation and encapsulation.

*Chapter 7, Implementing Interfaces and Inheriting Classes*, is about deriving new types from existing ones using OOP. You will learn how to implement interfaces, about base and derived classes, how to override a type member, how to use polymorphism, and how to cast between classes in an inheritance hierarchy.

*Chapter 8, Working with Relational Data Using the Entity Framework*, is about reading and writing to Microsoft SQL Server (and other databases) using classic ADO.NET and the object-relational mapping technology known as Entity Framework.

*Chapter 9, Querying and Manipulating Data with LINQ*, is about Language Integrated Queries (LINQ) — language extensions that add the ability to work with sequences of items, and filter, sort, and project them into different outputs.

*Chapter 10, Working with Files, Streams, and Serialization*, is about reading and writing to files and streams, text encoding, and serialization.

*Chapter 11, Protecting Your Data and Applications*, is about protecting your data using encryption and hashing, and checking who is running your application and what they are allowed to do.

*Chapter 12, Improving Performance and Scalability with Multitasking*, is about allowing multiple actions to be executed at the same time to improve performance, scalability, and user productivity.

*Chapter 13, Building Universal Windows Platform Apps Using XAML,* is about learning the basics of XAML, which can be used to define the user interface for a graphical app for the Universal Windows Platform (UWP). This app can then run on Windows 10, Windows 10 Mobile, Xbox One, and even HoloLens.

*Chapter 14, Building Web Applications and Services Using ASP.NET Core,* is about building web applications and services using a modern HTTP architecture on the server side using Microsoft ASP.NET Core 1.0. You will learn about the models, views, and controllers that make up MVC and the Web API.

*Chapter 15, Taking C# Cross-Platform,* is about introducing you to how you can take C# cross-platform using .NET Core, ASP.NET Core 1.0, Entity Framework Core 1.0, and Visual Studio Code.

*Chapter 16, Building a Quiz,* is about designing and building a quiz application that helps students learn C#, .NET Core, and related topics.

*Appendix A, Answers to the Test Your Knowledge Questions,* has the answers to the test questions at the end of each chapter.

*Appendix B, Creating a Virtual Machine for Your Development Environment,* shows how to set up a virtual machine in Microsoft Azure for use as a development environment.

# What you need for this book

Although you can develop and deploy C# on many platforms, including Mac OS X and Linux, for the best learning experience, you need two pieces of software:

- Microsoft Windows 10
- Microsoft Visual Studio Community 2015 with Update 1 (or later)

The best version of Windows to use is Microsoft Windows 10 because you need this version to create Universal Windows Platform apps in *Chapter 13, Building Universal Windows Platform Apps Using XAML.* Earlier versions of Windows, such as 7 or 8.1, will work for all other chapters. If you don't have a Windows computer, then you can use a virtual machine running Windows in the cloud. Refer to *Appendix B, Creating a Virtual Machine for Your Development Environment* for instructions.

The best version of Visual Studio to use is Microsoft Visual Studio Community 2015 with Update 1 (or later), which is the version I used while writing this book. In *Chapter 15, Taking C# Cross-Platform,* I will introduce you to Visual Studio Code, which runs on Windows, Linux, and Mac OS X, and can create cross-platform applications for all these OSes.

# Who this book is for

If you have heard that C# is a popular general-purpose, cross-platform programming language used to create everything from business applications, websites, and services to games for mobile devices, Xbox One, and the Windows 10 desktop-to-tablet-to-phone platform, then this book is for you.

# Conventions

In this book, you will find a number of text styles that distinguish between different kinds of information. Here are some examples of these styles and an explanation of their meaning.

Code words in text, database table names, folder names, filenames, file extensions, pathnames, dummy URLs, user input, and Twitter handles are shown as follows: " The code you will write will be stored in the file named `Program.cs`."

A block of code is set as follows:

```
// the best nieces and nephews in the world
names[0] = "Kate";
names[1] = "Jack";
names[2] = "Rebecca";
names[3] = "Tom";
```

When we wish to draw your attention to a particular part of a code block, the relevant lines or items are set in bold:

```
// the best nieces and nephews in the world
names[0] = "Kate";
names[1] = "Jack";
names[2] = "Rebecca";
names[3] = "Tom";
```

Any command-line input or output is written as follows:

```
csc my.cs /target:library
```

**New terms** and **important words** are shown in bold. Words that you see on the screen, for example, in menus or dialog boxes, appear in the text like this: "In Visual Studio, from the **View** menu, choose **Other Windows**, and then **C# Interactive**."

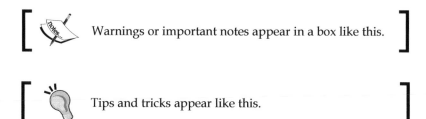

Warnings or important notes appear in a box like this.

Tips and tricks appear like this.

# Reader feedback

Feedback from our readers is always welcome. Let us know what you think about this book—what you liked or disliked. Reader feedback is important for us as it helps us develop titles that you will really get the most out of.

To send us general feedback, simply e-mail feedback@packtpub.com, and mention the book's title in the subject of your message.

If there is a topic that you have expertise in and you are interested in either writing or contributing to a book, see our author guide at www.packtpub.com/authors.

# Customer support

Now that you are the proud owner of a Packt book, we have a number of things to help you to get the most from your purchase.

# Downloading the example code

You can download the example code files for this book from your account at http://www.packtpub.com. If you purchased this book elsewhere, you can visit http://www.packtpub.com/support and register to have the files e-mailed directly to you.

You can download the code files by following these steps:

1. Log in or register to our website using your e-mail address and password.
2. Hover the mouse pointer on the **SUPPORT** tab at the top.
3. Click on **Code Downloads & Errata**.
4. Enter the name of the book in the **Search** box.
5. Select the book for which you're looking to download the code files.
6. Choose from the drop-down menu where you purchased this book from.
7. Click on **Code Download**.

Once the file is downloaded, please make sure that you unzip or extract the folder using the latest version of:

- WinRAR / 7-Zip for Windows
- Zipeg / iZip / UnRarX for Mac
- 7-Zip / PeaZip for Linux

# Errata

Although we have taken every care to ensure the accuracy of our content, mistakes do happen. If you find a mistake in one of our books—maybe a mistake in the text or the code—we would be grateful if you could report this to us. By doing so, you can save other readers from frustration and help us improve subsequent versions of this book. If you find any errata, please report them by visiting http://www.packtpub.com/submit-errata, selecting your book, clicking on the **Errata Submission Form** link, and entering the details of your errata. Once your errata are verified, your submission will be accepted and the errata will be uploaded to our website or added to any list of existing errata under the Errata section of that title.

To view the previously submitted errata, go to https://www.packtpub.com/books/content/support and enter the name of the book in the search field. The required information will appear under the **Errata** section.

# Piracy

Piracy of copyrighted material on the Internet is an ongoing problem across all media. At Packt, we take the protection of our copyright and licenses very seriously. If you come across any illegal copies of our works in any form on the Internet, please provide us with the location address or website name immediately so that we can pursue a remedy.

Please contact us at copyright@packtpub.com with a link to the suspected pirated material.

We appreciate your help in protecting our authors and our ability to bring you valuable content.

# Questions

If you have a problem with any aspect of this book, you can contact us at questions@packtpub.com, and we will do our best to address the problem.

# 1
# Hello, C#! Welcome, .NET Core!

This chapter is about setting up your development environment, understanding the similarities and differences between .NET Core, .NET Framework, and .NET Native, and using various tools to create the simplest application possible with C#.

Most people learn complex topics by imitation and repetition rather than reading a detailed explanation of theory. So, I will not explain every keyword and step. The idea is to get you to write some code, build an application, and see it run. You don't need to know the details of how it all works yet.

In the words of Samuel Johnson, author of the English dictionary of 1755, I have likely committed "a few wild blunders, and risible absurdities, from which no work of such multiplicity is free." I take sole responsibility for these and hope you appreciate the challenge of my attempt to "lash the wind" by writing this book about .NET Core 1.0 during its rocky birth in the early months of 2016.

This chapter covers the following topics:

- Setting up your development environment
- Understanding the .NET Framework, .NET Core, and .NET Native
- Writing and compiling code by using the Developer Command Prompt
- Writing and compiling code by using Microsoft Visual Studio 2015
- Targeting the .NET Core
- Managing source code with GitHub

# Setting up your development environment

Before you start programming, you will need to set up your **Interactive Development Environment** (IDE) that includes a code editor for C#. The best IDE to choose is Microsoft Visual Studio 2015, but it only runs on the Windows operating system.

## Using alternative C# IDEs

There are alternative IDEs for C#, for example, **MonoDevelop**, **JetBrains Project Rider**, and **Microsoft Visual Studio Code**. They each have versions available for Windows, Linux, and Mac OS X, allowing you to write code on one operating system and deploy to the same, or a different, one:

- For MonoDevelop IDE, visit `http://www.monodevelop.com/`
- For JetBrains Project Rider, visit `http://blog.jetbrains.com/dotnet/2016/01/13/project-rider-a-csharp-ide/`
- For Microsoft Visual Studio Code, visit `https://code.visualstudio.com/`

**Cloud9** is a web browser-based IDE, so it's even more cross-platform than the others. here is the link:

`https://c9.io/web/sign-up/free`

In *Chapter 15*, *Taking C# Cross-Platform*, I will show you how to use Visual Studio Code running on Mac OS X to create an ASP.NET Core 1.0 web application that can be deployed to Windows, Mac OS X, or Linux operating systems, or to Docker containers.

 Linux and Docker are popular server host platforms because they are relatively lightweight and more cost-effectively scalable when compared to operating system platforms that are designed for end users, such as Windows and Mac OS X.

# Using Visual Studio 2015 on Windows 10

You can use Windows 7 or later to complete most of the chapters in this book, but you will have a better experience if you use Windows 10.

> If you don't have Windows, I recommend that you create a virtual machine (VM) to use for development. You can choose any cloud provider, but Microsoft Azure has preconfigured VMs that include properly licensed Windows and Visual Studio 2015. You only pay for the minutes your VM is running, so it is a way for users of Linux, Mac OS X, and older Windows versions to have all the benefits of using Visual Studio 2015. Refer to *Appendix B, Creating a Virtual Machine for Your Development Environment* for more information.

Since October 2014, Microsoft has made a professional-quality edition of Visual Studio available to everyone for free. It is called the **Community Edition**.

> Microsoft has combined all its free developer offerings in a program called **Visual Studio Dev Essentials**. This includes the Community Edition, the free level of Visual Studio Team Services, Azure credits for test and development, and free training from Pluralsight, Wintellect, and Xamarin.

# Installing Microsoft Visual Studio 2015

Download and install **Microsoft Visual Studio Community 2015 with Update 1** or higher.

# Choosing the default installation

If you prefer a smaller, faster installation then choose **Default** because it only requires 8 GB and should complete the installation in about an hour. With this choice, as shown in the following screenshot, you will be able to complete the first two-thirds of this book. To complete the rest of the book, you can later add additional features, such as support for building Universal Windows Platform (UWP) apps, via **Programs and Features** in the **Control Panel**:

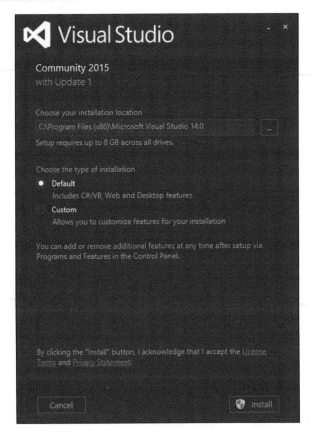

If you chose **Default**, then skip to the **Completing the Installation** section.

# Choosing the custom installation

If you have 34 GB of free disk space and can wait for several hours, then in the installation dialog, choose **Custom**, and then click on **Next**. Select the following features:

- Under **Windows and Web Development**, tick the following checkboxes:
  - **Microsoft SQL Server Data Tools**

- ° **Microsoft Web Developer Tools**
- ° **Universal Windows App Development Tools**

- Under **Cross Platform Mobile Development**, tick the following checkbox:
  - ° **C#/.NET (Xamarin)**

- Under **Common Tools**, tick the following checkboxes:
  - ° **Git for Windows**
  - ° **GitHub Extension for Visual Studio**

Click on **Next**:

 If you have the Home edition of Windows 10, then you will not be able to install emulators for Windows Phone because they require Hyper-V support.

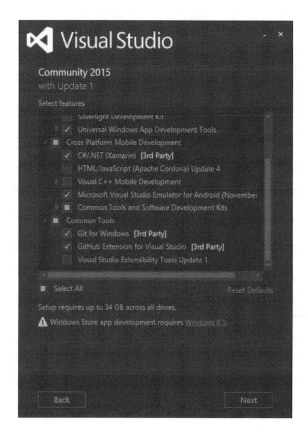

You can choose to install everything if you want support for languages such as C++, Python, and F#, but these will not be covered in this book.

## Completing the installation

On the license terms dialog, click on **Install**. Wait for the files to download and install.

 While you wait for Visual Studio to install, you can jump to the *Understanding .NET Framework, .NET Core, and .NET Native* section in this chapter.

## Signing in to Visual Studio

The first time that you run Visual Studio, you will be prompted to sign in:

If you have a Microsoft account, for example, a Hotmail, MSN, Live, or Outlook e-mail address, you can use that account. If you don't, then register for a new one at the following link:

```
https://signup.live.com/
```

# Choosing development settings

After signing in, you will be prompted to choose **Development Settings**. Choose **Visual C#** to configure keyboard shortcuts and a default window layout that works best for C# programmers, as shown in the following screenshot:

After you click on **Start Visual Studio**, you will see the Visual Studio user interface with the **Start Page** open in the central area. Like most Windows desktop applications, Visual Studio has a menu bar, a toolbar for common commands, and a status bar at the bottom. On the right is the **Solution Explorer** window that will list all of your open projects, as shown in the following screenshot:

To have quick access to Visual Studio in the future, right-click on its entry in the Windows taskbar and select **Pin this program to taskbar**:

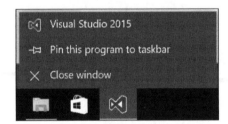

# Updating extensions and products

In the top-right corner of Visual Studio, you will see a flag that has a number next to it. These are notifications of extensions and product updates.

Click on the flag to display the **Notifications** window, as shown in the following screenshot:

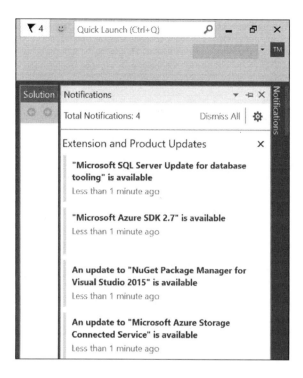

In the **Notifications** window, click on each entry to install the update. You can install these updates at a later time if you prefer, but it is best to keep your software up-to-date to avoid bugs and security holes. The following screenshot shows an extension downloading and installing:

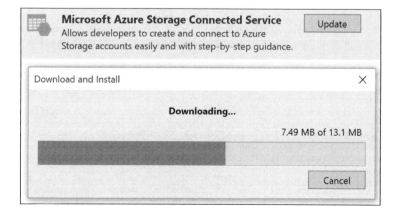

# Using older versions of Visual Studio

If you want to use a free version of Visual Studio older than 2015, then you can use one of the more limited Express editions. A lot of the code in this book will work with older versions if you bear in mind when the following features were introduced:

| Year | C# | Features |
|------|-----|----------|
| 2005 | 2 | Generics with `<T>` |
| 2008 | 3 | Lambda expressions with `=>` and manipulating sequences with LINQ (`from`, `in`, `where`, `orderby`, `ascending`, `descending`, `select`, `group`, `into`) |
| 2010 | 4 | Dynamic typing with `dynamic` and multithreading with `Task` |
| 2012 | 5 | Simplifying multithreading with `async` and `await` |
| 2015 | 6 | `string` interpolation with `$""`, importing static types with `using static`, and other refinements. |

# Understanding .NET Framework, .NET Core, and .NET Native

.NET Framework, .NET Core, and .NET Native are related platforms for developers to build applications and services upon.

# Understanding .NET Framework platform

Microsoft's .NET Framework is a development platform that includes a Common Language Runtime (CLR) that manages the execution of code and a rich library of classes for building applications.

Microsoft designed the .NET Framework to have the possibility of being cross-platform, but Microsoft put their implementation effort into making it work best with Windows.

Practically speaking, the .NET Framework is Windows-only.

# Understanding the Mono project

The open source community developed a cross-platform .NET implementation named the Mono project (`http://www.mono-project.com/`).

**Mono** is cross-platform, but it fell well behind Microsoft's implementation of .NET Framework. It has found a niche as the foundation of the **Xamarin** mobile platform.

# Understanding the .NET Core platform

Today, we live in a truly cross-platform world. Modern mobile and cloud development have made Windows a much less important operating system. So, Microsoft has been working on an effort to decouple the .NET Framework from its close ties with Windows.

While rewriting .NET to be truly cross-platform, Microsoft has taken the opportunity to refactor .NET, to remove major parts that are no longer considered "core".

This new product is branded as the .NET Core 1.0, which includes a cross-platform implementation of the CLR, known as **CoreCLR**, and a streamlined library of classes known as **CoreFX**.

# Streamlining .NET

.NET Core 1.0 is much smaller than the current version of the .NET Framework because a *lot* has been removed.

For example, Windows Forms and Windows Presentation Foundation (WPF) can be used to build graphical user interface (GUI) applications, but they are tightly-bound to Windows, so they have been removed from the .NET Core. The latest technology for building Windows apps is the Universal Windows Platform (UWP). You will learn about it in *Chapter 13, Building Universal Windows Platform Apps Using XAML.*

ASP.NET Web Forms and Windows Communication Foundation (WCF) are old web applications and service technologies that fewer developers choose to use today, so they have also been removed from the .NET Core. Instead, developers prefer to use ASP.NET MVC and ASP.NET Web API. These two technologies have been refactored and combined into a new product that runs on the .NET Core, named ASP.NET Core 1.0. You will learn about it in *Chapter 14, Building Web Applications and Services Using ASP.NET Core.*

The Entity Framework (EF) 6.x is an object-relational mapping technology for working with data stored in relational databases, such as Oracle and Microsoft SQL Server. It has gained baggage over the years, so the cross-platform version has been slimmed down and named Entity Framework Core 1.0. You will learn about it in *Chapter 8, Working with Relational Data Using the Entity Framework.*

Some data types in .NET that are included with both the .NET Framework and the .NET Core have been simplified by removing some members. For example, in the .NET Framework, the `File` class has both a `Close` and `Dispose` method, and either can be used to release the file resources. In .NET Core, there is only the `Dispose` method. This reduces the memory footprint of the assembly and simplifies the API.

The .NET Framework 4.6 is about 200 MB. The .NET Core 1.0 is about 11 MB. Eventually, the .NET Core may grow to a similar larger size. Microsoft's goal is not to make the .NET Core smaller than the .NET Framework. The goal is to componentize .NET Core to support modern technologies and to have fewer dependencies so that deployment requires only those components that your application really needs.

# The future of .NET

The .NET Core is the future of .NET, but in my opinion, we are not there yet. .NET Core 1.0 is a great start, but it will take another version or two to become as mature as the current version of the .NET Framework.

This book will focus features available in .NET Core, but will use the .NET Framework when features have not (yet) been implemented in the .NET Core.

One of the reasons we picked this cover image for this book is that you can think of .NET Core as a new dawn for .NET. The .NET Framework has become overgrown, like a dense forest, and the .NET Core is like finding a clearing or glade within it. It's a fresh start.

# Understanding the .NET Native platform

Another .NET initiative is .NET Native which compiles C# code to native CPU instructions ahead-of-time (AoT) rather than using the CLR to compile IL just-in-time (JIT) to native code later.

The .NET Native compiler improves execution speed and reduces the memory footprint for applications. It supports the following:

- UWP apps for Windows 10, Windows 10 Mobile, Xbox One, HoloLens, and Internet of Things (IoT) devices such as Raspberry Pi

- Server-side web development with ASP.NET Core 1.0

- Console applications for use on the command line

## Comparing .NET technologies

The following table summarizes and compares Microsoft's three .NET technologies:

| Platform | Feature set | C# compiles to | Host OSes |
|---|---|---|---|
| .NET Framework | Mature and extensive | Intermediate Language (IL) code | Windows only |
| .NET Core | Brand-new and somewhat limited | | Windows, Linux, Mac OS X, Docker |
| .NET Native | Brand-new and very limited | Native code | |

# Writing and compiling code using the Developer Command Prompt

When you install Visual Studio, other tools are installed too. One of those tools is the **Developer Command Prompt for VS2015** that has its path set to find developer tools such as the C# compiler.

# Writing code using Notepad

Start Notepad (or your favorite text editor) and enter the following code:

```
class Program { static void Main() { System.Console.
WriteLine("Hello C#!"); } }
```

You can type the code all on one line or spread it out over multiple lines and indent your lines to make it easier to read.

C# is case sensitive, meaning that you must type uppercase and lowercase characters exactly as shown in the preceding code. C# is not whitespace sensitive, meaning that it does not care if you use tabs and spaces and carriage-returns to lay out your code however you like.

From the **File** menu, choose **Save As**.

In the dialog box, change to drive C: (or any drive that you want to use to save your projects), click on the **New Folder** button, and name the folder Code.

In the **Save as type** field, select **All Files** from the drop-down list to avoid appending the .txt file extension, and enter the file name as myfirstapp.cs, as shown in the following screenshot:

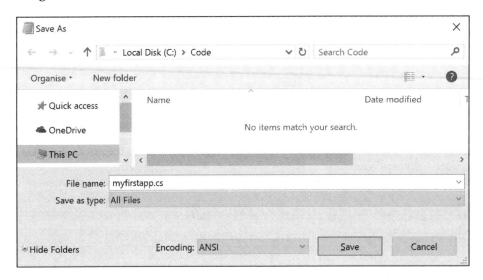

Your code in Notepad should look something like the following screenshot:

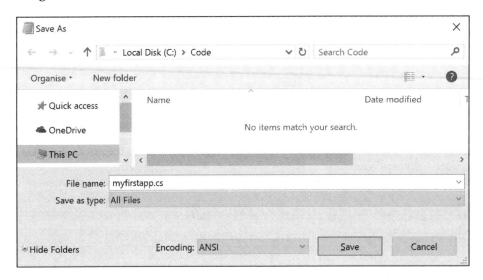

# Compiling code using the Developer Command Prompt

Start the Developer Command Prompt for VS2015 by typing the letters **deve** in the Windows 10 **Search** box, as you can see in the following screenshot. You will also find it on the **Start Menu** or **Start Screen** listed in **All apps** in the **Visual Studio 2015** folder:

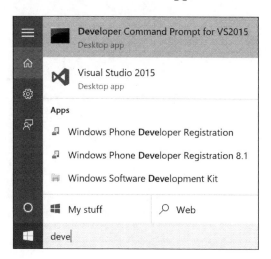

At the Command Prompt, enter the commands to do the following:

- Change to the C:\Code folder
- Compile the source code using the C# compiler
- Request a directory listing
- Run the application by entering the name of the EXE

Here are the commands:

```
cd C:\Code
csc myfirstapp.cs
dir
myfirstapp
```

The output in the Command Prompt window should look like this:

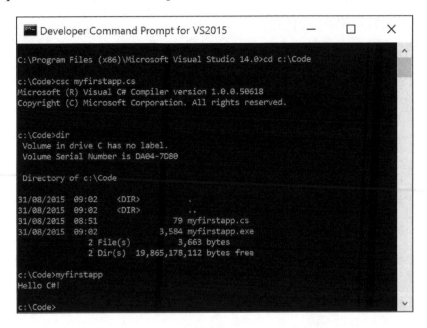

Note that your source code, the file named `myfirstapp.cs`, has been compiled into an assembly named `myfirstapp.exe`. When you enter the name of the assembly, it is loaded and executed by .NET Framework 4.6 and its CLR.

You can copy the `myfirstapp.exe` file onto any computer with Windows 10 and it will run correctly because all copies of Windows 10 have .NET Framework 4.6 installed. Actually, you can copy the file onto a computer with an older version of Windows as long as it has .NET Framework 4.0 or later installed.

# Fixing compiler errors

If the compiler displays errors, read them carefully, and fix them in Notepad. Save your changes and recompile.

At the Command Prompt, you can press the up and down arrows on your keyboard to cycle through previous commands you have entered.

A typical error might be using the wrong case, a missing semi-colon at the end of a line, or a mismatched pair of curly braces. For example, if you had mistyped a lowercase m for the `Main` method you would see this error message:

```
error CS5001: Program does not contain a static 'Main' method suitable
for an entry point
```

# Decompiling code using ILDASM

The C# compiler converts your source code into Intermediate Language (IL) code and stores the IL in an assembly (a DLL or EXE file).

IL code statements are like assembly language instructions, but they are executed by the .NET virtual machine known as the Common Language Runtime (CLR).

At runtime, the CLR loads the IL code from the assembly, JIT compiles it into native CPU instructions, and then it is executed by the CPU on your machine.

The benefit of this two-step compilation process is that Microsoft can create CLRs for Linux and Mac OS X as well as for Windows. The same IL code runs everywhere because of the second compilation process that generates code for the native operating system and CPU instruction set.

Regardless of which language the source is written in, all .NET applications use IL code for their instructions, stored in an assembly. Microsoft provides a tool that can open an assembly and reveal this IL code.

Actually, not all .NET applications use IL code! Some use the new .NET Native compiler to generate native code instead of IL code, improving performance and reducing memory footprint, but at the cost of portability.

# Disassembling compiled assemblies

Disassembling a compiled assembly is an advanced technique. I will walk you through the process, but do not worry about fully understanding what you are seeing yet!

Start the IL Disassembler by entering the following at the Developer Command Prompt:

```
ildasm myfirstapp.exe
```

You will see the **IL DASM** tool with the compiled EXE assembly loaded:

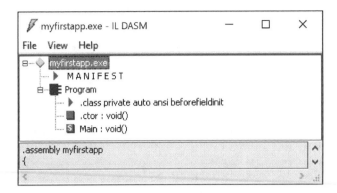

Double-click on **MANIFEST** in the tree view to show the metadata version (4.0.30319) of .NET and the **Microsoft Core Library** (mscorlib) assembly version (4.0.0.0) that this assembly needs to run. The following screenshot tells us that to run this assembly, we would need .NET Framework 4.0 or later installed:

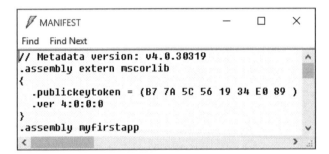

Close the MANIFEST window, expand **Program**, and then double-click on the **Main** method. Note the IL instructions: ldstr (load string), nop (no operation), and ret (return). Remember that IL is an assembly language that is executed by the .NET CLR:

```
.method private hidebysig static void  Main() cil managed
{
  .entrypoint
  // Code size       13 (0xd)
  .maxstack  8
  IL_0000:  nop
  IL_0001:  ldstr      "Hello C#!"
  IL_0006:  call       void [mscorlib]System.Console::WriteLine(string)
  IL_000b:  nop
  IL_000c:  ret
} // end of method Program::Main
```

Anyone can use this tool to see any .NET assembly's IL code. Don't panic! This is not a reason to avoid C#.

All applications are lists of instructions that must be visible to the machine that runs it. If the machine can read these instructions, so can anything else. Therefore, all software can be reverse-engineered. It's just a matter of the effort required. .NET just happens to make it *very* easy!

**ILSpy** is a popular open source tool that does everything IL DASM does and can also reverse-engineer the IL code into C# or Visual Basic .NET source code. I used this tool for a client who had lost the source code for an assembly and needed to recover it!

# Writing and compiling code using Microsoft Visual Studio 2015

We will now recreate the same application using Microsoft Visual Studio 2015.

I have been training students to use Visual Studio for over a decade, and I am always surprised at how many programmers fail to use the tool to their advantage.

Over the next few pages, I will slowly walk you through typing a line of code. It may seem redundant, but you will benefit from seeing what help and information Visual Studio provides as you enter your code. If you want to become a fast, accurate coder, letting Visual Studio write most of your code for you is a huge benefit!

## Writing code using Visual Studio 2015

Start Microsoft Visual Studio 2015.

Navigate to **File** | **New** | **Project** menu or press *Ctrl + Shift + N*.

At the top of the **New Project** dialog box, choose **.NET Framework 4.6.1** (or later). From the **Installed Templates** list on the left, choose **Visual C#**. In the list at the center, choose **Console Application**. Enter the name **Ch01_MyFirstApp**, set the location to C:\Code, enter **Chapter01** as the solution name, and click on **OK** or press *Enter*:

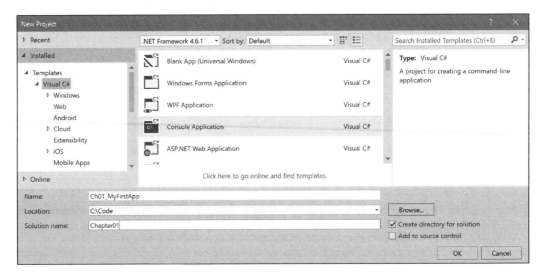

In the code editor, inside the Main method, press *Enter* to insert a new line between the innermost braces { }, and then type the letters sy, as you can see in the following screenshot:

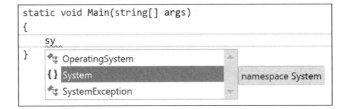

Note that IntelliSense shows a list of **keywords**, **namespaces**, and **types** that contain the letters sy, and highlights the first one that starts with sy, which happens to be the namespace that we want—System.

Type a dot (also known as decimal point or full stop). IntelliSense automatically completes the word **System** for you, enters the dot, and displays a list of types and namespaces, such as AccessViolationException and Action, in the System namespace, as shown in the following screenshot:

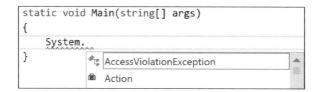

Type the letters con and IntelliSense shows a list of matching types and namespaces:

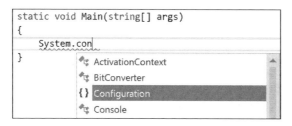

Press the down arrow on your keyboard to highlight **Console**, and then type a dot.

IntelliSense shows a list of the members of the Console class:

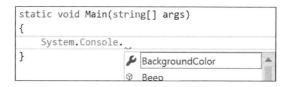

Members include properties (attributes of an object, such as BackgroundColor), methods (actions the object can perform, such as Beep), and other related things.

Type the letters wr. IntelliSense shows two matching members containing these letters:

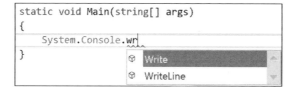

Use the down arrow to highlight **WriteLine** and then type an open parenthesis (.

IntelliSense autocompletes WriteLine and enters a pair of parentheses.

You will also see a tooltip telling you that the `WriteLine` method has 19 variations:

```
static void Main(string[] args)
{
    System.Console.WriteLine()
}       ▲ 1 of 19 ▼ void Console.WriteLine()
            Writes the current line terminator to the standard output stream.
```

Type a double quote (`"`). IntelliSense enters a pair of double quotes for you and leaves the keyboard cursor in between them.

Type the text `Hello C#!`, as shown in the following screenshot:

```
static void Main(string[] args)
{
    System.Console.WriteLine("Hello C#!")
}
```

The red squiggle at the end of the line indicates an error, because every C# statement must end in a semicolon. Move the cursor to the end of the line by pressing End, and type a semicolon to fix the error.

# Compiling code using Visual Studio

From the **Debug** menu, choose **Start Without Debugging** or press *Ctrl* + *F5*. Your completed application runs in a console window and closes when you press any key:

To save space and to make the output clearer, I will usually not include screenshots of output from console applications as I did previously. Instead, I will show the output like this:

```
Hello C#!
```

# Fixing mistakes with the error list

Let's make two deliberate errors.

Change the M of the Main method to the lowercase letter m.

Delete the e at the end of the method name WriteLine.

On the **Build** menu, choose **Build Ch01_MyFirstApp** or press *Shift + F6*.

After a few seconds, the status bar tells us that the build failed and the error list is activated. You can also view the error list by pressing *Ctrl + W, E*:

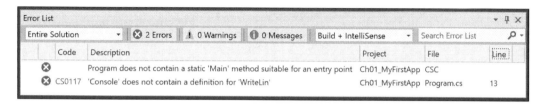

The **Error List** can be filtered to show **Errors**, **Warnings**, and informational **Messages** by clicking on the toggle buttons at the top of the window.

If an error shows the line number, for example Line 13 in the preceding screenshot, then you can double-click on the error to jump to the line causing the problem.

If it's a more general error, such as the missing Main method, the compiler can't tell you the line number. You might want a method named main as well as a method named Main (remember that C# is case sensitive so you're allowed to do that).

Fix the two (as shown in the preceding screenshot) errors before you continue. Note that the error list updates to show no errors.

# Experimenting with C# Interactive

Although Visual Studio has always had an **Immediate** window with limited **REPL (read-eval-print loop)** support, Visual Studio 2015 with Update 1 includes an enhanced window with full IntelliSense and color syntax code, named C# Interactive.

On the **View** menu, choose **Other Windows**, and then **C# Interactive**.

We will write some interactive code to download the About page from Microsoft's public website.

This is just an example. You don't need to understand the code yet!

At the **C# Interactive** prompt, we will enter commands to do the following:

- Reference the `System.Net.Http` assembly
- Import the `System.Net.Http` namespace
- Declare and instantiate an HTTP client variable
- Set the client's base address to Microsoft's website
- Wait asynchronously for a response to a GET request for the About page
- Read the status code returned by the web server
- Read the content type header
- Read the contents of the HTML page as a string

Type each of the following commands after the > prompt and then press *Enter*:

```
> #r "System.Net.Http"
> using System.Net.Http;
> var client = new HttpClient();
> client.BaseAddress = new Uri("http://www.microsoft.com/");
> var response = await client.GetAsync("about");
> response.StatusCode
OK
> response.Content.Headers.GetValues("Content-Type")
string[1] { "text/html" }
> await response.Content.ReadAsStringAsync()
"<!DOCTYPE html ><html xmlns:mscom=\"http://schemas.microsoft.com/
CMSvNext\" xmlns:md=\"http://schemas.microsoft.com/mscom-data\"
lang=\"en\" xmlns=\"http://www.w3.org/1999/xhtml\"><head><meta http-
equiv=\"X-UA-Compatible\" content=\"IE=edge\" /><meta charset=\"utf-8\"
/><meta name=\"viewport\" content=\"width=device-width, initial-
scale=1.0\" /><link rel=\"shortcut icon\" href=\"//www.microsoft.com/
favicon.ico?v2\" /><script type=\"text/javascript\" src=\"http://ajax.
aspnetcdn.com/ajax/jQuery/jquery-1.7.2.min.js\">\r\n        // Third
party scripts and code linked to or referenced from this website are
licensed to you by the parties that own such code, not by Microsoft. See
ASP.NET Ajax CDN Terms of Use - http://www.asp.net/ajaxlibrary/CDN.ashx.\
r\n    </script><script type=\"text/javascript\" language=\"javascript\"
>/*<![CDATA[*/if($(document).bind(\"mobileinit\",function(){$.mobile.aut
oInitializePage=!1}),navigator.userAgent.match(/IEMobile\\/10\\.0/)){var
msViewportStyle=document.createElement(\"style ...
```

```
C# Interactive                                          ▾ ⇅ ✕
↺  ≣  ↑  ↓
    Microsoft (R) Roslyn C# Compiler version 1.1.0.51109
    Loading context from 'CSharpInteractive.rsp'.
    Type "#help" for more information.
    > #r "System.Net.Http"
    > using System.Net.Http;
    > var client = new HttpClient();
    > client.BaseAddress = new Uri("http://www.microsoft.com/");
    > var response = await client.GetAsync("about");
    > response.StatusCode
    OK
    > response.Content.Headers.GetValues("Content-Type")
    string[1] { "text/html" }
    > await response.Content.ReadAsStringAsync()
    "<!DOCTYPE html ><html xmlns:mscom=\"http://schemas.microsoft.c
    >
100 %   ▾ ◄ ▮▮
C# Interactive  Package Manage...  Error List  Output  Find Results 1  Task Runner Expl...
```

# Other useful windows

Visual Studio has lots of other useful windows, including the following:

- The **Solution Explorer** window for managing all the projects and files you work on
- The **Team Explorer** window for source code management tools, such as GitHub
- The **Server Explorer** window for managing database connections

If you ever can't see a window you need, go to the **View** menu to make it reappear or learn its keyboard shortcut, as shown here:

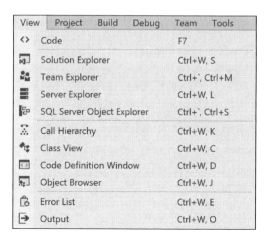

If your keyboard shortcuts are different from the ones in the preceding screenshot, it is because you picked a different set when you installed Visual Studio. You can reset your keyboard shortcuts to match the ones used in this book by clicking on the **Tools** menu, then clicking on **Import and Export Settings...**, choosing **Reset all settings**, and then choosing to reset to the **Visual C#** settings collection.

# Targeting the .NET Core

For 15 years, .NET programmers have been targeting the .NET Framework, so there are many projects that may need to move from Windows-only to cross-platform by retargeting to the .NET Core.

# Understanding the .NET Portability Analyzer

To ensure that a project will work cross-platform, we can install and run the Visual Studio 2015 extension named .NET Portability Analyzer.

It allows you to choose multiple platforms that you would like to target and then scans your compiled assemblies, passes a list of the types and methods that you use to a web service, and produces a report that lists which ones are not supported on each platform along with recommendations for fixes.

# Installing the .NET Portability Analyzer

In Visual Studio, go to the **Tools** menu and choose **Extensions and Updates...**.

On the left-hand side of the dialog, click on **Online**. In the **Search Visual Studio Gallery** box, type **portability** and press *Enter*.

Click on the **.NET Portability Analyzer** entry and then click on the **Download** button. Once the extension is installed, restart Visual Studio:

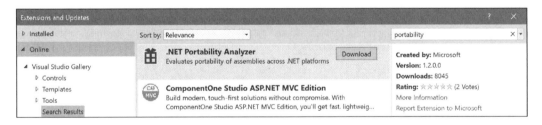

# Configuring the .NET Portability Analyzer

In Visual Studio, go to the **Tools** menu and choose **Options**.

In the **Options** dialog box, scroll down through the left-hand side list and choose **.NET Portability Analyzer**. In the **Target Platforms** section, deselect everything except for the following:

- .NET Core (Cross-platform) 1.0 (shown as 5.0 in the following screenshot)
- .NET Framework 4.5
- .NET Native 1.0
- ASP.NET Core 1.0 (shown as ASP.NET 5 in the screenshot below):

 Microsoft Azure has a Platform-as-a-Service (PaaS) feature named Cloud Services, which is limited to the .NET Framework 4.5; this is why it is a common target platform to check with the analyzer.

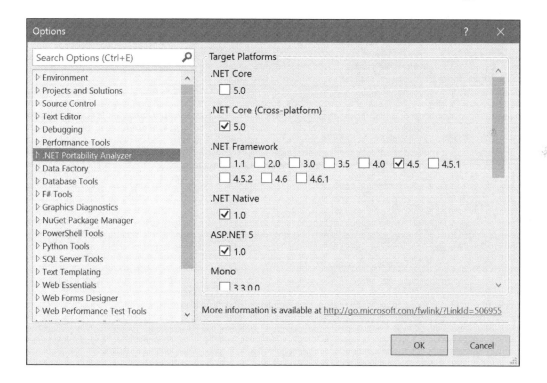

# Analyzing a solution

In Visual Studio, open the previous solution, named **Chapter01**. In the **Solution Explorer** window, right-click on the project named **Ch01_MyFirstApp** (not the solution), choose **Analyze**, and then choose **Analyze Assembly Portability**.

After a few seconds, a report will display in the main area.

 Be patient with the .NET Portability Analyzer because it has to send data to a web service and wait for a response.

Note that the `Console` class in the `System` namespace and its `WriteLine` method are supported by the following:

- .NET Core (Cross-Platform) 1.0 (shown as 5.0 in the following screenshot)
- .NET Framework 4.5
- ASP.NET Core 1.0 (shown as ASP.NET 5 in the following screenshot)

However, it is not supported by .NET Native 1.0:

## .NET Portability Report

*Submission Id c5a18f49-a75c-49bc-b3ef-fb17ed93ca81*

## Contents

- Portability Summary

## Portability Summary

| Assembly | .NET Core (Cross-platform),Version=v5.0 | .NET Framework,Version=v4.5 | .NET Native,Version=v1.0 | ASP.NET 5,Version=v1.0 |
|---|---|---|---|---|
| Ch01_MyFirstApp, Version=1.0.0.0, Culture=neutral, PublicKeyToken=null (.NETFramework,Version=v4.6) | 100.00 % | 100.00 % | 93.94 % | 100.00 % |

Ch01_MyFirstApp, Version=1.0.0.0, Culture=neutral, PublicKeyToken=null (.NETFramework,Version=v4.6)

| Target type | .NET Core (Cross-platform),Version=v5.0 | .NET Framework,Version=v4.5 | .NET Native,Version=v1.0 | ASP.NET 5,Version=v1.0 | Recommended changes |
|---|---|---|---|---|---|
| System.Console | ✔ | ✔ | ✘ | ✔ | |
| WriteLine (System.String) | ✔ | ✔ | ✘ | ✔ | |

At the time of writing this, the .NET Portability Analyzer has not been updated to show the new version branding for .NET Core and related products, which can be found at `http://www.hanselman.com/blog/ASPNET5IsDeadIntroducingASPNETCore10AndNETCore10.aspx`.

Press *Ctrl + W*, *E* to view the error list, which has also been populated. As we saw earlier, double-clicking on an error will jump the code editor to the line that could cause an issue:

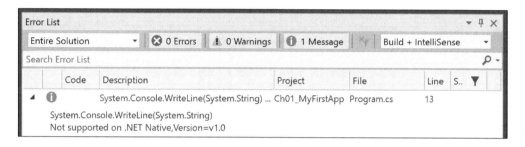

## .NET Portability and this book

I used the .NET Portability Analyzer while writing all the code in this book to ensure that, whenever possible, I can show you code that will work cross-platform using the .NET Core 1.0. If there are useful features that aren't cross-platform yet, then I will point that out in the text. Hopefully, they will be implemented in .NET Core in future versions.

# Creating new projects for the .NET Core

Let's recreate the console application, but this time, target the .NET Core from the start.

# Managing .NET Core development with Command Line Tools

There are two sets of command-line tools that you can use to manage the .NET Core:

- **.NET Version Manager, .NET Execution Environment, .NET Development Utilities** (dnvm, dnx, dnu): These were used by Microsoft during the initial development of the .NET Core between 2013 and 2015. They are installed as part of Visual Studio 2015. These tools will be deprecated with the final release of the .NET Core.

- **.NET CLI** (dotnet): This is a driver, which will be used by the final release of the .NET Core. It provides a simplified layer on top of other underlying tools. The .NET CLI must be installed separately.

> At the time of writing, the DNX tools are more advanced than the .NET CLI, so in *Chapter 15, Taking C# Cross-Platform*, I will need to show you how to use both sets of tools. For this chapter, we can use the newer CLI tool because we are only using basic features. I recommend that you browse http://cs6dotnetcore.azurewebsites.net/ for information about changes between the time of writing this book and the release of the final versions of .NET Core 1.0 and its related technologies and tools.

## Installing the .NET Command Line Tools

First, we must install the .NET Command Line Tools (CLI).

Start Microsoft Edge and go to the https://github.com/dotnet/cli.

Scroll down the page to find the **Installers** section and click on the link to download the **MSI** file for Windows. Open the file and install.

## Creating a .NET Core application using Command Line Tools

Start the Developer Command Prompt for VS2015. At the prompt, enter the following command:

```
dotnet
```

You should see the following output:

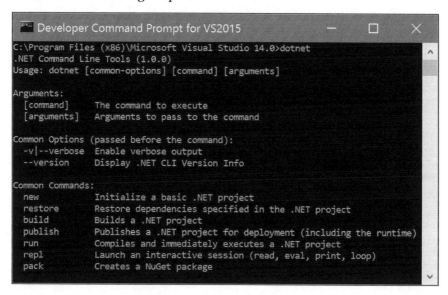

Enter the following at the prompt to create a new directory, change to it, create a new console application in the directory, and then list the files it created:

```
cd C:\Code\Chapter01
mkdir Ch01_MySecondApp
cd Ch01_MySecondApp
dotnet new
dir
```

You should see that the `dotnet` tool has created three new files for you: `NuGet.Config`, `Program.cs`, and `project.json`.

At the prompt, enter the following to start Notepad for editing the `Program` class:

```
notepad Program.cs
```

In Notepad, modify the `WriteLine` statement as follows:

```
Console.WriteLine("Hello C#, Welcome .NET Core!");
```

Save changes and exit Notepad.

At the prompt, enter the following commands:

```
dotnet restore
dotnet run
```

After a few seconds, all the dependency packages will be downloaded and your application will run, showing the following output:

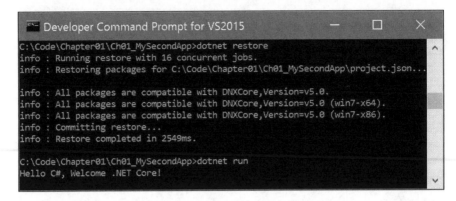

To compile the source code into an assembly containing IL code, enter the following command:

**dotnet build**

The output in the Command Prompt window should look like this:

Enter the following commands to change to a subdirectory, list the files in it, and execute the compiled console application:

**cd bin\Debug\dnxcore50**

**dir**

**Ch01_MySecondApp**

 The Debug is the name of the configuration and dnxcore50 is the name of the framework. This will change in the release version of the .NET Core.

# Creating a .NET Core application using Visual Studio 2015

Start Visual Studio 2015 and open the **Chapter01** solution.

In Visual Studio, navigate to **File | Add | New Project**.

In the **Add New Project** dialog box, in the **Installed Templates** list on the left-hand side, choose **Visual C#**. In the list at the center, choose **Console Application (Package)**. Enter the name **Ch01_DotNetCore**, and click on **OK** or press *Enter*:

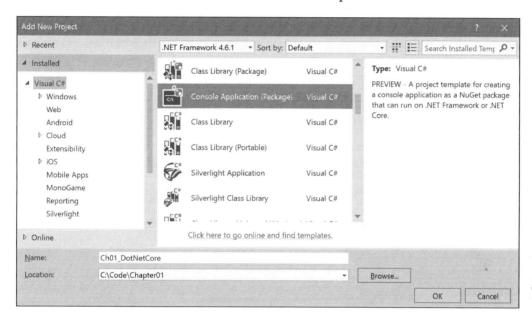

In the **Solution Explorer** window, right-click on the solution named **Chapter01** and choose **Properties**.

Set the **Startup Project** to **Current selection** and click on **OK**.

Inside the `Main` method of the `Program` class, enter the following statements:

```
Console.WriteLine("Welcome, .NET Core!");
Console.ReadLine();
```

As you type code, you will notice that Visual Studio shows you which types and methods might not be available when targeting .NET Core. For example, the **BufferHeight** property is available when targeting the .NET Framework but not the .NET Core, as shown in the following screenshot as DNX 4.5.1 and DNX Core 5.0 respectively:

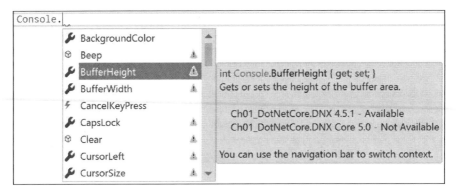

You can tell the compiler to include statements available only when .NET Framework is available by using conditional compilation symbols, as follows:

```
#if DNX451
    Console.BufferHeight = 300;
#elseif DNXCORE50
    // some alternative for .NET Core
#endif
```

 In *Chapter 5, Using Specialized .NET Types,* you will learn more about conditional compilation symbols so that you can create projects that target both the .NET Framework and the .NET Core with a single code base.

 The names of the conditional compilation symbols will change in the future. Visit https://github.com/dotnet/corefx/blob/master/Documentation/architecture/net-platform-standard.md for more information.

In the **Solution Explorer** window, double-click on **Properties** for the **Ch01_DotNetCore** project.

In the **Properties** window, click on the **Debug** tab, select the **Use Specific Runtime** checkbox, and select the latest version of the **.NET Core** platform for the **x64** CPU architecture, as shown in the following screenshot:

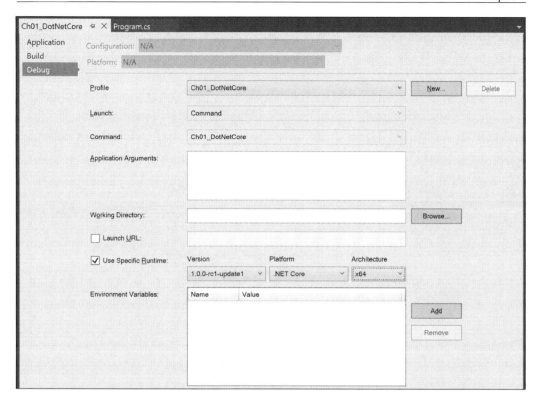

In the Visual Studio **Debug** menu, choose **Start** or press *F5*.

Note that the Command Prompt window shows that the console application is running the **dnx-coreclr-win-x64.1.0.0-rc1-update1** runtime:

 Throughout the first half of this book, I will show example code by creating console applications, so you can decide if you want to target the .NET Framework by choosing **Console Application**, or target the .NET Core by choosing **Console Application (Package)**.

# Managing source code with GitHub

Git is a commonly used source code management system. GitHub is a company, website, and desktop application that makes it easier to manage Git.

Visual Studio 2015 has built-in support for using Git with GitHub as well as Microsoft's own source code management system, named **Visual Studio Team Services**.

I used GitHub to store solutions to all the practical exercises at the end of each chapter.

# Using the Team Explorer window

In Visual Studio, navigate to **View | Team Explorer** menu to see the **Team Explorer** window:

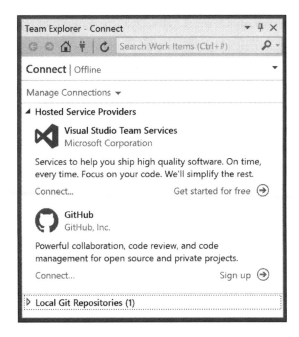

Although it is a good idea to sign up with an online source code management system provider, you can clone a GitHub repository without signing up for an account.

# Cloning a GitHub repository

In the **Team Explorer** window, expand **Local Git Repositories**, click on the **Clone** menu, and then enter the following URL of a Git repository to clone it:

```
https://github.com/markjprice/cs6dotnetcore.git
```

Enter a path for the cloned Git repository:

```
C:\Code\Repos\cs6dotnetcore
```

Click on the **Clone** button:

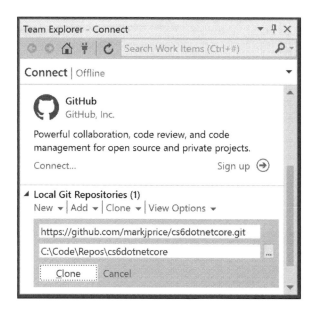

Wait for the Git repository to clone locally:

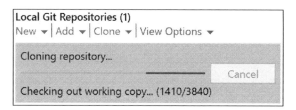

You will now have a local copy of the complete solutions to all the hands-on practice exercises for this book.

# Managing a GitHub repository

Double-click on the **cs6dotnetcore** repo to open a detail view.

You can click on the options in the **Project** section to view **Pull Requests** and **Issues**, and other aspects of a repository.

You can double-click on an entry in the **Solutions** section to open it in the **Solution Explorer**:

# Practicing and exploring

Test your knowledge and understanding by answering some questions, get some hands-on practice, and explore, with deeper research into the topics covered in this chapter.

## Exercise 1.1 – test your knowledge

Answer the following questions:

1. Why can a programmer use different languages to write applications that run on .NET?
2. What do you type at the Command Prompt to compile the C# source code?
3. What is the Visual Studio 2015 keyboard shortcut to save, compile, and run an application, without attaching the debugger?
4. What is the Visual Studio 2015 keyboard shortcut to view the error list?
5. What does `ildasm.exe` do?
6. Is the .NET Core better than the .NET Framework?
7. How is .NET Native different from the .NET Core?
8. What does the .NET Portability Analyzer do?
9. What is the difference between Git and GitHub?
10. What is the name of the entry-point method of a .NET application and how should it be declared?

## Exercise 1.2 – practice managing Visual Studio Windows

Practice closing and viewing windows, such as **Error List** and **Toolbox**.

You can pin, unpin, float, and rearrange windows by dragging their title bars. As you do so, Visual Studio will show blue tinted boxes and overlays to help you to understand where the window will be moved when you release the mouse button.

 You can always reset Visual Studio back to one of the default layouts by clicking on the **Tools** menu and **Import and Export Settings…**.

# Exercise 1.3 – practice coding anywhere

You do not need Visual Studio to practice writing C#. Simply go to the .NET Fiddle website (`https://dotnetfiddle.net/`) and start coding. It's also a great way to share snippets of C# code with other developers:

# Exercise 1.4 – explore topics

Use the following links to read more details about the topics covered in this chapter:

- **Visual Studio IDE User's Guide**: `https://msdn.microsoft.com/en-us/library/dn762121.aspx`

- **Solutions and Projects**: `https://msdn.microsoft.com/en-us/library/b142f8e7.aspx`

- **Using IntelliSense**: `https://msdn.microsoft.com/en-us/library/hcw1s69b.aspx`

- **Identifying and Customizing Keyboard Shortcuts in Visual Studio**: `https://msdn.microsoft.com/en-us/library/5zwses53.aspx`

- **Making your libraries compatible with .NET Core and other .NET Platforms**: `https://github.com/dotnet/corefx/blob/master/Documentation/project-docs/support-dotnet-core-instructions.md`

- **.NET Core: A general purpose managed framework**: `http://dotnet.github.io`

- **Leveraging existing code across .NET platforms**: `http://blogs.msdn.com/b/dotnet/archive/2014/08/06/leveraging-existing-code-across-net-platforms.aspx`

- **.NET Command Line Interface (CLI)**: `https://github.com/dotnet/cli`

- **Use Visual Studio and Team Foundation Server with Git**: `https://msdn.microsoft.com/Library/vs/alm/Code/git/overview`

- **The easiest way to connect to your GitHub repositories in Visual Studio**: `https://visualstudio.github.com/`

# Summary

In this chapter, we set up the development environment, we used the Developer Command Prompt to compile and decompile an application, we used Visual Studio to create the same application and explore the features that make it so easy to use for development, and we discussed the differences between the .NET Framework, the .NET Core, and .NET Native.

In the next chapter, you will learn to speak C#.

# 2
# Speaking C#

This chapter is about the C# language — the grammar and vocabulary that you will use every day to write the source code for your applications.

Programming languages have many similarities to human languages, except that in programming languages, you can make up our own words, just like Dr. Seuss!

> *"And then, just to show them, I'll sail to Ka-Troo*
> *And bring back an It-Kutch a Preep and a Proo*
> *A Nerkle a Nerd and a Seersucker, too!"*
> *If I Ran the Zoo*

To learn to speak C#, you need to create some simple applications. To avoid overloading you with too much information too soon, the first few chapters of this book will use the simplest type of application: a console application.

This chapter covers the following topics:

- Understanding C# basics
- Declaring variables
- Building console applications
- Operating on variables

# Understanding C# basics

Let's start with looking at the basics of the grammar and vocabulary of C#. In this chapter, you will create multiple console applications, each showing a feature of the C# language. To manage these projects, we will put them all in a single solution. Visual Studio 2015 can only have one solution open at any one time, but each solution can group together multiple projects. A project can build a console application, a Windows desktop application, a web application, and dozens of others.

Start Microsoft Visual Studio 2015. In Visual Studio, press *Ctrl + Shift + N* or choose the **File | New | Project**... menu.

In the **New Project** dialog, in the **Installed Templates** list, expand **Other Project Types**, and select **Visual Studio Solutions**. In the list at the center, select **Blank Solution**, type the name **Chapter02**, change the location to C:\Code, and then click on **OK**, as shown in the following screenshot:

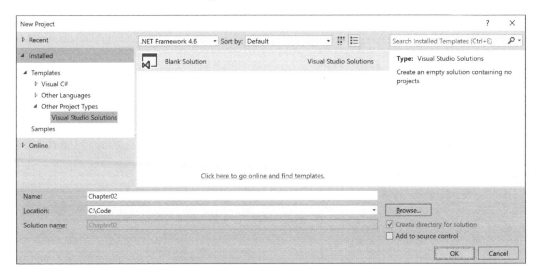

If you were to run **File Explorer**, you would see that Visual Studio has created a folder named **Chapter02** with a Visual Studio solution named **Chapter02** inside it, as follows:

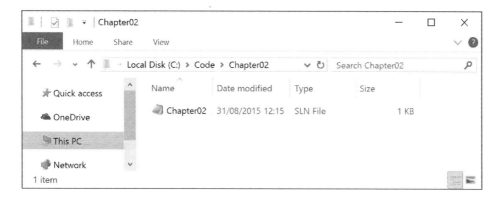

In Visual Studio, navigate to **File | Add | New Project...**, as shown in the following screenshot. This will add a new project to the blank solution:

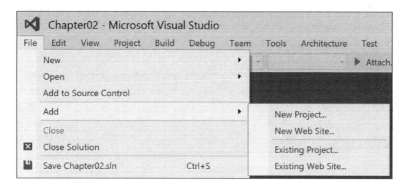

In the **Add New Project** dialog, in the **Installed Templates** list, select **Visual C#**. In the list at the center, select **Console Application**, type the name **Ch02_Basics**, ensure that **.NET Framework 4.6** (or later) is selected at the top, and then click on **OK**.

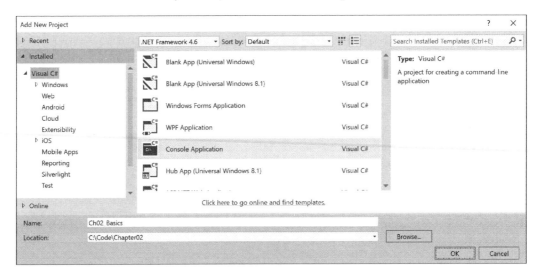

If you were to run **File Explorer**, you would see that Visual Studio has created a new folder with some files and subfolders inside it. You don't need to know what all these do yet. The code you will write will be stored in the file named Program.cs, as shown in the following screenshot:

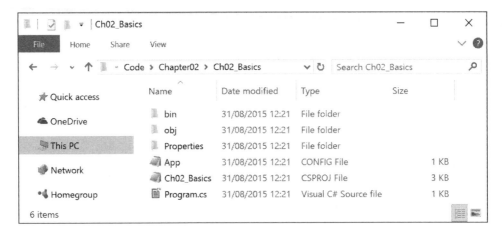

In Visual Studio, the **Solution Explorer** window on the right-hand side shows the same files as the ones in the preceding screenshot of the file system:

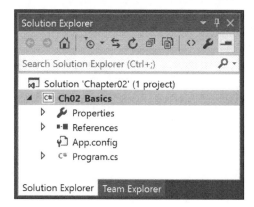

 Some folders and files, for example, the bin folder, are hidden by default in **Solution Explorer**. At the top of the window is a toolbar button named **Show All Files**. Toggle this button to show and hide folders and files.

# The C# grammar

The grammar of C# includes statements and blocks.

## Statements

In English, we indicate the end of a sentence with a full stop. A sentence can be composed of multiple words and phrases. The order of words is part of the grammar. For example, in English, we say: the black cat. The adjective, black, comes before the noun, cat. French grammar has a different order; the adjective comes after the noun, "le chat noir".

C# indicates the end of a statement with a semicolon. A statement can be composed of multiple variables and expressions. In the following statement, `FullName` is a variable and `FirstName + LastName` is an expression:

```
var FullName = FirstName + LastName;
```

You can add comments to explain your code using a double slash `//`.

The compiler ignores everything after the `//` until the end of the line; for example:

```
var TotalPrice = Cost + Tax; // Tax is 20% of the Cost
```

 Visual Studio will add or remove the comment (double slashes) at the start of the currently selected line(s) if you press *Ctrl + K + C* or *Ctrl + K + U*.

To write a multi-line comment, use `/*` at the beginning and `*/` at the end of comment, as shown in the following code:

```
/*
This is a multi-line
comment.
*/
```

## Blocks

In English, we indicate a paragraph with blank lines. C# indicates a **block** of code with curly brackets { }. Blocks often start with a declaration to indicate what the block is defining. For example, a block can define a namespace, a class, a method, or a statement. You will learn what these are later.

In your current project, note the grammar of C# written for you by the Visual Studio template. If you are using Visual Studio 2015, the first five lines will be slightly faded out in your editor window to indicate that they aren't necessary (but leave them in for now).

In the following code block, I have added some comments and a single statement inside the `Main` method:

```
using System;
using System.Collections.Generic;
using System.Linq;
using System.Text;
using System.Threading.Tasks; // ; is the end of a statement

namespace Ch02_Basics
{
    class Program
    {
        static void Main(string[] args)
        { // the start of a block
            Console.WriteLine("Hello C#"); // a statement
        } // the end of a block
    }
}
```

# The C# vocabulary

Some of the 79 predefined, reserved keywords that you will see in this chapter include `using`, `namespace`, `class`, `static`, `int`, `string`, `double`, `bool`, `var`, `if`, `switch`, `break`, `while`, `do`, `for`, and `foreach`.

Visual Studio shows C# keywords in blue to make them easier to spot. In the following screenshot, `namespace`, `class`, `static`, `void`, and `string` are part of the vocabulary of C#:

```
Program.cs*  ⊕ ✕
C# Ch02_Basics                                                    ▾
      ⊟using System;
       using System.Collections.Generic;
       using System.Linq;
       using System.Text;
       using System.Threading.Tasks;

      ⊟namespace Ch02_Basics
       {
      ⊟    class Program
           {
      ⊟        static void Main(string[] args)
               {
               }
           }
       }
```

There are another 25 contextual keywords that only have a special meaning in a specific context. But that still means there are only 104 actual C# keywords in the language.

English has more than 250,000 distinct words. How does C# get away with only having 104 keywords? Why is C# so difficult to learn if it has so few words?

One of the key differences between a human language and a programming language is that developers need to be able to define new "words" with new meanings.

Apart from the 104 keywords in the C# language, this book will teach you about some of the hundreds of thousands of "words" that other developers have defined. You will also learn how to define your own "words".

Programmers all over the world have to learn English because most programming languages use English words like namespace and class. There are programming languages that use other human languages, such as Arabic, but they are rare. This YouTube video shows a demonstration of an Arabic programming language: https://www.youtube.com/watch?v=77KAHPZUR8g.

# Writing the code

Simple editors such as Notepad don't help you write correct English, as shown in the following screenshot:

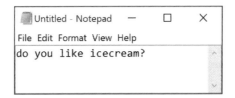

Notepad won't help you write correct C# either.

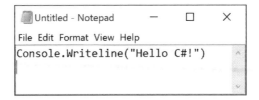

Microsoft Word helps you write English by highlighting spelling mistakes with red squiggles (it should be *ice cream*) and grammatical errors with blue squiggles (sentences should have an upper-case first letter).

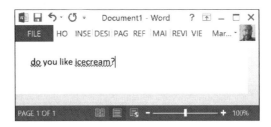

Similarly, Visual Studio helps you write C# code by highlighting spelling mistakes (the method name should be WriteLine with an uppercase L) and grammatical errors (statements must end with a semicolon).

Visual Studio constantly watches what you type and gives you feedback by highlighting problems with colored squiggly lines under your code and showing the **Error List** window as you can see in the following screenshot. You can ask Visual Studio to do a complete check of your code by choosing **Build-Solution** or pressing *F6*.

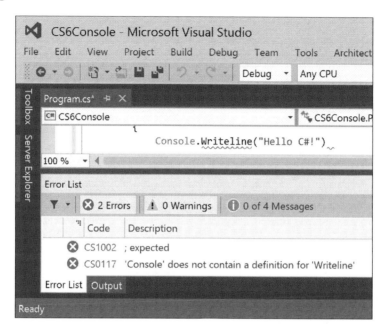

# Verbs are methods

In English, verbs are doing or action words. In C#, doing or action words are called **methods**. There are literally hundreds of thousands of methods available to C#.

In English, verbs change how they are written according to when in time the action happens. For example, Amir *was jumping* in the past, Beth *jumps* in the present, they *jumped* in the past, and Daz *will jump* in the future.

In C#, methods such as `WriteLine` change how they are called or executed according to the specifics of the action. This is called **overloading**, which we will cover in more detail in *Chapter 6, Building Your Own Types with Object-Oriented Programming*. Consider the following example:

```
// outputs a carriage-return
Console.WriteLine();
// outputs the greeting and a carriage-return
Console.WriteLine("Hello Ahmed");
```

```
// outputs a formatted number and date
Console.WriteLine("Temperature on {0:D} is {1}°C.",
    DateTime.Today, 23.4);
```

A different analogy is that some words are spelled the same but have different meanings depending on the context.

# Nouns are types, fields, and variables

In English, nouns are names that refer to things. In C#, their equivalents are types, fields, and variables. There are tens of thousands of types available in C#.

# Counting types and methods

Let's write some code to find out how many types and methods are available to C# in our simple console application.

Don't worry about how this code works. It uses a technique called **reflection**, which is beyond the scope of this book.

Start by adding the following statement at the top of the `Program.cs` file:

```
using System.Reflection;
```

Inside the `Main` method, type the following code:

```
// loop through the assemblies that this application references
foreach (var r in Assembly.GetExecutingAssembly()
    .GetReferencedAssemblies())
{
    // load the assembly so we can read its details
    var a = Assembly.Load(r.FullName);
    // declare and set a variable to count the total number of methods
    int methodCount = 0;
    // loop through all the types in the assembly
    foreach (var t in a.DefinedTypes)
    {
        // add up the counts of methods
        methodCount += t.GetMethods().Count();
    }
    // output the count of types and their methods
    Console.WriteLine($"{a.DefinedTypes.Count():N0} types with
{methodCount:N0} methods in {r.Name} assembly.");
}
```

Press *Ctrl + F5* to save, compile, and run your application without the debugger attached, or click on the **Debug** menu and then **Start Without Debugging**.

You will see the following output that shows the actual number of types and methods that are available to you in the simplest application:

```
3,233 types with 38,529 methods in mscorlib assembly.
974 types with 9,301 methods in System.Core assembly.
```

 The actual numbers displayed may be different depending on the version of the .NET Framework that you are using. The numbers we see here are for version 4.6.1.

Add the following four lines of code at the top of the `Main` method. By declaring variables that use types in other assemblies, those assemblies are loaded with our application. This allows our code to see all the types and methods in them:

```
static void Main(string[] args)
{
    System.Data.SqlClient.SqlConnection connection;
    System.Xml.XmlReader reader;
    System.Xml.Linq.XElement element;
    System.Net.Http.HttpClient client;
```

Press *Ctrl + F5* and view the output in the console:

```
3,233 types with 38,529 methods in mscorlib assembly.
1,105 types with 14,621 methods in System.Data assembly.
1,247 types with 19,139 methods in System.Xml assembly.
91 types with 1,632 methods in System.Xml.Linq assembly.
102 types with 1,201 methods in System.Net.Http assembly.
974 types with 9,301 methods in System.Core assembly.
```

Now you have a better sense of why learning C# is a challenge. There are many types with many methods to learn about, and other programmers are constantly defining new ones!

# Declaring variables

All applications process data. Data comes in, data is processed, and data goes out.

Data usually comes into our program from files, databases, or user input. Data can be put temporarily in variables that will be stored in the memory of the running program. When the program ends, the data in memory is lost. Data is usually output to files and databases or to the screen or a printer.

When using variables, you should think about, first, how much space it takes in memory, and, next, how fast it can be processed.

We control this by picking an appropriate type. You can think of simple common types such as `int` and `double` as being differently sized storage boxes. A smaller box would take less memory but may not be processed as quickly.

# Naming variables

There are naming conventions for variables and it is best practice to follow them, as shown in the following table:

| Naming convention | Examples | Usage |
|---|---|---|
| Camel case | `cost`, `orderDetail`, `dateOfBirth` | Local variables and private members |
| Pascal/title case | `Cost`, `OrderDetail`, `DateOfBirth` | Type names and nonprivate members |

The following code block shows an example of declaring and initializing a local variable. Note that you can output the name of a variable using a keyword introduced in C# 6, that is, `nameof`:

```
double heightInMetres = 1.88;
Console.WriteLine($"The variable {nameof(heightInMetres)} has the
value {heightInMetres}.");
```

# Storing text

For text, a single letter such as A is stored as a `char` type and is assigned using single-quotes around the literal value.

```
char letter = 'A';
```

Multiple characters like `Bob` are stored as a `string` type and are assigned using double quotes around the literal value:

```
string name = "Bob";
```

# Storing numbers

Numbers are data that we want to perform an arithmetic calculation on (for example, multiplying).

> A telephone number is not really a number. To decide whether a variable needs to be stored as a number or not, ask yourself whether you need to multiply two telephone numbers together or whether the number includes special characters such as (414)-555-1234. In these cases, the number is really a sequence of characters so should be stored as a string.

Numbers can be natural numbers, such as 42, used for counting (also called whole numbers), they can also be negative numbers, such as -42 (called **integers**), or they can be **real** numbers, such as 3.9 (with a fractional part), which are called **single** or **double-precision floating point** numbers in computing.

You might know that computers store everything as bits. A **bit** is either 0 or 1. This is called a **binary** number system. Humans use a **decimal** number system.

## Storing whole numbers

The following table shows how computers store the number 10. Note the 1 bits in the 8 and the 2 columns; 8 + 2 = 10.

| 128 | 64 | 32 | 16 | 8 | 4 | 2 | 1 |
|-----|-----|-----|-----|---|---|---|---|
| 0 | 0 | 0 | 0 | 1 | 0 | 1 | 0 |

So, `10` in decimal is `00001010` in binary.

Computers can always exactly represent integers (positive and negative whole numbers) using the `int` type or one of its sibling types such as `short`.

# Storing real numbers

Computers cannot always exactly represent floating point numbers. The `float` and `double` types store real numbers using single and double precision floating points.

The following table shows how a computer stores the number `12.75`. Note the 1 bits in the 8, 4, ½, and ¼ columns.

8 + 4 + ½ + ¼ = 12¾ = 12.75.

| 128 | 64 | 32 | 16 | 8 | 4 | 2 | 1 | . | ½ | ¼ | 1/8 | 1/16 |
|-----|----|----|----|----|----|----|----|----|----|----|----|----|
| 0 | 0 | 0 | 0 | 1 | 1 | 0 | 0 | . | 1 | 1 | 0 | 0 |

So, `12.75` in decimal is `00001100.1100` in binary.

As you can see, the number 12.75 can be exactly represented using bits. But some numbers can't, as you will see shortly.

## Sizes of numbers in memory

In Visual Studio, click on **File | Add | New Project...**. In the **Add New Project** dialog, in the **Installed Templates** list, select **Visual C#**. In the list at the center, select **Console Application**, type the name **Ch02_Numbers**, and then click on **OK**.

In the **Solution Explorer** window, right-click on the solution and select **Properties** or press *Alt + Enter*. For **Startup Project**, select **Current selection**. From now on you can simply click on a project in the Solution Explorer and then press *Ctrl + F5* to save, compile, and run that project.

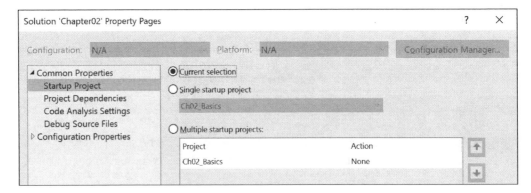

Type the following code inside the `Main` method:

```
Console.WriteLine($"int uses {sizeof(int)} bytes and can store numbers
in the range {int.MinValue:N0} to {int.MaxValue:N0}.");
Console.WriteLine($"double uses {sizeof(double)} bytes and can store
numbers in the range {double.MinValue:N0} to {double.MaxValue:N0}.");
Console.WriteLine($"decimal uses {sizeof(decimal)} bytes and can
store numbers in the range {decimal.MinValue:N0} to {decimal.
MaxValue:N0}.");
```

Press *Ctrl* + *F5* and view the output in the console:

```
int uses 4 bytes and can store numbers in the range -2,147,483,648 to
2,147,483,647.
```

```
double uses 8 bytes and can store numbers in the range -179,769,313,486,2
32,000,000,000,000,000,000,000,000,000,000,000,000,000,000,000,000,00
0,000,000,000,000,000,000,000,000,000,000,000,000,000,000,000,000,000
,000,000,000,000,000,000,000,000,000,000,000,000,000,000,000,000,000,
000,000,000,000,000,000,000,000,000,000,000,000,000,000,000,000,000,0
00,000,000,000,000,000,000,000,000,000,000,000,000,000,000,000,000,00
0,000,000,000,000,000,000 to 179,769,313,486,232,000,000,000,000,000,
000,000,000,000,000,000,000,000,000,000,000,000,000,000,000,000,000,0
00,000,000,000,000,000,000,000,000,000,000,000,000,000,000,000,000,00
0,000,000,000,000,000,000,000,000,000,000,000,000,000,000,000,000,000
,000,000,000,000,000,000,000,000,000,000,000,000,000,000,000,000,000,
000,000,000,000,000,000,000,000,000,000,000,000,000,000,000,000,000,0
00,000.
```

```
decimal uses 16 bytes and can store numbers in the range -79,228,162,514,
264,337,593,543,950,335 to 79,228,162,514,264,337,593,543,950,335.
```

Note that an `int` variable uses four bytes of memory and can store positive or negative numbers up to about 2 billion.

A `double` variable uses eight bytes of memory and can store much bigger values! A `decimal` variable uses 16 bytes of memory and can store big numbers, but not as big as a `double`.

Why might a `double` variable be able to store bigger numbers than a `decimal` variable yet use half the space in memory? Let's find out!

## Comparing double and decimal

In Visual Studio, click on **File** | **Add** | **New Project…**. In the **Add New Project** dialog, in the **Installed Templates** list, select **Visual C#**. In the list at the center, select **Console Application**, type the name **Ch02_NumberAccuracy**, and then click on **OK**.

Enter the following code. Do not worry about understanding the syntax right now, although it isn't too hard to follow:

```
double a = 0.1;
double b = 0.2;
if (a + b == 0.3)
{
    Console.WriteLine($"{a} + {b} equals 0.3");
}
else
{
    Console.WriteLine($"{a} + {b} does NOT equal 0.3");
}
```

Press *Ctrl* + *F5* and view the output in the console:

**0.1 + 0.2 does NOT equal 0.3**

The double type is NOT guaranteed to be accurate. Only use double when accuracy, especially when comparing two numbers, is not important, for example, when measuring a person's height.

The problem with the preceding code is how the computer stores the number 0.1 or multiples of 0.1. To represent 0.1 in binary, the computer stores 1 in the 1/16 column, 1 in the 1/128 column, 1 in the 1/1024 column, and so on. The number 0.1 in decimal is 0.0001001001001 repeating forever:

| 4 | 2 | 1 | . | ½ | ¼ | 1/8 | 1/16 | 1/32 | 1/64 | 1/128 | 1/256 | 1/512 | 1/1024 | 1/2048 |
|---|---|---|---|---|---|-----|------|------|------|-------|-------|-------|--------|--------|
| 0 | 0 | 0 | . | 0 | 0 | 0   | 1    | 0    | 0    | 1     | 0     | 0     | 1      | 0      |

Never compare double values using ==. During the First Gulf War, an American patriot missile battery used double values in its calculations. The inaccuracy caused it to fail to track and intercept an incoming Iraqi Scud missile, and 28 soldiers were killed, as you can read about at this link: https://www.ima.umn.edu/~arnold/disasters/patriot.html.

Copy and paste the code you wrote before that used doubles and then modify it to look like the following code:

```
decimal c = 0.1M; // M indicates a decimal literal value
decimal d = 0.2M;
if (c + d == 0.3M)
{
    Console.WriteLine($"{c} + {d} equals 0.3");
}
else
{
    Console.WriteLine($"{c} + {d} does NOT equal 0.3");
}
```

Press *Ctrl + F5* and view the output in the console:

**0.1 + 0.2 equals 0.3**

The decimal type is accurate because it actually stores the number as a large integer and shifts the decimal point. For example, 0.1 is stored as 1 with a note to shift the decimal point one place to the left. 12.75 is stored as 1275 with a note to shift the decimal point two places to the left.

**Best Practice**

Use int for whole numbers and double for real numbers. Use decimal for money, CAD drawings, general engineering, and wherever accuracy of a real number is important.

The double type has some useful special values: double.NaN means not-a-number and double.Infinity means an infinitely large value. You can use these special values when comparing the value of double variables.

# Storing Booleans

Booleans (bool) can only contain one of the two values: true or false, as shown in the following code. They are most commonly used to branch and loop, as you will see in *Chapter 3, Controlling the Flow, Converting Types, and Handling Exceptions*:

```
bool happy = true;
bool sad = false;
```

# The object type

There is a special type named `object` that can store any type of data, but its flexibility comes at the cost of messier code and poor performance due to boxing and unboxing operations when storing a value type. You should avoid it whenever possible.

Add a new **Console Application** project named **Ch02_SpecialTypes** and add the following code to the `Main` method:

```
object height = 1.88; // storing a double in an object
object name = "Amir"; // storing a string in an object
int length1 = name.Length; // gives compile error!
int length2 = ((string)name).Length; // cast to access members
```

The `object` type has been available since the first version of C# but C# 2 and higher versions have better alternatives, which we will cover later, that provide the flexibility we want without the performance overhead.

# The dynamic type

There is another special type named `dynamic` that can also store any type of data, and, like `object`, its flexibility comes at the cost of performance. Unlike `object`, the value stored in the variable can have its members invoked without an explicit cast, as shown in the following code:

```
dynamic anotherName = "Ahmed"; // storing a string in a dynamic object
int length = anotherName.Length; // this compiles but might throw an
exception at run-time!
```

The limitation of `dynamic` is that Visual Studio cannot show IntelliSense to help you write the code because the compiler doesn't check at build time. Instead, the CLR checks for the member at runtime. The `dynamic` keyword was introduced in C# 4.

# Local variables

Local variables are declared inside methods and they only exist during the call to that method. Once the method returns, the memory allocated to any local variables is released.

Add a new **Console Application** project named **Ch02_Variables**. Enter the following code to declare and assign values to some local variables inside the `Main` method. Note that we specify the type before the name of each variable:

```
int population = 66000000;
double weight = 1.88; // in kilograms
decimal price = 4.99M; // in pounds sterling
string fruit = "Apples"; // strings use double-quotes
char letter = 'Z'; // chars use single-quotes
```

Visual Studio 2015 will show green squiggles under each of the variable names to warn you that the variable is assigned but its value is never used.

# Inferring the type of a local variable

You can use the `var` keyword to declare local variables. The compiler will infer the type from the literal value you assign after the assignment = operator.

A literal number without a decimal point is inferred as an `int` variable unless you add the `L` suffix, in which case it infers a `long` variable. A literal number with a decimal point is inferred as a `double` unless you add the `M` suffix, in which case it infers a `decimal` variable, or the `F` suffix, in which case it infers a `float` variable. Double quotes indicate a `string` variable, single quotes indicate a `char`, and the `true` and `false` values indicates a `bool`.

Modify your code to use `var`:

```
var population = 66000000;
var weight = 1.88; // in kilograms
var price = 4.99M; // in pounds sterling
var fruit = "Apples"; // strings use double-quotes
var letter = 'Z'; // chars use single-quotes
var happy = true;
```

Although using `var` is convenient, some developers avoid using it to make it easier for a code reader to understand the types in use in the code. Personally, I use it whenever the type is obvious. For example, the first statement is just as clear as the second in stating what the type of the xml variable is but is shorter than the second statement:

```
var xml = new XmlDocument();
XmlDocument xml = new XmlDocument();
```

# Making a value type nullable

Most of the primitive types except `string` are value types. This means they must have a value. You can determine the default value of a type using the `default()` operator. The default value of an `int` variable is 0 (zero):

```
int defaultValueOfInt = default(int); // 0
```

Strings are reference types. This means that they can have a `null` value. The `null` value is a special value that indicates that the variable does not reference anything (yet).

Sometimes it is convenient to allow a value type to be `null`. You can do this by adding a question mark as a suffix to the type when declaring a variable, as shown in the following code:

```
int ICannotBeNull = 4;
ICannotBeNull = default(int); // 0
int? ICouldBeNull = null;
int result1 = ICouldBeNull.GetValueOrDefault(); // 0
ICouldBeNull = 4;
int result2 = ICouldBeNull.GetValueOrDefault(); // 4
```

# Storing multiple values in an array

When you need to store multiple values of the same type, you can declare an array. For example, you might need to store four names in a string array.

Add the following lines of code to the end of the `Main` method. It declares an array for storing four strings. Then, it stores strings at index positions 0 to 3 (note that arrays count from zero, so the last item is one less than the length of the array). Finally, it loops through each item in the array using a `for` statement that we cover in more detail in *Chapter 3, Controlling the Flow, Converting Types, and Handling Exceptions*:

```
// declaring the size of the array
string[] names = new string[4];
// storing items at index positions
names[0] = "Kate";
names[1] = "Jack";
names[2] = "Rebecca";
names[3] = "Tom";
for (int i = 0; i < names.Length; i++)
{
    Console.WriteLine(names[i]); // read the item at this index
}
```

Arrays are always of a fixed size, so you need to decide how many items you want to store before instantiating them. Arrays are useful for temporarily storing multiple items, but collections are more flexible when adding and removing items dynamically. We cover collections in *Chapter 4, Using Common .NET Types.*

# Building console applications

Console applications are text based and are run at the Command Prompt. They typically perform simple tasks that need to be scripted such as compiling a file or encrypting a section of a configuration file. They can have arguments passed to them to control their behavior, for example, to compile a source file into a shared library:

```
csc my.cs /target:library
```

To encrypt the database connection strings section in a `Web.config` file, use the following command:

```
aspnet_regiis -pdf "connectionStrings" "c:\mywebsite\"
```

# Displaying output to the user

The two most common tasks that a console application performs are writing and reading lines. We have already been using the `WriteLine` method to output. If we didn't want a carriage return at the end of lines, we could have used the `Write` method.

C# 6 has a handy new feature named string interpolation. This allows us to easily output one or more variables in a nicely formatted manner. A string prefixed with `$` can use curly braces around the name of a variable to output the current value of that variable at that position in the string.

In the **Ch02_Variables** project, enter the following code in the `Main` method:

```
Console.Write($"The population of the UK is {population}. ");
Console.WriteLine($"The population of the UK is {population:N0}. ");
Console.WriteLine($"{weight}kg of {fruit} costs {price:C}.");
```

Press *Ctrl + F5* and view the output in the console:

```
The population of the UK is 66000000. The population of the UK is
66,000,000.

1.88kg of Apples costs £4.99.
```

The variable can be formatted using special format codes. N0 means a number with commas for thousands and no decimal places. C means currency. The currency format will be determined by the current thread. If you run this code on a PC in the UK, you get pounds sterling. If you run this code on a PC in Germany, you get Euros.

# Getting input from the user

We can get input from the user using the ReadLine method. This method waits for the user to type some text. As soon as the user presses *Enter*, whatever the user has typed is returned as a string.

Let's ask the user for their name and age. Later, we will convert the age into a number, but we will leave it as a string for now:

```
Console.Write("Type your name and press ENTER: ");
string name = Console.ReadLine();
Console.Write("Type your age and press ENTER: ");
string age = Console.ReadLine();
Console.WriteLine($"Hello {name}, you look good for {age}.");
```

Press *Ctrl + F5* and view the output in the console. Enter a name and an age:

```
Type your name and press ENTER: Gary
Type your age and press ENTER: 34
Hello Gary, you look good for 34.
```

# Importing a namespace

You might have noticed that unlike our very first application we have not been typing System before Console.

System is a namespace. Namespaces are like an address for a type. To refer to someone exactly, you might use Oxford.HighStreet.BobSmith, which tells us to look for a person named Bob Smith on the High Street in the city of Oxford.

The line System.Console.WriteLine tells the compiler to look for a method named WriteLine in a type named Console in a namespace named System.

To simplify our code, Visual Studio added a line at the top of the code file to tell the compiler to always look in the System namespace for types that haven't been prefixed with their namespace. We call this importing the namespace.

```
using System;
```

# Simplifying the usage of the console in C# 6

In C# 6, the `using` statement can be used to further simplify our code.

Add the following line to the top of the file:

```
using static System.Console;
```

Now, we don't need to enter the `Console` type throughout our code. We can use Find and Replace to remove it. Select the first `Console.` line in your code (ensure that you select the dot after the word `Console`).

Press *Ctrl + H* to do a Quick Replace (ensure that the **Replace...** box is empty).

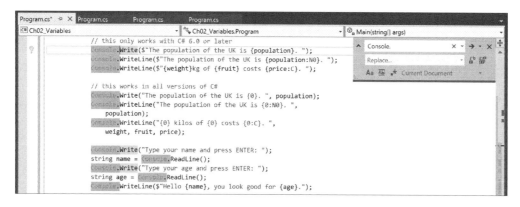

Press *Alt + A* to replace all and then click on **OK**.

Close the replace box by clicking on the cross in its top-right corner.

We can use a Visual Studio feature to clean up the extra `using` statements that we don't need.

Click on the using statements, click on the light bulb icon that appears (or press *Ctrl + .*), and then select **Remove Unnecessary Usings**:

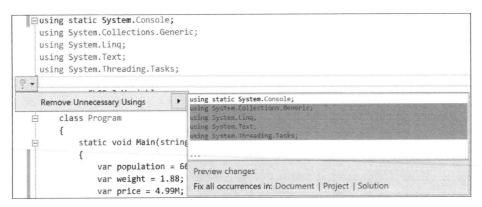

Our complete application now looks like the following code:

```
using static System.Console;

namespace Ch02_Variables
{
    class Program
    {
        static void Main(string[] args)
        {
            var population = 66000000;
            var weight = 1.88; // in kilograms
            var price = 4.99M; // in pounds sterling
            var fruit = "Apples"; // strings use double-quotes
            var letter = 'Z'; // chars use single-quotes
            var happy = true;

            int ICannotBeNull = 4;
            ICannotBeNull = default(int); // 0
            int? ICouldBeNull = null;
            var result1 = ICouldBeNull.GetValueOrDefault(); // 0
            ICouldBeNull = 4;
            var result2 = ICouldBeNull.GetValueOrDefault(); // 4

            // declaring the size of the array
            string[] names = new string[4];
            // storing items at index positions
            names[0] = "George";
            names[1] = "Jerry";
```

```
        names[2] = "Elaine";
        names[3] = "Cosmo";
        for (int i = 0; i < names.Length; i++)
        {
            WriteLine(names[i]); // read the item at this index
        }

        Write($"The population of the UK is {population}. ");
        WriteLine($"The population of the UK is {population:N0}.
");

        WriteLine($"{weight}kg of {fruit} costs {price:C}. ");

        Write("Type your name and press ENTER: ");
        string name = ReadLine();
        Write("Type your age and press ENTER: ");
        string age = ReadLine();
        WriteLine($"Hello {name}, you look good for {age}.");
    }
  }
}
```

# Reading arguments and working with arrays

You have probably been wondering what the string[] args argument is in the Main method. It is an array used to pass arguments into a console application.

Add a new **Console Application** project named **Ch02_Arguments**.

Remember how we could pass the name of the file we wanted to compile to the compiler when we used the C# compiler at the Command Prompt? We can do the same thing with our own applications. For example, we can enter the following at the Command Prompt:

Ch02_Arguments apples bananas cherries

We would be able to read the fruit names by reading them from the args array.

Remember that arrays use the square bracket syntax to indicate multiple values. Arrays have a property named Length that tells us how many items are currently in the array. If there is at least one item, then we can access it by knowing its index. Indexes start counting from zero so the first item in an array is item 0.

Add a statement to statically import the System.Console type. Write a statement to output the number of arguments passed to the application. Remove the unnecessary using statements. Your code should now look like this:

```
using static System.Console;
namespace Ch02_Arguments
{
    class Program
    {
        static void Main(string[] args)
        {
            WriteLine($"There are {args.Length} arguments.");
        }
    }
}
```

> Remember to statically import the System.Console type to simplify your code, as these instructions will not be repeated.

Press *Ctrl + F5* and view the output in the console:

**There are 0 arguments.**

To pass in some arguments, view the **Solution Explorer** window, and inside the **Ch02_Arguments** project, double-click on **Properties**:

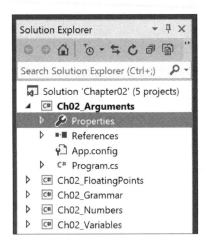

In the **Properties** window, select the **Debug** tab, and in the **Command line arguments** box, enter a space-separated list of four arguments as shown in the code and screenshot that follows:

```
firstarg second-arg third:arg "fourth arg"
```

Note that you can use almost any character in an argument including hyphens and colons. If you need to use a space inside an argument, you must wrap it in double quotes.

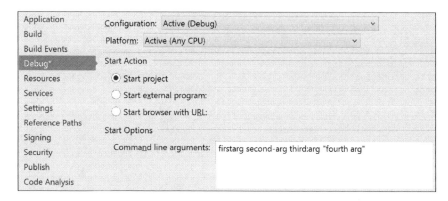

Press *Ctrl* + *F5* and view the output in the console:

```
There are 4 arguments.
```

To enumerate or iterate (that is, loop through) the values of those four arguments, add these three lines of highlighted code after outputting the length of the array:

```
WriteLine($"There are {args.Length} arguments.");
foreach (string arg in args)
{
    WriteLine(arg);
}
```

We will now use these arguments to allow the user to pick a color for the background, foreground, width and height of the console window.

Change the arguments in the **Properties** window to look like this:

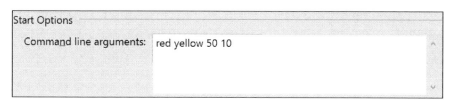

Import the System namespace by adding the following line to the top of the code file if it is not already there:

```
using System;
```

Add the highlighted code on top of the existing code like this:

```
ForegroundColor = (ConsoleColor)Enum.Parse(typeof(ConsoleColor),
args[0], true);
BackgroundColor = (ConsoleColor)Enum.Parse(typeof(ConsoleColor),
args[1], true);
WindowWidth = int.Parse(args[2]);
WindowHeight = int.Parse(args[3]);

WriteLine($"There are {args.Length} arguments.");
foreach (var arg in args)
{
    WriteLine(arg);
}
```

We needed to import the System namespace so that the compiler knows about the ConsoleColor and Enum types. If you cannot see either of these types in the IntelliSense list, it is because you are missing the using System; statement.

Press *Ctrl + F5*. The console window is now a different size and uses different colors for the foreground and background text.

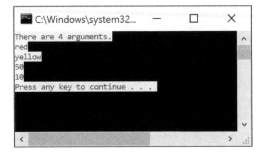

# Operating on variables

**Operators** apply simple operations, such as addition and multiplication, to operands, such as numbers. They usually return a new value that is the result of the operation.

Most operators are binary, meaning that they work on two operands:

```
var result = FirstOperand operator SecondOperand;
```

Some operators are **unary** meaning they work on a single operand. A **ternary** operator works on three operands.

# Experimenting with unary operators

Two common unary operators are used to increment ++ and decrement -- a number.

In Visual Studio, from the **View** menu, choose **Other Windows**, and then **C# Interactive**. Enter the following code:

```
> int i = 3;
> i
3
```

Note that when you enter a full statement ending in a semicolon, it is executed when you press *Enter*.

The first statement uses the assignment operator = to assign the value 3 to the variable i. When you enter a variable name at the prompt, it returns the variable's current value.

Enter the following statements and before pressing *Enter*, try to guess what the value of x and y will be:

```
> int x = 3;
> int y = x++;
```

Now check the values of x and y. You might be surprised to see that y has the value 3:

```
> x
4
> y
3
```

The variable y has the value 3 because the ++ operator executes after the assignment. This is known as postfix. If you need to increment before assignment, use prefix, as follows:

```
> int x = 3;
> int y = ++x;
> x
4
> y
4
```

You can decrement a variable using the -- operator.

**Best Practice**

Due to the confusion between prefix and postfix for the increment and decrement operators when combined with assignment, the Swift programming language designers plan to drop support for this operator in version 3. My recommendation for usage in C# is to never combine the use of ++ and -- operators with an assignment =. Perform the operations as separate statements.

# Experimenting with arithmetic operators

Arithmetic operators allow you to perform arithmetics on numbers. Enter the following in the **C# Interactive** window:

```
> 11 + 3
14
> 11 - 3
8
> 11 * 3
33
> 11 / 3
3
> 11 % 3
2
> 11.0 / 3
3.6666666666666665
```

To understand the divide (/) and modulus (%) operators when applied to integers (whole numbers), you need to think back to primary school.

Imagine you have eleven sweets and three friends. How can you divide the sweets between your friends? You can give three sweets to each of your friends and there will be two left over. Those two are the modulus, also known as remainder. If you have twelve sweets, then each friend gets four of them and there are none left over. So the remainder is 0.

If you start with a real number (such as 11.0), then the divide operator returns a floating point value, such as 3.6666666666665, rather than a whole number.

# Comparison and Boolean operators

Comparison and Boolean operators either return `true` or `false`. In the next chapter, we will use comparison operators in the `if` and `while` statements to check for conditions.

# Practicing and exploring

Test your knowledge and understanding by answering some questions, get some hands-on practice, and explore the topics covered in this chapter with deeper research.

# Exercise 2.1 – test your knowledge

What type would you choose for the following "numbers"?

1. A person's telephone number
2. A person's height
3. A person's age
4. A person's salary
5. A book's ISBN
6. A book's price
7. A book's shipping weight
8. A country's population
9. The number of stars in the Universe
10. The number of employees in each of the small or medium businesses in the UK (up to about 50,000 employees per business)

# Exercise 2.2 – practice number sizes and ranges

Create a **Console Application** project named **Ch02_Exercise02** that outputs the number of bytes in memory that each of the following number types use and the minimum and maximum possible values they can have: `sbyte`, `byte`, `short`, `ushort`, `int`, `uint`, `long`, `ulong`, `float`, `double`, and `decimal`.

Read the online MSDN documentation for Composite Formatting, available at `https://msdn.microsoft.com/en-us/library/ txafckwd(v=vs.110).aspx`, to learn how to align text in a console application.

The output of your application should look something like the following screenshot:

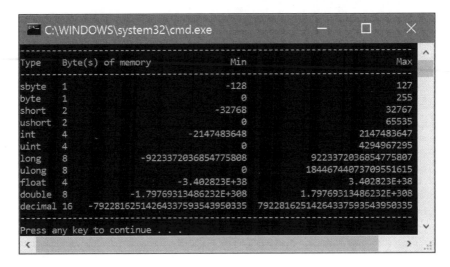

# Exercise 2.3 – explore topics

Use the following links to read more about the topics covered in this chapter:

- **C# Keywords**: `https://msdn.microsoft.com/en-us/library/x53a06bb.aspx`

- **Integral Types Table (C# Reference)**: `https://msdn.microsoft.com/en-us/library/exx3b86w.aspx`

- **Floating-Point Types Table (C# Reference)**: `https://msdn.microsoft.com/en-us/library/9ahet949.aspx`

- **decimal (C# Reference)**: `https://msdn.microsoft.com/en-us/library/364x0z75.aspx`

- **bool (C# Reference)**: `https://msdn.microsoft.com/en-us/library/c8f5xwh7.aspx`

- **char (C# Reference)**: `https://msdn.microsoft.com/en-us/library/x9h8tsay.aspx`

- **string (C# Reference)**: https://msdn.microsoft.com/en-us/library/362314fe.aspx

- **var (C# Reference)**: https://msdn.microsoft.com/en-us/library/bb383973.aspx

- **Nullable Types (C# Programming Guide)**: https://msdn.microsoft.com/en-us/library/1t3y8s4s.aspx

- **Standard Numeric Format Strings**: https://msdn.microsoft.com/en-us/library/dwhawy9k(v=vs.110).aspx

- **Custom Numeric Format Strings**: https://msdn.microsoft.com/en-us/library/0c899ak8(v=vs.110).aspx

- **Custom Date and Time Format Strings**: https://msdn.microsoft.com/en-us/library/8kb3ddd4(v=vs.110).aspx

- **Composite Formatting**: https://msdn.microsoft.com/en-us/library/txafckwd(v=vs.110).aspx

- **Console Class**: https://msdn.microsoft.com/en-us/library/system.console(v=vs.110).aspx

- **C# Operators**: https://msdn.microsoft.com/en-us/library/6a71f45d.aspx

- **Languages features in C# 6 and VB 14**: https://github.com/dotnet/roslyn/wiki/Languages-features-in-C%23-6-and-VB-14

# Summary

In this chapter, you learned how to declare variables with an explicit type or inferred with the var keyword, we discussed some of the built-in types for numbers, text, and Booleans, we covered how to choose between number types, and we experimented with some operators.

In the next chapter, you will learn about branching, looping, converting between types, and handling exceptions.

# 3

# Controlling the Flow, Converting Types, and Handling Exceptions

This chapter is about writing code that makes decisions, repeats blocks of statements, converts between types, and handles errors (known as exceptions). You will also learn about the best places to look for help.

This chapter covers the following topics:

- Selection statements
- Iteration statements
- Casting and converting between types
- Handling exceptions
- Checking for overflow
- Looking for help

## Selection statements

Every application needs to be able to select from choices and branch along different code paths. The two selection statements in C# are `if` and `switch`, also known as `if-else` and `switch-case`. You can use `if` for all your code but `switch` can simplify your code in some common scenarios.

Start Microsoft Visual Studio 2015. In Visual Studio, press *Ctrl* + *Shift* + *N* or choose **File** | **New** | **Project…**.

In the **New Project** dialog, in the **Installed Templates** list, select **Visual C#**. In the list at the center, select Console Application, type the name **Ch03_SelectionStatements**, change the location to **C:\Code**, type the solution name **Chapter03**, and then click on **OK**.

At the top of the Program.cs file, statically import the System.Console type, as follows:

```
using static System.Console;
```

# The if-else statement

The if-else statement determines which branch to follow by evaluating a Boolean expression. The else block is optional. if-else statements can be nested and combined. Each Boolean expression can be independent of the others.

Add the following statements to the Main method to check whether this console application has any arguments passed to it:

```
if (args.Length == 0)
{
    WriteLine("There are no arguments.");
}
else
{
    WriteLine("There is at least one argument.");
}
```

Since there is only a single statement inside each block, this code *can* be written without the curly braces, as follows:

```
if (args.Length == 0)
    WriteLine("There are no arguments.");
else
    WriteLine("There is at least one argument.");
```

This style of the if-else statement is *not* recommended because it can introduce serious bugs, for example, the infamous #gotofail bug in Apple's iPhone operating system. For 18 months after Apple's iOS 6 was released, it had a bug in its **Secure Sockets Layer** (SSL) encryption code, which meant that any user running Safari to connect to secure websites, such as their bank, for the purpose of payment transactions and other online banking activities, were not properly secure because an important check was being accidently skipped.

```
https://gotofail.com/
```

Just because you can leave out the curly braces, doesn't mean you should. Your code is not "more efficient" without them, instead, it is less maintainable and potentially more dangerous, as this tweet points out:

**Chris Adamson** @invalidname · May 26
Had a colleague remove my {} surrounding a 1-line if clause today. No, not angry. It's on his conscience now. #gotofail

↩     ↻ 10     ★ 15     •••

# The switch-case statement

The `switch-case` statement is different from the `if-else` statement because it compares a single expression against a list of possible cases. Every case is related to the single expression. Every case must end with the `break` keyword (such as case 1 in the following code) or the `goto case` keywords, (such as case 2 in the following code) or they should have no statements (such as case 3 in the following code).

Enter the following code after the `if-else` statement you wrote previously. Note that the first line is a label that can be jumped to and the second line generates a random number. The `switch` statement branches based on the value of this random number:

```
A_label:
    var number = (new Random()).Next(1, 7);
    WriteLine($"My random number is {number}");
    switch (number)
    {
        case 1: // must be a literal value
            WriteLine("One");
            break; // jumps to end of switch statement
        case 2:
            WriteLine("Two");
            goto case 1;
        case 3:
        case 4:
            WriteLine("Three or four");
            goto case 1;
        case 5:
            // go to sleep for half a second
            System.Threading.Thread.Sleep(500);
            goto A_label;
```

```
        default:
            WriteLine("Default");
            break;
    } // end of switch statement
```

You can use the `goto` keyword to jump to another case or a label. The `goto` keyword is frowned upon by most programmers but can be the best solution in some scenarios. Use it sparingly.

Run the program by pressing *Ctrl + F5*. Run it multiple times to see what happens in various cases of random numbers, as shown in the following output:

**There are no arguments.**

**My random number is 5**

**My random number is 3**

**Three or four**

**One**

# Autoformatting code

Let's take a diversion for a minute to talk about formatting. Code is easier to read and understand if it is consistently indented and spaced out.

If your code can compile, then Visual Studio can automatically format it so it's nicely spaced and indented.

Type the following code (Visual Studio will autoformat even at the end of each line so when it does so, force the code to be improperly spaced out as shown):

```
var x    =3;
if(x==3)
{ WriteLine("three");
}
```

Press *Shift + F6* and wait for your code to build, and then press *Ctrl + K, D*. Your code will now look like this:

```
var x = 3;
if (x == 3)
{
    WriteLine("three");
}
```

# Iteration statements

Iteration statements repeat a block either while a condition is `true` or for each item in a sequence. The choice of which statement to use is based on a combination of ease of understanding to solve the logic problem and personal preference.

Add a new Console Application project named **Ch03_IterationStatements**.

Set the solution's startup project to be the current selection.

# The while statement

The `while` statement evaluates a Boolean expression and continues to loop while it is `true`.

Type the following code inside the `Main` method (remember to statically import the `System.Console` type!):

```
int x = 0;
while (x < 10)
{
    WriteLine(x);
    x++;
}
```

Press *Ctrl* + *F5* and view the output in the console:

```
0
1
2
3
4
5
6
7
8
9
```

# The do-while statement

The do-while statement is like while except the Boolean expression is checked at the bottom of the block instead of the top, which means that it always executes at least once.

If you want to try the code for the do-while statement, then select all the previous statements and press *Ctrl + K, C* to comment them out and then enter the following code and run it:

```
int x = 0;
do
{
    WriteLine(x);
    x++;
} while (x < 10);
```

When you then press *Ctrl + F5*, you will see that the results are the same as those we got earlier.

# The for statement

The for statement is like while except that it is more succinct. It combines an initializer statement that executes once at the start of the loop, a Boolean expression to check whether the loop should continue, and an incrementer that executes at the bottom of the loop.

The for statement is commonly used with an integer counter, although it doesn't have to be as shown in the following code:

```
for (int y = 0; y < 10; y++)
{
    WriteLine(y);
}
```

# The foreach statement

The foreach statement is a bit different from the other three. It is used to perform a block of statements on each item in a sequence (for example, an array or collection). Each item is read-only and if the sequence is modified during iteration, for example, by adding or removing an item, then an exception will be thrown.

Type the following code inside the `Main` method, which creates an array of `string` variables and then uses a `foreach` statement to enumerate and output the length of each of them:

```
string[] names = { "Adam", "Barry", "Charlie" };
foreach (string name in names)
{
    WriteLine($"{name} has {name.Length} characters.");
}
```

Press *Ctrl* + *F5* and view the output in the console:

```
Adam has 4 characters.
Barry has 5 characters.
Charlie has 7 characters.
```

## How does the foreach statement actually work?

Technically, the `foreach` statement will work on any type that implements an interface called `IEnumerable`, but you don't need to worry about what an interface is for now. You will learn about interfaces in *Chapter 7, Implementing Interfaces and Inheriting Classes*.

If you use a tool like `ildasm`, then you will see that the compiler turns the `foreach` statement in the preceding code into something like this:

```
IEnumerator e = names.GetEnumerator();
while(e.MoveNext())
{
    string name = (string)e.Current; // Current is read-only!
    WriteLine($"{name} has {name.Length} characters.");
}
```

 Due to the use of an iterator, the variable declared in a `foreach` statement cannot be used to modify the value of the current item.

# Casting and converting between types

You will often need to convert between different types.

Add a new Console Application project named **Ch03_CastingConverting**.

## Casting from numbers to numbers

It is safe to implicitly cast an `int` variable into a `double` variable.

In the `Main` method, enter the following statements:

```
int a = 10;
double b = a;
WriteLine(b);
```

You cannot implicitly cast a `double` variable into an `int` variable because it is potentially unsafe and would lose data.

In the `Main` method, enter the following statements:

```
double c = 9.8;
int d = c; // compiler gives an error for this line
WriteLine(d);
```

Press *Ctrl* + *W*, *E* to view the **Error List**, as shown in the following screenshot:

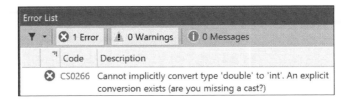

You must explicitly cast a `double` into an `int` variable using a pair of round brackets around the type you want to cast the `double` into. The pair of round brackets is the cast operator. Even then you must beware that the part after the decimal point will be trimmed off without warning.

Modify the assignment statement for the variable d, as shown in the following code:

```
double c = 9.8;
int d = (int)c;
WriteLine(d); // d is 9 losing the .8 part
```

We must do a similar operation when moving values between larger integers and smaller integers. Again, beware that you might lose information because any value too big will get set to -1!

Enter the following code:

```
long e = 10;
int f = (int)e;
WriteLine($"e is {e} and f is {f}");
e = long.MaxValue;
f = (int)e;
WriteLine($"e is {e} and f is {f}");
```

Press *Ctrl* + *F5* and view the output in the console:

**e is 10 and f is 10**

**e is 9223372036854775807 and f is -1**

# Using the Convert type

An alternative to using the casting operator is to use the System.Convert type.

At the top of the Program.cs file, type the following code:

```
using static System.Convert;
```

We can now use a lot of ToSomeType methods.

```
double g = 9.8;
int h = ToInt32(g);
WriteLine($"g is {g} and h is {h}");
```

Note that one difference between casting and converting is that converting rounds the double value up to 10 instead of trimming the part after the decimal point.

Press *Ctrl* + *F5* and view the output in the console:

**g is 9.8 and h is 10**

The System.Convert type can convert to and from all the C# number types as well as Booleans, strings, and dates and times.

# Rounding numbers

You have now seen that the cast operator trims the decimal part of a real number and that the convert methods round up or down. But what is the rule for rounding?

In British primary schools, children are taught to round *up* if the decimal part is .5 or higher and round *down* if the decimal part is less.

Enter the following code beneath the code that you have already written to see the effect of converting four double variables to int variables:

```
double i = 9.49;
double j = 9.5;
double k = 10.49;
double l = 10.5;
WriteLine($"i is {i}, ToInt(i) is {ToInt32(i)}");
WriteLine($"j is {j}, ToInt(j) is {ToInt32(j)}");
WriteLine($"k is {k}, ToInt(k) is {ToInt32(k)}");
WriteLine($"l is {l}, ToInt(l) is {ToInt32(l)}");
```

Press *Ctrl + F5* and view the output in the console:

```
i is 9.49, ToInt(i) is 9
j is 9.5, ToInt(j) is 10
k is 10.49, ToInt(k) is 10
l is 10.5, ToInt(l) is 10
```

Note that the rule for rounding in C# is subtly different. It will round *up* if the decimal part is .5 or higher *and* the non-decimal part is odd, but it will round *down* if the non-decimal part is even. It always rounds *down* if the decimal part is less than .5.

This rule is known as **Banker's Rounding** and it is preferred because it reduces bias. Sadly, other languages such as JavaScript use the primary school rule.

[

**Best Practice**
For every programming language that you use, check its rounding rules. They may not work the way you expect!
]

# Converting from any type to a string

The most common conversion is from any type into a string variable, so all types have a method named ToString that they inherit from the System.Object class (which can be simplified using the object keyword).

The `ToString` method converts the current value of any variable into a textual representation. Some types can't be sensibly represented as text so they return their namespace and type name. Enter the following statements beneath the code that you have already written to declare four variables of types `int`, `bool`, `DateTime`, and `object`, and see what their implementations of `ToString` return:

```
int number = 12;
WriteLine(number.ToString());
bool boolean = true;
WriteLine(boolean.ToString());
DateTime now = DateTime.Now;
WriteLine(now.ToString());
object me = new object();
WriteLine(me.ToString());
```

Press *Ctrl* + *F5* and view the output in the console:

```
12
True
04/03/2016 13:48:54
System.Object
```

# Parsing from strings to numbers or dates and times

The second most common conversion is from strings to numbers or dates and times. The opposite of `ToString` is `Parse`. Only a few types have a `Parse` method.

Add a new Console Application project named **Ch03_Parsing**.

Add the following statements to the bottom of the `Main` method:

```
int age = int.Parse("27");
DateTime birthday = DateTime.Parse("4 July 1980");
WriteLine($"I was born {age} years ago.");
WriteLine($"My birthday is {birthday}.");
WriteLine($"My birthday is {birthday:D}.");
```

Press *Ctrl* + *F5* and view the output in the console:

```
I was born 27 years ago.
My birthday is 04/07/1980 00:00:00.
My birthday is 04 July 1980.
```

One problem with the `Parse` method is that it gives errors if the string cannot be converted.

Add the following statements to the bottom of the `Main` method:

```
int count = int.Parse("abc");
```

Press *Ctrl* + *F5* and view the output in the console:

**Unhandled Exception: System.FormatException: Input string was not in a correct format.**

To avoid errors, you can use the `TryParse` method instead. `TryParse` attempts to convert the input string and returns `true` if it can convert it and `false` if it cannot. The `out` keyword is required to allow the `TryParse` method to set the `count` variable when the conversion works.

Replace the `int count` declaration with the following statements:

```
Write("How many eggs are there? ");
int count;
string input = Console.ReadLine();
if (int.TryParse(input, out count))
{
    WriteLine($"There are {count} eggs.");
}
else
{
    WriteLine("I could not parse the input.");
}
```

Run the application twice. The first time, enter 12. You will see the following output:

**How many eggs are there? 12**

**There are 12 eggs.**

The second time, enter `twelve`. You will see the following output:

**How many eggs are there? twelve**

**I could not parse the count.**

 You can also use the `Convert` type, but like the `Parse` method, it gives an error if it cannot convert.

# Handling exceptions

You've seen several scenarios when errors have occurred. C# calls that an exception being thrown. A best practice is to avoid writing code that will throw an exception whenever possible, but sometimes you can't. In those scenarios, you must catch the exception and handle it.

As you have seen, the default behavior of a console application is to display details about the exception in the console window and then stop running the application.

The default behavior of a Windows desktop application is to display details about the exception in a dialog box and allow the user to choose to either continue or stop running the application.

You can have more control over how you want to handle exceptions using the try-catch statement.

Add a new Console Application project named **Ch03_HandlingExceptions**.

# The try-catch statement

When you know that a statement can cause an error, you should wrap that statement in a try block. For example, parsing from a string to a number can cause an error. We do not have to do anything inside the catch block. When the following code executes, the error will get caught and not displayed and the Console Application will continue running.

In the Main method, add the following statements:

```
WriteLine("Before parsing");
Write("What is your age? ");
string input = Console.ReadLine();
try
{
    int age = int.Parse(input);
    WriteLine($"You are {age} years old.");
}
catch
{

}
WriteLine("After parsing");
```

Run the program by pressing *Ctrl + F5* and enter a valid age, for example, 43:

```
Before parsing
What is your age? 43
You are 43 years old.
After parsing
```

Run the program and enter an invalid age, for example, kermit;

```
Before parsing
What is your age? kermit
After parsing
```

It can be useful to see the type of error that occurred.

# Catching all exceptions

Modify the catch statement to look like this:

```
catch(Exception ex)
{
    WriteLine($"{ex.GetType()} says {ex.Message}");
}
```

Run the program and again enter an invalid age, for example, kermit:

```
Before parsing
What is your age? kermit
System.FormatException says Input string was not in a correct format.
After parsing
```

# Catching specific exceptions

Now that we know which specific type of exception occurred, we can improve our code by catching just that type of exception and customizing the message that we display to the user.

Leave the existing catch block but add the following code above it:

```
catch (FormatException)
{
    WriteLine("The age you entered is not a valid number format.");
}
```

```
catch (Exception ex)
{
    WriteLine($"{ex.GetType()} says {ex.Message}");
}
```

Run the program and again enter an invalid age, for example, `kermit`:

```
Before parsing
What is your age? kermit
The age you entered is not a valid number format.
After parsing
```

The reason we want to leave the more general catch below is because there might be other types of exception that can occur. Run the program and enter a number that is too big for an integer, for example, `9876543210`:

```
Before parsing
What is your age? 9876543210
System.OverflowException says Value was either too large or too small for
an Int32.
After parsing
```

Let's add another catch for this new type of exception:

```
catch(OverflowException)
{
    WriteLine("Your age is a valid number format but it is either too
big or small.");
}
catch (FormatException)
{
    WriteLine("The age you entered is not a valid number format.");
}
```

Rerun the program one more time and enter a number that is too big:

```
Before parsing
What is your age? 9876543210
Your age is a valid number format but it is either too big or small.
After parsing
```

The order in which you catch exceptions is important. The correct order is related to the inheritance hierarchy of the exception types. You will learn about inheritance in *Chapter 6, Building Your Own Types with Object-Oriented Programming*. But don't worry too much about this – the compiler will give you build errors if you catch exceptions in the wrong order anyway.

# The finally statement

Sometimes we would want to ensure that some code executes regardless of whether an exception occurs or not. To do this, we use a finally statement.

Add a new Console Application project named **Ch03_Finally**.

A common scenario in which you would want to use finally is when working with files and databases. When you open a file or a database, you are using resources outside of .NET. These are called **unmanaged resources** and must be disposed of when you are done working with them. To guarantee that they are disposed of, we can call the Dispose method inside of a finally block.

You will learn about files and databases in more detail in later chapters. For now, focus on the code that we write in the finally block.

Import the System.IO namespace at the top of the code file:

```
using System.IO;
```

Type the following code in the Main method:

```
FileStream file = null;
StreamWriter writer = null;
try
{
    file = File.OpenWrite(@"c:\Code\file.txt");
    writer = new StreamWriter(file);
    writer.WriteLine("Hello C#!");
}
catch (Exception ex)
{
    // if the folder doesn't exist the exception will be caught
    WriteLine($"{ex.GetType()} says {ex.Message}");
}
```

```
finally
{
    if(writer != null)
    {
        writer.Dispose();
        WriteLine("The writer's unmanaged resources have been
disposed.");
    }
    if (file != null)
    {
        file.Dispose();
        WriteLine("The file's unmanaged resources have been
disposed.");
    }
}
```

Press *Ctrl + F5* and view the output in the console:

**The writer's unmanaged resources have been disposed.**

**The file's unmanaged resources have been disposed.**

# Simplifying disposal with the using statement

If you don't need to catch any exceptions, then you can simplify the code that needs to check for a non-null object and then call its `Dispose` method, as follows:

```
using (FileStream file2 = File.OpenWrite(@"c:\Code\file2.txt"))
{
    using (StreamWriter writer2 = new StreamWriter(file2))
    {
        writer.WriteLine("Hello C#!");
    } // automatically calls Dispose if the object is not null
} // automatically calls Dispose if the object is not null
```

The compiler changes your code into the longer version but without a `catch` block. You are allowed to use nested `try-catch` statements, so if you do want to catch any exceptions you can do this.

Add this code after the existing code. It will create a file named `file2.txt`:

```
using (FileStream file2 = File.OpenWrite(@"c:\Code\file2.txt"))
{
    using (StreamWriter writer2 = new StreamWriter(file2))
    {
        try
        {
```

```
            Writer2.WriteLine("Hello C#!");
        }
        catch (Exception ex)
        {
            WriteLine($"{ex.GetType()} says {ex.Message}");
        }
    }
}
```

 Many types, including `FileStream` and `StreamWriter` mentioned earlier, provide a `Close` method as well as a `Dispose` method. In the .NET Framework, you can use either because they do the same thing. In the .NET Core, Microsoft has simplified the API so you must use `Dispose`.

# Checking for overflow

Earlier, we saw that when casting between number types it was possible to lose information, for example, when casting from a `long` variable to an `int` variable. If the value stored in a type is too big, it will overflow.

Add a new Console Application project named **Ch03_CheckingForOverflow**.

## The checked statement

The `checked` statement tells .NET to throw an exception when an overflow happens instead of allowing to it happen silently.

We set the initial value of an `int` variable to its maximum value minus one. Then, we increment it several times, outputting its value each time. Note that once x gets above its maximum value, it overflows to its minimum value and continues incrementing from there.

Type the following code in the `Main` method and run the program:

```
int x = int.MaxValue - 1;
WriteLine(x);
x++;
WriteLine(x);
x++;
WriteLine(x);
x++;
WriteLine(x);
```

Press *Ctrl* + *F5* and view the output in the console:

2147483646

2147483647

-2147483648

-2147483647

Now let's get the compiler to warn us about the overflow using the checked statement:

```
checked
{
    int x = int.MaxValue - 1;
    WriteLine(x);
    x++;
    WriteLine(x);
    x++;
    WriteLine(x);
    x++;
    WriteLine(x);
}
```

Press *Ctrl+F5* and view the output in the console:

2147483646

2147483647

**Unhandled Exception: System.OverflowException: Arithmetic operation resulted in an overflow.**

Just like any other exception, we could wrap these statements in a try-catch block and display a nicer error message for the user:

```
try
{
    // previous code goes here
}
catch(OverflowException)
{
    WriteLine("The code overflowed but I caught the exception.");
}
```

Press *Ctrl* + *F5* and view the output in the console:

2147483646

2147483647

**The code overflowed but I caught the exception.**

# The unchecked statement

A related keyword is unchecked. Type the following statement at the end of the previous statements. The compiler will not compile this statement because it knows it would overflow:

```
int x = int.MaxValue + 1;
```

Press *F6* to build and notice the error, as shown in the following screenshot:

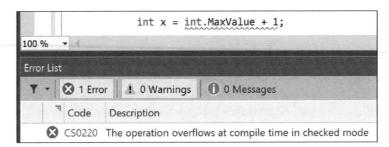

Note that this is a **compile-time** check. To disable compile-time checks, we can wrap the statement in an unchecked block, as shown in the following code:

```
unchecked
{
    int x = int.MaxValue + 1;
    WriteLine(x);
    x--;
    WriteLine(x);
    x--;
}
```

Press *Ctrl* + *F5* and view the output in the console:

```
2147483646
2147483647
The code overflowed but I caught the exception.
-2147483648
2147483647
2147483646
```

Of course it would be pretty rare that you would want to explicitly switch off a check like this because it allows an overflow to occur. But, perhaps, you can think of a scenario where you might want that behavior.

# Looking for help

This section is about how to find quality information about programming on the Web.

## MSDN

The definitive resource for getting help about C# and .NET is the **Microsoft Developer Network (MSDN)**.

Visual Studio is integrated with MSDN, so if you press *F1* inside a C# keyword or type, then it will open your browser and take you to the official documentation.

Almost all the reference URLs at the end of chapters in this book will take you to MSDN.

## Getting the definition of code

Another useful keystroke is *F12*. This will show what the original source code looks like. It uses a similar technique as IL DASM to reverse engineer the source code from Microsoft assemblies.

Enter the following code, click inside int, and then press *F12* (or right-click and choose **Go To Definition**):

```
int x;
```

In the new code window that appears, you can see that int is in the mscorlib.dll assembly, it is named Int32, it is in the System namespace, and int is therefore an alias for System.Int32.

```
C#  MetadataAsSourceProject                      ▾  ⁛ System.Int32                             ▾  ⚙ T
     ⊞ Assembly mscorlib, Version=4.0.0.0, Culture=neutral, PublicKeyToken=b77a5c561934e089

     ⊞ using ...

     ⊟ namespace System
       {
     ⊞     ...public struct Int32 : IComparable, IFormattable, IConvertible, IComparable<Int32>
             {
     ⊞           ...public const Int32 MaxValue = 2147483647;
     ⊞           ...public const Int32 MinValue = -2147483648;
```

Microsoft defined `Int32` using a `struct` keyword, meaning that it is a value type stored on the stack. You can also see that `Int32` implements interfaces such as `IComparable` and has constants for its maximum and minimum possible values.

In the code editor window, find the `Parse` methods and click on the small box with a plus symbol in the `Parse` methods to expand the code like I have done in the following screenshot:

```
//
// Summary:
//     Converts the string representation of a number to its 32-bit signed integer equivalent.
//
// Parameters:
//   s:
//     A string containing a number to convert.
//
// Returns:
//     A 32-bit signed integer equivalent to the number contained in s.
//
// Exceptions:
//   T:System.ArgumentNullException:
//     s is null.
//
//   T:System.FormatException:
//     s is not in the correct format.
//
//   T:System.OverflowException:
//     s represents a number less than System.Int32.MinValue or greater than System.Int32.MaxValue.
public static Int32 Parse(string s);
```

In the comment, you will see that Microsoft has documented what exceptions might occur if you call this method (`ArgumentNullException`, `FormatException`, and `OverflowException`).

Now we know that we need to wrap a call to this method in a `try-catch` statement and which exceptions to catch.

# StackOverflow

**StackOverflow** is the most popular third-party website for getting answers to difficult programming questions. It is so popular that search engines such as **DuckDuckGo** have a special way to write a query to search the site.

Go to DuckDuckGo.com and enter the following query:

```
!so securestring
```

You will get the following results:

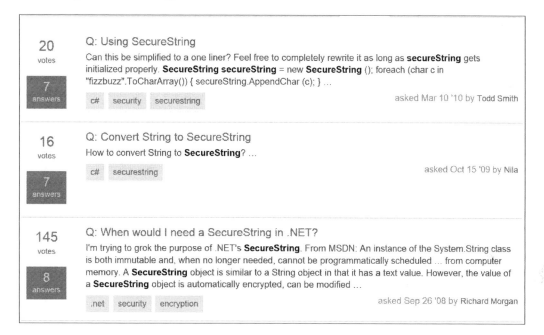

# Google

You can search **Google** with advanced search options to increase the likelihood of finding what you need.

For example, if you are searching for information about **garbage collection** using a simple Google query, you would see a Wikipedia definition of garbage collection in computer science and then a list of garbage collection services in your local area.

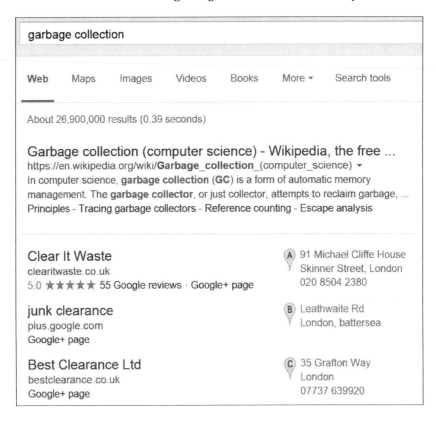

We can improve the search by restricting it to a useful site like StackOverflow, as shown in the following screenshot:

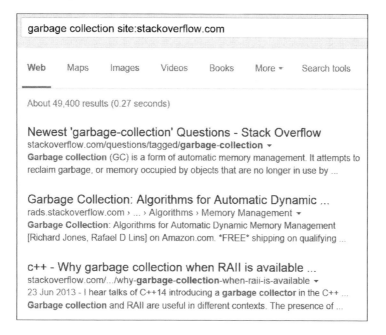

We can improve the search even more by removing languages that we might not care about, such as C++, as shown in the following screenshot:

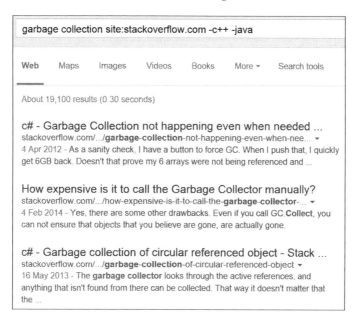

# Design patterns

A design pattern is a general solution to a common problem. Programmers have been solving the same problems over and over. When the community discovers a good reusable solution, we call it a design pattern. Many design patterns have been documented over the years.

Microsoft has a group called **patterns & practices** that specializes in documenting and promoting design patterns for Microsoft products.

**Best Practice**

Before writing new code, search to see if someone else has already solved the problem in a general way.

# Practice and explore

Test your knowledge and understanding by answering some questions, get some hands-on practice, and explore with deeper research into this chapter's topics.

# Exercise 3.1 – test your knowledge

Answer the following questions:

1. What happens when you divide an `int` variable by `0`?
2. What happens when you divide a `double` variable by `0`?
3. What happens when you overflow an `int` variable, that is, set it to a value beyond its range?
4. What is the difference between `x = y++;` and `x = ++y;`?
5. What is the difference between `break`, `continue`, and `return` when used inside a `loop` statement?
6. What are the three parts of a `for` statement and which of them are required?
7. What is the difference between the `=` and `==` operators?

# Exercise 3.2 – explore loops and overflow

What will happen if this code executes?

```
int max = 500;
for (byte i = 0; i < max; i++)
{
    WriteLine(i);
}
```

Add a new Console Application named **Ch03_Exercise02** and enter the preceding code. Run the application by pressing *Ctrl + F5*. What happens?

What code could you *add* (don't change any of the preceding code) to warn us about the problem?

# Exercise 3.3 – practice loops and operators

FizzBuzz is a group word game for children to teach them about division. Players take turns to count incrementally, replacing any number divisible by three with the word "fizz", any number divisible by five with the word "buzz", and any number divisible by both with "fizzbuzz".

Some interviewers give applicants simple FizzBuzz-style problems to solve during interviews. Most good programmers should be able to write out on paper or whiteboard a program to output a simulated FizzBuzz game in under a couple of minutes.

Want to know something worrisome? Many computer science graduates can't. You can even find senior programmers who take more than 10-15 minutes to write a solution.

> *"199 out of 200 applicants for every programming job can't write code at all. I repeat: they can't write any code whatsoever."*
>
> *-Reginald Braithwaite*

This quote is taken from `http://blog.codinghorror.com/why-cant-programmers-program/`.

Refer to the following link for more information:

`http://imranontech.com/2007/01/24/using-fizzbuzz-to-find-developers-who-grok-coding/`

Create a Console Application named **Ch03_Exercise03** that outputs a simulated FizzBuzz game counting up to `100`. The output should look something like this:

```
1, 2, Fizz, 4, Buzz, Fizz, 7, 8, Fizz, Buzz, 11, Fizz, 13, 14, FizzBuzz,
16, 17, Fizz, 19, Buzz, Fizz, 22, 23, Fizz, Buzz, 26, Fizz, 28, 29,
FizzBuzz, 31, 32, Fizz, 34, Buzz, Fizz, 37, 38, Fizz, Buzz, 41, Fizz, 43,
44, FizzBuzz, 46, 47, Fizz, 49, Buzz, Fizz, 52, 53, Fizz, Buzz, 56, Fizz,
58, 59, FizzBuzz, 61, 62, Fizz, 64, Buzz, Fizz, 67, 68, Fizz, Buzz, 71,
Fizz, 73, 74, FizzBuzz, 76, 77, Fizz, 79, Buzz, Fizz, 82, 83, Fizz, Buzz,
86, Fizz, 88, 89, FizzBuzz, 91, 92, Fizz, 94, Buzz, Fizz, 97, 98, Fizz,
Buzz
```

## Exercise 3.4 – practice exception handling

Create a Console Application named **Ch03_Exercise04** that asks the user for two numbers in the range 0-255 and then divides the first number by the second:

```
Enter a number between 1 and 255: 100

Enter another number between 1 and 255: 8

100 divided by 8 is 12
```

Write exception handlers to catch any thrown errors:

```
Enter a number between 1 and 255: apples

Enter another number between 1 and 255: bananas

FormatException: Input string was not in a correct format.
```

## Exercise 3.5 – explore topics

Use the following links to read in more detail about the topics covered in this chapter:

- **Selection Statements (C# Reference)**: https://msdn.microsoft.com/en-us/library/676s4xab.aspx

- **Iteration Statements (C# Reference)**: https://msdn.microsoft.com/en-us/library/32dbftby.aspx

- **Jump Statements (C# Reference)**: https://msdn.microsoft.com/en-us/library/d96yfwee.aspx

- **Casting and Type Conversions (C# Programming Guide)**: https://msdn.microsoft.com/en-us/library/ms173105.aspx

- **Exception Handling Statements (C# Reference)**: https://msdn.microsoft.com/en-us/library/s7fekhdy.aspx

- **Checked and Unchecked (C# Reference)**: https://msdn.microsoft.com/en-us/library/khy08726.aspx

- **Namespace Keywords (C# Reference)**: https://msdn.microsoft.com/en-us/library/cxtk6h5e.aspx

- **StackOverflow**: http://stackoverflow.com/

- **Google Advanced Search**: http://www.google.com/advanced_search

- **Design Patterns**: https://msdn.microsoft.com/en-us/library/ff649977.aspx

- **patterns & practices**: https://msdn.microsoft.com/en-us/library/ff921345.aspx

# Summary

In this chapter, you learned how to branch and loop, how to convert between types, how to handle exceptions, and most importantly, how to find help!

You are now ready to learn more about what is underneath C# — .NET types.

# Using Common .NET Types

$4$

This chapter is about .NET types and how they are related to C#. You will learn about .NET Framework and .NET Core, and their class library assemblies of common types that allow your applications to connect existing components together to perform common practical tasks.

This chapter covers the following topics:

- Using assemblies and namespaces
- Storing and manipulating text
- Storing data with collections

## Using assemblies and namespaces

The .NET Framework and the .NET Core are made up of several pieces, which are as follows:

- **Language compilers**: These turn your source code (written with languages such as C#, F#, Visual Basic, and others) into **intermediate language (IL)** code stored in assemblies (applications and class libraries). C# 6 introduced a completely rewritten compiler known as Roslyn.

- **Common Language Runtimes (CLR** and **CoreCLR)**: These runtimes load assemblies, compile the IL code stored in them into native code instructions for your computer's CPU, and execute the code within an environment that manages resources such as threads and memory.

- **Base Class Libraries (BCL** and **CoreFX)**: These are prebuilt assemblies of types for performing common tasks when building applications. You can use them to quickly build anything you want, rather like combining LEGO pieces.

# Comparing .NET Framework with .NET Core

The .NET Framework is a superset of .NET Core.

Although .NET Core has less functionality today, going forward, Microsoft has said that new features will be first added to .NET Core and then ported back to .NET Framework.

In this book, I will use the term **.NET** when introducing features that apply to both the .NET Framework and the .NET Core.

# Base Class Libraries and CoreFX

The .NET Framework's BCL and the .NET Core's CoreFX are libraries of prebuilt code that are divided into assemblies and namespaces that make it easier to manage the tens of thousands of types available. It is important to understand the difference between an assembly and a namespace.

## Assemblies

An **assembly** is where a type is stored in the filesystem. Assemblies are a mechanism for deploying code. For example, the `System.Data.dll` assembly contains types for managing databases.

When using the .NET Framework, the `System.Data.dll` assembly can be found in the **Global Assembly Cache (GAC)** centralized folder `C:\Program Files (x86)\ Reference Assemblies\Microsoft\Framework\.NETFramework\v4.6\`.

When using .NET Core, the equivalent assembly would be found in a private subfolder alongside other dependency assemblies.

## Namespaces

A **namespace** is the address of a type. Namespaces are a mechanism to uniquely identify a type by providing a full address rather than just a short name.

In the real world, *Bob* of *34 Sycamore Street* is different from *Bob* of *12 Willow Drive*.

In .NET, the `IActionFilter` interface of the `System.Web.Mvc` namespace is different from the `IActionFilter` interface of the `System.Web.Http.Filters` namespace.

# Referencing an assembly

If an assembly is compiled as a class library (it provides types for other assemblies to use), then it has the file extension **DLL (dynamic link library)** and cannot be executed standalone.

If an assembly is compiled as an application, then it has the file extension **EXE (executable)** and can be executed standalone.

Any assembly (both applications and class libraries) can reference one or more class library assemblies, but you cannot have circular references, so assembly *B* cannot reference assembly *A* if assembly *A* already references assembly *B*. Visual Studio will warn you if you attempt to add a reference that would cause a circular reference.

# Referencing Microsoft Core Library

Every application compiled for .NET has an automatic reference to **Microsoft Core Library** (`mscorlib.dll`). This special assembly contains types that almost all applications would need, such as the `int` and `string` types.

The name Microsoft Core Library has nothing to do with .NET Core.

To use types in other assemblies, they must be manually referenced. Most Visual Studio project templates add some common assembly references for you, for example, the `System.Xml.dll` assembly for working with XML.

# An example of assembly references

The following diagram shows a console application that needs to connect to a database, process an XML file, connect to an HTTP server, and query data using LINQ so that it has references to the assemblies that contain types to perform those tasks:

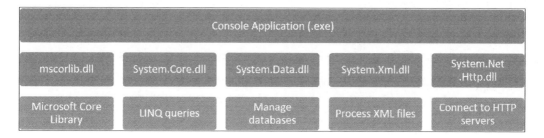

# Relating assemblies and namespaces

The following steps will help you to relate assemblies and namespaces:

1. Start Microsoft Visual Studio 2015.

2. In Visual Studio, press *Ctrl + Shift + N* or navigate to **File | New | Project...**

3. In the **New Project** dialog, in the **Installed Templates** list, select **Visual C#**. In the list at the center, select **Console Application**, type the name **Ch04_AssembliesAndNamespaces**, change the location to C:\Code, type the solution name **Chapter04**, and then click on **OK**.

4. In the **Solution Explorer** window, expand **References**. Note that a console application project already has references to several assemblies, including **System.Xml**.

   If you don't need any of these assemblies, then you can remove the reference by selecting it and pressing *Del*, or right-clicking and choosing **Remove**:

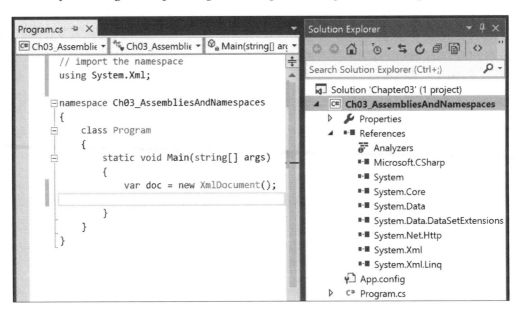

5. Inside the Main method, type the following code:

   ```
   var doc = new XmlDocument();
   ```

   The XmlDocument type is not recognized because we have not told the compiler what the namespace of the type is. Although this project already has a reference to the assembly that contains the type, we also need to either prefix the type name with its namespace, or import the namespace. We can get Visual Studio to fix this problem for us.

# Importing a namespace

You need to perform the following steps to import a namespace:

1. Click inside the `XmlDocument` type. Visual Studio displays a light bulb showing that it recognizes the type and can automatically fix the problem for you, as shown in the following screenshot:

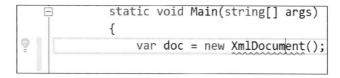

2. Click on the light bulb or press *Ctrl+*.

3. Choose `using System.Xml;` from the menu showing several other options as well. This will import the namespace by adding a `using` statement to the top of the file:

Once a namespace is imported for a code file, then all the types within the namespace are available for use in that code file just by typing their name.

Add another line of code to create an `XmlDataDocument` instance:

```
var data = new XmlDataDocument();
```

 You will see a green squiggle under the type name, which is a warning telling us that this type is obsolete and will be removed in a future release. Ignore that because it's not relevant to what you are learning now. As long as a type name is teal (bluish-green) it means the compiler understands it.

In the **Solution Explorer** window, inside **References**, right-click on **System.Xml**, and choose **Remove**.

After a few seconds, Visual Studio displays a red squiggle under XmlDocument, as shown in the following screenshot, and the text turns black instead of teal. This indicates that Visual Studio doesn't recognize the XmlDocument type:

```
var doc = new XmlDocument();
var data = new XmlDataDocument();
```

This is because we no longer have a reference to the assembly that contains the XmlDocument type. Just having the import statement (using System.Xml;) is not enough to find the type.

The color syntax highlighting behavior may be different in older versions of Visual Studio.

However, the XmlDataDocument type is not affected (it is still teal). This is because XmlDataDocument is not in the System.Xml assembly. It is actually in the System.Data assembly and our project still has a reference to that assembly.

A type can be in any assembly and any namespace. They do not have to be related. It is up to the creator of a type to decide what makes most sense for the type. For example, the Microsoft employee who was responsible for the XmlDataDocument type decided that it should be stored in the System.Data assembly but logically grouped with types in the System.Xml namespace.

The following table summarizes the assembly and namespace locations of the two types that we have been looking at:

| Type | Assembly | Namespace |
|---|---|---|
| XmlDocument | System.Xml | System.Xml |
| XmlDataDocument | System.Data | System.Xml |

To fix the current compile error, we need to add back the reference to the System.Xml assembly.

In the **Solution Explorer** window, right-click on **References**, choose **Add Reference...**, and in the **Reference Manager** dialog box that appears, select **Assemblies** on the left-hand side, scroll down through the list, select the checkbox next to **System.Xml**, and then click on **OK**:

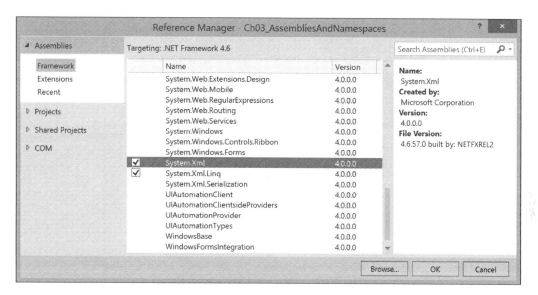

# Browsing assemblies and namespaces

A useful tool for understanding the relationship between assemblies and namespaces is the **Object Browser**.

On the **View** menu, choose **Object Browser**, or press *Ctrl + W, J*.

 Remember that keyboard shortcuts are dependent upon your settings. If you have chosen an option other than Visual C# for your development settings, then your keyboard shortcut for the **Object Browser** window may be different!

The **Object Browser** window shows that inside the `System.Data` assembly is the namespace `System.Xml`, and that contains the `XmlDataDocument` type:

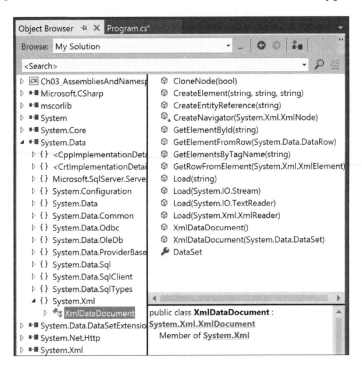

If you expand the `System.Xml` assembly, you will see that it adds far more types to the `System.Xml` namespace.

If you select an assembly, you will see its location in the file system, for example, `C:\Program Files (x86)\Reference Assemblies\Microsoft\Framework\.NETFramework\v4.6\System.Xml.dll`:

**Best Practice**

Use class library assemblies to group together types with related functionality. Carefully consider the namespace that your types should belong to. Although Microsoft puts all .NET types underneath the `System` namespace, they often put other types underneath a `Microsoft.ApplicationName` namespace. You should follow their example and therefore use your organization name and application names. For example, `Packt.Publishing` might be a good namespace for a `Book` type.

# Relating C# keywords to .NET types

One of the common questions I get from new C# programmers is, "What is the difference between `string` with a lowercase and `String` with an uppercase?"

The short answer is easy: none.

The long answer is that all C# type keywords are aliases for a .NET type in a class library assembly.

When you use the keyword `string`, the compiler turns it into a `System.String` type. When you use the type `int`, the compiler turns it into a `System.Int32` type. You can even see this if you hover your mouse over an `int` type, as follows:

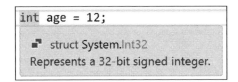

**Best Practice**

Use the C# keyword instead of the actual type because the keywords do not need the namespace imported.

The following table shows the 16 C# type keywords and their actual .NET types:

| Keyword | .NET type | Keyword | .NET type |
|---------|-----------|---------|-----------|
| string | System.String | char | System.Char |
| sbyte | System.SByte | byte | System.Byte |
| short | System.Int16 | ushort | System.UInt16 |
| int | System.Int32 | uint | System.UInt32 |
| long | System.Int64 | ulong | System.UInt64 |
| float | System.Single | double | System.Double |
| decimal | System.Decimal | bool | System.Boolean |
| object | System.Object | dynamic | System.Dynamic.DynamicObject |

Other .NET programming language compilers can do the same thing. For example, the Visual Basic .NET language has a type named `Integer` that is its alias for `System.Int32`.

# Storing and manipulating text

The most common type of data for variables is text. The most common types in .NET for working with text are shown in the following table:

| Namespace | Type |
|---|---|
| System | Char |
| System | String |
| System.Text | StringBuilder |
| System.Text.RegularExpressions | Regex |

# Getting the length of a string

Add a new console application project named **Ch04_ManipulatingText**. Set the solution's startup project to be the current selection.

Sometimes, you need to find out the length of a piece of text stored in a string variable. Modify the code to look like this:

```
using static System.Console;

namespace Ch04_ManipulatingText
{
    class Program
    {
        static void Main(string[] args)
        {
            string city = "London";
            WriteLine($"{city} is {city.Length} characters long.");
        }
    }
}
```

# Getting the characters of a string

A string variable uses an array of char internally to store the text. It also has an indexer, which means that we can use the array syntax to read its characters. Add the following statement:

```
WriteLine($"First char is {city[0]} and third is {city[2]}.");
```

# Splitting a string

Sometimes you need to split some text wherever there is a character such as a comma.

Add more lines of code to define a single string with comma-separated city names. You can use the `Split` method and specify a character that you want to treat as the separator. An array of strings is then created which you can enumerate using a `foreach` statement:

```
string cities = "Paris,Berlin,Madrid,New York";
string[] citiesArray = cities.Split(',');
foreach (string item in citiesArray)
{
    WriteLine(item);
}
```

# Extracting part of a string

Sometimes you need to get part of some text. For example, if you had a person's full name stored in a string with a space character between the first and last name, then you could find the position of the space using the `IndexOf` method, and then extract the first name and last name as two parts using the `Substring` method shown as follows:

```
string fullname = "Alan Jones";
int indexOfTheSpace = fullname.IndexOf(' ');
string firstname = fullname.Substring(0, indexOfTheSpace);
string lastname = fullname.Substring(indexOfTheSpace + 1);
WriteLine($"{lastname}, {firstname}");
```

 If the format of the full name was different, for example, "Lastname, Firstname", then the code would be slightly different.

# Checking a string for content

Sometimes you need to check whether a piece of text starts or ends with some characters or contains some characters. For example, the following code checks whether the company variable starts with the letter M and contains the letter N:

```
string company = "Microsoft";
bool startsWithM = company.StartsWith("M");
bool containsN = company.Contains("N");
WriteLine($"Starts with M: {startsWithM}, contains an N:
{containsN}");
```

Press *Ctrl + F5* to run the application and check the output:

```
London is 6 characters long.
First char is L and third is n.
Paris
Berlin
Madrid
New York
Jones, Alan
Starts with M: True, contains an N: False
```

# Other string members

Here are some other `string` members:

| Member | Description |
|---|---|
| `Trim`, `TrimStart`, and `TrimEnd` | These trim whitespace characters such as spaces, tabs, and new lines |
| `ToUpper` and `ToLower` | These convert to uppercase or lowercase |
| `Insert` and `Remove` | These insert or remove some text |
| `Replace` | This replaces some text |
| `String.Concat` (or use +) | This concatenates two strings |
| `String.Join` | This concatenates strings with a character in between each one |
| `String.IsEmptyOrNull` | This checks whether a string is empty or null |
| `String.Empty` | This can be used instead of allocating memory each time you use a literal string value using an empty pair of double quotes ("") |

# Building strings efficiently

You can concatenate two strings to make a new string using the `String.Concat` method or simply using the + operator. But, this is a bad practice because .NET must create a completely new string in memory. This might not be noticeable if you are only concatenating two strings but if you concatenate inside a loop, it can have a significant negative impact on performance and memory use.

# Validating input with regular expressions

Regular expressions are useful for validating input from the user. They are very powerful and can get very complicated. Almost all programming languages have support for regular expressions, and use a common set of special characters to define them.

Add a new console application project named **Ch04_RegularExpressions**. At the top of the file, import the following namespace and type:

```
using System.Text.RegularExpressions;
using static System.Console;
```

In the Main method, add the following statements:

```
Write("Enter your age: ");
string input = ReadLine();
Regex ageChecker = new Regex(@"\d");
if(ageChecker.IsMatch(input))
{
    WriteLine("Thank you!");
}
else
{
    WriteLine($"This is not a valid age: {input}");
}
```

> The @ character in front of a string switches off the ability to enter escape characters in a string variable. Escape characters are prefixed with a backslash (\). For example, \t means a tab and \n means new line. When writing regular expressions, we can disable this feature. Prefixing a string with @ allows a backslash to be a backslash.

Press *Ctrl + F5*, and see the output. If you enter a valid age, it will say "Thank you!"

```
Enter your age: 34
Thank you!
```

If you enter carrots, you will see the error message:

```
Enter your age: carrots
This is not a valid age: carrots
```

However, if you enter `bob30smith` it says "Thank you!"

```
Enter your age: bob30smith
Thank you!
```

The regular expression we used is \d, which means one digit. However, it does not limit what is entered *before* and *after* the digit.

Change the regular expression to ^\d$, like this:

```
Regex ageChecker = new Regex(@"^\d$");
```

Rerun the application. Now, it rejects anything except a single digit.

We want to allow one or more digits. To do this, we add a + (plus) after the \d. Change the regular expression to look like this:

```
Regex ageChecker = new Regex(@"^\d+$");
```

Rerun the application and see how the regular expression now only allows positive whole numbers of any length.

# The syntax of a regular expression

Here are some common special symbols that you can use in regular expressions:

| Symbol | Meaning | Symbol | Meaning |
|---|---|---|---|
| ^ | Start of input | $ | End of input |
| \d | A single digit | \D | A single NON-digit |
| \w | Whitespace | \W | NON-whitespace |
| [A-Za-z0-9] | Range(s) of characters | [AEIOU] | Set of characters |
| + | One or more | ? | One or none |
| . | A single character | | |
| {3} | Exactly three | {3,5} | Three to five |
| {3,} | Three or more | {,3} | Up to three |

# Examples of regular expressions

Here are some examples of regular expressions:

| Expression | Meaning |
|---|---|
| \d | A single digit somewhere in the input |
| a | The a character somewhere in the input |
| Bob | The word Bob somewhere in the input |
| ^Bob | The word Bob at the start of the input |
| Bob$ | The word Bob at the end of the input |
| ^\d{2}$ | Exactly two digits |
| ^[0-9]{2}$ | Exactly two digits |
| ^[A-Z]{4,}$ | At least four uppercase letters only |
| ^[A-Za-z]{4,}$ | At least four upper or lowercase letters only |
| ^[A-Z]{2}\d{3}$ | Two uppercase letters and three digits only |
| ^d.g$ | The letter d, then any character, and then the letter g, so it would match both dig and dog or any character between the d and g |
| ^d\.g$ | The letter d, then a dot (.), and then the letter g, so it would match d.g only |

**Best Practice**

Use regular expressions to validate input from the user. The same regular expressions can be reused in C# and other languages, such as JavaScript.

# Storing data with collections

If you need to store multiple values, you can use a collection. A **collection** is a data structure in memory that can manage multiple items in different ways, although all collections have some shared functionality.

There are two main namespaces for collections:

- System.Collections: Avoid the types in this namespace because they store any type that derives from System.Object, that is, every type (which is flexible but not type safe, thus leading to errors and boxing of value types, which can be slow and inefficient).

- System.Collections.Generic: The types in this namespace were introduced in C# 2 with .NET 2.0 and are better because they allow you to specify the type you want to store (which is safer, faster, and more efficient).

All collections have a `Count` property to tell you how many items are in it. For example, if we had a collection named `passengers` we could do this:

```
int howMany = passengers.Count;
```

All collections can be iterated using the `foreach` statement. To perform some action on all the items in the `passengers` collection, we can do this:

```
foreach (var passenger in passengers)
{
    // do something with each passenger
}
```

# Understanding collections

There are several different collection categories: lists, dictionaries, stacks, queues, sets, and many other more specialized collections.

# Lists

**Lists** are best when you want to manually control the order of items in a collection. Each item in a list has a unique index (or position) that is automatically assigned. Items can be any type (although they should all be the same type) and items can be duplicated. Indexes are `int` types and start from 0, so the first item in a list is at index 0, as shown in the following table:

| Index | Item |
|-------|--------|
| 0 | London |
| 1 | Paris |
| 2 | London |
| 3 | Sydney |

If a new item (for example, **Santiago**) is inserted between **London** and **Sydney**, the index of **Sydney** is automatically incremented. Therefore, you must be aware that an item's index can change after inserting or removing items, as shown in the following table:

| Index | Item |
|-------|----------|
| 0 | London |
| 1 | Paris |
| 2 | London |
| 3 | Santiago |
| 4 | Sydney |

# Dictionaries

**Dictionaries** are best when each value (or item) has a unique subvalue (or a made-up value) that can be used as a key to quickly find the value in the collection later on. The key must be unique. If you are storing a list of people, you can use a government-issued identity number as the key.

Think of the key as being like an index entry in a real-world dictionary. It allows you to quickly find the definition of a word because the words (that is, keys) are kept sorted, and if we know we're looking for the definition of *Manatee*, we would jump to the middle of the dictionary to start looking, because the letter M is in the middle of the alphabet. Dictionaries in programming are similarly optimized when looking something up.

Both the key and the value can be any type. This example uses strings for both:

| Key | Value |
|-----|-------|
| BSA | Bob Smith |
| MW | Max Williams |
| BSB | Bob Smith |
| AM | Amir Mohammed |

# Stacks

**Stacks** are best when you want to implement the last-in, first-out (LIFO) behavior. With a stack, you can only directly access the one item at the top of the stack, although you can enumerate to read through the whole stack of items. You cannot, for example, access the second item in a stack.

For example, word processors use a stack to remember the sequence of actions you have recently performed, so that when you press *Ctrl + Z*, it will undo the last action in the stack, and then the next last action, and so on.

# Queues

**Queues** are best when you want to implement the first-in, first out (FIFO) behavior. With a queue you can only directly access the one item at the front of the queue, although you can enumerate to read through the whole queue of items. You cannot, for example, access the second item in a queue.

For example, background processes use a queue to process work items in the order that they arrive, just like people standing in line at the post office.

# Sets

**Sets** are best when you want to perform set operations between two collections. For example, you may have two collections of city names and you want to know which names appear in both sets (known as the **intersect** between the sets).

# Working with lists

Add a new console application project named **Ch04_Lists**.

In the Main method, type the following code, which illustrates some of the common ways of working with lists:

```
var cities = new List<string>();
cities.Add("London");
cities.Add("Paris");
cities.Add("Milan");
WriteLine("Initial list");
foreach (string city in cities)
{
    WriteLine($"  {city}");
}
WriteLine($"The first city is {cities[0]}.");
WriteLine($"The last city is {cities[cities.Count - 1]}.");
cities.Insert(0, "Sydney");
WriteLine("After inserting Sydney at index 0");
foreach (string city in cities)
{
    WriteLine($"  {city}");
}
cities.RemoveAt(1);
cities.Remove("Milan");
WriteLine("After removing two cities");
foreach (string city in cities)
{
    WriteLine($"  {city}");
}
```

The angle brackets after the List<T> type are a feature of C# called **generics**. It's just a fancy term for making a collection **strongly typed**, that is, the compiler knows more specifically what type of object is allowed to be stored in the collection. Generics improve the performance and correctness of your code. Strongly typed collections are different from **statically typed collections**. The old System.Collection types are statically typed to contain weakly typed System.Object items. The newer System.Collection.Generic types are statically typed to contain strongly typed <T> instances. Ironically, the term "generics" just means a *more specific* static type!

Press *Ctrl* + *F5* to see the output:

```
Initial list
    London
    Paris
    Milan
The first city is London.
The last city is Milan.
After inserting Sydney at index 0
    Sydney
    London
    Paris
    Milan
After removing two cities
    Sydney
    Paris
```

# Working with dictionaries

Add a new console application project named **Ch04_Dictionaries**.

In the Main method, type the following code that illustrates some of the common ways of working with dictionaries:

```
var keywords = new Dictionary<string, string>();
keywords.Add("int", "32-bit integer data type");
keywords.Add("long", "64-bit integer data type");
keywords.Add("float", "Single precision floating point number");
WriteLine("Keywords and their definitions");
foreach (KeyValuePair<string, string> item in keywords)
```

```
    {
        WriteLine($"  {item.Key}: {item.Value}");
    }
    WriteLine($"The definition of long is {keywords["long"]}");
```

Run the application by pressing *Ctrl + F5*.

```
Keywords and their definitions
    int: 32-bit integer data type
    long: 64-bit integer data type
    float: Single precision floating point number
The definition of long is 64-bit integer data type
```

# Sorting collections

A `List<T>` class can be sorted by calling its `Sort` method (but remember that the indexes of each item will change).

> Sorting a list of strings or other built-in types works automatically, but if you create a collection of your own type, then that type must implement an interface named `IComparable`. You will learn how to do this in *Chapter 7, Implementing Interfaces and Inheriting Classes*.

The `Dictionary<T>`, `Stack<T>`, or `Queue<T>` classes cannot be sorted, because you wouldn't usually want that functionality. For example, you would never sort a queue of guests checking into a hotel. But sometimes, you might want to sort a dictionary or a set.

The differences between these sorted collections are often subtle, but can have an impact on the memory requirements and performance of your application, so it is worth putting some effort into picking the best for your requirements. The following table summarizes some examples of sorted collection:

| Collection | Description |
|---|---|
| `SortedDictionary<TKey, TValue>` | This represents a collection of key/value pairs that are sorted on the key |
| `SortedList<TKey, TValue>` | This represents a collection of key/value pairs that are sorted by key, based on the associated `IComparer<T>` implementation |
| `SortedSet<T>` | This represents a collection of objects that is maintained in a sorted order |

# Avoiding old collections

Avoid the old collections, listed in the following table, and use the more modern equivalents instead.

In 2005, Microsoft introduced generics that can be used to control more specifically which types can be stored in a collection. A collection that can only contain the `int` types is safer than one that can contain any object. The `<T>` parameter should be replaced with the type you want to store.

| Avoid these collections<br><br>Namespaces: System.Collections, System.Collections.Specialized | Use these collections instead<br><br>Namespace: System.Collections. Generics |
|---|---|
| `ArrayList` | `List<T>` |
| `Hashtable, HybridDictionary, ListDictionary` | `Dictionary<TKey, TValue>` |
| `Stack` | `Stack<T>` |
| `Queue` | `Queue<T>` |
| `SortedList` | `SortedList<T>` |
| `StringCollection` | `List<string>` |
| `StringDictionary` | `Dictionary<string, string>` |

# Using specialized collections

There are a few other collections for special situations. For example, the `NameValueCollection` can be used to automate filling in a form on a web page and posting the named values to the web server:

| Collection | Description |
|---|---|
| `System.Collections. BitArray` | This manages a compact array of bit values, which are represented as Booleans, where `true` indicates that the bit is on (1) and `false` indicates the bit is off (0) |
| `System.Collections. Specialized. NameValueCollection` | This represents a collection of associated string keys and string values that can be accessed either with the key or with the index |
| `System.Collections. Generics.LinkedList<T>` | This represents a doubly-linked list where every item has a reference to its previous and next item |

# Practicing and exploring

Test your knowledge and understanding by answering some questions, get some hands-on practice, and explore with deeper research into topics of this chapter.

## Exercise 4.1 – test your knowledge

Use the Web to answer the following questions:

1. Does every assembly you create have a reference to the `mscorlib.dll` assembly?

2. What is the maximum number of characters that can be stored in a `string`?

3. When and why should you use a `SecureString`?

4. When should you use a `LinkedList`?

5. When should you use a `SortedDictionary` class rather than a `SortedList` class?

6. Why should you *not* use the official standard for e-mail addresses to create a regular expression for validating a user's e-mail address?

## Exercise 4.2 – practice regular expressions

Create a console application named **Ch04_Exercise02** that prompts the user to enter a regular expression, and then prompts the user to enter some input and compare the two for a match until the user presses *Esc*:

```
The default regular expression checks for at least one digit.

Enter a regular expression (or press ENTER to use the default): ^[a-z]+$

Enter some input: apples

apples matches ^[a-z]+$? True

Press ESC to end or any key to try again.

Enter a regular expression (or press ENTER to use the default): ^[a-z]+$

Enter some input: abc123xyz

abc123xyz matches ^[a-z]+$? False

Press ESC to end or any key to try again.
```

# Exercise 4.3 – explore topics

Use the following links to read in more detail the topics covered in this chapter:

- **.NET Blog: A first hand look from the .NET engineering team**: http://blogs.msdn.com/b/dotnet/

- **Assemblies and the Global Assembly Cache (C# and Visual Basic)**: https://msdn.microsoft.com/en-us/library/ms173099.aspx

- **String Class**: https://msdn.microsoft.com/en-us/library/system.string(v=vs.110).aspx

- **StringBuilder Class**: https://msdn.microsoft.com/en-us/library/system.text.stringbuilder(v=vs.110).aspx

- **Regex Class**: https://msdn.microsoft.com/en-us/library/system.text.regularexpressions.regex(v=vs.110).aspx

- **How to: Search Strings Using Regular Expressions (C# Programming Guide)**: https://msdn.microsoft.com/en-us/library/ms228595.aspx

- **Regular Expression Language - Quick Reference**: https://msdn.microsoft.com/en-us/library/az24scfc(v=vs.110).aspx

- **RegExr: Learn, Build, & Test RegExr**: http://regexr.com/

- **Collections (C# and Visual Basic)**: https://msdn.microsoft.com/en-us/library/ybcx56wz.aspx

- **List<T> Class**: https://msdn.microsoft.com/en-us/library/6sh2ey19(v=vs.110).aspx

- **Dictionary<TKey, TValue> Class**: https://msdn.microsoft.com/en-us/library/xfhwa508(v=vs.110).aspx

- **Stack<T> Class**: https://msdn.microsoft.com/en-us/library/3278tedw(v=vs.110).aspx

- **Queue<T> Class**: https://msdn.microsoft.com/en-us/library/7977ey2c(v=vs.110).aspx

- **SortedList<TKey, TValue> Class**: https://msdn.microsoft.com/en-us/library/ms132319(v=vs.110).aspx

- **SortedDictionary<TKey, TValue> Class**: https://msdn.microsoft.com/en-us/library/f7fta44c(v=vs.110).aspx

# Summary

In this chapter, you explored the relationship between assemblies and namespaces, you learned about the best types to use for storing and manipulating text, and which collections to use for storing multiple items.

In the next chapter, you will learn about more specialized .NET types.

# 5

# Using Specialized .NET Types

This chapter is about specialized .NET types used to debug and diagnose problems, unit test your code, support multiple languages and cultures, and access features and applications outside of .NET.

This chapter covers the following topics:

- Debugging and diagnostics
- Unit testing an application
- Internationalizing an application
- Interoperating with unmanaged code

## Debugging and diagnostics

In this section, you will learn how to debug problems at design time, trace problems at runtime, and use types such as `Debug`, `Trace`, `Process`, and `Stopwatch` that are in the `System.Diagnostics` namespace.

## Debugging an application

In Visual Studio, press *Ctrl + Shift + N* or navigate to **File | New | Project...**.

In the **New Project** dialog, from the **Installed Templates** list, select **Visual C#**. In the list at the center, select **Console Application**, type the name **Ch05_Debugging**, change the location to `C:\Code`, type the solution name **Chapter05**, and then click on **OK**.

Modify the template code to look like this:

```
using static System.Console;

namespace Ch05_Debugging
{
    class Program
    {
        static double Add(double a, double b)
        {
            return a * b; // deliberate bug!
        }
        static void Main(string[] args)
        {
            double a = 4.5; // or use var
            double b = 2.5;
            double answer = Add(a, b);
            WriteLine($"{a} + {b} = {answer}");
            ReadLine(); // wait for user to press ENTER
        }
    }
}
```

Press *Ctrl + F5* and take a look at the output:

```
4.5 + 2.5 = 11.25
```

There is a bug! `4.5` added to `2.5` should be `7` and not `11.25`. We will use the **debugging tools** in Visual Studio 2015 to squash the bug.

# Setting a breakpoint

Breakpoints allow us to mark a line of code that we want to pause at to find bugs. Click on the open curly bracket at the beginning of the `Main` method and go to the **Debug | Toggle Breakpoint** menu, or press *F9*.

A red highlight will appear with a red circle in the grey margin bar on the left-hand side, to indicate that a breakpoint has been set. Breakpoints can be toggled off with the same command. You can also click in the margin to toggle the breakpoint on and off, as shown in the following screenshot:

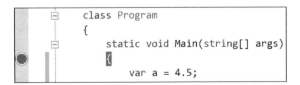

Go to **Debug | Start Debugging**, or press the **Start** toolbar button, or press *F5*. Visual Studio starts and then pauses when it hits the breakpoint. This is known as **break mode**. The line that will be executed next is highlighted in yellow, and a yellow arrow points at the line from the grey margin bar, as shown in the following screenshot:

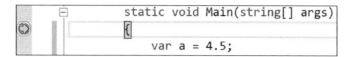

 You can drag the yellow arrow and its highlight. When you continue executing, it will run from the new position. This is useful for moving back a few statements to rerun them or to skip over some statements.

# The debugging toolbar

Visual Studio enables some extra toolbar buttons to make it easy to access debugging features. Here are a few of those:

- **Continue** / *F5* (green triangle): This button will run the code at full speed from the current position
- **Stop Debugging** / *Shift + F5* (red square): This button will stop the program
- **Restart** / *Ctrl + Shift + F5* (circular black arrow): This button will stop and then immediately restart the program
- **Step into** / *F11*, **Step over** / *F10*, and **Step out** / *Shift + F11* (blue arrows over dots): These buttons will step through the code in various ways

The following screenshot illustrates Visual Studio's extra toolbar buttons:

# Debugging windows

Visual Studio makes some extra windows visible so that you can monitor useful information such as variables while you step through your code. If you cannot find one of these windows, then on the **Debug** menu, choose **Windows**, and then select the window you want to view.

 Most of the debug windows are only available when you are in the **Break** mode.

The **Locals** window shows the name, value, and type for any local variables. Keep an eye on this window while you step through your code:

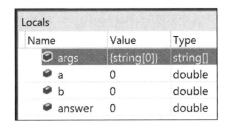

In *Chapter 1, Hello, C#! Welcome, .NET Core!*, I introduced you to the **C# Interactive** window. The similar, but more basic, **Immediate Window** also allows live interaction with your code.

For example, you can ask a question such as, "What is 1+2?" by typing ?1+2 and pressing *Enter*. You can also use the question mark to find out the current value of a variable:

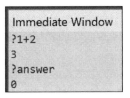

You can execute statements of code:

As long as you have Visual Studio 2015 with Update 1, the **C# Interactive** window is better.

# Stepping through code

From the **Debug** menu, choose **Debug | Step Into**, or click on the **Step Into** button in the toolbar, or press *F11*. The yellow highlight steps forward one line, as shown in the following screenshot:

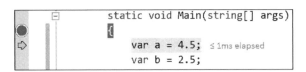

Choose **Debug** | **Step Over** or press *F10*. The yellow highlight steps forward one line. At the moment, there is no difference between using **Step Into** or **Step Over**.

Press *F10* again so that the yellow highlight is on the line that calls the Add method:

```
static void Main(string[] args)
{
    var a = 4.5;
    var b = 2.5;
    var answer = Add(a, b);
    WriteLine($"{a} + {b} =
```

The difference between **Step Into** or **Step Over** can be seen when you are about to execute a method call. If you press **Step Into**, the debugger steps into the method so that you can step through every line in that method. If you press **Step Over**, the whole method is executed in one go (it does *not* skip over the method!).

Use **Step Into** to step inside the method. Hover your mouse over the multiply (*) operator. A tooltip will appear showing that this operator is multiplying a by b to give the result 11.25. We can see that this is the bug. You can pin the tooltip by clicking on the pin icon as I have done here:

```
static double Add(double a, double b)
{   ≤ 20ms elapsed
    return a * b;        a * b  11.25
}
```

Fix the bug by changing the * to +.

We don't need to step through all the lines in the Add method, so choose **Step Out** or press *Shift + F11*. Press *F11* or choose **Step Into** to assign the return value of the Add method to the variable answer.

The **Locals** window highlights the most recent change in red text. The answer is correct, so choose **Continue** or press *F5*:

| Name | Value | Type |
|------|-------|------|
| args | {string[0]} | string[] |
| a | 4.5 | double |
| b | 2.5 | double |
| answer | 7 | double |

# Customizing breakpoints

You can also right-click on a breakpoint and choose additional options, such as **Conditions**, as shown in the following screenshot:

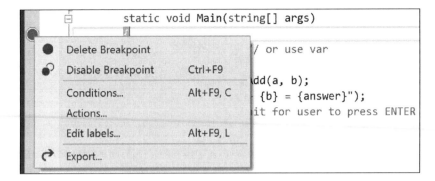

The conditions for a breakpoint include an expression that must be true and a hit count to reach for the breakpoint to apply.

In the example, as you can see in the following screenshot, I have set a condition to only apply the breakpoint if both the answer variable is greater than 9 and we have hit the breakpoint three times:

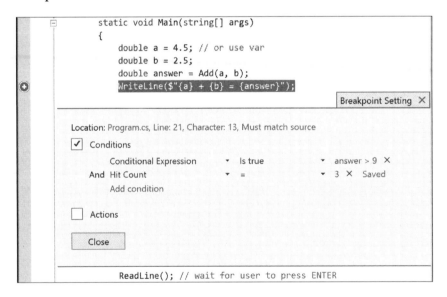

You have now fixed a bug using some of Visual Studio's debugging features.

# Monitoring performance and resource usage

To write the best applications, we need to be able to monitor the speed and efficiency of our code.

## Evaluating the efficiency of types

What is the best type to use for a particular scenario? To answer this question, we need to carefully consider what we mean by best. We should consider the following four factors:

- **Functionality**: This can be decided by checking whether the type provides the features you need
- **Memory size**: This can be decided by the number of bytes of memory the type takes up
- **Performance**: This can be decided by how fast the type is
- **Future needs**: This depends on the changes in requirements and maintainability

There will be scenarios, such as storing numbers, where multiple types have the same functionality, so we would need to consider the memory and performance in order to make a choice.

If we need to store millions of numbers, then the best type to use would be the one that requires the least number of bytes of memory. If we only need to store a few numbers but we need to perform lots of calculations on them, then the best type to use would be the one that runs fastest on a particular CPU.

You have seen the use of the `sizeof()` operator to show the number of bytes a single instance of a type uses in memory. When we are storing lots of values in more complex data structures, such as arrays and lists, then we need a better way of measuring memory usage.

You can read lots of advice online and in books, but the only way to know for sure what the best type would be for your code is to compare the types yourself. In the next section, you will learn how to write the code to monitor the actual memory requirements and the actual performance when using different types.

Although today a `short` variable might be the best choice, it might be a better choice to use an `int` variable, even though it takes twice as much space in memory, because we might need a wider range of values to be stored in the future.

There is another metric we should consider: maintenance. This is a measure of how much effort another programmer would have to put in, to understand and modify your code. If you use a nonobvious type choice, it might confuse the programmer who comes along later and needs to fix a bug or add a feature. There are analyzing tools that will generate a report that shows how easily maintainable your code is.

# Monitoring performance and memory use

The System.Diagnostics namespace has lots of useful types for monitoring your code. The first one we will look at is the Stopwatch type.

Add a new console application project named **Ch05_Monitoring**. Set the solution's start up project to be the current selection.

Modify the template code to look like this:

```
using System;
using System.Diagnostics;
using System.Linq;
using static System.Console;
using static System.Diagnostics.Process;

namespace Ch05_Monitoring
{
    class Recorder
    {
        static Stopwatch timer = new Stopwatch();
        static long bytesPhysicalBefore = 0;
        static long bytesVirtualBefore = 0;
        public static void Start()
        {
            GC.Collect();
            GC.WaitForPendingFinalizers();
            GC.Collect();
            bytesPhysicalBefore = GetCurrentProcess().WorkingSet64;
            bytesVirtualBefore = GetCurrentProcess().
VirtualMemorySize64;
            timer.Restart();
        }
        public static void Stop()
        {
            timer.Stop();
            long bytesPhysicalAfter = GetCurrentProcess().
WorkingSet64;
```

```
        vlong bytesVirtualAfter = GetCurrentProcess().
VirtualMemorySize64;
            WriteLine("Stopped recording.");
            WriteLine($"{bytesPhysicalAfter - bytesPhysicalBefore:N0}
physical bytes used.");
            WriteLine($"{bytesVirtualAfter - bytesVirtualBefore:N0}
virtual bytes used.");
            WriteLine($"{timer.Elapsed} time span ellapsed.");
            WriteLine($"{timer.ElapsedMilliseconds:N0} total
milliseconds ellapsed.");
        }
    }
    class Program
    {
        static void Main(string[] args)
        {
            Write("Press ENTER to start the timer: ");
            ReadLine();
            Recorder.Start();
            int[] largeArrayOfInts = Enumerable.Range(1, 10000).
ToArray();
            Write("Press ENTER to stop the timer: ");
            ReadLine();
            Recorder.Stop();
            ReadLine();
        }
    }
}
```

The Start method of the Recorder class uses the **garbage collector
(GC)** type to ensure that all the currently allocated memory is collected
before recording the amount of used memory. This is an advanced
technique that you should almost never use in production code.

You have created a class named Recorder with two methods to start and stop
recording the time and memory used by any code you run. The Main method
starts recording when the user presses *Enter*, creates an array of ten thousand int
variables, and then stops recording when the user presses *Enter* again.

The `Stopwatch` type has some useful members, as shown in the following table:

| Member | Description |
|--------|-------------|
| The `Restart` method | This resets the elapsed time to zero and then starts the stopwatch |
| The `Stop` method | This stops the stopwatch |
| The `Elapsed` property | This is the elapsed time stored as a `TimeSpan` (hours:minutes:seconds) |
| The `ElapsedMilliseconds` property | This is the elapsed time in milliseconds stored as a long integer |

The `Process` type has some useful members:

| Member | Description |
|--------|-------------|
| `VirtualMemorySize64` | This displays the amount of the virtual memory, in bytes, allocated for the process |
| `WorkingSet64` | This displays the amount of physical memory, in bytes, allocated for the process |

Press *Ctrl* + *F5* to start the application without the debugger attached. The application will start recording the time and memory used when you press *Enter*, and then stop recording when you press *Enter* again:

```
Press ENTER to start the timer:
Press ENTER to stop the timer:
Stopped recording.
942,080 physical bytes used.
0 virtual bytes used.
00:00:03.1166037 time span ellapsed.
3,116 total milliseconds ellapsed.
```

# Measuring the efficiency of processing strings

Now that you've seen how the `Stopwatch` and `Process` types can be used to monitor your code, we will use them to evaluate the best way to process `string` variables.

Add a new console application project named **Ch05_BuildingStrings**. Add the following `using` statements:

```
using System;
using System.Diagnostics;
using System.Linq;
```

```
using System.Text;
using static System.Console;
using static System.Diagnostics.Process;
```

Copy and paste the class definition for the `Recorder` class from the earlier project.

**Best Practice**

Although copy and paste is a valid technique for code reuse in some scenarios, it would be better to create a class library assembly for the `Recorder` class so that we can share it between multiple projects without maintaining multiple copies. You will learn how to do this in *Chapter 6, Building Your Own Types with Object-Oriented Programming*.

Add the following code to the `Main` method. It creates an array of ten thousand `int` variables and then concatenates them with commas for separators using a `string` and a `StringBuilder`:

```
int[] numbers = Enumerable.Range(1, 10000).ToArray();
Recorder.Start();
WriteLine("Using string");
string s = "";
for (int i = 0; i < numbers.Length; i++)
{
    s += numbers[i] + ", ";
}
Recorder.Stop();
Recorder.Start();
WriteLine("Using StringBuilder");
StringBuilder builder = new StringBuilder();
for (int i = 0; i < numbers.Length; i++)
{
    builder.Append(numbers[i]);
    builder.Append(", ");
}
Recorder.Stop();
ReadLine();
```

Press *Ctrl* + *F5* to see the output:

```
Using string
Stopped recording.
7,540,736 physical bytes used.
69,632 virtual bytes used.
00:00:00.0871730 time span ellapsed.
```

```
87 total milliseconds ellapsed.

Using StringBuilder
Stopped recording.
8,192 physical bytes used.
0 virtual bytes used.
00:00:00.0015680 time span ellapsed.
1 total milliseconds ellapsed.
```

We can summarize the results as follows:

- The `string` class used about 7.5 MB of memory and took 87 milliseconds
- The `StringBuilder` class used 8 KB of memory and took 1.5 milliseconds

In this scenario, `StringBuilder` is about one hundred times faster and about one thousand times more memory efficient when concatenating text!

**Best Practice**

Avoid using the `String.Concat` method or the + operator with `string` variables. Instead, use `StringBuilder` or the C# 6 $ string interpolation to concatenate variables together, especially inside loops.

# Monitoring with Debug and Trace

You have seen the use of the `Console` type and its `WriteLine` method to provide output to the console window. We also have a pair of types named `Debug` and `Trace` that have more flexibility in where they write out to.

The `Debug` and `Trace` classes can write to any **trace listener**. A trace listener is a type that can be configured to write output anywhere you like when the `Trace.WriteLine` method is called. There are several trace listeners provided by .NET, and you can even make your own by inheriting from the `TraceListener` type.

## Writing to the default trace listener

One, the `DefaultTraceListener`, is configured automatically and writes to Visual Studio's output window; you can configure others manually using code or a configuration file.

Add a new console application project named **Ch05_Tracing**. Modify the template code to look like this:

```
using System.Diagnostics;
using static System.Console;
namespace Ch05_Tracing
{
    class Program
    {
        static void Main(string[] args)
        {
            Debug.WriteLine("Debug says Hello C#!");
            Trace.WriteLine("Trace says Hello C#!");
            WriteLine("Press ENTER to close.");
            ReadLine();
        }
    }
}
```

Press *F5* to start Visual Studio with the debugger attached. In Visual Studio's output window, you will see the two messages. If you cannot see the output window, press *Ctrl + W, O* or navigate to **View | Output** menu.

Ensure that you show output from **Debug**, as shown in the following screenshot:

# Configuring trace listeners

Now, we will configure some trace listeners that will also write to a text file and to the Windows application event log.

In Visual Studio's **Solution Explorer**, double-click on the file named `App.config` and modify it to look like this:

```
<?xml version="1.0" encoding="utf-8" ?>
<configuration>
  <system.diagnostics>
    <sharedListeners>
```

```
        <add name="file" type="System.Diagnostics.
TextWriterTraceListener" initializeData="C:\Code\Trace.txt" />
        <add name="appeventlog" type="System.Diagnostics.
EventLogTraceListener" initializeData="Application" />
    </sharedListeners>
    <trace autoflush="true">
      <listeners>
        <add name="file" />
        <add name="appeventlog" />
      </listeners>
    </trace>
  </system.diagnostics>
  <startup>
    <supportedRuntime version="v4.0" sku=".NETFramework,Version=v4.6"
/>
  </startup>
</configuration>
```

You have configured two shared listeners—one that writes to a text file and another that writes to the application event log.

Press *F5* to start Visual Studio with the debugger attached. In the console application, press *Enter* to close it. This will release the file that it is writing to. Click on the Windows Start menu, type **event**, and then click on **Event Viewer**:

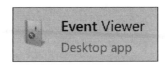

In the **Event Viewer** window, expand **Windows Logs**, choose **Application**, choose the most recent log entry, and then click on the **Details** tab. You should see that the **Friendly View** option of the **EventData** is the message we output:

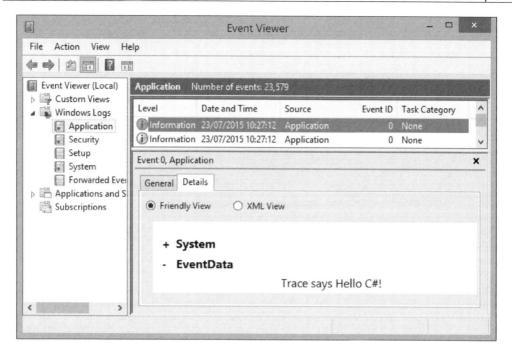

Run **File Explorer**, look in the `C:\Code` folder, and open the file named `Trace.txt`. If you open it with Notepad, it will look like this:

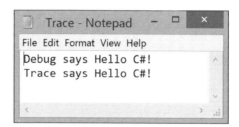

# Configuring compiler symbols for .NET Framework

You might be wondering what the difference between `Debug` and `Trace` is. When you compile and run any application, it can be configured with the debug or trace compiler symbols on or off. By default, both are enabled. You can see this by double-clicking on **Properties** in the **Solution Explorer** window, and then clicking on the **Debug** tab.

You can see that both the debug and trace symbols are enabled. You can define your own symbols by entering them in the **Conditional compilation symbols** box, as shown in the following screenshot, where I have defined two symbols named **KERMIT** and **FOZZIE**:

# Defining compiler symbols for .NET Core

If you chose to create a **Console Application (Package)** project to target the .NET Core, then you must define compiler symbols using the **project.json** file.

In the `project.json` file, add the `configurations` section, as shown in the following code, that specifies options for the two possible solution configurations — Debug and Release:

```
{
  "version": "1.0.0-*",
  "description": "Ch05_Tracing Console Application",
  "authors": [ "markjprice" ],
  "tags": [ "" ],
  "projectUrl": "",
  "licenseUrl": "",

  "configurations": {
    "Debug": {
      "compilationOptions": {
        "define": [ "DEBUG", "TRACE", "KERMIT", "FOZZIE" ]
      }
    },
    "Release": {
      "compilationOptions": {
        "define": [ "RELEASE", "TRACE" ],
        "optimize": true
      }
    }
  },
```

# Checking compiler symbols

Modify the content of the `Main` method to look like this. We are using conditional compilation `#if` statements to only write to the trace listeners if the **KERMIT** and **FOZZIE** symbols have been defined. Note that they are Booleans so we can use operators like AND (`&&`) on them:

```
namespace Ch05_Tracing
{
    class Program
    {
        static void Main(string[] args)
        {
            Debug.WriteLine("Debug says Hello C#!");
            Trace.WriteLine("Trace says Hello C#!");

#if KERMIT
            Trace.WriteLine("KERMIT is on!");
#endif
#if KERMIT && FOZZIE
            Trace.WriteLine("KERMIT and FOZZIE are on!");
#endif
```

Press *F5* to start Visual Studio with the debugger attached.

In Visual Studio's output window, you will see all the messages:

**Debug says Hello C#!**

**Trace says Hello C#!**

**KERMIT is on!**

**KERMIT and FOZZIE are on!**

In Visual Studio's toolbar, go to the drop-down menu that shows the list of configurations and choose **Release**. In this configuration, only the TRACE directive is set:

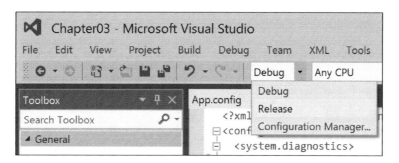

Press *F5* to start Visual Studio with the debugger attached. If you see a warning message, choose **Continue Debugging**. In Visual Studio's **Output** window, you will see only the Trace message:

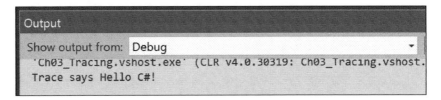

The idea is that you can safely put as many `Debug.WriteLine` statements throughout your code, knowing that when you finally compile and deploy the release version of your application they will all be automatically removed.

**Best Practice**

Use `Debug.WriteLine` statements liberally throughout your code, knowing that they will be stripped out automatically when you compile the release version of your application.

If you need more flexibility, then you can also define your own symbols, but for these, you must manually check that your own symbol has been defined using `#if` statements.

But what about the `Trace.WriteLine` statements? They are left in your release code, so they should be used more sparingly. Even these can be configured using trace switches.

## Switching trace levels

In the `App.config` file, add the following section inside `<system.diagnostics>`. It can go before or after the `<trace>` and `<sharedListeners>` sections:

```
<switches>
  <add name="PacktSwitch" value="3"/>
</switches>
```

The value of a switch can be set using a number or a word. For example, the number 3 can be replaced with the word **Info**, as shown in the following table:

| Number | Word | Description |
|--------|------|-------------|
| 0 | Off | This will output nothing |
| 1 | Error | This will output only errors |
| 2 | Warning | This will output errors and warnings |
| 3 | Info | This will output errors, warnings, and info messages |
| 4 | Verbose | This will output all levels |

In the `Main` method, add the following statements before prompting the user to press *Enter*:

```
var ts = new TraceSwitch("PacktSwitch", "");
Trace.WriteLineIf(ts.TraceError, "TraceError");
Trace.WriteLineIf(ts.TraceWarning, "TraceWarning");
Trace.WriteLineIf(ts.TraceInfo, "TraceInfo");
Trace.WriteLineIf(ts.TraceVerbose, "TraceVerbose");
Trace.Close(); // release any file or database listeners
WriteLine("Press ENTER to close.");
ReadLine();
```

This code will check the value of the switch named `PacktSwitch` and only output if the level has been set.

**Best Practice**

Call the `Close` method of the `Trace` type to release any locks that might be held after writing to a text file trace listener. This is necessary only if you are writing to listeners that are buffered or apply locking, such as files and databases. However, it doesn't hurt to do this every time.

Press *F5* to start Visual Studio with the debugger attached. If you see a warning message, choose **Continue Debugging**. In Visual Studio's **Output** window, you will see only the Trace messages up to level 3 (Info):

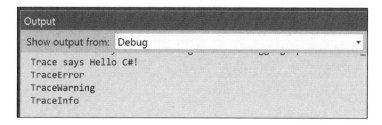

# Unit testing an application

Microsoft has a proprietary unit testing framework known as MS Test, which is closely integrated with Visual Studio. However, to use a unit testing framework that is compatible with .NET Core, we will use the third-party framework **xUnit.net**.

## Creating a unit of code that needs testing

Add a new Class Library project named **Ch05_Calculator**. In the **Solution Explorer** window, right-click on the **Class1.cs** file and choose **Rename**. Change its name to **Calculator**.

Modify the code to look like this:

```
namespace Ch05_Calculator
{
    public class Calculator
    {
        public double Add(double a, double b)
        {
            return a * b;
        }
    }
}
```

## Creating a unit test project

Add a new Class Library project named **Ch05_CalculatorUnitTests**. In the **Solution Explorer**, right-click on **References** and choose **Manage NuGet Packages**.

In the **NuGet Package Manager** window, click on the **Browse** tab, and then search for **xunit**. Click on **Install** for the latest stable version:

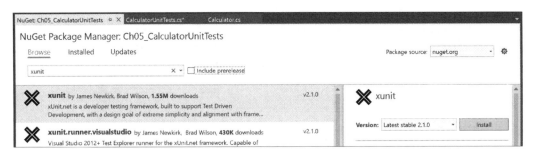

In the **Solution Explorer**, right-click on **References** and choose **Add Reference....** In the **Reference Manager** window, select the checkbox for **Ch05_Calculator** and then click on **OK**. In the **Solution Explorer** window, right-click on the **Class1.cs** file and choose **Rename**. Change its name to **CalculatorUnitTests**.

Modify the code to look like this:

```
using Ch05_Calculator;
using Xunit;

namespace Ch05_CalculatorUnitTests
{
    public class CalculatorUnitTests
    {
        [Fact]
        public void TestAdding2And2()
        {
            // arrange
            double a = 2;
            double b = 2;
            double expected = 4;
            var calc = new Calculator();
            // act
            double actual = calc.Add(a, b);
            // assert
            Assert.Equal(expected, actual);
        }
        [Fact]
        public void TestAdding2And3()
        {
            // arrange
            double a = 2;
            double b = 3;
            double expected = 5;
            var calc = new Calculator();
            // act
            double actual = calc.Add(a, b);
            // assert
            Assert.Equal(expected, actual);
        }
    }
}
```

A well-written unit test will have three parts:

- **Arrange**: This part will declare and instantiate variables for input and output
- **Act**: This part will execute the unit that you are testing
- **Assert**: This part will make one or more assertions about the output

# Running unit tests

You must install a runner to execute your tests. There is a runner for Visual Studio, but we will use the one that executes in a console application because it is cross-platform.

In the **Solution Explorer** window, right-click on **References** and choose **Manage NuGet Packages**. In the **NuGet Package Manager**, click on the **Browse** tab, and then search for xunit.runner.console. Click on **Install** for the latest stable version.

Open a Command Prompt and navigate to C:\Code\Chapter05\. Enter the following command at the prompt to run your tests:

```
packages\xunit.runner.console.2.1.0\tools\xunit.console Ch05_
CalculatorUnitTests\bin\Debug\Ch05_CalculatorUnitTests.dll
```

You should see the following results:

Fix the bug in the `Add` method, rebuild the unit test project, and then rerun the unit tests at the Command Prompt. You should see the following results:

```
Developer Command Prompt for VS2015                    —    □    ×
C:\Code\Chapter05>packages\xunit.runner.console.2.1.0\tools\xunit.console Ch05_C
alculatorUnitTests\bin\Debug\Ch05_CalculatorUnitTests.dll
xUnit.net Console Runner (64-bit .NET 4.0.30319.42000)
  Discovering: Ch05_CalculatorUnitTests
  Discovered:  Ch05_CalculatorUnitTests
  Starting:    Ch05_CalculatorUnitTests
  Finished:    Ch05_CalculatorUnitTests
=== TEST EXECUTION SUMMARY ===
   Ch05_CalculatorUnitTests  Total: 2, Errors: 0, Failed: 0, Skipped: 0, Time: 0
.235s

C:\Code\Chapter05>
```

# Internationalizing an application

**Internationalization** is the process of enabling your application to run correctly all over the world. It has two parts: **globalization** and **localization**.

Globalization is about writing your code to accommodate multiple languages and regions. The combination of a language and a region is known as a culture. It is important for your code to know both the language and region because date and currency formats are different in Quebec and Paris despite them both using French.

There are **International Standards Organization (ISO)** codes for all culture combinations. For example, in the code da-DK, da indicates the Danish language and DK indicates the country of Denmark.

Localization is about customizing the user interface to support a particular language. Since localization is just about the language, it doesn't need to know about the region.

Internationalization is a huge topic that entire books have been written about. In this section, you will get a brief introduction to the basics using the `CultureInfo` type in the `System.Globalization` namespace.

 .NET Core 1.0 does not currently allow threads to get or set their `CurrentCulture` or `CurrentUICulture` properties. An alternative for getting these two properties (but not setting) is to use the `CultureInfo` class's static properties, but you cannot set them.

# Globalizing an application

Add a new console application project named **Ch05_Internationalization**. At the top of the file, import the following types and namespaces:

```
using static System.Console;
using System;
using System.Threading;
using System.Globalization;
```

In the `Main` method, enter the following statements:

```
Thread t = Thread.CurrentThread;
WriteLine($"The current globalization culture is {t.CurrentCulture.
Name}: {t.CurrentCulture.DisplayName}");
WriteLine($"The current localization culture is {t.CurrentUICulture.
Name}: {t.CurrentUICulture.DisplayName}");
WriteLine();
WriteLine("en-US: English (United States)");
WriteLine("da-DK: Danish (Denmark)");
WriteLine("fr-CA: French (Canada)");
Write("Enter an ISO culture code: ");
string newculture = ReadLine();
if (!string.IsNullOrEmpty(newculture))
{
    var ci = new CultureInfo(newculture);
    Thread.CurrentThread.CurrentCulture = ci;
    Thread.CurrentThread.CurrentUICulture = ci;
}
Write("Enter your name: ");
string name = ReadLine();
Write("Enter your date of birth: ");
string dob = ReadLine();
Write("Enter your salary: ");
string salary = ReadLine();
DateTime date = DateTime.Parse(dob);
int minutes = (int)DateTime.Today.Subtract(date).TotalMinutes;
decimal earns = decimal.Parse(salary);
WriteLine($"{name} was born on a {date:dddd} and is {minutes:N0}
minutes old and earns {earns:C}.");
```

When you run an application, it automatically sets its thread to use the culture of the operating system. I am running my code in London, UK, so the thread is already set to English (United Kingdom).

The code prompts the user to enter an alternative ISO code. This allows your applications to replace the default culture at runtime.

The application then uses standard format codes to output the day of the week dddd, the number of minutes with thousand separators N0, and the salary with the currency symbol C. These adapt automatically based on the thread's culture.

Press *Ctrl + F5*. Enter **en-GB** for the ISO code and then enter some sample data. You will need to enter a date in a format valid for British English:

```
Enter an ISO culture code: en-GB

Enter your name: Alice

Enter your date of birth: 30/3/1967

Enter your salary: 23500

Alice was born on a Thursday, is 25,469,280 minutes old and earns
£23,500.00.
```

Rerun the application and try a different culture such as Danish in Denmark (da-DK). You will need to enter a date in a format valid for the culture you chose:

```
Enter an ISO culture code: da-DK

Enter your name: Mikkel

Enter your date of birth: 12.3.1980

Enter your salary: 34000

Mikkel was born on a onsdag, is 18.656.640 minutes old and earns kr.
34.000,00.
```

# Localizing an application

The application does not currently change the prompts. They have been hardcoded to always ask in English. We can improve this using localization. Choose **Project | Add New Item...** or press *Ctrl + Shift + A*.

In the dialog box, type **resource** into the search box, change the name of the resources file that you are adding to **Prompts.resx**, and then click on **Add**:

Add the following entries and then close the resource editor:

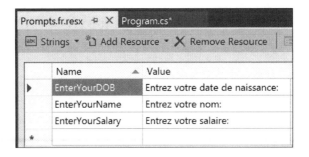

In the **Solution Explorer** window, copy and paste the **Prompts.resx** file by selecting it and pressing *Ctrl* + *C* and then *Ctrl* + *V*.

Rename the new copy to **Prompts.fr.resx**. The **fr** indicates that this new copy should be used for French. Open it and modify the entry values as follows:

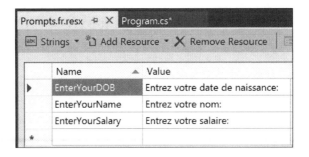

Modify the following statements in the `Main` method:

```
Write($"{Prompts.EnterYourName} ");
string name = ReadLine();
Write($"{Prompts.EnterYourDOB} ");
string dob = ReadLine();
Write($"{Prompts.EnterYourSalary} ");
string salary = ReadLine();
```

Press *Ctrl* + *F5*. With an ISO culture code of *fr-FR*, this will load the French prompts:

```
Enter an ISO culture code: fr-FR

Entrez votre nom: Michel

Entrez votre date de naissance: 4 5 1967

Entrez votre salaire: 72000

Michel was born on a jeudi, is 25 418 880 minutes old and earns 72 000,00
?.
```

With any other ISO code, it will load English prompts (think of a resource file without an ISO code in its name as being the default). You could use Microsoft Bing or Google Translate to create your resource files.

**Best Practice**

Consider whether your application needs to be internationalized and plan for that before you start coding! Write down all the pieces of text in the user interface that will need to be localized. Think about all the data that will need to be globalized (date formats, number formats, and sorting text behavior).

# Interoperating with unmanaged code

.NET applications are loaded, executed, and managed by the CLR. We use the term **unmanaged** to refer to any code that is outside the control of the CLR.

If a .NET developer needs to interact with unmanaged code, they can use two technologies: **Component Object Model (COM) Interop** and **Platform Invoke** (also known as **P/Invoke**).

Both of these technologies are specific to Windows and, therefore, are only supported by the .NET Framework, not by the .NET Core.

# Automating Microsoft Excel using COM Interop

Most of the popular Microsoft Office products support being automated using COM. If you have Microsoft Excel (for Windows) installed, then you can complete this exercise.

Add a new console application project named **Ch05_AutomatingExcel**. In the **Solution Explorer** window, right-click on **References** and choose **Add Reference…**.

In the **Reference Manager** window, on the left-hand side, click on **COM**, and then select the checkbox for **Microsoft Excel 16.0 Object Library** (or the latest version that you have installed). Click on **OK**:

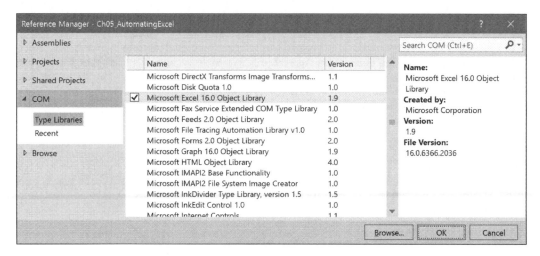

At the top of the code, import the following types and namespaces:

```
using static System.Console;
using static System.Convert;
using Microsoft.Office.Interop.Excel;
```

In the `Main` method, enter the following statements:

```
const int xlPie = 5;
Write("Enter a number: ");
double number = ToDouble(ReadLine());
var excel = new Application();
excel.Visible = true;
excel.Workbooks.Add();
excel.Range["A1"].Value = number;
```

```
excel.Range["A2"].Formula = "=A1*2";
excel.Range["A1:A2"].Select();
excel.ActiveSheet.Shapes.AddChart2(251, xlPie).Select();
excel.ActiveChart.SetSourceData(Source: excel.
Range["Sheet1!$A$1:$A$2"]);
```

When you run the console application, it starts Excel, makes it visible (because it runs hidden in the background by default), adds a blank new workbook, sets the cell A1 to contain the number the user entered, doubles it using a formula, then selects the cells and uses the numbers as a source for a pie chart:

To make it even easier to learn how to automate Excel, switch on the **Developer** tab in Excel and then use it to record a macro. The code recorded is Visual Basic for Applications, but that is easy to translate to C#.

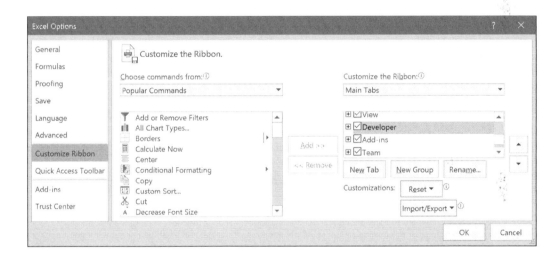

# Accessing the Win32 API with P/Invoke

All Windows applications make calls to the Win32 API to provide their functionality. That's what makes them Windows applications.

Technologies such as .NET are layers on top of the Win32 API. Most of the Win32 API functions have been exposed via .NET types, but not all. If a .NET developer needs to access a Win32 API that isn't already exposed, then they can use P/Invoke.

Add a new console application project named **Ch05_HackNotepad**. At the top of the file, import the following types and namespaces:

```
using static System.Console;
using static System.Diagnostics.Process;
using System.Runtime.InteropServices;
using System;
```

In the `Program` class, enter the following statements:

```
[DllImport("user32.dll", SetLastError = true)]
static extern IntPtr FindWindow(string lpClassName, string
lpWindowName);
[DllImport("user32.dll", SetLastError = true, CharSet = CharSet.Auto)]
public static extern bool SetWindowText(IntPtr hwnd, string lpString);
```

In the `Main` method, enter the following statements:

```
Write("Enter a message: ");
string message = ReadLine();
WriteLine("Press any key to start Notepad.");
ReadKey();
Start("notepad.exe").WaitForInputIdle();
// use a Win32 API call to get reference to Notepad
IntPtr notepad = FindWindow("Notepad", null);
if (notepad != IntPtr.Zero)
{
    // if it is running, set it's window text with a message
    SetWindowText(notepad, "Notepad has been hacked! " + message);
}
else
{
    WriteLine("Notepad is not running!");
}
```

When you run the console application, it prompts the user to enter a message, starts an instance of Notepad, finds the Notepad window, and sets its title to a customized message.

A more practical example would be impersonating a user other than the current one while executing some statements. To do this, you would need to use P/Invoke to import the `LogonUser` function from `advapi32.dll` and the `CloseHandle` function from `kernel32.dll`. For more details, visit https://msdn.microsoft.com/en-us/library/w070t6ka(v=vs.110).aspx.

# Practicing and exploring

Test your knowledge and understanding by answering some questions, get some hands-on practice, and explore with deeper research into the topics covered in this chapter.

## Exercise 5.1 – test your knowledge

Answer the following questions:

1. What is the difference between pressing *F5*, *Ctrl* + *F5*, *Shift* + *F5*, and *Ctrl* + *Shift* + *F5*?
2. Want is the ISO culture code for Welsh?
3. Which information can you find out about a process?
4. Can your applications write to the security event log in Windows?
5. How accurate is the `Stopwatch`?
6. What is the difference between localization, globalization, and internationalization?

## Exercise 5.2 – practice using Debug and Trace

Create a console application named **Ch05_Exercise02** that writes the message "I am debugging." only when the DEBUG symbol is set, writes the message "I am tracing." only when the TRACE symbol is set, and the message "I am confused!" only when TRACE and a custom conditional compilation symbol named CONFUSED is set.

## Exercise 5.3 – explore topics

Use the following links to read more about the topics covered in this chapter:

- **Debugging in Visual Studio**: https://msdn.microsoft.com/en-us/library/sc65sadd.aspx

- **Start, Break, Step, Run through Code, and Stop Debugging in Visual Studio**: https://msdn.microsoft.com/en-us/library/y740d9d3.aspx

- **Breakpoints and Tracepoints**: https://msdn.microsoft.com/en-us/library/ktf38f66.aspx

- **System.Diagnostics Namespaces**: https://msdn.microsoft.com/en-us/library/gg145030(v=vs.110).aspx

- **Stopwatch Class**: https://msdn.microsoft.com/en-us/library/system.diagnostics.stopwatch(v=vs.110).aspx

- **Process Class**: https://msdn.microsoft.com/en-us/library/system.diagnostics.process(v=vs.110).aspx

- **Debug Class**: https://msdn.microsoft.com/en-us/library/system.diagnostics.debug(v=vs.110).aspx

- **xUnit.net**: http://xunit.github.io/

- **Globalizing and Localizing .NET Framework Applications**: https://msdn.microsoft.com/en-us/library/h6270d0z(v=vs.110).aspx

- **System.Globalization Namespace**: https://msdn.microsoft.com/en-us/library/system.globalization.aspx

# Summary

In this chapter, you learned how to use the Visual Studio debugging and diagnostic features, how to unit test your code, how to internationalize your code, and how to interoperate with code outside of .NET.

In the next chapter, you will learn how to build your own types using object-oriented programming techniques.

# 6

# Building Your Own Types with Object-Oriented Programming

This chapter is about making your own types using object-oriented programming (OOP). You will learn about all the different categories of members that a type can have, including fields to store data and methods to perform actions. You will use OOP concepts such as aggregation and encapsulation.

This chapter will cover the following topics:

- Talking about OOP
- Building class libraries
- Storing data with fields
- Writing and calling methods
- Controlling access with properties and indexers
- Simplifying methods with operators
- Raising and handling events

## Talking about OOP

An object in the real world is a thing, like a car or a person. An object in programming often represents something in the real world, such as a product or bank account, but can also be something more abstract.

In C#, we use a `class` (usually) or a `struct` (rarely) to define each type of object. You can think of a type as being a blueprint or template for an object.

**Encapsulation** is the combination of the data and actions that are related to an object. For example, a `BankAccount` type might have data such as `Balance` and `AccountName`, as well as actions such as `Deposit` and `Withdraw`. When encapsulating, you often want to control what is allowed to access those data and actions.

**Composition** is about what an object is made of. For example, a car is composed of different parts such as four wheels, several seats, an engine, and so on.

**Aggregation** is about what is related to an object. For example, a person could sit in the driver's seat and becomes the car's driver.

**Inheritance** is about reusing code by having a **sub**class derive from a **base** or **super** class. All functionality in the base class becomes available in the derived class.

**Abstraction** is about capturing the core idea of an object and ignoring the details or specifics. Abstraction is a tricky balance. If you make a class more abstract, more classes would be able to inherit from it, but there will be less functionality share.

**Polymorphism** is about allowing a derived class to override an inherited action to provide custom behavior.

# Building class libraries

Class library assemblies group types together into easily deployable units (DLL files). So far, you have only created console applications to contain all your code. To make the code that you write reusable across multiple projects, you should put it in class library assemblies, just like Microsoft does.

 Put types that you might reuse in a class library.

## Creating a class library to share code

Start Microsoft Visual Studio 2015. In Visual Studio, press *Ctrl* + *Shift* + *N* or go to **File** | **New** | **Project...**.

In the **New Project** dialog, in the **Installed Templates** list, select **Visual C#**. In the center list, select **Class Library**, type **Name** as **Ch06_PacktLibrary**, change **Location** to `C:\Code`, type **Solution name** as **Chapter06**, and then click on **OK**.

 Make sure you choose class library and *not* a console application!

# Defining a class

In **Solution Explorer**, right-click on the file named `Class1.cs` and choose **Rename**. Type the name as **Person**. When you are prompted to rename all other references to the class, click on **Yes**:

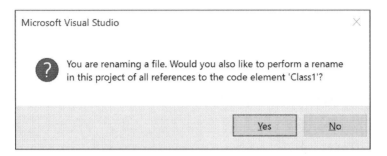

Change the namespace to **Packt.CS6** because it is important to put your classes in a logically named namespace. Your code should now look like this:

```
namespace Packt.CS6
{
    public class Person
    {
    }
}
```

Notice that I chose to apply the C# keyword `public` before the class. This allows all code to access this class. If you do not explicitly apply the `public` keyword, then it would only be accessible within the assembly that defined it. We need it to be accessible outside the assembly too. This type does not yet have any members encapsulated within it. We will create some soon.

Members can be fields, methods, or specialized versions of both. They are described here:

- **Fields** are used to store data. These are the three specialized fields:
    - **Constants**: The data in this field never changes
    - **Read-only fields**: The data in this field cannot change after the class is instantiated
    - **Events**: These point to methods that you want to call automatically when something happens, such as clicking on a button

- **Methods** are used to execute statements. These are the four specialized methods:

    ◦ **Constructors**: These are a type of method that execute when you use the `new` keyword to allocate memory and instantiate a class

    ◦ **Properties**: These are a type of method that execute when you want to control access to fields

    ◦ **Indexers**: These are a type of method that execute when you want to control access to fields

    ◦ **Operators**: These are a type of method that execute when you want to apply an operator

# Instantiating a class

In this section, we will make an instance of the `Person` class.

Add a new console application project named **Ch06_PeopleApp**.

[  Make sure you choose console application and *not* a class library! ]

This project needs a reference to the class library we just made.

In **Solution Explorer**, right-click on **References** and choose **Add Reference...**:

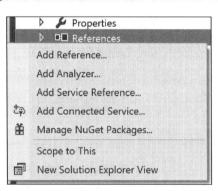

In the **Reference Manager** dialog box, in the list on the left-hand side, choose **Projects**, select the **Ch06_PacktLibrary** assembly, and then click on **OK**:

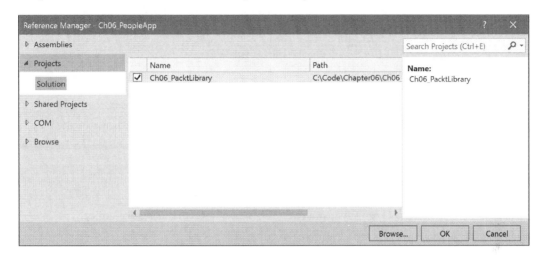

At the top of the file, type the following code to import the namespace for our class and to statically import the `Console` type:

```
using Packt.CS6;
using static System.Console;
```

In the `Main` method, type the following code to create an instance of the `Person` type by using the `new` keyword. The `new` keyword allocates memory for the object and initializes any internal data. We could use `Person` in place of the `var` keyword, but the use of `var` involves less typing and is just as clear:

```
var p1 = new Person();
WriteLine(p1.ToString());
```

Press *Ctrl* + *F5*. If you see the following dialog box, then dismiss it:

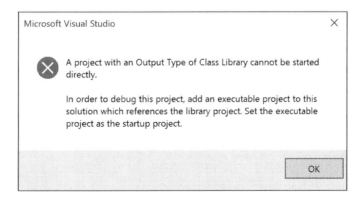

Set the solution's startup project to the current selection. Click inside the
**Ch06_PeopleApp** project or inside the `Program.cs` file, and press *Ctrl + F5* again.

Although our `Person` class did not explicitly choose to inherit from a type, all types
indirectly inherit from a special type named `System.Object`. The implementation of
the `ToString` method in the `System.Object` type simply outputs the full namespace
and type name like this:

**Packt.CS6.Person**

Back in the original `Person` class, we could have explicitly told the compiler that
`Person` inherits from the `System.Object` type like this:

```
public class Person : System.Object
```

> When class A inherits from class B, we say that B is the base or super class
> and A is the derived or subclass. In this case, `System.Object` is the base
> or super class and `Person` is the derived or subclass.

You can also use the C# alias `object` keyword:

```
public class Person : object
```

Modify the code to explicitly inherit from the `object` type. Then, click inside the
keyword and press *F12*. You will see the Microsoft-defined `System.Object` type and
its members. You do not need to understand any of this yet, but notice that it has a
method named `ToString`, as you can see in the following screenshot:

```
namespace System
{
    public class Object
    {
        public Object();

        ~Object();

        public static bool Equals(Object objA, Object objB);
        public static bool ReferenceEquals(Object objA, Object objB);
        public virtual bool Equals(Object obj);
        public virtual int GetHashCode();
        public Type GetType();
        public virtual string ToString();
        protected Object MemberwiseClone();
    }
}
```

Assume other programmers know that if inheritance is not specified, the class will inherit from `System.Object`.

# Storing data with fields

Next, we will define some fields in the class to store information about a person.

## Defining fields

Inside the `Person` class, write the following code. At this point, we have decided that a person is composed of a name and a date of birth. We have **encapsulated** these two values inside the person. We have also made the fields public so that they are visible outside the class itself:

```
public class Person
{
    // fields
    public string Name;
    public DateTime DateOfBirth;
}
```

You can use any type for a field, including arrays and collections; for example, if you need to store multiple values.

You might want to click, hold, and drag the tab for one of your open files to arrange them so that you can see both files at once, like this:

Notice, that like we did with the class, we applied the `public` keyword to these fields. If we hadn't, then they would be `private` to the class, which means they are accessible only inside the class.

There are four access modifier keywords that you can apply to a class member such as a field or method. Part of encapsulation is choosing how visible the members are:

| Access Modifier | Description |
|---|---|
| `private` (default) | Member is accessible inside the type only |
| `internal` | Member is accessible inside the type and any type in the same assembly |
| `protected` | Member is accessible inside the type and any type that inherits from the type |
| `internal` `protected` | Member is accessible inside the type, any type in the same assembly, and any type that inherits from the type |
| `public` | Member is accessible everywhere |

 Explicitly apply one of the access modifiers to all type members rather than use the default, which is `private`.

Inside the `Main` method, change the code to look like this:

```
var p1 = new Person();
p1.Name = "Bob Smith";
p1.DateOfBirth = new DateTime(1965, 12, 22);
WriteLine($"{p1.Name} was born on {p1.DateOfBirth:dddd, d MMMM
yyyy}");
```

Run the application by pressing *Ctrl* + *F5*, and view the output:

```
Bob Smith was born on Wednesday, 22 December 1965
```

You can also initialize fields using a short-hand object initializer syntax using curly brackets.

Add the following code underneath the existing code to create another new person. Note the different format code for the date of birth when writing to the console:

```
var p2 = new Person { Name = "Alice Jones", DateOfBirth = new
DateTime(1998, 3, 17) };
WriteLine($"{p2.Name} was born on {p2.DateOfBirth:d MMM yy}");
```

Run the application and view the output:

```
Alice Jones was born on 17 Mar 98
```

# Storing a value using the enum keyword

Sometimes, a value needs to be one of a limited list of options. For example, a person may have a favorite ancient world wonder. Sometimes, a value needs to be combination of a limited list of options. For example, a person may have a bucket list of ancient world wonders they want to visit. We can store this data using an enum type.

An enum is a very efficient way of storing one or more choices, because internally, it uses int values in combination with a lookup table of string descriptions.

Add a new class to the **Ch06_PacktLibrary** project named **WondersOfTheAncientWorld** by pressing *Shift + Alt + C* or going to **Project | Add Class....**

Modify the code file to make it look like this. Notice that the class keyword has been changed to enum and made public:

```
namespace Packt.CS6
{
    public enum WondersOfTheAncientWorld
    {
        GreatPyramidOfGiza,
        HangingGardensOfBabylon,
        StatueOfZeusAtOlympia,
        TempleOfArtemisAtEphesus,
        MausoleumAtHalicarnassus,
        ColossusOfRhodes,
        LighthouseOfAlexandria
    }
}
```

In the Person class, add the following statement to your list of fields:

```
public WondersOfTheAncientWorld FavouriteAncientWonder;
```

Back in the Main method of **Ch06_PeopleApp**, add the following statements:

```
p1.FavouriteAncientWonder = WondersOfTheAncientWorld.
StatueOfZeusAtOlympia;
WriteLine($"{p1.Name}'s favourite wonder is {p1.
FavouriteAncientWonder}");
```

Run the application and view the output:

```
Bob Smith's favourite wonder is StatueOfZeusAtOlympia
```

For the bucket list, we could create a collection of instances of the enum, but there is a better way. We can combine multiple choices into a single value using **flags**.

Modify the enum to look like this. Notice that I have used the left shift operator (<<) to set individual bits within the flag. I could also have set the values to 1, 2, 4, 8, 16, 32, and so on:

```
namespace Packt.CS6
{
    [System.Flags]
    public enum WondersOfTheAncientWorld : byte
    {
        None = 0,
        GreatPyramidOfGiza = 1,
        HangingGardensOfBabylon = 1 << 1,
        StatueOfZeusAtOlympia = 1 << 2,
        TempleOfArtemisAtEphesus = 1 << 3,
        MausoleumAtHalicarnassus = 1 << 4,
        ColossusOfRhodes = 1 << 5,
        LighthouseOfAlexandria = 1 << 6
    }
}
```

Notice that we are assigning explicit values for each choice that would not overlap when looking at the bits stored in memory. We must also mark the enum with the System.Flags attribute. Normally, an enum uses an int variable internally, but since we don't need values that big, we can make it more efficient by telling it to use a byte variable (with 8 bit columns).

If we want to indicate that our bucket list includes the Hanging Gardens and the Mausoleum at Halicarnassus, then we would want the 16 and 2 bits set to 1. In other words, we would store the value 18:

| 128 | 64 | 32 | 16 | 8 | 4 | 2 | 1 |
|-----|----|----|----|----|----|----|----|
| 0 | 0 | 0 | 1 | 0 | 0 | 1 | 0 |

In the Person class, add the following statement to your list of fields:

```
public WondersOfTheAncientWorld BucketList;
```

Back in the `Main` method of **Ch06_PeopleApp**, add the following statements to set the bucket list using the | operator (logical OR) to combine `enum` values. We could also set the value using the number `18` cast into the `enum` type as in the comment:

```
p1.BucketList = WondersOfTheAncientWorld.HangingGardensOfBabylon |
WondersOfTheAncientWorld.MausoleumAtHalicarnassus;
// p1.BucketList = (WondersOfTheAncientWorld)18;
WriteLine($"{p1.Name}'s bucket list is {p1.BucketList}");
```

Run the application and view the output:

```
Bob Smith's bucket list is HangingGardensOfBabylon,
MausoleumAtHalicarnassus
```

 Use enum values to store combinations of discreet options. Derive an enum from `byte` if there are up to eight options, from `short` if there are up to 16 options, from `int` if there are up to 32 options, and from `long` if there are up to 64 options.

# Storing multiple values using collections

Let's add a field to store a person's children. This is an example of **aggregation** because children are instances of a class that is related to the current person, but are not part of the person themselves:

```
public List<Person> Children = new List<Person>();
```

Note that we need to ensure the collection is initialized to a new instance of a collection before we can add items to the collection.

In the `Main` method, add the following code:

```
p1.Children.Add(new Person());
p1.Children.Add(new Person());
WriteLine($"{p1.Name} has {p1.Children.Count} children.");
```

Run the application and view the output:

```
Bob Smith has 2 children.
```

# Making a field static

The fields that we have created so far have all been instance members, meaning that a copy of each field exists for each instance of the class that is created.

Sometimes, you want to define a field that only has one copy, which is shared across all instances. These are called **static** members.

In the **Ch06_PacktLibrary** project, add a new class named `BankAccount`. Modify the code as follows:

```
namespace Packt.CS6
{
    public class BankAccount
    {
        public string AccountName;
        public decimal Balance;
        public static decimal InterestRate;
    }
}
```

Notice that each instance of `BankAccount` will have its own `AccountName` and `Balance`, but all instances will share a single `InterestRate` field.

In **Ch06_PeopleApp** and its `Main` method, add the following code, where we will set the shared interest rate and then create two instances of the `BankAccount` type:

```
BankAccount.InterestRate = 0.012M;
var ba1 = new BankAccount();
ba1.AccountName = "Mrs. Jones";
ba1.Balance = 2400;
WriteLine($"{ba1.AccountName} earned {ba1.Balance * BankAccount.
InterestRate} interest.");
var ba2 = new BankAccount();
ba2.AccountName = "Ms. Gerrier";
ba2.Balance = 98;
WriteLine($"{ba2.AccountName} earned {ba2.Balance * BankAccount.
InterestRate} interest.");
```

Run the application and view the output:

**Mrs. Jones earned £28.80 interest.**

**Ms. Gerrier earned £1.18 interest.**

# Making a field constant

If the value of a field will never *ever* change, you can use `const` and assign the value at compile time.

Inside the `Person` class, add the following code:

```
// constants
public const string Species = "Homo Sapien";
```

Inside the `Main` method, change the code to look like the following statement. Note that to read a constant field, you must write the name of the class, not the name of an instance of the class:

```
WriteLine($"{p1.Name} is a {Person.Species}");
```

Run the application and view the output:

```
Bob Smith is a Homo Sapien
```

Examples of `const` fields in Microsoft types include `System.Int32.MaxValue` and `System.Math.PI`, because neither value will *ever* change, as you can see in the following screenshot:

> (constant) int int.MaxValue = 2147483647
> Represents the largest possible value of an int. This field is constant.
>
> (constant) double Math.PI = 3.1415926535897931
> Represents the ratio of the circumference of a circle to its diameter, specified by the constant, π.

Constants should be avoided for two important reasons:

- The value must be known at compile time, and it must be expressible as a literal string, Boolean, or number value
- Every reference to the `const` field is replaced with the literal value at compile time, which will, therefore, not be reflected if the value changes in a future version

# Making a field read only

A better choice for fields that should not change is to mark them as read-only.

Inside the `Person` class, write the following code:

```
// read-only fields
public readonly string HomePlanet = "Earth";
```

Inside the `Main` method, add the following code statement. Notice that to get a read-only field, you must write the name of an instance of the class, not the type name, unlike constants:

```
WriteLine($"{p1.Name} was born on {p1.HomePlanet}");
```

Run the application and view the output:

**Bob Smith was born on Earth**

Use read-only fields over `const` fields for two important reasons:

- The value can be calculated or loaded at runtime and can be expressed using any executable statement. So, a read-only field can be set using a constructor.
- Every reference to the field is a live reference, so any future changes will be correctly reflected by calling code.

# Initializing fields with constructors

Fields often need to be initialized at runtime. You do this in a constructor that will be called when you make an instance of the class using the `new` keyword. Constructors execute before any fields are set by the code that is using the type.

Inside the `Person` class, add the following code:

```
// read-only fields
public readonly string HomePlanet = "Earth";
public readonly DateTime Instantiated;

// constructors
public Person()
{
    Name = "Unknown"; // set a default name
    Instantiated = DateTime.Now;
}
```

Inside the `Main` method, add the following code:

```
var p3 = new Person();
WriteLine($"{p3.Name} was instantiated at {p3.Instantiated:hh:mm:ss}
on {p3.Instantiated:dddd, d MMMM yyyy}");
```

Run the application and view the output:

```
Unknown was instantiated at 11:58:12 on Sunday, 3 January 2016
```

You can have multiple constructors in a type. Inside the `Person` class, add the following code:

```
public Person(string initialName)
{
    Name = initialName;
    Instantiated = DateTime.Now;
}
```

Inside the `Main` method, add the following code:

```
var p4 = new Person("Aziz");
WriteLine($"{p4.Name} was instantiated at {p4.Instantiated:hh:mm:ss}
on {p4.Instantiated:dddd, d MMMM yyyy}");
```

Notice that when you enter the statement to call the constructor, it shows the name of the parameter to be passed, as shown in the following screenshot:

Run the application and view the output:

```
Aziz was instantiated at 11:59:25 on Sunday, 3 January 2016
```

Constructors are a special category of method. Let's look at methods in more detail.

# Writing and calling methods

Methods are type members that execute a block of statements. A method that performs some actions but does not return a value is marked as returning `void`. A method that performs some actions and returns a value is marked as returning the type of that return value.

Inside the `Person` class, statically import the `System.Console` type and then add the following code:

```
// methods
public void WriteToConsole()
{
    WriteLine($"{Name} was born on {DateOfBirth:dddd, d MMMM yyyy}");
}
public string GetOrigin()
{
    return $"{Name} was born on {HomePlanet}";
}
```

Inside the `Main` method, add the following code:

```
p1.WriteToConsole();
WriteLine(p1.GetOrigin());
```

Run the application and view the output:

**Bob Smith was born on Wednesday, 22 December 1965**

**Bob Smith was born on Earth**

Methods can have parameters passed to them in order to change their behavior. Parameters are defined a bit like variable declarations but inside the parentheses of the method.

Inside the `Person` class, add the following code:

```
public string SayHello()
{
    return $"{Name} says 'Hello!'";
}
public string SayHelloTo(string name)
{
    return $"{Name} says 'Hello {name}!'";
}
```

Inside the `Main` method, add the following code:

```
WriteLine(p1.SayHello());
WriteLine(p1.SayHelloTo("Emily"));
```

Run the application and view the output:

**Bob Smith says 'Hello!'**

**Bob Smith says 'Hello Emily!'**

# Overloading methods

When typing a statement that calls a method, you can press *Ctrl + K, I* or go to the **Edit | IntelliSense | Quick Info** to see **Quick Info** of a method:

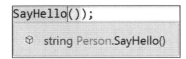

Here is the `SayHelloTo` method's Quick Info:

Instead of having two different method names, we could give both methods the same name. This is allowed because the methods each have a different signature. A method signature is the list of parameter types that can be passed when calling the method.

In the `Person` class, change the name of the `SayHelloTo` method to `SayHello`. Now, when you view the quick info for the method, it tells you that it has one additional overload:

 Use overloaded methods to simplify your class by making it appear to have fewer methods.

# Optional parameters and named arguments

Another way to simplify methods is to make parameters optional. You make a parameter optional by assigning a default value inside the method parameter list. Optional parameters must always come last in the list of parameters.

You will now create a method with three optional parameters.

Inside the `Person` class, add the following code:

```
public void OptionalParameters(string command = "Run!", double number
= 0.0, bool active = true)
{
    WriteLine($"command is {command}, number is {number}, active is
{active}");
}
```

Inside the `Main` method, add the following code. Notice IntelliSense Quick Info, that appears as you call the method, showing the three optional parameters in square brackets:

```
p1.OptionalParameters();
```

Watch Visual Studio as you type the code and you will see a tooltip as in the following screenshot:

```
p1.OptionalParameters();
```
void Person.OptionalParameters([**string command** = **"Run!"**], [double number = 0], [bool active = true])

When you run the application, you will see the following output:

**command is Run!, number is 0, active is True**

Add the following line that passes a string for the command and a double for the number parameters:

```
p1.OptionalParameters("Jump!", 98.5);
```

Run the application and see the output:

**command is Jump!, number is 98.5, active is True**

The default values for command and number have been replaced, but the default for active is still true.

Optional parameters are often combined with naming parameters when you call the method, because naming a parameter allows the values to be passed in a different order than how they were declared:

```
p1.OptionalParameters(number: 52.7, command: "Hide!");
```

Run the application and see the output:

**command is Hide!, number is 52.7, active is True**

You can even use named parameters to skip over optional parameters:

```
p1.OptionalParameters("Poke!", active: false);
```

Run the application and see the output:

```
command is Poke!, number is 0, active is False
```

# Splitting classes using partial

When working on large projects with multiple team members, it is useful to be able to split the definition of a complex class across multiple files. You do this using the `partial` keyword.

Imagine we want to add a new method to the `Person` class without having to ask another programmer to close the `Person.cs` file. If the class is defined as `partial`, then we can split it over as many separate files as we like.

In the `Person` class, add the `partial` keyword:

```
namespace Packt.CS6
{
    public partial class Person
    {
```

In the **Project** menu, go to **Add Class...** or press *Shift + Alt + C*. Enter the name **Person2**.

We cannot enter `Person` because Visual Studio isn't smart enough to understand what we want to do. Instead, we must now rename the new class to `Person`, change the namespace, and add the `public partial` keywords:

```
namespace Packt.CS6
{
    public partial class Person
    {
```

The rest of the code we write can now be put in this new `Person2.cs` file.

# Controlling access with properties and indexers

Earlier, you created a method named `GetOrigin` that returned a `string` containing the name and origin of the person. Languages such as Java do this a lot. C# has a better way: properties.

A property is simply a method (or pair of methods) that act like a field when you want to get or set a value, thereby simplifying the syntax.

## Defining read-only properties

In the `Person2.cs` file, inside the `Person` class, add the following code to define three properties.

The first property will perform the same role as the `GetOrigin` method, using the `property` syntax that works with all versions of C# (although it uses the C# 6-only string interpolation syntax).

The second property will return a greeting message using the new C# 6 lambda expression (`=>`) syntax.

The third property will calculate the person's age.

Here is the code:

```
// property defined using C# 1 - 5 syntax
public string Origin
{
    get
    {
        return $"{Name} was born on {HomePlanet}";
    }
}

// two properties defined using C# 6 lambda expression syntax
public string Greeting => $"{Name} says 'Hello!'";


public int Age => (int)(DateTime.Today.Subtract(DateOfBirth).TotalDays
/ 365.25);
```

In the `Main` method, add the following code. You can see that to get (or read) a property, you need to treat it like a field:

```
var max = new Person { Name = "Max", DateOfBirth = new DateTime(1972,
1, 27) };
WriteLine(max.Origin);
WriteLine(max.Greeting);
WriteLine(max.Age);
```

Run the application and view the output:

**Max was born on Earth**

**Max says 'Hello!'**

43

# Defining settable properties

To create a settable property, you must use the older syntax and provide a pair of methods, not just a `get` part but also a `set` part.

In the `Person2.cs` file, add the following code to define a `string` property that has both a `get` and `set` method (aka getter and setter). Although you have not manually created a field to store the person's favorite ice cream, it is there, automatically created by the compiler for you:

```
public string FavouriteIceCream { get; set; } // auto-syntax
```

Sometimes, you need more control over what happens when a property is set. In this scenario, you must use a more detailed syntax and manually create a private field to store the value for the property:

```
private string favouritePrimaryColour;
public string FavouritePrimaryColour
{
    get
    {
        return favouritePrimaryColour;
    }
    set
    {
        switch (value.ToLower())
        {
            case "red":
            case "green":
            case "blue":
```

```
                favouritePrimaryColour = value;
                break;
            default:
                throw new ArgumentException($"{value} is not a primary
    colour. Choose from: red, green, blue.");
        }
    }
}
```

In the `Main` method add the following code:

```
max.FavouriteIceCream = "Chocolate Fudge";
WriteLine($"Max's favourite ice-cream flavour is {max.
FavouriteIceCream}.");
max.FavouritePrimaryColour = "Red";
WriteLine($"Max's favourite primary colour is {max.
FavouritePrimaryColour}.");
```

Run the application and view the output:

**Max's favourite ice-cream flavour is Chocolate Fudge.**

**Max's favourite primary colour is Red.**

If you try to set the color to any value other than red, green, or blue, then the code will throw an exception. The calling code could then use a `try-catch` statement to display the error message.

 Use properties instead of fields when you want to validate what value can be stored, when you want to data bind in XAML (we will cover this in *Chapter 13, Building Universal Windows Platform Apps Using XAML*), and when you want to read and write to fields without using methods.

# Defining indexers

Indexers allow the calling code to use the array syntax to access a property. For example, the string class defines an indexer so that the calling code can access individual characters in the string individually. We will define an indexer to simplify access to the children of a person.

In the `Person2.cs` file, add the following code to define an indexer to get and set a child using the index (position) of the child:

```
// indexers
public Person this[int index]
{
    get
    {
        return Children[index];
    }
    set
    {
        Children[index] = value;
    }
}
```

> You can overload indexers so that different types can be used to call them. For example, as well as passing an `int`, you could also pass a `string`.

In the `Main` method, add the following code. After adding two children, we will access the first and second child using the longer `Children` field and the shorter indexer syntax:

```
max.Children.Add(new Person { Name = "Charlie" });
max.Children.Add(new Person { Name = "Ella" });
WriteLine($"Max's first child is {max.Children[0].Name}");
WriteLine($"Max's second child is {max.Children[1].Name}");
WriteLine($"Max's first child is {max[0].Name}");
WriteLine($"Max's second child is {max[1].Name}");
```

Run the application and view the output:

```
Max's first child is Charlie
Max's second child is Ella
Max's first child is Charlie
Max's second child is Ella
```

> Only use indexers if it makes sense to use the square bracket/array syntax. For example, a Microsoft type that uses indexers is `DbDataReader`. It loads one record at a time from a database table and allows you to use the indexer syntax to read column values based on the index or name of the column.

# Simplifying methods with operators

We might want two instances of a person to be able to procreate. We could do this with the following method:

```
// method to "multiply"
public Person Procreate(Person partner)
{
    var baby = new Person("Baby");
    Children.Add(baby);
    partner.Children.Add(baby);
    return baby;
}
```

Now, we can get two people to make a baby:

```
var harry = new Person { Name = "Harry" };
var mary = new Person { Name = "Mary" };
var baby1 = harry.Procreate(mary);
WriteLine($"{mary.Name} has {mary.Children.Count} children.");
WriteLine($"{harry.Name} has {harry.Children.Count} children.");
```

Run the application and view the output:

```
Mary has 1 children.

Harry has 1 children.
```

An alternative would be to define an operator to allow two people to "multiply". To allow this, we need to define a static operator for the * symbol:

```
// operator to "multiply"
public static Person operator *(Person p1, Person p2)
{
    return p1.Procreate(p2);
}
```

Add the following code at the end of the `Main` method, but before writing the children count to the console:

```
var baby1 = harry.Procreate(mary);
var baby2 = harry * mary;
WriteLine($"{mary.Name} has {mary.Children.Count} children.");
```

Run the application and view the output:

```
Mary has 2 children.

Harry has 2 children.
```

# Raising and handling events

Methods are often described as actions that an object can do. For example, a List class can add an item to itself or clear itself.

Events are often described as actions that happen to an object. For example, in a user interface, a Button has a Click event, click being something that happens to a button.

Another way of thinking of events is a way of exchanging messages between two objects.

# Calling methods using delegates

You have already seen the most common way to call or execute a method: use the "dot" syntax to access the method using its name.

The other way to call or execute a method is to use a delegate. If you have used languages that support function pointers, then you can think of a delegate as being a type-safe method pointer. In other words, a delegate is just the memory address of a method that matches the same signature as the delegate.

For example, imagine there is a method that must have a string passed as its only parameter and it returns an int:

```
public int MethodIWantToCall(string input)
{
    return input.Length;
}
```

I could call this method directly like this:

```
int answer = p1.MethodIWantToCall("Frog");
```

Alternatively, I could define a delegate with a matching signature to call the method indirectly. Notice that the names of parameters do not have to match. Only the types of parameters and return values must match:

```
delegate int DelegateWithMatchingSignature(string s);
```

Now, I can create an instance of the delegate, point it at the method, and finally call the delegate (which calls the method!):

```
var d = new DelegateWithMatchingSignature(p1.MethodIWantToCall);
int answer2 = d("Frog");
```

You are probably thinking, "What's the point of that?" Well, it provides flexibility.

We could use delegates to create a queue of methods that need to be called in order. Delegates have built-in support for asynchronous operations that run on a different thread for better performance. Most importantly, delegates allow us to create events.

 Delegates and events are one of the most advanced features of C# and can take a few attempts to understand, so don't worry if you're feeling lost!

# Defining events

Microsoft has predefined two delegates for use as events. They look like this:

```
public delegate void EventHandler(object sender, EventArgs e);
public delegate void EventHandler<TEventArgs>(object sender,
TEventArgs e);
```

 When you want to define an event in your own type, you should use one of these two predefined delegates.

Add the following code to `Person2.cs`. The code defines an event named `Shout`. It also defines a field to store `AngerLevel` and a method named `Poke`.

Each time a person is poked, their anger level increments. Once their anger level reaches three, they raise the `Shout` event, but only if the event delegate is pointing at a method (that is, NOT null):

```
// events
public event EventHandler Shout;
public int AngerLevel;
public void Poke()
{
    AngerLevel++;
    if (AngerLevel >= 3)
    {
        if (Shout != null)
        {
            Shout(this, EventArgs.Empty);
        }
    }
}
```

In the `Main` method, start typing the following code to assign an event handler:

```
p1.Shout +=
```

Notice the IntelliSense that appears when you type the `+=` operator, as shown in the following screenshot:

```
p1.Shout +=
                    P1_Shout;    (Press TAB to insert)
```

Press *Tab* and then *Enter* to accept the name of the method. Visual Studio inserts a method that correctly matches the signature of the event delegate. This method will be automatically called when the event is raised.

[  In older versions of Visual Studio, you had to press the *Tab* key twice. ]

Scroll down to find the method Visual Studio created for you and delete the statement that throws a `NotImplementedException`. Replace it with the following code:

```
private static void P1_Shout(object sender, EventArgs e)
{
    Person p = (Person)sender;
    WriteLine($"{p.Name} is this angry: {p.AngerLevel}.");
}
```

Back in the `Main` method, add the following code after handling the `Shout` event:

```
p1.Shout += P1_Shout;
p1.Poke();
p1.Poke();
p1.Poke();
p1.Poke();
```

Run the application. Notice that Bob only gets angry enough to shout once he's been poked three times:

```
Bob Smith is this angry: 3.
Bob Smith is this angry: 4.
```

# Practicing and exploring

Test your knowledge and understanding by answering some questions, get some hands-on practice, and explore this chapter's topics with deeper research.

## Exercise 6.1 – test your knowledge

Answer the following questions:

1. What are the four access modifiers and what do they do?
2. What is the difference between the `static`, `const`, and `readonly` keywords?
3. How many parameters can a method have?
4. What does a constructor do?
5. Why do you need to apply the `[Flags]` attribute to an `enum` keyword when you want to store combined values?
6. What is a delegate?
7. What is an event?
8. Why is the `partial` keyword useful?

## Exercise 6.2 – practice writing mathematical methods

Create a console application named **Ch06_Exercise02** and add three static methods to the `Program` class to perform the following tasks:

- Numbers used to count are called "cardinal" numbers, for example, 1, 2, 3. Numbers used to order are "ordinal" numbers, for example, 1st, 2nd, 3rd. Write a method named `CardinalToOrdinal` that converts a cardinal `int` into an ordinal `string`, for example, converts 1 into 1st, 2 into 2nd, and so on.

- The factorial of 5 is 120, because factorials are calculated by multiplying the number by one less than itself and so on like this: 5 x 4 x 3 x 2 x 1 = 120. The factorial of 3 is 6 because it is 3 x 2 x 1 = 6. Write a method named `Factorial` that calculates the factorial for an `int` variable passed to it as a parameter. You could either use a loop or a technique called **recursion**, which means a method that calls itself.

- Prime factors are the combination of smallest prime numbers that when multiplied together will produce the original number. For example, the prime factors of 30 are 2 x 3 x 5. The prime factors of 4 are 2 x 2. Write a method named `PrimeFactors` that, when passed an `int` variable as a parameter, returns a `string` showing the prime factors as stated earlier.

In the `Main` method, prompt the user to press A, B, or C to choose between the three mathematical functions. Then, prompt the user to enter a number as input and then show the output.

# Exercise 6.3 – explore topics

Use the following links to read more about this chapter's topics:

- **.NET Framework class library**: https://msdn.microsoft.com/en-us/library/gg145045(v=vs.110).aspx

- **Framework design guidelines**: https://msdn.microsoft.com/en-us/library/vstudio/ms229042(v=vs.110).aspx

- **Fields (C# programming guide)**: https://msdn.microsoft.com/en-us/library/ms173118.aspx

- **Access modifiers (C# programming guide)**: https://msdn.microsoft.com/en-us/library/ms173121.aspx

- **Constructors (C# programming guide)**: https://msdn.microsoft.com/en-us/library/ace5hbzh.aspx

- **Methods (C# programming guide)**: https://msdn.microsoft.com/en-us/library/ms173114.aspx

- **Named and optional arguments (C# programming guide)**: https://msdn.microsoft.com/en-us/library/dd264739.aspx

- **Method parameters (C# reference)**: https://msdn.microsoft.com/en-us/library/8f1hz171(v=vs.140).aspx

- **Properties (C# programming guide)**: https://msdn.microsoft.com/en-us/library/x9fsa0sw.aspx

- **Indexers (C# programming guide)**: https://msdn.microsoft.com/en-us/library/6x16t2tx.aspx

- **Operator (C# reference)**: https://msdn.microsoft.com/en-us/library/s53ehcz3.aspx

- **Delegates (C# programming guide)**: https://msdn.microsoft.com/en-us/library/ms173171.aspx

- **Events (C# programming guide)**: https://msdn.microsoft.com/en-us/library/awbftdfh.aspx

# Summary

In this chapter, you learned about making your own types using OOP. You learned about all the different categories of members that a type can have, including fields to store data and methods to perform actions. You used OOP concepts such as aggregation and encapsulation.

In the next chapter, you will take these concepts further by implementing interfaces and inheriting from existing classes.

# 7

# Implementing Interfaces and Inheriting Classes

This chapter is about deriving new types from existing ones using object-oriented programming (OOP). You will learn how to implement interfaces, about base and derived classes, how to override a type member, how to use polymorphism, how to create extension methods, and how to cast between classes in an inheritance hierarchy.

This chapter covers the following topics:

- Implementing interfaces
- Managing memory with reference and value types
- Inheriting from classes
- Casting within inheritance hierarchies
- Documenting your types
- Inheriting and extending .NET types

## Implementing interfaces

**Interfaces** are a way of connecting different types together to make new things. Think of them like the studs on top of LEGO bricks that allow them to "stick" together, or electrical standards for plugs and sockets.

If a type implements a particular interface, then it is making a promise to the rest of .NET that it supports a certain feature.

# Common interfaces

Here are some common interfaces that your types might want to implement:

| Interface | Method(s) | Description |
|-----------|-----------|-------------|
| IComparable | CompareTo(other) | This defines a comparison method that a type implements to order or sort its instances |
| IComparer | Compare(first, second) | This defines a comparison method that a secondary type implements to order or sort instances of a primary type |
| IDisposable | Dispose() | This defines a disposal method to release unmanaged resources more efficiently than waiting for a finalizer |
| IFormattable | ToString(format, culture) | This defines a culture-aware method to format the value of an object into a string representation |
| IFormatter | Serialize(stream, object), Deserialize(stream) | This defines methods to convert an object to and from a stream of bytes for storage or transfer |

# Comparing objects when sorting

One of the most common interfaces that you will want to implement is `IComparable`. It allows arrays and collections that contain instances of your type to be sorted.

In Visual Studio, open the **Chapter06** solution and the `Program.cs` file in the **Ch06_PeopleApp** project. Add the following code to the `Main` method. It creates an array of `Person` instances, attempts to sort it, and then outputs the array:

```
Person[] people =
{
    new Person { Name = "Simon" },
    new Person { Name = "Jenny" },
    new Person { Name = "Adam" },
    new Person { Name = "Richard" }
};
Array.Sort(people);
foreach (var person in people)
{
    WriteLine($"{person.Name}");
}
```

Run the application by pressing *Ctrl + F5*. You will see this runtime error:

```
Unhandled Exception: System.InvalidOperationException: Failed to compare
two elements in the array. ---> System.ArgumentException: At least one
object must implement IComparable.
```

As the error explains, to fix the problem our type must implement `IComparable`.

In the **Ch06_PacktLibrary** project in the `Person2.cs` file, add the following code to the end of the class definition:

```
public partial class Person : IComparable<Person>
```

Visual Studio will draw a red squiggle under the new code you have added to warn you that you have not yet implemented the method you have promised to.

Visual Studio can write the skeleton implementation for you if you click on the light bulb and choose the first option, that is, **Implement interface**.

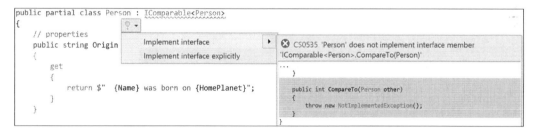

Scroll down to find the method that Visual Studio wrote for you and delete the statement that throws the `NotImplementedException` error. Modify the method to look like this:

```
public int CompareTo(Person other)
{
    return Name.CompareTo(other.Name);
}
```

I have chosen to compare two `Person` instances by comparing their name fields. People will therefore be sorted alphabetically by their name.

Run the application. This time it works:

```
Adam
Jenny
Richard
Simon
```

# Defining a separate comparer

Sometimes you won't have access to the source code for a type and it might not implement the IComparable interface. Luckily, there is another way to sort instances of a type. You can create a secondary type that implements a slightly different interface named IComparer.

In the **Ch06_PacktLibrary** project, add a new class named PersonComparer that implements the IComparer interface, as shown in the following block of code. It will compare two people by comparing the length of their Name field, or if the names are the same length, then by comparing the names alphabetically:

```
using System.Collections.Generic;
namespace Packt.CS6
{
    public class PersonComparer : IComparer<Person>
    {
        public int Compare(Person x, Person y)
        {
            int temp = x.Name.Length.CompareTo(y.Name.Length);
            if (temp == 0)
            {
                return x.Name.CompareTo(y.Name);
            }
            else
            {
                return temp;
            }
        }
    }
}
```

In the Main method, add the following code:

```
Array.Sort(people, new PersonComparer());
foreach (var person in people)
{
    WriteLine($"{person.Name}");
}
```

Run the application. This time, when we sort the people array, we explicitly ask the sorting algorithm to use the PersonComparer type instead, so the people are sorted with the shortest names first:

**Adam**

**Jenny**

**Simon**

**Richard**

**Best Practice**
If anyone might want to sort an array or collection of instances of your type, then implement the `IComparable` interface.

# Managing memory with reference and value types

There are two categories of memory: **stack** memory and **heap** memory. Stack memory is fast but limited and heap memory is slower but plentiful.

There are two C# keywords that you use to create object types: `class` and `struct`. Both can have the same members. The difference between the two is how memory is allocated and the lifetime of their variables.

Technically, how memory is allocated is an implementation detail and not part of the C# or .NET specifications. Alternative implementations could choose to store instances of a `struct` type on the heap! You can read more about how value types are stored here: `https://blogs.msdn.microsoft.com/ericlippert/2010/09/30/the-truth-about-value-types/`.

When you define a type using `class`, you are defining a **reference** type. This means that the memory for the object itself is allocated on the heap along with some overhead consisting of a pointer to the object's method table and an object that is used to synchronize access from multiple threads, and only the memory address of the object (and a little overhead) is stored on the stack.

When you define a type using `struct`, you are defining a **value** type. This means that the memory for the object itself is allocated on the stack.

If your type defined by using the `struct` keyword uses reference types for any of its fields, then those fields will be stored on the heap!

These are most of the `struct` types, that is, value types in .NET:

- **These are number value types**: byte, sbyte, short, ushort, int, uint, long, ulong, float, double, decimal
- **These are character and Boolean value types**: char, bool
- **These are System.Drawing value types**: Color, Point, Rectangle

Almost all the other types in .NET are classes, that is, reference types, including `string`.

[  You cannot inherit from a `struct`. ]

# Defining a type using the struct keyword

In **Solution Explorer**, ensure that the **Ch06_PacktLibrary** project has the focus. Next, from the **Project** menu, choose **Add Class...** or press *Shift + Alt + C*.

In the dialog box enter `DisplacementVector` for the name.

[  There isn't a template for `struct`, so you have to use `class` and then change it manually. ]

Modify the code to look like this:

```
namespace Packt.CS6
{
    public struct DisplacementVector
    {
        public int X;
        public int Y;
        public DisplacementVector(int initialX, int initialY)
        {
            X = initialX;
            Y = initialY;
        }
        public static DisplacementVector operator +(DisplacementVector
vector1, DisplacementVector vector2)
        {
            return new DisplacementVector(vector1.X + vector2.X,
vector1.Y + vector2.Y);
        }
    }
}
```

In the **Ch06_PeopleApp** project, in the `Main` method, add the following code:

```
var dv1 = new DisplacementVector(3, 5);
var dv2 = new DisplacementVector(-2, 7);
var dv3 = dv1 + dv2;
WriteLine($"({dv1.X}, {dv1.Y}) + ({dv2.X}, {dv2.Y}) = ({dv3.X},
{dv3.Y})");
```

Run the application and view the output:

```
(3, 5) + (-2, 7) = (1, 12)
```

**Best Practice**

If your type uses 16 bytes or less of stack memory, only uses `struct` keywords for its field types, and you will never want to inherit from it, then Microsoft recommends that you use a `struct` keyword. If your type uses more than 16 bytes of stack memory, uses `classes` for its field types, and if you would want to inherit from your type, then use a `class`. By the way, if you are wondering what I mean by "inherit", then read on…

# Releasing unmanaged resources

In the previous chapter, we saw that constructors can be used to initialize fields. A type may have multiple constructors.

Imagine that a constructor allocates an unmanaged resource (that is, anything that is not controlled by .NET). The unmanaged resource must be manually released because .NET cannot do it for us.

Each type can have a single **finalizer** (also known as destructor) that will be called by the CLR when the resources need to be released. A finalizer has the same name as a constructor (that is, the type name) but it is prefixed with a tilde (~) as shown in the following code example:

```
public class Animal
{
    public Animal()
    {
        // allocate an unmanaged resource
    }
    ~Animal() // Finalizer aka destructor
    {
        // deallocate the unmanaged resource
    }
}
```

This is the minimum you should do in this scenario. The problem with just providing a finalizer is that the .NET garbage collector requires two garbage collections to completely release the allocated resources for this type.

Though optional, it is recommended to also provide a method to allow a developer who uses your type to explicitly release resources so that the garbage collector can then release the object in a single collection. There is a standard mechanism to do this in .NET by implementing the IDisposable interface, as shown in the following code example:

```
public class Animal : IDisposable
{
    public Animal()
    {
        // allocate unmanaged resource
    }
    ~Animal() // Finalizer aka destructor
    {
        if (disposed) return;
        Dispose(false);
    }
    bool disposed = false; // have resources been released?
    public void Dispose()
    {
        Dispose(true);
        GC.SuppressFinalize(this);
    }
    protected virtual void Dispose(bool disposing)
    {
        if (disposed) return;
        // deallocate the *unmanaged* resource
        // ...
        if (disposing)
        {
            // deallocate any other *managed* resources
            // ...
        }
        disposed = true;
    }
}
```

Note that there are two `Dispose` methods. The public method will be called by a developer using your type. The `Dispose` method with a `bool` parameter is used internally to implement the deallocation of resources, both unmanaged and managed. When the public `Dispose` method is called, both unmanaged and managed resources need to be deallocated, but when the finalizer runs, only unmanaged resources need to be deallocated.

Also, note the call to `GC.SuppressFinalize(this)` — this is what notifies the garbage collector that it no longer needs to run the finalizer and removes the need for a second collection.

## Ensuring that dispose is called

When someone uses a type that implements `IDisposable`, they can ensure that the public `Dispose` method is called with the `using` statement, as shown in the following code:

```
using(Animal a = new Animal())
{
    // code that uses the Animal instance
}
```

The compiler converts your code into something like the following, which guarantees that even if an exception occurs, the `Dispose` method will still be called:

```
Animal a = new Animal();
try
{
    // code that uses the Animal instance
}
finally
{
    if (a != null) a.Dispose();
}
```

# Inheriting from classes

Inheritance is a mechanism for code reuse where a derived (or sub) class is based on a base (or super) class thereby having access to all of the base class' members. The `Person` type we created earlier implicitly derived (inherited) from `System.Object`. Now, we will create a new class that explicitly inherits from `Person`.

In **Solution Explorer**, ensure that the **Ch06_PacktLibrary** project has the focus. Next, from the **Project** menu, choose **Add Class...** or press *Shift + Alt + C*. Name the class `Employee`.

Modify its code as follows:

```
using System;
namespace Packt.CS6
{
    public class Employee : Person
    {
    }
}
```

Add a new console application named **Ch07_InheritanceApp**.

Add a reference to the **Ch06_PacktLibrary** assembly.

Modify the `Program.cs` file to import the `Packt.CS6` namespace and add statements to the `Main` method to create an instance of the `Employee` class:

```
using Packt.CS6;
using System;
using static System.Console;
namespace Ch07_InheritanceApp
{
    class Program
    {
        static void Main(string[] args)
        {
            Employee e1 = new Employee { Name = "John Jones",
DateOfBirth = new DateTime(1990, 7, 28) };
            e1.WriteToConsole();
        }
    }
}
```

Run the application and view the output:

`John Jones was born on Saturday, 28 July 1990`

Note that the `Employee` class has inherited all the members of `Person`.

# Extending classes

Now, we will add some employee-specific members to extend the class.

In the `Employee` class, add the following code to define two properties:

```
public string EmployeeCode { get; set; }
public DateTime HireDate { get; set; }
```

Back in the `Main` method, add the following code:

```
e1.EmployeeCode = "JJ001";
e1.HireDate = new DateTime(2014, 11, 23);
WriteLine($"{e1.Name} was hired on {e1.HireDate:dd/MM/yy}");
```

Run the application and view the output:

```
John Jones was hired on 23/11/14
```

# Hiding members

So far, the `WriteToConsole` method is inherited from `Person`, and it only outputs the employee's name and date of birth. We might want to change what this method does for an employee.

In the `Employee` class, add the following code to redefine the `WriteToConsole` method:

```
using System;
using static System.Console;
namespace Packt.CS6
{
    public class Employee : Person
    {
        public string EmployeeCode { get; set; }
        public DateTime HireDate { get; set; }
        public void WriteToConsole()
        {
            WriteLine($"{Name}'s birth date is {DateOfBirth:dd/MM/yy}
and hire date was {HireDate:dd/MM/yy}");
        }
    }
}
```

Run the application and view the output:

```
John Jones's birth date is 28/07/90 and hire date was 01/01/01
John Jones was hired on 23/11/14
```

Note that Visual Studio warns you that your method now hides the method with the same name that you inherited from the `Person` class.

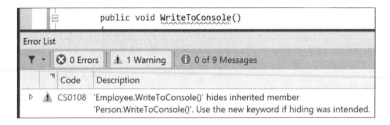

You can remove this warning by applying the `new` keyword to the method:

```
public new void WriteToConsole()
```

# Overriding members

Rather than hiding a method, it is usually better to **override** it. You can only override members if the base class chooses to allow overriding by applying the `virtual` keyword.

In the `Main` method, add the following statement:

```
WriteLine(e1.ToString());
```

Run the application. The `ToString` method is inherited from `System.Object`. The implementation outputs the namespace and type name, as follows:

```
Packt.CS6.Employee
```

Let's override this behavior for the `Person` class.

Open the `Person.cs` file and at the bottom of the `Person.cs` file (but inside the class brackets), type the word `override` and enter a space after the word. You will see that Visual Studio shows a list of methods that have been marked as virtual so that they can be overridden.

Use the arrow keys on your keyboard to choose ToString and then press *Enter*.

Modify the code to look like this:

```
// overridden methods
public override string ToString()
{
    return $"{Name} is a {base.ToString()}";
}
```

Run the application. Now, when the ToString method is called, it outputs the person's name as well as the base class's implementation of ToString:

**John Jones is a Packt.CS6.Employee**

# Preventing inheritance and overriding

You can prevent someone from inheriting from your class by applying the sealed keyword to its definition. No one can inherit from Mr. Money Bags:

```
public sealed class MrMoneyBags
{
}
```

You can prevent someone from further overriding a method in your class by applying the sealed keyword to the method. No one can change the way Lady Gaga sings:

```
public class Singer
{
    public virtual void Sing()
    {
    }
}

public class LadyGaga : Singer
{
    public override sealed void Sing()
    {
    }
}
```

 You can only seal a method that you have overridden so the sealed keyword is always used in combination with the override keyword.

# Polymorphism

You have now seen two ways to change the behavior of an inherited method. We can hide an inherited method using new (known as non-polymorphic inheritance) or we can override it if it is virtual (polymorphic inheritance).

Both ways can call the base class using the base keyword, so what is the difference?

It all depends on the type of the variable holding a reference to the object. For example, a variable of the Person type can hold a reference to a Person class *or any type that derives from* Person.

In the Employee class, add the following code:

```
public override string ToString()
{
    return $"{Name}'s code is {EmployeeCode}";
}
```

In the Main method, write the following code:

```
Employee aliceInEmployee = new Employee { Name = "Alice", EmployeeCode = "AA123" };
Person aliceInPerson = aliceInEmployee;
aliceInEmployee.WriteToConsole();
aliceInPerson.WriteToConsole();
WriteLine(aliceInEmployee.ToString());
WriteLine(aliceInPerson.ToString());
```

Run the application and view the output:

```
Alice's birth date is 01/01/01 and hire date was 01/01/01
Alice was born on Monday, 1 January 0001
Alice's code is AA123
Alice's code is AA123
```

Note that when a method is hidden with new, the compiler is not smart enough to know that the object is an employee, so it calls the WriteToConsole method in Person.

When a method is overridden with `virtual` and `override`, the compiler is smart enough to know that although the variable is declared as a `Person` class, the object itself is an `Employee` and therefore the `Employee` implementation of `ToString` is called.

| Variable type | Method defined with | Method executed |
|---|---|---|
| Person | | `WriteToConsole` in `Person` |
| Employee | new | `WriteToConsole` in `Employee` |
| Person | virtual | `ToString` in `Employee` |
| Employee | override | `ToString` in `Employee` |

> Polymorphism is literally academic to most programmers. If you **grok** the concept, that's great, but if not, you shouldn't worry about polymorphism. `http://www.urbandictionary.com/define.php?term=grok`

# Casting within inheritance hierarchies

Casting is subtly different from converting between different types.

## Implicit casting

In the previous example, you saw how an instance of a derived type can be stored in a variable of its base type (or its base's base type and so on). When we do this, it is called implicit casting.

## Explicit casting

Going the other way, for example, attempting to store an instance of a base type in a variable of a derived type, is an explicit cast and you must use parentheses to do it.

In the `Main` method, add the following code:

```
Employee e2 = aliceInPerson;
```

Visual Studio gives a compile error, as shown in the following screenshot:

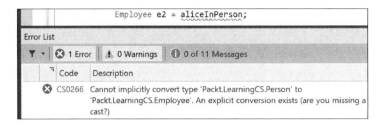

Change the code as follows:

```
Employee e2 = (Employee)aliceInPerson;
```

# Handling casting exceptions

The compiler is now happy *but* because `aliceInPerson` might be a different derived type, such as a `Student` instead of an `Employee`, we need to be careful. This statement might throw an `InvalidCastException`.

We can handle this by writing a `try-catch` statement, but there is a better way. We can check the current type of the object using the `is` keyword.

Wrap the explicit cast statement in an `if` statement, as follows:

```
if (aliceInPerson is Employee)
{
    WriteLine($"{nameof(aliceInPerson)} IS an Employee");
    Employee e2 = (Employee)aliceInPerson;
    // do something with e2
}
```

Run the application and view the output:

**aliceInPerson IS an Employee**

Alternatively, you can use the `as` keyword to cast. Instead of throwing an exception, the `as` keyword returns `null` if the type cannot be cast.

```
Employee e3 = aliceInPerson as Employee;
if (e3 != null)
{
    WriteLine($"{nameof(aliceInPerson)} AS an Employee");
    // do something with e3
}
```

Since accessing a `null` variable can throw a `NullReferenceException` error, you should always check for `null` before using the result.

Run the application and view the output:

```
aliceInPerson AS an Employee
```

 **Best Practice**
Use the `is` and `as` keywords to avoid throwing exceptions when casting between derived types.

# Documenting your types

One of the files that you can add to a Visual Studio project is **Class Diagram**.

From the **Project** menu, choose **Add New Item** or press *Ctrl + Shift + A*. In the **Search** box, enter **diagram** and change the filename to **PacktLibrary.cd**, as shown in the following screenshot:

In the **View** menu, choose **Class View**. In the **Class View** window, expand **Ch06_PacktLibrary**, expand **Packt.CS6**, and then drag and drop the **Person** file into the middle of the class diagram, as shown in the following screenshot:

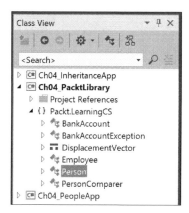

In the following diagram, you will see the **Person** class and the interface that it implements:

In the preceding diagram, right-click on the background, choose **Change Members Format**, and then **Display Full Signature**.

Click on the downward pointing chevron in the top-right corner of the class to expand its details and stretch the box to make it wide enough for you to see all the details.

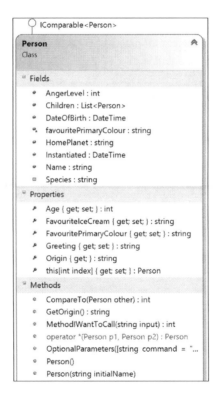

Drag and drop the `Employee` class onto the diagram to show the inheritance hierarchy.

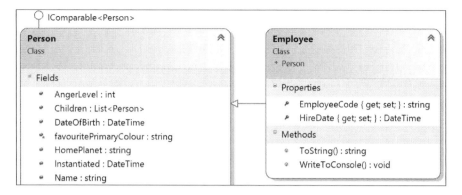

Right-click on the `Employee` class and choose **Class Details**. This window can be used to modify or add new members to a class.

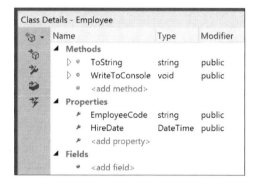

# Inheriting and extending .NET types

.NET has prebuilt class libraries containing hundreds of thousands of types. Rather than creating your own completely new types, you can often start by inheriting from one of Microsoft's.

# Inheriting from the Exception class

In the **Ch06_PacktLibrary** project, add a new class named `BankAccountException`, as shown in the following code:

```
using System;

namespace Packt.CS6
{
    public class BankAccountException : Exception
    {
        public BankAccountException() : base() { }
        public BankAccountException(string message) : base(message) {
}
        public BankAccountException(string message, Exception
innerException) : base(message, innerException) { }
    }
}
```

In the `BankAccount` class that you created in the previous chapter, add the following method:

```
public void Withdraw(decimal amount)
{
    if ((Balance - amount) < 0M)
    {
        throw new BankAccountException("Balance cannot be less than
zero!");
    }
    else
    {
        Balance -= amount;
    }
}
```

In **Ch07_InheritanceApp**, in the `Main` method, add the following statements to test what happens when we try to withdraw too much from a bank account:

```
try
{
    var ba = new BankAccount();
    ba.Balance = 100;
    WriteLine($"Balance is {ba.Balance}");
    ba.Withdraw(150);
    WriteLine($"Balance is {ba.Balance}");
}
catch (BankAccountException ex)
```

```
    {
        WriteLine($"{ex.GetType().Name}: {ex.Message}");
    }
```

Run the application and view the output:

```
Balance is 100
```

```
BankAccountException: Balance cannot be less than zero!
```

> **Best Practice**
> When defining your own exceptions, give them the three conventional constructors.

# Extending types when you can't inherit

Earlier, we saw how the `sealed` modifier can be used to prevent inheritance.

Microsoft has applied the `sealed` keyword to the `System.String` class so that no one can inherit and potentially break the behavior of strings.

Can we still add new methods to strings? Yes, we can if we use a language feature named **extension methods** that was introduced with C# 3.

## Using static methods to reuse functionality

Since the first version of C#, we have been able to create static methods to reuse functionality, such as the ability to validate that a string contains an e-mail address.

In the **Ch06_PacktLibrary** project, add a new class named `MyExtensions`, as shown in the following code:

```
using System.Text.RegularExpressions;

namespace Packt.CS6
{
    public class MyExtensions
    {
        public static bool IsValidEmail(string input)
        {
            // use simple regular expression to check
            // that the input string is a valid email
            return Regex.IsMatch(input,
                @"[a-zA-Z0-9\.-_]+@[a-zA-Z0-9\.-_]+");
        }
    }
}
```

Add a new Console Application named **Ch07_ExtensionMethods**.

Add a reference to the **Ch06_PacktLibrary** assembly.

Modify the `Program.cs` file to import the `Packt.CS6` namespace and add statements to the `Main` method to validate two examples of e-mail addresses:

```
using static System.Console;
using Packt.CS6;

namespace Ch07_ExtensionMethods
{
    class Program
    {
        static void Main(string[] args)
        {
            string email1 = "pamela@test.com";
            string email2 = "ian&test.com";

            WriteLine($"{email1} is a valid e-mail address:
{MyExtensions.IsValidEmail(email1)}.");
            WriteLine($"{email2} is a valid e-mail address:
{MyExtensions.IsValidEmail(email2)}.");
        }
    }
}
```

Run the application and view the output:

```
pamela@test.com is a valid e-mail address: True.
ian&test.com is a valid e-mail address: False.
```

This works, but extension methods can reduce the amount of code we have to type and simplify the usage of this function.

# Using extension methods to reuse functionality

In the `MyExtensions` class, add the `static` modifier before the class, and add the `this` modifier before the `string` type, like this:

```
public static class MyExtensions
{
    public static bool IsValidEmail(this string input)
    {
```

These two changes inform the compiler that it should treat the method as a method that extends the `System.String` type.

Back in the `Program` class, add some new statements to use the method as an extension method for strings:

```
WriteLine($"{email1} is a valid e-mail address: {email1.
IsValidEmail()}.");
WriteLine($"{email2} is a valid e-mail address: {email2.
IsValidEmail()}.");
```

Note the subtle change in the syntax. The `IsValidEmail` method now appears to be an instance member of the `string` type.

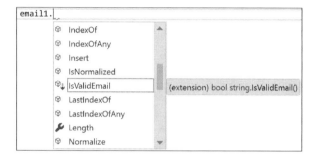

 Extension methods cannot replace or override existing instance methods, so you cannot, for example, redefine the `Insert` method of the `string` class. The extension method will appear as an overload but the instance method will be called in preference to the extension method with the same name and signature.

Although extension methods don't seem to give a big benefit compared to simply using static methods, in *Chapter 9, Querying and Manipulating Data with LINQ*, you will see some extremely useful examples of extension methods.

# Practice and explore

Test your knowledge and understanding by answering some questions. Get some hands-on practice and explore with deeper research into this chapter's topics.

# Exercise 7.1 – test your knowledge

Answer the following questions:

1. How are a base class and a derived class related?
2. What is the difference between `is` and `as`?
3. Which keyword is used to prevent a class from being derived from or a method from being overridden?
4. Which keyword is used to prevent a class from being instantiated with the `new` keyword?
5. Which keyword is used to allow a member to be overridden?
6. What's the deal with polymorphism?
7. What are the signatures of the constructors that all exceptions should have?
8. What is an extension method and how do you define one?

# Exercise 7.2 – practice creating an inheritance hierarchy

Add a new console application named **Ch07_Exercise02**.

Create a class named `Shape` with properties named `Height`, `Width`, and `Area`.

Add three classes that derive from it—`Rectangle`, `Square`, and `Circle`—with any additional members you feel are appropriate and that override and implement the `Area` property correctly.

# Exercise 7.3 – explore topics

Use the following links to read more about the topics covered in this chapter:

- **Interfaces (C# Programming Guide)**: `https://msdn.microsoft.com/en-us/library/ms173156.aspx`
- **IComparable<T> Interface**: `https://msdn.microsoft.com/en-us/library/4d7sx9hd(v=vs.110).aspx`
- **Classes (C# Programming Guide)**: `https://msdn.microsoft.com/en-us/library/x9afc042.aspx`
- **Reference Types (C# Reference)**: `https://msdn.microsoft.com/en-us/library/490f96s2(v=vs.140).aspx`

- **Structs (C# Programming Guide)**: `https://msdn.microsoft.com/en-us/library/saxz13w4.aspx`

- **Value Types (C# Reference)**: `https://msdn.microsoft.com/en-us/library/s1ax56ch(v=vs.140).aspx`

- **Inheritance (C# Programming Guide)**: `https://msdn.microsoft.com/en-us/library/ms173149.aspx`

- **Polymorphism (C# Programming Guide)**: `https://msdn.microsoft.com/en-us/library/ms173152.aspx`

- **Cleaning Up Unmanaged Resources**: `http://msdn.microsoft.com/en-us/library/498928w2.aspx`

- **Destructors (C# Programming Guide)**: `http://msdn.microsoft.com/en-us/library/66x5fx1b.aspx`

- **IDisposable Interface**: `http://msdn.microsoft.com/en-us/library/system.idisposable.aspx`

# Summary

In this chapter, you learned about deriving types using inheritance and object-oriented programming (OOP). You learned about base and derived classes, how to override a type member, how to use polymorphism, and how to cast between types.

In the next chapter, you will learn about working with relational data using the Entity Framework.

# 8

# Working with Relational Data Using the Entity Framework

This chapter is about reading and writing to Microsoft SQL Server (and other databases) using classic ADO.NET and the object-relational mapping technology known as the Entity Framework.

This chapter will cover the following topics:

- Relational Database Management Systems
- Using ADO.NET
- Using Entity Framework 6
- Using Entity Framework Core

## Relational Database Management Systems

One of the most common places to store data is in a **Relational Database Management System (RDBMS)**. Common ones include Microsoft SQL Server, Oracle, and MySQL.

## Connecting to Microsoft SQL Server LocalDb

Microsoft offers various editions of its SQL Server product. We will use a free version that can run standalone and is known as LocalDb. The latest version of LocalDb is installed as part of Visual Studio 2015.

When you write code to connect to a database, you need to know its **server name**. The name depends on the version you choose to use. Here are some examples:

- **Visual Studio 2015 installs SQL Server 2014**: `(localdb)\mssqllocaldb`
- **Visual Studio 2012/2013 installs SQL Server 2012**: `(localdb)\v11.0`
- **If you install SQL Server Express**: `.\sqlexpress`

# The Northwind sample database

To learn how to manage a database, it would be useful to have a sample one to practice on that has a medium complexity and a decent amount of sample records. Microsoft offers several sample databases, most of which are too complex for our needs. So, we will use a database that was first created in the early 1990s known as **Northwind**.

Use the link `https://github.com/markjprice/cs6dotnetcore` to download the `Northwind.sql` file.

In Microsoft Visual Studio 2015, go to **File | Open | File...** or press *Ctrl + O*.

Browse to the `Northwind.sql` file and choose **Open**.

In the editor window, right-click and choose **Execute...** or press *Ctrl + Shift + E*.

In the dialog box, enter the server name as `(localdb)\mssqllocaldb` and click on **Connect**, as shown in the following screenshot:

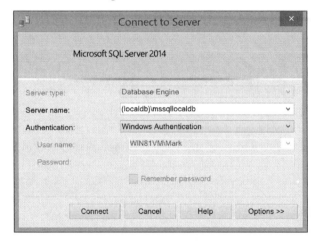

 LocalDb sometimes takes too long to start the first time, and you might see a timeout error. Simply click on **Connect** again, and it should work.

When you see the **Command(s) completed successfully** message, then the Northwind database has been created, and we can connect to it.

In Microsoft Visual Studio 2015, choose **View | Server Explorer...** or press *Ctrl + W, L*.

In the **Server Explorer** window, right-click on **Data Connections** and choose **Add Connection**.

In the dialog box, enter the server name as (localdb)\mssqllocaldb, enter the database name as Northwind, and click on **OK**:

In **Server Explorer** window, expand the data connection and its tables. You should see a dozen tables, including the **Products** table:

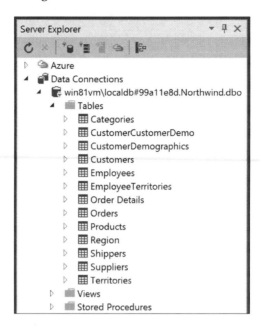

Right-click on the **Products** table and choose **Show Table Data**:

To see the details of the **Products** table columns and types, right-click on **Products** and choose **Show Table Definition**:

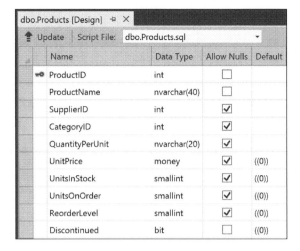

Here is a diagram of Northwind that you can refer to as we write queries:

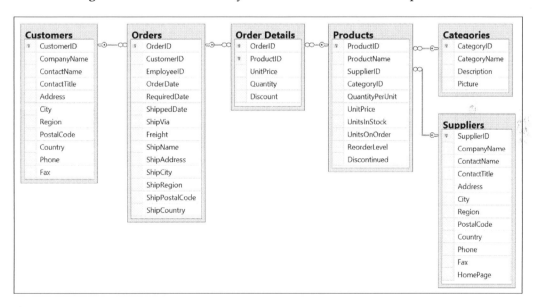

# Choosing a .NET data provider

Before we dive into the practicalities of managing data in a RDBMS, let's briefly talk about choosing between **.NET data providers**.

To manage data, we need classes that know how to efficiently "talk" to the database. .NET data providers are sets of classes that are optimized for a specific RDBMS.

.NET data providers are **native** if they are optimized for one type of RDBMS. Some .NET data providers act as a **bridge** to older data technologies such as OLEDB. The following table summarizes your choices:

| To manage this RDBMS | .NET data provider namespace |
| --- | --- |
| Microsoft SQL Server 7.0 or later | `System.Data.SqlClient` |
| Oracle 8.1.7 or later | `System.Data.OracleClient` |
| Other databases with native providers | Download a provider from the manufacturer's website |
| Microsoft SQL Server 6.5 and earlier, Microsoft Access MDB files, or any other RDBMS that does not have a native provider | `System.Data.OleDb` |
| Only an RDBMS that does not have an OLE DB provider or a native provider | `System.Data.Odbc` |

# Using ADO.NET

When Microsoft first created .NET, it had one data access technology, and it was named ADO.NET. Since then, Microsoft has added additional technologies but reused the name ADO.NET, so it can get confusing. The following are your two main choices today:

- **ADO.NET**: This is the original .NET data access technology that has classes that inherit from abstract base classes such as `DbConnection` and `DbDataReader`. I often refer to this as classic ADO.NET.

- **ADO.NET Entity Framework**: This is a layer on top of ADO.NET that adds object-relational mapping (ORM) capabilities. I often refer to this as Entity Framework or just EF.

Both are supported on .NET Core. Use classic ADO.NET for performance, to maintain existing code that already uses it, and when your tables must always be accessed through stored procedures instead of directly. Use Entity Framework when developer productivity is more important than performance and when you are allowed to execute dynamically generated SQL statements against your tables.

# Connecting to the database

To connect to an RDBMS, we need to know some information about it:

- The name of the server computer that is running the RDBMS
- The name of the database
- Security information such as username and password or if we should pass the currently logged-on user's credentials automatically

We specify this information in a connection string. For backward compatibility, there are multiple possible keywords we can use. Here are some examples:

- **Data Source** or **server** or **addr**: This is the name of the server (and optional instance)
- **Initial Catalog** or **database**: This is the name of the database
- **Integrated Security** or **trusted_connection**: This keyword is set to `true` or `SSPI` to pass the thread's current user credentials

Start Microsoft Visual Studio 2015. In Visual Studio, press *Ctrl* + *Shift* + *N* or go to **File | New | Project...**.

In the **New Project** dialog, in the **Installed Templates** list, select **Visual C#**. In the center list, select **Console Application**, type name as **Ch08_ADONET**, change the location to `C:\Code`, type solution name as **Chapter08**, and then click on **OK**.

To connect to the database, we need a class that inherits from `DbConnection`. The one for SQL Server is named `SqlConnection`. To use it, we must import the `System.Data.SqlClient` namespace.

Add the following code to the top of the `Program.cs` file:

```
using static System.Console;
using System.Data.SqlClient;
```

Add the following code inside the `Main` method. Note the @ symbol at the beginning of the connection string. This disables escape characters because we need to use a back slash (\) in the server and instance name:

```
var connection = new SqlConnection(@"Data Source=(localdb)\
mssqllocaldb;Initial Catalog=Northwind;Integrated Security=true;");
connection.Open();
WriteLine($"The connection is {connection.State}.");
connection.Close();
WriteLine($"The connection is {connection.State}.");
```

Run the application by pressing *Ctrl + F5* and view the output:

```
The connection is Open.
The connection is Closed.
```

If you see an exception similar to the following, then check the connection string for typos. If you enter an invalid database name, you will see this exception:

```
Unhandled Exception: System.Data.SqlClient.SqlException: Cannot open
database "Northwnd" requested by the login. The login failed.
Login failed for user 'WIN81VM\Mark'.
```

If you enter an invalid server or instance name, you will see this exception:

```
Unhandled Exception: System.Data.SqlClient.SqlException: A network-
related or instance-specific error occurred while establishing
a connection to SQL Server. The server was not found or was not
accessible. Verify that the instance name is correct and that SQL
Server is configured to allow remote connections. (provider: SQL Network
Interfaces, error: 50 - Local Database Runtime error occurred. The
specified LocalDB instance does not exist.)
```

If you make a mistake in the server or instance name, then the connection will wait for 30 seconds before returning the exception!

# Executing commands and reading result sets

Now that we have a successful connection to the database we can issue SQL statements such as SELECT to query records and INSERT to add new records.

This book does not teach the SQL language. To learn about Microsoft SQL Server and the SQL language, refer to SQL Server 2014 Development Essentials at https://www.packtpub.com/networking-and-servers/sql-server-2014-development-essentials.

We will work with the Categories table because it is small and simple. First, we will execute a statement to get all the categories. Then, we will add a new category, list the categories again to see the new category, and finally delete the category we inserted.

Inside the `Program` class, add a method shown as follows:

```
// a method we will call three times to list the categories
private static void ListCategories(SqlConnection connection)
{
    var getCategories = new SqlCommand("SELECT CategoryID,
CategoryName FROM Categories", connection);

    SqlDataReader reader = getCategories.ExecuteReader();

    // find out the index positions of the columns that you want to
read
    int indexOfID = reader.GetOrdinal("CategoryID");
    int indexOfName = reader.GetOrdinal("CategoryName");

    while (reader.Read())
    {
        // use the typed GetXxx methods to efficiently read the column
values
        WriteLine($"{reader.GetInt32(indexOfID)}: {reader.
GetString(indexOfName)}");
    }
    reader.Close();
}
```

Modify the code in the `Main` method to add statements between the `Open` and `Close` method calls as shown in the following code. The code:

- Lists the eight categories in the original table
- Prompts the user to enter a new category name
- Truncates the name entered down to a maximum of 15 characters
- Inserts the new category using a parameter to avoid SQL injection attacks
- Lists the nine categories now in the table
- Deletes the new category
- Lists the eight categories in the original table

```
WriteLine("Original list of categories:");
ListCategories(connection);

Write("Enter a new category name: ");
string name = ReadLine();
// the category name column only allows up to 15 chars so truncate if
necessary
if (name.Length > 15) name = name.Substring(0, 15);
```

```
var insertCategory = new SqlCommand($"INSERT INTO
Categories(CategoryName) VALUES(@NewCategoryName)", connection);
insertCategory.Parameters.AddWithValue("@NewCategoryName", name);
int rowsAffected = insertCategory.ExecuteNonQuery();
WriteLine($"{rowsAffected} row(s) were inserted.");

WriteLine("List of categories after inserting:");
ListCategories(connection);

var deleteCategory = new SqlCommand($"DELETE FROM Categories WHERE
CategoryName = @DeleteCategoryName", connection);
deleteCategory.Parameters.AddWithValue("@DeleteCategoryName", name);
rowsAffected = deleteCategory.ExecuteNonQuery();
WriteLine($"{rowsAffected} row(s) were deleted.");

WriteLine("List of categories after deleting:");
ListCategories(connection);
```

Press *Ctrl + F5*. When prompted, enter a new category name, for example, `Tasty Treats`:

```
The connection is Open.

Original list of categories:

1: Beverages

2: Condiments

3: Confections

4: Dairy Products

5: Grains/Cereals

6: Meat/Poultry

7: Produce

8: Seafood

Enter a new category name: Tasty Treats

1 row(s) were inserted.

List of categories after inserting:

1: Beverages

2: Condiments

3: Confections

4: Dairy Products

5: Grains/Cereals

6: Meat/Poultry

7: Produce
```

```
8: Seafood

9: Tasty Treats

1 row(s) were deleted.

List of categories after deleting:

1: Beverages

2: Condiments

3: Confections

4: Dairy Products

5: Grains/Cereals

6: Meat/Poultry

7: Produce

8: Seafood

The connection is Closed.
```

# Loading a connection string from configuration

Instead of hard coding the connection string in your source code, it is better to load it from a file so that it can be easily changed in the future without recompiling.

In **Solution Explorer** window, inside the **Ch08_ADONET** project, right-click on **References** and choose **Add Reference....** In the dialog box, select **System. Configuration** and click on **OK**.

At the top of the file, import the System.Configuration namespace, as shown here:

```
using System.Configuration;
```

Modify the existing code that instantiates SqlConnection to load the connection string at runtime from the configuration file:

```
var connection = new SqlConnection(ConfigurationManager.
ConnectionStrings["Northwind"].ConnectionString);
```

Double-click on the App.config file to open it, and add the following element for connectionStrings inside the existing configuration element:

```
<?xml version="1.0" encoding="utf-8" ?>
<configuration>
  <connectionStrings>
    <add name="Northwind"
        providerName="System.Data.SqlClient"
```

```
        connectionString="Data Source=(localdb)\mssqllocaldb;Initial
Catalog=Northwind;Integrated Security=true;" />
    </connectionStrings>
```

Press *Ctrl + F5* and check whether the application still functions as it did earlier.

> Every time you run this console application, you will notice that the ID for the new category increments by one. This is because Microsoft SQL Server uses an IDENTITY column, which remembers if a previous category has already been allocated the previous ID and won't reuse it to maintain data integrity.

> In *Chapter 12, Improving Performance and Scalability with Multitasking,* you will see how you can improve the preceding code using asynchronous operations to prevent the current thread from blocking.

# Using Entity Framework 6

The **Entity Framework (EF)** was first released as part of **.NET Framework 3.5 with Service Pack 1** back in late 2008. Since then it has evolved, as Microsoft has observed how programmers use an **object-relational mapping (ORM)** tool in the real world.

The version included with Visual Studio 2015 is **Entity Framework 6.1.3 (EF6)**. It is mature, stable, and supports the "old" EDMX design-time way of defining complex inheritance models, and a few other advanced features. However, EF6 is only supported by the .NET Framework, not by the .NET Core.

The next version, **Entity Framework Core 1.0 (EF Core)**, has been renamed and had its version reset to 1.0 to emphasize that it is a reset of functionality. Although EF Core has a similar name, you should be aware that it is different in many ways to EF6. Take a look at its pros and cons:

- Pros
    - EF Core is available for the .NET Core as well as the .NET Framework, which means it can be used cross-platform, on Linux and Max OS X as well as Windows
    - EF Core supports modern cloud-based, non-relational, schema-less data stores such as Microsoft Azure Table Storage and Redis

- Cons

  ° EF Core does not support the EDMX design-time XML file format

  ° EF Core does not (yet) support complex inheritance models and other advanced features of EF6

 Use EF6 for Windows platform applications until EF Core becomes more stable and implements more features. Use EF Core for cross-platform development.

# Building an Entity Framework 6 model

Using EF6 is easy because tooling support is built into Visual Studio 2015.

We will create a console application that lists the details of every product that costs more than an amount entered by the user.

Add a new console application project named **Ch08_EF6**.

Set the solution's startup project to be the current selection.

On the **Project** menu, choose **Add New Item…**, and in the dialog box, choose **ADO.NET Entity Data Model** and name it **Northwind**:

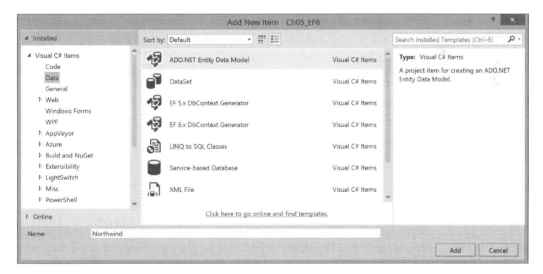

In the first step of the wizard, choose **Code First from database** and then click on **Next**:

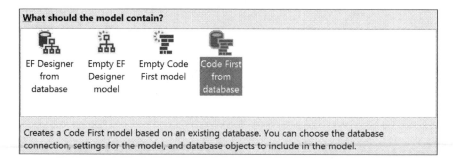

Do not choose either of the first two options because those use the EDMX design-time file that is not supported in EF Core. Even when using EF6, I recommend that you get used to the Code First way of defining the Entity data model.

In the second step of the wizard, click on **New Connection**:

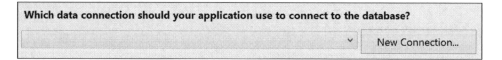

In the **Connection Properties** dialog, enter server name as **(localdb)\mssqllocaldb** and choose database name as **Northwind**. Then, click on **OK**:

 If you have connection problems, then check which version of SQL Server LocalDb you have installed, and use the appropriate server and instance name.

Click on **Next** to go to the step of the wizard for picking database objects, check the box to choose all **Tables**, and then click on **Finish**:

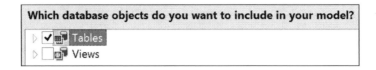

In **Solution Explorer**, double-click on the App.config file and notice that a connection string named Northwind has been defined:

```
<connectionStrings>
  <add name="Northwind" connectionString="data source=(localdb)\
mssqllocaldb;initial catalog=Northwind;integrated security=True;Mult
ipleActiveResultSets=True;App=EntityFramework" providerName="System.
Data.SqlClient" />
</connectionStrings>
```

In **Solution Explorer**, double-click on the Northwind.cs file and notice that it is a class that inherits from DbContext. This class represents the context of all interaction with the database and will track any changes we make to the local data so that those changes can be saved to the actual database:

```
public partial class Northwind : DbContext
```

Notice that the Northwind class has properties that represent the tables within the database. The DbSet type has built-in methods to add, delete, and find records:

```
public virtual DbSet<Category> Categories { get; set; }
```

Notice the overridden method named OnModelCreating that adds extra information to the model that cannot be inferred using conventions. For example, the following statement tells the model that the CustomerID column is of fixed length:

```
modelBuilder.Entity<Customer>()
    .Property(e => e.CustomerID)
    .IsFixedLength();
```

In **Solution Explorer**, double-click on the Customer.cs file and notice that it is a normal class. We call this a **POCO (Plain Old CLR Object)** class, because it does not need to inherit from any special type. It represents an entity (record or row) in a table in the database:

```
public partial class Customer
```

Each class has properties that represent the columns in the Customer table:

```
[StringLength(5)]
public string CustomerID { get; set; }
```

# Entity Framework Code First models

The Entity Framework uses a combination of **conventions, annotation attributes**, and **Fluent API** statements to build a model at runtime so that any actions performed using the classes can be automatically translated into actions performed on the actual database.

## EF Code First conventions

The code generated uses the following conventions:

- If a connection string exists with the same name as the class derived from DbContext, then it is loaded and used to connect to the database automatically.
- The name of a table is assumed to match the name of a DbSet<T> property in the DbContext class, for example, Customers.
- The names of the columns are assumed to match the names of properties in the class, for example, CustomerID.
- The string .NET type is assumed to be an nvarchar type in the database.
- The int .NET type is assumed to be an int type in the database.
- A property that is named ID or the name of the class has ID as the suffix, it is assumed to be a primary key. If this property is any integer type or the Guid type, then it is also assumed to be an IDENTITY (automatically assigned value when inserting).

There are other conventions, and you can even define your own, but that is beyond the scope of this book.

## EF annotation attributes

Conventions often aren't enough to completely map the classes to the database objects. A simple way of adding more metadata to your model is to apply annotation attributes.

For example, in the database, the maximum length of the company name of a customer is 40, and the value cannot be null (empty). In the class, the wizard applies attributes to specify this:

```
[Required]
[StringLength(40)]
public string CompanyName { get; set; }
```

When there isn't an obvious map between .NET types and database types, an attribute can be used. For example, in the database, the column type of UnitPrice for the Products table is money. .NET does not have a money type, so it should use decimal instead:

```
[Column(TypeName = "money")]
public decimal? UnitPrice { get; set; }
```

In the Category table, Description can be longer than the 8,000 characters that can be stored in an nvarchar variable, so it needs to map to ntext instead:

```
[Column(TypeName = "ntext")]
public string Description { get; set; }
```

There are other attributes, but they are beyond the scope of this book.

# EF Fluent API

The last way that the model can be defined is using the **Fluent API**. It can be used instead of attributes or in addition to them. For example, look at the following two attributes in the Customer class:

```
[Required]
[StringLength(40)]
public string CompanyName { get; set; }
```

They could be deleted and replaced with this Fluent API statement in the Northwind class' OnModelBuilding method:

```
modelBuilder.Entity<Customer>()
    .Property(customer => customer.CompanyName)
    .IsRequired()
    .HasMaxLength(40);
```

# Querying an Entity Data Model

In the `Main` method, add the following statements to:

- Prompt the user for a price
- Create an instance of the `Northwind` class that will manage the database
- Write a simple query using LINQ
- Loop through the results

```
WriteLine("List of products that cost more than a given price with
most expensive first.");
string input;
decimal price;
do
{
    Write("Enter a product price: ");
    input = ReadLine();
} while (!decimal.TryParse(input, out price));

var db = new Northwind();

IQueryable<Product> query = db.Products
    .Where(product => product.UnitPrice > price)
    .OrderByDescending(product => product.UnitPrice);

foreach (Product item in query)
{
    WriteLine($"{item.ProductID}: {item.ProductName} costs {item.
UnitPrice:$#,##0.00}");
}
```

 You will learn much more about LINQ in *Chapter 9, Querying and Manipulating Data with LINQ*.

Press *Ctrl + F5*. Enter 50 when prompted to enter a product price:

```
List of products that cost more than a given price with most expensive
first.

Enter a product price: 50

38: Côte de Blaye costs $263.50

29: Thüringer Rostbratwurst costs $123.79

9: Mishi Kobe Niku costs $97.00
```

```
20: Sir Rodney's Marmalade costs $81.00
18: Carnarvon Tigers costs $62.50
59: Raclette Courdavault costs $55.00
51: Manjimup Dried Apples costs $53.00
```

# Logging SQL statements

There are two ways to find out how the LINQ query is being translated into the underlying database's query language. The first is to convert the query into a string.

Add the following code before the `for` statement that loops through the results:

```
WriteLine(query.ToString());
```

Rerun the application with *Ctrl + F5* and enter 50 again. You will see the Transact-SQL statement that was dynamically generated at runtime and then executed in the database to fetch the data we asked for:

```
List of products that cost more than a given price with most expensive
first.
Enter a product price: 50
SELECT
    [Project1].[ProductID] AS [ProductID],
    [Project1].[ProductName] AS [ProductName],
    [Project1].[SupplierID] AS [SupplierID],
    [Project1].[CategoryID] AS [CategoryID],
    [Project1].[QuantityPerUnit] AS [QuantityPerUnit],
    [Project1].[UnitPrice] AS [UnitPrice],
    [Project1].[UnitsInStock] AS [UnitsInStock],
    [Project1].[UnitsOnOrder] AS [UnitsOnOrder],
    [Project1].[ReorderLevel] AS [ReorderLevel],
    [Project1].[Discontinued] AS [Discontinued]
    FROM ( SELECT
        [Extent1].[ProductID] AS [ProductID],
        [Extent1].[ProductName] AS [ProductName],
        [Extent1].[SupplierID] AS [SupplierID],
        [Extent1].[CategoryID] AS [CategoryID],
        [Extent1].[QuantityPerUnit] AS [QuantityPerUnit],
        [Extent1].[UnitPrice] AS [UnitPrice],
```

```
        [Extent1].[UnitsInStock] AS [UnitsInStock],

        [Extent1].[UnitsOnOrder] AS [UnitsOnOrder],

        [Extent1].[ReorderLevel] AS [ReorderLevel],

        [Extent1].[Discontinued] AS [Discontinued]

        FROM [dbo].[Products] AS [Extent1]

        WHERE [Extent1].[UnitPrice] > @p__linq__0

    )  AS [Project1]

    ORDER BY [Project1].[UnitPrice] DESC
38: Côte de Blaye costs $263.50

29: Thüringer Rostbratwurst costs $123.79

9: Mishi Kobe Niku costs $97.00

20: Sir Rodney's Marmalade costs $81.00

18: Carnarvon Tigers costs $62.50

59: Raclette Courdavault costs $55.00

51: Manjimup Dried Apples costs $53.00
```

A better way is to use the database logging feature.

Comment out the previous statement to output the query as a `string`. Then, add the following code after creating the db variable:

```
var db = new Northwind();
db.Database.Log = new Action<string>(message => { WriteLine(message);
});
```

Rerun the application and enter 50 again.

In the following output, you will see all the activity happening between our application and the database, including every time a connection is opened and closed, and useful timings for performance testing.

 Ignore the statements that use INFORMATION_SCHEMA.TABLES and [dbo].[__MigrationHistory]. These are internal checks made by EF.

```
List of products that cost more than a given price with most expensive
first.
Enter a product price: 50
Opened connection at 30/08/2015 13:59:40 +01:00
SELECT
    [Project1].[ProductID] AS [ProductID],
```

```
        [Project1].[ProductName] AS [ProductName],

        [Project1].[SupplierID] AS [SupplierID],

        [Project1].[CategoryID] AS [CategoryID],

        [Project1].[QuantityPerUnit] AS [QuantityPerUnit],

        [Project1].[UnitPrice] AS [UnitPrice],

        [Project1].[UnitsInStock] AS [UnitsInStock],

        [Project1].[UnitsOnOrder] AS [UnitsOnOrder],

        [Project1].[ReorderLevel] AS [ReorderLevel],

        [Project1].[Discontinued] AS [Discontinued]
    FROM ( SELECT

        [Extent1].[ProductID] AS [ProductID],

        [Extent1].[ProductName] AS [ProductName],

        [Extent1].[SupplierID] AS [SupplierID],

        [Extent1].[CategoryID] AS [CategoryID],

        [Extent1].[QuantityPerUnit] AS [QuantityPerUnit],

        [Extent1].[UnitPrice] AS [UnitPrice],

        [Extent1].[UnitsInStock] AS [UnitsInStock],

        [Extent1].[UnitsOnOrder] AS [UnitsOnOrder],

        [Extent1].[ReorderLevel] AS [ReorderLevel],

        [Extent1].[Discontinued] AS [Discontinued]

        FROM [dbo].[Products] AS [Extent1]

        WHERE [Extent1].[UnitPrice] > @p__linq__0

    )  AS [Project1]

    ORDER BY [Project1].[UnitPrice] DESC
-- p__linq__0: '50' (Type = Decimal, IsNullable = false, Precision = 2)
-- Executing at 30/08/2015 13:59:40 +01:00
-- Completed in 7 ms with result: SqlDataReader
38: Côte de Blaye costs $263.50
29: Thüringer Rostbratwurst costs $123.79
9: Mishi Kobe Niku costs $97.00
20: Sir Rodney's Marmalade costs $81.00
18: Carnarvon Tigers costs $62.50
59: Raclette Courdavault costs $55.00
51: Manjimup Dried Apples costs $53.00
Closed connection at 30/08/2015 13:59:40 +01:00
```

> Notice that internally, EF6 uses classic ADO.NET types such as
> `SqlConnection` and `SqlDataReader`. For this reason, EF will always
> be slower than using classic ADO.NET. If performance is your goal, then
> use classic ADO.NET in preference to EF.

# Manipulating data with Entity Data Models

It is easy to insert, update, and delete entities using EF.

## Inserting entities

After the `foreach` statement, add the following code to insert a product and relist
all products:

```
var newProduct = new Product
{
    ProductName = "Bob's Burger",
    UnitPrice = 500M
};
// mark product as added in change tracking
db.Products.Add(newProduct);
// save tracked changes to database
db.SaveChanges();
foreach (var item in query)
{
    WriteLine($"{item.ProductID}: {item.ProductName} costs {item.
UnitPrice:$#,##0.00}");
}
```

Rerun the application and enter 50. You will see that the product has been inserted:

```
78: Bob's Burger costs $500.00
```

The following statement is logged, showing how the row was inserted within a
transaction:

```
Opened connection at 30/08/2015 14:04:22 +01:00

Started transaction at 30/08/2015 14:04:22 +01:00

INSERT [dbo].[Products]([ProductName], [SupplierID], [CategoryID],
[QuantityPerUnit], [UnitPrice], [UnitsInStock], [UnitsOnOrder],
[ReorderLevel], [Discontinued])

VALUES (@0, NULL, NULL, NULL, @1, NULL, NULL, NULL, @2)
```

```
SELECT [ProductID]
FROM [dbo].[Products]
WHERE @@ROWCOUNT > 0 AND [ProductID] = scope_identity()
-- @0: 'Bob's Burger' (Type = String, Size = 40)
-- @1: '500' (Type = Decimal, Precision = 19, Scale = 4)
-- @2: 'False' (Type = Boolean)
-- Executing at 30/08/2015 14:04:22 +01:00
-- Completed in 12 ms with result: SqlDataReader
Committed transaction at 30/08/2015 14:04:22 +01:00
Closed connection at 30/08/2015 14:04:22 +01:00
```

# Updating entities

Add the following code to increase the price by $20 of the product with a primary key value for its Product ID of 78 and then relist the products:

```
Product updateProduct = db.Products.Find(78);
updateProduct.UnitPrice += 20M;
db.SaveChanges();
foreach (var item in query)
{
    WriteLine($"{item.ProductID}: {item.ProductName} costs {item.
UnitPrice:$#,##0.00}");
}
```

Rerun the application and notice that the existing entity for Bob's Burger has increased in price by $20:

```
78: Bob's Burger costs $520.00
```

Did you see the update statement that was dynamically generated and executed against the database and logged to the console? It looked something like this:

```
Opened connection at 30/08/2015 14:10:07 +01:00
Started transaction at 30/08/2015 14:10:07 +01:00
UPDATE [dbo].[Products]
SET [UnitPrice] = @0
WHERE ([ProductID] = @1)
-- @0: '520.0000' (Type = Decimal, Precision = 19, Scale = 4)
-- @1: '78' (Type = Int32)
```

```
-- Executing at 30/08/2015 14:10:07 +01:00
-- Completed in 2 ms with result: 1
Committed transaction at 30/08/2015 14:10:07 +01:00
Closed connection at 30/08/2015 14:10:07 +01:00
```

Notice the following aspects:

- When you call the `SaveChanges` method, EF implicitly creates a transaction so that if something goes wrong, it would automatically rollback all the changes, and if everything works *ok*, it would commit the transaction
- EF is repeatedly opening and closing the connection

We can improve performance by manually controlling when we open and close the connection.

Add the following code immediately after creating the db object:

```
var db = new Northwind();
// if you manually open a connection it will stop
// automatically opening and closing repeatedly
db.Database.Connection.Open();
```

Add the following code at the end of the `Main` method:

```
db.Database.Connection.Close();
```

If you rerun the application, you will see that the connection is only opened and closed once.

# Transactions

Every time you call the `SaveChanges` method, an **implicit transaction** is started. If every operation succeeds, then the transaction is committed.

Transactions maintain the integrity of your database by applying locks to prevent reads and writes while a sequence of operations is occurring.

Transactions are ACID, which is explained here:

- **A** is for atomic. Either all the operations in the transaction commit or none of them do.
- **C** is for consistent. The state of the database before and after a transaction is consistent. This is dependent on your code logic.

- **I** is for isolated. During a transaction, changes are hidden from other processes. There are multiple isolation levels that you can pick from (see the following table). The stronger the level, the better the integrity of the data. However, more locks must be applied which will negatively affect other processes. Snapshot is a special case, because it creates multiple copies of rows to avoid locks, but this will increase the size of your database while transactions occur.

- **D** is for durable. If a failure occurs during a transaction, it can be recovered. The opposite of durable is volatile.

| Isolation level | Lock(s) | Integrity problems allowed |
|---|---|---|
| ReadUncommitted | None | Dirty reads, non-repeatable reads, and phantom data |
| ReadCommitted | When editing, it applies read lock(s) to block other users from reading the record(s) until the transaction ends | Non-repeatable reads and phantom data |
| RepeatableRead | When reading, it applies edit lock(s) to block other users from editing the record(s) until the transaction ends | Phantom data |
| Serializable | Applies key-range locks to prevent any action that would affect the results, including inserts and deletes | None |
| Snapshot | None | None |

# Defining an explicit transaction

You can define an explicit transaction using the `TransactionScope` type.

Add a reference to the **System.Transactions** assembly and import the `System.Transactions` namespace.

Before the instantiation of the `db` variable, add the following statement to instantiate an explicit transaction scope. Also, add options to weaken the isolation level to allow dirty reads and other integrity issues, reduce locks to improve performance, and to automatically rollback if the transaction is not disposed within 10 seconds, to prevent deadlocks:

```
var options = new TransactionOptions
{
    IsolationLevel = IsolationLevel.ReadUncommitted,
    Timeout = TimeSpan.FromSeconds(10)
```

```
};
using (var scope = new TransactionScope(TransactionScopeOption.
Required, options))
{
    var db = new Northwind();
```

You will also need to enter a close brace, }, after you close the database connection. When the close brace executes, the transaction scope will dispose and check whether everything worked. If it did, then all participants in the transaction would be asked to commit. If an exception occurs, then all participants would be asked to rollback:

```
    db.Database.Connection.Close();
}
```

 Always specify a transaction timeout so that deadlocks cannot occur.

# Loading patterns with EF

There are three **loading patterns** that can be used with EF: **lazy loading**, **eager loading**, and **explicit loading**.

## Lazy loading entities

Add a new console application project named **Ch08_LoadingPatterns**.

Add an **ADO.NET Entity Data Model** for the Northwind database, as we did earlier.

Back in `Program.cs`, add the following code to the top of the file:

```
using System;
using static System.Console;
```

Add the following code to the `Main` method:

```
var db = new Northwind();
db.Database.Log = new Action<string>(message => { WriteLine(message);
});
var query = db.Categories;
foreach (var item in query)
{
    WriteLine(item.CategoryName);
}
```

Press *Ctrl + F5* to run the application and notice that Transact-SQL queried only the Categories table:

```
SELECT
    [Extent1].[CategoryID] AS [CategoryID],
    [Extent1].[CategoryName] AS [CategoryName],
    [Extent1].[Description] AS [Description],
    [Extent1].[Picture] AS [Picture]
    FROM [dbo].[Categories] AS [Extent1]
-- Executing at 23/08/2015 12:17:02 +01:00
-- Completed in 14 ms with result: SqlDataReader
Beverages
Condiments
Confections
Dairy Products
Grains/Cereals
Meat/Poultry
Produce
Seafood
```

Each item in foreach is an instance of the Category class, which has a property named Products, that is, the list of products in that category. Since the original query only selected from the Categories table, this property is empty for each category.

Let's see what happens when we attempt to output how many products there are in each category. Temporarily comment out the line for logging:

```
// db.Database.Log = new Action<string>(message => {
WriteLine(message); });
```

Modify the WriteLine statement inside foreach:

```
WriteLine($"{item.CategoryName} has {item.Products.Count} products.");
```

Rerun the application. Notice that the correct number of products is output:

```
Beverages has 12 products.
Condiments has 12 products.
Confections has 13 products.
Dairy Products has 10 products.
```

```
Grains/Cereals has 7 products.
```

```
Meat/Poultry has 6 products.
```

```
Produce has 5 products.
```

```
Seafood has 12 products.
```

This is due to a feature of EF known as **lazy loading**.

Uncomment the logging line and rerun the application. You will notice that when the code accesses the `Products` property, EF automatically checks to see whether they are loaded. If not, EF loads them for us "lazily."

For example, just before outputting the count of seafood products, this query is executed:

```
SELECT
    [Extent1].[ProductID] AS [ProductID],
    [Extent1].[ProductName] AS [ProductName],
    [Extent1].[SupplierID] AS [SupplierID],
    [Extent1].[CategoryID] AS [CategoryID],
    [Extent1].[QuantityPerUnit] AS [QuantityPerUnit],
    [Extent1].[UnitPrice] AS [UnitPrice],
    [Extent1].[UnitsInStock] AS [UnitsInStock],
    [Extent1].[UnitsOnOrder] AS [UnitsOnOrder],
    [Extent1].[ReorderLevel] AS [ReorderLevel],
    [Extent1].[Discontinued] AS [Discontinued]
    FROM [dbo].[Products] AS [Extent1]
    WHERE [Extent1].[CategoryID] = @EntityKeyValue1
-- EntityKeyValue1: '8' (Type = Int32, IsNullable = false)
-- Executing at 30/08/2015 14:16:26 +01:00
-- Completed in 0 ms with result: SqlDataReader
Seafood has 12 products.
```

The problem with lazy loading is that multiple round trips to the database server are required to eventually fetch all the data.

# Eager loading entities

Sometimes, it is better to disable lazy loading and manually specify that all the data is brought across the network immediately using eager loading (aka early loading).

Add the following line of code after creating the db variable to disable lazy loading:

```
db.Configuration.LazyLoadingEnabled = false;
```

If you rerun the application, you will now find that all the product counts are zero:

**Beverages has 0 products.**

**Condiments has 0 products.**

**Confections has 0 products.**

**Dairy Products has 0 products.**

**Grains/Cereals has 0 products.**

**Meat/Poultry has 0 products.**

**Produce has 0 products.**

**Seafood has 0 products.**

To perform eager loading, modify the query line to make it look like this:

```
var query = db.Categories.Include("Products");
```

Rerun the application. You will see that EF generates a SELECT statement with a subquery in order to fetch the related products for each category, all in one go:

```
SELECT
    [Project1].[CategoryID] AS [CategoryID],
    [Project1].[CategoryName] AS [CategoryName],
    [Project1].[Description] AS [Description],
    [Project1].[Picture] AS [Picture],
    [Project1].[C1] AS [C1],
    [Project1].[ProductID] AS [ProductID],
    [Project1].[ProductName] AS [ProductName],
    [Project1].[SupplierID] AS [SupplierID],
    [Project1].[CategoryID1] AS [CategoryID1],
    [Project1].[QuantityPerUnit] AS [QuantityPerUnit],
    [Project1].[UnitPrice] AS [UnitPrice],
    [Project1].[UnitsInStock] AS [UnitsInStock],
    [Project1].[UnitsOnOrder] AS [UnitsOnOrder],
    [Project1].[ReorderLevel] AS [ReorderLevel],
```

```
        [Project1].[Discontinued] AS [Discontinued]
   FROM ( SELECT
        [Extent1].[CategoryID] AS [CategoryID],
        [Extent1].[CategoryName] AS [CategoryName],
        [Extent1].[Description] AS [Description],
        [Extent1].[Picture] AS [Picture],
        [Extent2].[ProductID] AS [ProductID],
        [Extent2].[ProductName] AS [ProductName],
        [Extent2].[SupplierID] AS [SupplierID],
        [Extent2].[CategoryID] AS [CategoryID1],
        [Extent2].[QuantityPerUnit] AS [QuantityPerUnit],
        [Extent2].[UnitPrice] AS [UnitPrice],
        [Extent2].[UnitsInStock] AS [UnitsInStock],
        [Extent2].[UnitsOnOrder] AS [UnitsOnOrder],
        [Extent2].[ReorderLevel] AS [ReorderLevel],
        [Extent2].[Discontinued] AS [Discontinued],
        CASE WHEN ([Extent2].[ProductID] IS NULL) THEN CAST(NULL AS int)
ELSE 1
END AS [C1]
        FROM   [dbo].[Categories] AS [Extent1]
        LEFT OUTER JOIN [dbo].[Products] AS [Extent2] ON [Extent1].
[CategoryID]
= [Extent2].[CategoryID]
    ) AS [Project1]
    ORDER BY [Project1].[CategoryID] ASC, [Project1].[C1] ASC
```

# Explicit loading entities

The last type of loading we will look at is explicit loading. It works similar to lazy loading, but you are in control of exactly which related data is loaded and when.

Modify your code to make it look like this:

```csharp
using System;
using System.Linq;
using static System.Console;
namespace Ch08_LoadingPatterns
{
    class Program
    {
```

```
static void Main(string[] args)
{
    WriteLine("Loading Patterns with the Entity Framework");
    var db = new Northwind();
    IQueryable<Category> query;
    Write("Enable lazy loading? (Y/N): ");
    var lazyloading = (ReadKey().Key == ConsoleKey.Y);
    db.Configuration.LazyLoadingEnabled = lazyloading;
    WriteLine();
    Write("Enable logging? (Y/N): ");
    var logging = (ReadKey().Key == ConsoleKey.Y);
    if (logging)
    {
        db.Database.Log = new Action<string>(message => {
WriteLine(message); });
    }
    WriteLine();
    Write("Enable eager loading? (Y/N): ");
    var eagerloading = (ReadKey().Key == ConsoleKey.Y);
    if (eagerloading)
    {
        query = db.Categories.Include("Products");
    }
    else
    {
        query = db.Categories;
    }
    WriteLine();
    Write("Enable explicit loading? (Y/N): ");
    var explicitloading = (ReadKey().Key == ConsoleKey.Y);
    WriteLine();
    foreach (var item in query)
    {
        if (explicitloading)
        {
            Write($"Explicitly load products for {item.
CategoryName}? (Y/N): ");
            if (ReadKey().Key == ConsoleKey.Y)
            {
                var products = db.Entry(item).Collection(c =>
c.Products);
                if (!products.IsLoaded) products.Load();
            }
            WriteLine();
```

```
            }
                WriteLine($"{item.CategoryName} has {item.Products.
    Count} products.");
                }
            }
        }
    }
```

Rerun the application, disable lazy loading, disable logging, disable eager loading, and enable explicit loading.

For each category, press Y or N to load its products as you wish. For example, this is the output when I ran it. I chose to load products for only four of the eight categories:

```
Enable lazy-loading? (Y/N): n

Enable logging? (Y/N): n

Enable eager-loading? (Y/N): n

Enable explicit-loading? (Y/N): y

Explicitly load products for Beverages? (Y/N): y

Beverages has 12 products.

Explicitly load products for Condiments? (Y/N): n

Condiments has 0 products.

Explicitly load products for Confections? (Y/N): n

Confections has 0 products.

Explicitly load products for Dairy Products? (Y/N): y

Dairy Products has 10 products.

Explicitly load products for Grains/Cereals? (Y/N): y

Grains/Cereals has 7 products.

Explicitly load products for Meat/Poultry? (Y/N): y

Meat/Poultry has 6 products.

Explicitly load products for Produce? (Y/N): n

Produce has 0 products.

Explicitly load products for Seafood? (Y/N): n

Seafood has 0 products.
```

 Carefully consider which loading pattern is best for your code. The default of lazy loading can literally make you into a lazy database developer!

# Using Entity Framework Core

Add a new **Console Application (Package)** project named **Ch08_EFCore**.

 Notice that we have chosen **Console Application (Package)** to target .NET Core.

To use EF Core, you must install a provider for the RDBMS you want to use. You can find an up-to-date list of data providers here:

`http://ef.readthedocs.org/en/latest/providers/index.html`

To install the provider for SQL Server, on the **Tools** menu, choose **NuGet Package Manager** and then choose **Package Manager Console**.

In **Package Manager Console**, ensure package source is set to `nuget.org` and default project is set to `Ch08_EFCore`. Then, enter the following command in the prompt:

```
install-package entityframework.microsoftsqlserver
```

 By the time you read this book, the final release version should be available so that the preceding command will work. If you get an error with the preceding line, add the `-pre` flag to the end to install the pre-release version.

At the time of writing this book, the pre-release version of EF Core is **7.0.0-rc1-final**, as you can see in the following screenshot:

Later, we will run migration commands, so you will need to install the following package too:

```
install-package entityframework.commands
```

By the time you read this book, the final release version should be available so that the preceding command will work. If you get an error with the preceding line, add the `-pre` flag to the end to install the pre-release version.

At the time of writing this book, there are no graphical tools or wizards to help you write the code, so we will have to do it all manually.

On the **Project** menu, choose **Add Class…** or press *Shift + Alt + C* and name it **Category**.

Modify its code to look like the following code block. Note the following aspects:

- The initialization of the `Products` property with an empty `Hashset` (to avoid `NullReferenceExceptions` when reading its `Count` property)

- The `Products` property is `virtual` (so that EF Core can inherit from our class and implement automatic lazy loading)

```
using System.Collections.Generic;
using System.ComponentModel.DataAnnotations.Schema;
namespace Ch08_EFCore
{
    [Table("Categories")]
    public class Category
    {
        public int CategoryID { get; set; }
        public string CategoryName { get; set; }
        public virtual ICollection<Product> Products { get; set; }
        public Category()
        {
            Products = new HashSet<Product>();
        }
    }
}
```

At the time of writing this book, EF Core does not have an automatic pluralizer or singularizer, so we must explicitly specify the table name using an attribute (or we could have used the Fluent API).

Add a class named `Product` and modify its code to look like the following code block. Notice the attribute to explicitly specify the column to use for the relationship between `Categories` and `Products`:

```
using System.ComponentModel.DataAnnotations.Schema;
namespace Ch08_EFCore
{
    [Table("Products")]
    public class Product
```

```
    {
        public int ProductID { get; set; }
        public string ProductName { get; set; }
        public decimal? UnitPrice { get; set; }
        public int CategoryID { get; set; }
        [ForeignKey("CategoryID")]
        public virtual Category Category { get; set; }
    }
}
```

Add a class named `Northwind` and modify its code to look like the following code block:

```
using Microsoft.Data.Entity;
namespace Ch08_EFCore
{
    public class Northwind : DbContext
    {
        public DbSet<Category> Categories { get; set; }
        public DbSet<Product> Products { get; set; }
        protected override void OnConfiguring(DbContextOptionsBuilder
optionsBuilder)
        {
            optionsBuilder.UseSqlServer(@"Data Source=(localdb)\
mssqllocaldb;initial catalog=Northwind;integrated security=true;");
            base.OnConfiguring(optionsBuilder);
        }
    }
}
```

> EF Core prefers code over the old XML `.config` files to specify the connection string. This is because it removes the dependency on `.config` XML files. You should still load the connection string from an external source, but you can now store it wherever you want.

In `Program.cs` file, import the `Microsoft.Data.Entity` namespace, statically import the `System.Console` type, and add the following statements inside the `Main` method:

```
var db = new Northwind();
var query = db.Categories.Include(c => c.Products);
foreach (var item in query)
{
```

```
    WriteLine($"{item.CategoryName} has {item.Products.Count}
products.");
}
ReadLine(); // wait for user to press ENTER when debugging
```

Open the project's **Properties** and on the **Debug** tab, select **Use Specific Runtime** and choose **.NET Core** and **x64**.

Run the application with *F5*, and view the output, which is the same as it was for EF6:

**Beverages has 12 products.**

**Condiments has 12 products.**

**Confections has 13 products.**

**Dairy Products has 10 products.**

**Grains/Cereals has 7 products.**

**Meat/Poultry has 6 products.**

**Produce has 5 products.**

**Seafood has 12 products.**

Note that this console application has a titlebar that shows that it targets .NET Core executed by the CoreCLR and the 64-bit CPU architecture, so it could be deployed to Windows, Max OS X, and Linux.

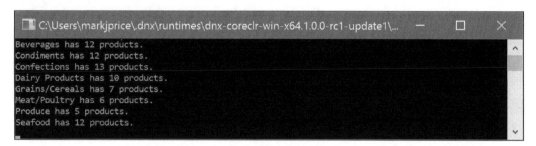

# Practicing and exploring

Test your knowledge and understanding by answering some questions, getting some hands-on practice, and exploring this chapter's topics with deeper research.

## Exercise 8.1 – test your knowledge

Answer the following questions:

1. Which .NET data provider would you use to work with Microsoft Access .MDB database files?

2. Which .NET data provider would you use to work with Microsoft SQL Server 2012 Express Edition?

3. What must you do with DbConnection variable before executing a DbCommand variable?

4. When would you use CommandBehavior.SequentialAccess?

5. When would you use classic ADO.NET instead of Entity Framework?

6. When defining a DbContext class, what type would you use for the property that represents a table, for example, the Products property of a Northwind context?

7. What are the EF conventions for primary keys?

8. When would you use an annotation attribute in an entity class?

9. Why might you choose the Fluent API in preference to annotation attributes?

10. What is the difference between Database First and Code First in EF6?

## Exercise 8.2 – explore the EF Core documentation

Go to the following website and read the official Entity Framework Core 1.0 documentation. Follow the tutorials to create Windows desktop and web applications and services. If you have a Mac or a Linux virtual machine, follow the tutorials to use EF Core on those alternative platforms.

http://ef.readthedocs.org/en/latest/

# Exercise 8.3 – explore topics

Use the following links to read more on this chapter's topics:

- **.NET Framework data providers**: `https://msdn.microsoft.com/en-us/library/a6cd7c08(v=vs.110).aspx`

- **Retrieving and modifying data in ADO.NET**: `https://msdn.microsoft.com/en-us/library/ms254937(v=vs.110).aspx`

- **Data points – looking ahead to Entity Framework 7**: `https://msdn.microsoft.com/en-us/magazine/dn890367.aspx`

# Summary

In this chapter, you learned how to connect to a database, how to execute an SQL statement and process the results, and how to build Code First data models for an existing database such as Northwind.

In the next chapter, you will learn how to write a LINQ query to select, filter, sort, join, and group data of all types.

# 9
# Querying and Manipulating Data with LINQ

This chapter is about **Language Integrated Queries (LINQ)**, language extensions that add the ability to work with sequences of items and filter, sort, and project them into different outputs.

This chapter covers the following topics:

- Writing LINQ queries
- Using multiple threads with Parallel LINQ
- Creating your own LINQ extension methods
- Working with LINQ to XML

## Writing LINQ queries

In the previous chapter, you wrote a few simple LINQ queries, but I didn't properly explained how LINQ works.

LINQ has several parts; some are required and some are optional:

- **Extension methods** (required): These are `Where`, `OrderBy`, `Select`, and so on. These provide the functionality of LINQ.
- **LINQ providers** (required): LINQ to Objects, LINQ to Entities, LINQ to XML, LINQ to OData, LINQ to Amazon, and so on, are LINQ providers. These convert standard LINQ operations into specific commands for different types of data.
- **Lambda expressions** (optional): These can be used instead of named methods to simplify LINQ extension method calls.

- **LINQ query comprehension syntax** (optional): These include `from`, `in`, `where`, `orderby`, `descending`, `select`, and so on. These are C# keywords that are aliases for some of the LINQ extension methods, and their use can simplify the queries you write, especially if you already have experience with other query languages such as **Structured Query Language (SQL)**.

> When programmers are first introduced to LINQ, they often believe that the query comprehension syntax is LINQ, but ironically, that is one of the parts of LINQ that is optional!

# Extending sequences with the Enumerable class

The extension methods, such as `Where` and `Select`, are appended by the `Enumerable` static class to any type, known as a **sequence**, that implements `IEnumerable<T>`.

For example, an array of a type `T` implements the `IEnumerable<T>` class, where `T` is the type of items in the array, so all arrays support LINQ to query and manipulate them.

All collections, such as `List<T>`, `Dictionary<TKey, TValue>`, `Stack<T>`, and `Queue<T>` implement `IEnumerable<T>`, so they can be queried and manipulated with LINQ.

# Filtering entities with Where

The most common reason for using LINQ is to filter items in a sequence using the `Where` extension method.

Start Microsoft Visual Studio 2015. In Visual Studio, press *Ctrl + Shift + N* or navigate to **File | New | Project...**.

In the **New Project** dialog, in the **Installed Templates** list, select **Visual C#**. In the list at the center, select **Console Application**, type the name **Ch09_LinqToObjects**, change the location to `C:\Code`, type the solution name **Chapter09**, and then click on **OK**.

Statically import the `System.Console` type.

In the `Main` method, add the following statements:

```
var names = new string[] { "Michael", "Pam", "Jim", "Dwight",
"Angela", "Kevin", "Toby", "Creed" };
var query = names.Where(
```

As you type the open parenthesis after `Where`, note the IntelliSense. It tells us that to call `Where`, we must pass in an instance of a `Func<string, bool>` delegate. This delegate must target a method with a matching signature, as you can see in the following screenshot::

```
var names = new string[] { "Michael", "Pam", "Jim", "Dwight", "Angela", "Kevin", "Toby", "Creed" };
var query = names.Where(|)
```
▲ 1 of 2 ▼ (extension) IEnumerable<string> IEnumerable<string>.Where<string>(Func**<string, bool> predicate**)

For each `string` variable passed to the method, the method must return a Boolean value. If the method returns `true`, it indicates that we should include the `string` in the results, and if the method returns `false`, it indicates that we should exclude it.

# Targeting a named method

Let's define a method that only includes names that are longer than four characters.

Add the following method under the `Main` method:

```
static bool NameLongerThanFour(string name)
{
    return name.Length > 4;
}
```

Complete the `Where` call and loop through the query items, as shown in the following code:

```
var query = names.Where(new Func<string, bool>(NameLongerThanFour));
foreach (var item in query)
{
    WriteLine(item);
}
```

Run the application by pressing *Ctrl + F5* and view the output:

```
Michael
Dwight
Angela
Kevin
Creed
```

# Simplifying the code by removing the explicit delegate instantiation

We can simplify the code by deleting the explicit instantiation of the `Func<string, bool>` delegate. The C# compiler will instantiate the `Func<string, bool>` delegate for us, so you never need to explicitly do it.

Modify the query to look like this:

```
var query = names.Where(NameLongerThanFour);
```

Rerun the application and note that the output is the same as before.

# Targeting a lambda expression

We can simplify our code even further using a **lambda expression** in place of the named method.

Although it can look complicated and magical at first, a lambda expression is simply a *nameless function*. It uses the `=>` (read as "goes to") symbol to indicate the return value.

Modify the query to look like the following statement:

```
var query = names.Where(name => name.Length > 4);
```

Note that the syntax for a lambda expression includes all the important parts of the `NameLongerThanFour` method, but nothing extraneous. A lambda expression only needs to define the following:

- The names of input parameters
- A return value expression

The type of the `name` input parameter is inferred from the fact that the sequence contains strings and the return type must be a `bool` value for `Where` to work, so the expression after the `=>` symbol must return a `bool` value.

The compiler does most of the work for us, so our code can be as concise as possible.

Rerun the application and note that the output is the same as earlier.

# Sorting sequences with OrderBy

Extension methods can be chained if the previous method returns another sequence, that is, a type that implements the `IEnumerable<T>` class.

Append a call to `OrderBy` to the end of the existing query as shown here:

```
var query = names
    .Where(name => name.Length > 4)
    .OrderBy(name => name.Length);
```

 I like to format the line so that each extension method call happens on its own line. I think this makes LINQ queries easier to read.

Rerun the application and note that the names are now sorted with shortest first:

Kevin

Creed

Dwight

Angela

Michael

 To put the longest name first, you would use `OrderByDescending`.

## Sorting by multiple properties with the ThenBy method

We might want to sort the array of names by more than one property.

Append a call to `ThenBy` to the end of the existing query as shown here:

```
var query = names
    .Where(name => name.Length > 4)
    .OrderBy(name => name.Length)
    .ThenBy(name => name);
```

Rerun the application and note the slight difference in the sort order. Within a group of names of the same length, the names are sorted alphabetically by the full value of the string, so Creed comes before Kevin, and Angela comes before Dwight:

Creed

Kevin

Angela

Dwight

Michael

# Working with sets

Sets are one of the most fundamental concepts in mathematics. A set is a collection of one or more objects. You might remember being taught about Venn diagrams in school. Common set operations include the **intersect** or **union** between sets.

Add a new console application project named **Ch09_Sets**. Set the solution's start up project to be the current selection.

Statically import the `System.Console` type.

This application will define three arrays of strings for cohorts of apprentices and then perform some common set operations.

On the top of the `Main` method, add the following method, that outputs any sequence of `string` variables as a comma-separated single `string` to the console output along with an optional description:

```
private static void Output(IEnumerable<string> cohort, string
description = "")
{
    WriteLine(description);
    WriteLine(string.Join(", ", cohort.ToArray()));
}
```

In the `Main` method, write the following statements:

```
var cohort1 = new string[] { "Rachel", "Gareth", "Jonathan", "George"
};
var cohort2 = new string[] { "Jack", "Stephen", "Daniel", "Jack",
"Jared" };
var cohort3 = new string[] { "Declan", "Jack", "Jack", "Jasmine",
"Conor" };
Output(cohort1, "Cohort 1");
Output(cohort2, "Cohort 2");
Output(cohort3, "Cohort 3");
WriteLine();
Output(cohort2.Distinct(), "cohort2.Distinct(): removes duplicates");
Output(cohort2.Union(cohort3), "cohort2.Union(cohort3): combines two
sequences and removes any duplicates");
Output(cohort2.Concat(cohort3), "cohort2.Concat(cohort3): combines two
sequences but leaves in any duplicates");
Output(cohort2.Intersect(cohort3), "cohort2.Intersect(cohort3):
returns items that are in both sequences");
Output(cohort2.Except(cohort3), "cohort2.Except(cohort3): removes
items from the first sequence that are in the second sequence");
```

```
Output(cohort1.Zip(cohort2, (c1, c2) => $"{c1} matched with {c2}"),
"cohort1.Zip(cohort2, (c1, c2) => $\"{c1} matched with {c2}\"):
matches items based on position in the sequence");
```

Run the application by pressing *Ctrl + F5* and view the output:

```
Cohort 1
Rachel, Gareth, Jonathan, George
Cohort 2
Jack, Stephen, Daniel, Jack, Jared
Cohort 3
Declan, Jack, Jack, Jasmine, Conor


cohort2.Distinct(): removes duplicates
Jack, Stephen, Daniel, Jared
cohort2.Union(cohort3): combines two sequences and removes any duplicates
Jack, Stephen, Daniel, Jared, Declan, Jasmine, Conor
cohort2.Concat(cohort3): combines two sequences but leaves in any
duplicates
Jack, Stephen, Daniel, Jack, Jared, Declan, Jack, Jack, Jasmine, Conor
cohort2.Intersect(cohort3): returns items that are in both sequences
Jack
cohort2.Except(cohort3): removes items from the first sequence that are
in the second sequence
Stephen, Daniel, Jared
cohort1.Zip(cohort2, (c1, c2) => $"{c1} matched with {c2}"): matches
items based on position in the sequence
Rachel matched with Jack, Gareth matched with Stephen, Jonathan matched
with Daniel, George matched with Jack
```

Note that with `Zip`, if there are unequal numbers of items in the two sequences, then some items will not have a matching partner, like poor Jared.

# Projecting entities with Select statement

To learn about **projection**, it is best to have some more complex sequences to work with, so in the next project, we will use the Northwind sample database.

Add a new console application project named **Ch09_Projection**. Add a new **ADO.NET Entity Data Model** item named **Northwind**. Use **Code First from database**, connect to the **Northwind** database with the server and instance name `(localdb)\mssqllocaldb`, and select all the tables.

In the `Main` method, write the following statements:

```
var db = new Northwind();

var query = db.Products
    .Where(product => product.UnitPrice < 10M)
    .OrderByDescending(product => product.UnitPrice);

foreach (var item in query)
{
    WriteLine($"{item.ProductID}: {item.ProductName} costs {item.
UnitPrice:$#,##0.00}");
}
```

Run the application by pressing *Ctrl + F5* and view the output:

```
41: Jack's New England Clam Chowder costs $9.65
45: Rogede sild costs $9.50
47: Zaanse koeken costs $9.50
19: Teatime Chocolate Biscuits costs $9.20
23: Tunnbröd costs $9.00
75: Rhönbräu Klosterbier costs $7.75
54: Tourtière costs $7.45
52: Filo Mix costs $7.00
13: Konbu costs $6.00
24: Guaraná Fantástica costs $4.50
33: Geitost costs $2.50
```

Although this query outputs the information we want, it does so inefficiently because it returns entire rows of all columns from the table. We can see this by outputting the query.

Add the following statement before the `foreach` statement:

```
WriteLine(query.ToString());
```

Rerun the applications and note that the SQL logged statement includes all columns:

```
SELECT
    [Extent1].[ProductID] AS [ProductID],
    [Extent1].[ProductName] AS [ProductName],
    [Extent1].[SupplierID] AS [SupplierID],
```

```
    [Extent1].[CategoryID] AS [CategoryID],
    [Extent1].[QuantityPerUnit] AS [QuantityPerUnit],
    [Extent1].[UnitPrice] AS [UnitPrice],
    [Extent1].[UnitsInStock] AS [UnitsInStock],
    [Extent1].[UnitsOnOrder] AS [UnitsOnOrder],
    [Extent1].[ReorderLevel] AS [ReorderLevel],
    [Extent1].[Discontinued] AS [Discontinued]
    FROM [dbo].[Products] AS [Extent1]
    WHERE [Extent1].[UnitPrice] < cast(10 as decimal(18))
    ORDER BY [Extent1].[UnitPrice] DESC
```

Change the LINQ to call the `Select` method to project the results into a new anonymous type with only the three columns that we actually need, like this:

```
var query = db.Products
    .Where(product => product.UnitPrice < 10M)
    .OrderByDescending(product => product.UnitPrice)
    .Select(product => new { product.ProductID, product.ProductName,
product.UnitPrice });
```

Rerun the application and note that the SQL now only includes three columns that we need:

```
SELECT
    [Extent1].[ProductID] AS [ProductID],
    [Extent1].[ProductName] AS [ProductName],
    [Extent1].[UnitPrice] AS [UnitPrice]
    FROM [dbo].[Products] AS [Extent1]
    WHERE [Extent1].[UnitPrice] < cast(10 as decimal(18))
    ORDER BY [Extent1].[UnitPrice] DESC
```

 You might also have noticed that the sequences implement `IQueryable<T>` instead of `IEnumerable<T>`. This is an indication that we are using a LINQ provider that uses deferred execution and builds the query in memory using expression trees. The query will not be executed until the last possible moment and only then will it be converted into another query language, such as Transact-SQL for Microsoft SQL Server. Enumerating the query with `foreach` or calling a method such as `ToArray` will force immediate execution of the query.

# Joining and grouping

Add a new console application project named **Ch09_JoiningGrouping**.

Add a new **ADO.NET Entity Data Model** item named **Northwind**. Use **Code First from database**, connect to the **Northwind** database with the server and instance name (localdb)\mssqllocaldb, and select all the tables.

In the Main method, write the following statements:

```
var db = new Northwind();

var categories = db.Categories.Select(c => new { c.CategoryID,
c.CategoryName }).ToArray();
var products = db.Products.Select(p => new { p.ProductID,
p.ProductName, p.CategoryID }).ToArray();

// join every product to its category to return 77 matches
var queryJoin = categories.Join(products,
    category => category.CategoryID,
    product => product.CategoryID,
    (c, p) => new { c.CategoryName, p.ProductName, p.ProductID });

foreach (var item in queryJoin)
{
    WriteLine($"{item.ProductID}: {item.ProductName} is in {item.
CategoryName}.");
}
```

Run the application and view the output. Note that there is a single line output for each of the 77 products, and the results show all products in the Beverages category first, then the Condiments category, and so on:

1: Chai is in Beverages.

2: Chang is in Beverages.

24: Guaraná Fantástica is in Beverages.

34: Sasquatch Ale is in Beverages.

35: Steeleye Stout is in Beverages.

38: Côte de Blaye is in Beverages.

39: Chartreuse verte is in Beverages.

43: Ipoh Coffee is in Beverages.

67: Laughing Lumberjack Lager is in Beverages.

70: Outback Lager is in Beverages.

75: Rhönbräu Klosterbier is in Beverages.

76: Lakkalikööri is in Beverages.

3: Aniseed Syrup is in Condiments.

4: Chef Anton's Cajun Seasoning is in Condiments.

Change the query to sort by ProductID:

```
var queryJoin = categories.Join(products,
    category => category.CategoryID,
    product => product.CategoryID,
    (c, p) => new { c.CategoryName, p.ProductName, p.ProductID })
    .OrderBy(cp => cp.ProductID);
```

Rerun the application and view the output:

1: Chai is in Beverages.

2: Chang is in Beverages.

3: Aniseed Syrup is in Condiments.

4: Chef Anton's Cajun Seasoning is in Condiments.

5: Chef Anton's Gumbo Mix is in Condiments.

6: Grandma's Boysenberry Spread is in Condiments.

7: Uncle Bob's Organic Dried Pears is in Produce.

8: Northwoods Cranberry Sauce is in Condiments.

9: Mishi Kobe Niku is in Meat/Poultry.

10: Ikura is in Seafood.

11: Queso Cabrales is in Dairy Products.

12: Queso Manchego La Pastora is in Dairy Products.

13: Konbu is in Seafood.

14: Tofu is in Produce.

15: Genen Shouyu is in Condiments.

Add some new statements, as shown below, to the existing code to use the GroupJoin method, and in the output, show the group name and then all the items within each group:

```
// group all products by their category to return 8 matches
var queryGroup = categories.GroupJoin(products,
    category => category.CategoryID,
    product => product.CategoryID,
    (c, Products) => new { c.CategoryName, Products = Products.
OrderBy(p => p.ProductName) });

foreach (var item in queryGroup)
```

```
    {
        WriteLine($"{item.CategoryName} has {item.Products.Count()}
    products.");
        foreach (var product in item.Products)
        {
            WriteLine($"  {product.ProductName}");
        }
    }
```

Rerun the application. Note that the products inside each category have been sorted by their name as the query asked:

```
Beverages has 12 products.
  Chai
  Chang
  Chartreuse verte
  Côte de Blaye
  Guaraná Fantástica
  Ipoh Coffee
  Lakkalikööri
  Laughing Lumberjack Lager
  Outback Lager
  Rhönbräu Klosterbier
  Sasquatch Ale
  Steeleye Stout
Condiments has 12 products.
  Aniseed Syrup
  Chef Anton's Cajun Seasoning
  Chef Anton's Gumbo Mix
```

# Sweetening the syntax with syntactic sugar

C# 3 introduced some new keywords in 2008 to make it easier for programmers with experience in SQL to write LINQ queries. This **syntactic sugar** is sometimes called the **LINQ query comprehension syntax**.

 LINQ query comprehension syntax is limited in functionality. You must use extension methods to access all the features of LINQ.

Consider the following code:

```
var query = names
    .Where(name => name.Length > 4)
    .OrderBy(name => name.Length)
    .ThenBy(name => name);
```

Instead of writing the preceding code, you can write this:

```
var query = from name in names
            where name.Length > 4
            orderby name.Length, name
            select name;
```

C# compiles the query comprehension syntax into the equivalent query using extension methods and lambda expressions.

Not all extension methods have a C# keyword equivalent, for example, the `Skip` and `Take` extension methods. The following query cannot be written using only the query syntax:

```
var query = names
    .Where(name => name.Length > 4)
    .OrderBy(name => name.Length)
    .ThenBy(name => name)
    .Skip(1)
    .Take(2);
```

Luckily, you can wrap query syntax in parentheses and then switch to using extension methods, as follows:

```
var query = (from name in names
             where name.Length > 4
             orderby name.Length, name
             select name)
            .Skip(1)
            .Take(2);
```

**Best Practice**
Learn both extension methods with lambda expressions and the comprehension syntax ways of writing LINQ queries because you are likely to have to maintain code that uses both.

# Using multiple threads with Parallel LINQ

By default, only one thread is used to execute a LINQ query. **Parallel LINQ (PLINQ)** is an easy way to enable multiple threads to execute a query.

To see it in action, we will start with some code that only uses a single thread to double 200 million integers.

Add a new console application project named **Ch09_PLINQ**. Import the System.Diagnostics namespace and statically import the System.Console type.

Add the following statements to the Main method:

```
var watch = Stopwatch.StartNew();
Write("Press ENTER to start. ");
ReadLine();
watch.Start();
IEnumerable<int> numbers = Enumerable.Range(1, 200000000);
var squares = numbers.Select(number => number * 2).ToArray();
watch.Stop();
WriteLine($"{watch.ElapsedMilliseconds:#,##0} ellapsed milliseconds.");
```

Press *Ctrl + F5* to run the application, but *do not* press *Enter* yet.

Right-click on the Windows Taskbar or press *Ctrl + Alt + Delete*, and then click on **Task Manager**.

At the bottom of the **Task Manager** window, click on the **More details** button. At the top of the **Task Manager** window, click on the **Performance** tab.

Right-click on the **CPU Utilization** graph, choose **Change graph to**, and then **Logical processors**, as you can see in the following screenshot:

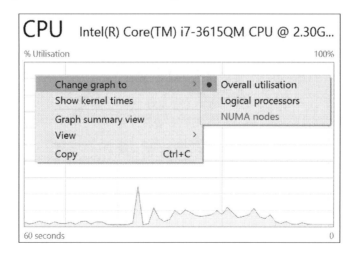

If you do not have multiple CPUs, then this exercise won't show much!

Rearrange the **Task Manager** window and your console application so that they are side by side.

Wait for the CPUs to settle and then press *Enter* to start the stopwatch and run the query. Your output should look like this:

```
Press ENTER to start.

19,404 ellapsed milliseconds.
```

The **Task Manager** window should show that while the code executed, one CPU was used the most. However, other CPUs could execute background tasks, such as the garbage collector, so they won't be completely flat:

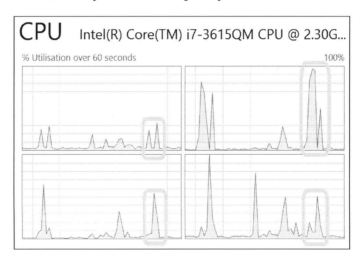

Close the console application, and back in the `Main` method, modify the query to make a call to the `AsParallel` extension method as follows:

```
var squares = numbers.AsParallel().Select(number => number *
2).ToArray();
```

Press *Ctrl* + *F5* to run the application again. Wait for the **Task Manager** window to settle and then press *Enter* to start the stopwatch and run the query. This time, the application should complete in less time (although it might not be as much less as you might hope for—managing those multiple threads takes extra effort!), as shown in the following output:

```
Press ENTER to start.
17,971 ellapsed milliseconds.
```

The **Task Manager** window should show that all CPUs were used equally to execute the LINQ query, as shown in the following screenshot:

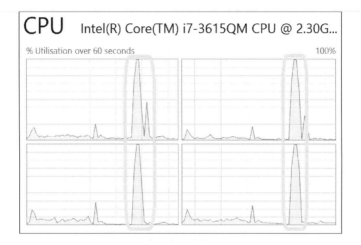

 You will learn more about managing multiple threads in *Chapter 12, Improving Performance and Scalability with Multitasking*.

# Creating your own LINQ extension methods

In *Chapter 7, Implementing Interfaces and Inheriting Classes*, you learned how to create your own extension methods. To create LINQ extension methods, all you have to do is extend the IEnumerable<T> type.

Add a new **Class Library** project named **Ch09_MyLINQExtensions**. Rename the Class1.cs file to MyLINQExtensions.

Modify the class to look like the following code. Note that the `ProcessSequence` extension method doesn't actually modify the sequence because it exists only as an example. It would be up to you to process the sequence in whatever manner you want. The `SummariseSequence` extension method also doesn't do anything especially useful. It simply returns the number of items in the sequence by using the built-in `LongCount` extension method. Again, it would be up to you to decide exactly what this method should do and what type it should return:

```
using System.Collections.Generic;

namespace System.Linq
{
    public static class MyLINQExtensions
    {
        // this is a chainable LINQ extension method
        public static IEnumerable<T> ProcessSequence<T>(this
IEnumerable<T> sequence)
        {
            return sequence;
        }

        // this is a scalar LINQ extension method
        public static long SummariseSequence<T>(this IEnumerable<T>
sequence)
        {
            return sequence.LongCount();
        }
    }
}
```

To use your LINQ extension methods in a project, you would simply need to reference the class library assembly because the `System.Linq` namespace is usually already imported.

In the **Ch09_LinqToObjects** project, add a reference to the **Ch09_MyLINQExtensions** assembly.

Modify the LINQ query to call your chainable extension method as follows:

```
var query = names
    .ProcessSequence()
    .Where(name => name.Length > 4)
    .OrderBy(name => name.Length)
    .ThenBy(name => name);
```

If you run the console application, then you will see the same output as before because your method doesn't actually modify the sequence. But you now know how to extend LINQ with your own functionality.

# Working with LINQ to XML

**LINQ to XML** is a provider that allows you to use LINQ to query and manipulate XML.

## Generating XML using LINQ to XML

Add a new console application project named **Ch09_LINQandXML**. Add a new **ADO.NET Entity Data Model** item named Northwind. Use **Code First from database**, connect to the Northwind database on the server named (localdb)\ mssqllocaldb, and select all the tables.

Import System.Xml.Linq. In the Main method, write the following statements:

```
var db = new Northwind();
var products = db.Products.ToArray();

var xml = new XElement("products",
                from p in products
                select new XElement("product",
                    new XAttribute("id", p.ProductID),
                    new XAttribute("price", p.UnitPrice),
                    new XElement("name", p.ProductName)));

Console.WriteLine(xml.ToString());
```

Run the application. Notice that the structure of the XML generated matches the elements and attributes that the LINQ to XML statement declaratively described in the preceding code:

```
<products>
  <product id="1" price="18.0000">
    <name>Chai</name>
  </product>
  <product id="2" price="19.0000">
    <name>Chang</name>
  </product>
  <product id="3" price="10.0000">
    <name>Aniseed Syrup</name>
  </product>
```

# Reading XML by using LINQ to XML

The .NET Framework uses XML to store its configuration. You might want to use LINQ to XML to more easily query those files.

In the **Solution Explorer** window, double-click on the `App.config` file for the **Ch09_LINQandXML** project and add the following into the <configuration> element:

```
<appSettings>
  <add key="color" value="red" />
  <add key="size" value="large" />
  <add key="price" value="23.99" />
</appSettings>
```

Back in the `Program` class, add the following statements to load the configuration file for this console application, use LINQ to XML to search for an element named `appSettings` and its descendants named `add`, then project the XML into an array of an anonymous type with a `Key` and `Value` property, and then enumerate through the array to show the results:

```
XDocument doc = XDocument.Load("Ch09_LINQandXML.exe.config");

var appSettings = doc.Descendants("appSettings").Descendants("add")
    .Select(node => new
    {
        Key = node.Attribute("key").Value,
        Value = node.Attribute("value").Value
    })
    .ToArray();

foreach (var item in appSettings)
{
    WriteLine($"{item.Key}: {item.Value}");
}
```

Press *Ctrl + F5* to run the application and view the output:

```
color: red
size: large
price: 23.99
```

# Practicing and exploring

Test your knowledge and understanding by answering some questions, get some hands-on practice, and explore, with deeper research into the topics covered in this chapter.

# Exercise 9.1 – test your knowledge

Answer the following questions:

1. What are the two requirements to use LINQ?

2. Which LINQ extension method would you use to return a subset of properties from a type?

3. Which LINQ extension method would you use to filter a sequence?

4. List five LINQ extension methods that perform aggregation.

5. What is the difference between the `Select` and `SelectMany` extension methods?

# Exercise 9.2 – practice querying with LINQ

Create a console application named **Ch09_Exercise02** that prompts the user for a city and then lists the company names for Northwind customers in that city, as shown in the following output:

```
Enter the name of a city: London

There are 6 customers in London:

Around the Horn

B's Beverages

Consolidated Holdings

Eastern Connection

North/South

Seven Seas Imports
```

Enhance the application by displaying a list of all unique cities that customers already reside in as a prompt to the user before they enter their preferred city:

```
Aachen, Albuquerque, Anchorage, Århus, Barcelona, Barquisimeto, Bergamo,
Berlin, Bern, Boise, Bräcke, Brandenburg, Bruxelles, Buenos Aires, Butte,
Campinas, Caracas, Charleroi, Cork, Cowes, Cunewalde, Elgin, Eugene,
Frankfurt a.M., Genève, Graz, Helsinki, I. de Margarita, Kirkland,
Kobenhavn, Köln, Lander, Leipzig, Lille, Lisboa, London, Luleå, Lyon,
Madrid, Mannheim, Marseille, México D.F., Montréal, München, Münster,
Nantes, Oulu, Paris, Portland, Reggio Emilia, Reims, Resende, Rio de
Janeiro, Salzburg, San Cristóbal, San Francisco, Sao Paulo, Seattle,
Sevilla, Stavern, Strasbourg, Stuttgart, Torino, Toulouse, Tsawassen,
Vancouver, Versailles, Walla Walla, Warszawa
```

# Exercise 9.3 – explore topics

Use the following links to read more details about the topics covered in this chapter:

- **Query Syntax and Method Syntax in LINQ (C#)**: `https://msdn.microsoft.com/en-us/library/bb397947.aspx`

- **101 LINQ Samples**: `https://code.msdn.microsoft.com/101-LINQ-Samples-3fb9811b`

- **Parallel LINQ (PLINQ)**: `https://msdn.microsoft.com/en-us/library/dd460688(v=vs.110).aspx`

- **LINQ to XML**: `https://msdn.microsoft.com/en-us/library/bb387098.aspx`

- **LINQPad – The .NET Programmer's Playground**: `https://www.linqpad.net/`

# Summary

In this chapter, you learned how to write LINQ queries to select, project, filter, sort, join, and group data in many different formats, including XML, which are tasks you will perform every day.

In the next chapter, you will learn how to manage files and streams, encode and decode text, and perform serialization.

# 10
# Working with Files, Streams, and Serialization

This chapter is about reading and writing to files and streams, encoding and decoding text, and serialization.

This chapter will cover the following topics:

- Managing the filesystem
- Reading and writing with streams
- Encoding text
- Serializing object graphs

## Managing the filesystem

Your applications will often need to perform input and output with files and directories. The `System.IO` namespace contains classes for this purpose.

## Managing directories

Start Microsoft Visual Studio 2015. In Visual Studio, press *Ctrl + Shift + N* or choose **File | New | Project...**.

In the **New Project** dialog, in the **Installed Templates** list, select **Visual C#**. In the center list, select **Console Application**, type **Name** as **Ch10_FileSystem**, change location to `C:\Code`, type solution name as **Chapter10**, and then click on **OK**.

At the top of the `Program.cs` file, add the following import statements:

```
using static System.Console;
using System.IO;
```

In the `Main` method, write the following statements to check for the existence of a directory, and then, create and delete it:

```
// define a directory
string dir = @"C:\Code\Ch10_Example\";
// check if it exists
WriteLine($"Does {dir} exist? {Directory.Exists(dir)}");
// create a directory
Directory.CreateDirectory(dir);
WriteLine($"Does {dir} exist? {Directory.Exists(dir)}");
// delete a directory
Directory.Delete(dir);
WriteLine($"Does {dir} exist? {Directory.Exists(dir)}");
```

Run the application by pressing *Ctrl + F5* and notice the output:

```
Does C:\Code\Ch10_Example\ exist? False
Does C:\Code\Ch10_Example\ exist? True
Does C:\Code\Ch10_Example\ exist? False
```

# Managing files

In the `Main` method, add the following statements to:

- Check for the existence of a file
- Create a text file
- Write a line of text to the file
- Copy the file to a backup
- Delete the original file
- Read the backup file's contents

```
string textFile = @"C:\Code\Ch10.txt";";
string backupFile = @"C:\Code\Ch10.bak";

// check if a file exists
WriteLine($"Does {textFile} exist? {File.Exists(textFile)}");

// create a new text file and write a line to it
StreamWriter textWriter = File.CreateText(textFile);
```

```
textWriter.WriteLine("Hello C#!");
textWriter.Dispose();
WriteLine($"Does {textFile} exist? {File.Exists(textFile)}");

// copy a file and overwrite if it already exists
File.Copy(textFile, backupFile, true);
WriteLine($"Does {backupFile} exist? {File.Exists(backupFile)}");

// delete a file
File.Delete(textFile);
WriteLine($"Does {textFile} exist? {File.Exists(textFile)}");

// read from a text file
string textReader = File.OpenText(backupFile);
WriteLine(textReader.ReadToEnd());
textReader.Dispose();
```

Rerun the application and notice the output:

**Does C:\Code\Ch10.txt exist? False**

**Does C:\Code\Ch10.txt exist? True**

**Does C:\Code\Ch10.bak exist? True**

**Does C:\Code\Ch10.txt exist? False**

**Hello C#!**

 In the .NET Framework, you can use either the Close or Dispose method when you are finished with StreamReader or StreamWriter. In the .NET Core, you can only use Dispose, because Microsoft has simplified the API.

# Managing paths

Sometimes you need to work with paths, for example, you might want to extract just the folder name, just the file name, or just the extension. Sometimes, you need to generate temporary folders and file names. You can do this with the Path class.

Add the following statements to the Main method:

```
WriteLine($"File Name: {Path.GetFileName(textFile)}");
WriteLine($"File Name without Extension: {Path.GetFileNameWithoutExten
sion(textFile)}");
WriteLine($"File Extension: {Path.GetExtension(textFile)}");
WriteLine($"Random File Name: {Path.GetRandomFileName()}");
WriteLine($"Temporary File Name: {Path.GetTempFileName()}");
```

Rerun the application:

**File Name: Ch10.txt**

**File Name without Extension: Ch10**

**File Extension: .txt**

**Random File Name: u45w1zki.co3**

**Temporary File Name: C:\Users\Mark\AppData\Local\Temp\tmpDF0B.tmp**

# Getting file information

To get more information about a file or directory, you can create an instance of the `FileInfo` or `DirectoryInfo` class.

Add the following statements to the end of the `Main` method:

```
string backup = @"C:\Code\Ch10.bak";
string info = new FileInfo(backup);
WriteLine($"{backup} contains {info.Length} bytes.");
WriteLine($"{backup} was last accessed {info.LastAccessTime}.");
WriteLine($"{backup} has readonly set to {info.IsReadOnly}.");
```

Rerun the application and see the output.:

**C:\Code\Ch10.bak contains 11 bytes.**

**C:\Code\Ch10.bak was last accessed 29/08/2015 16:25:47.**

**C:\Code\Ch10.bak has readonly set to False.**

# Reading and writing with streams

A **stream** is a sequence of bytes.

There is an abstract class named `Stream` that represents a stream. There are many classes that inherit from this base class, so they all work the same way. In the following table are some of the common members of the `Stream` class:

| Member | Description |
|---|---|
| CanRead, CanWrite | Determines whether you can read to and write from the stream |
| Length, Position | Determines the total number of bytes and the current position within the stream |
| Close() | Closes the stream and releases its resources |
| Flush() | If the stream has a buffer, then it is cleared and written to the underlying stream |

| Member | Description |
|---|---|
| Read() | Reads a specified number of bytes from the stream into a byte array and advances the position |
| ReadByte() | Reads the next byte from the stream and advances the position |
| Seek() | Moves the position to the specified position (if CanSeek is true) |
| Write() | Writes the contents of a byte array into the stream |
| WriteByte() | Writes a byte to the stream |

**Storage streams** can be read and written to, and the bytes will be stored in that location. The following table has examples of storage stream classes:

| Class | Description |
|---|---|
| FileStream | Stored in the filesystem |
| MemoryStream | Stored in memory in the current process |
| NetworkStream | Stored at a network location |

**Function streams** can only be "plugged onto" other streams to add functionality. The following table has examples of function stream classes:

| Class | Description |
|---|---|
| CryptoStream | Encrypts and decrypts the stream |
| GZipStream, DeflateStream | Compresses and decompresses the stream |
| AuthenticatedStream | Sends credentials across the stream |

Although there will be occasions where you need to work with streams at a low level, most often, you can plug helper classes into the chain to make things easier. Here are some helper classes to handle common scenarios:

| Class | Description |
|---|---|
| StreamReader | Reads from streams as text |
| StreamWriter | Writes to streams as text |
| XmlReader | Reads from streams as XML |
| XmlWriter | Writes to streams as XML |
| BinaryReader | Reads from streams as .NET types |
| BinaryWriter | Writes to streams as .NET types |

# Writing to text and XML streams

Add a new console application project named **Ch10_Streams**. Set the solution's start-up project to be the current selection.

Import the System.IO and System.Xml namespaces, statically import the System.Console type, and add the following statement to the Main method:

```
// define an array of strings
string[] callsigns = new string[] { "Husker", "Starbuck", "Apollo",
"Boomer", "Bulldog", "Athena", "Helo", "Racetrack" };

// define a file to write to using a text writer helper
string textFile = @"C:\Code\Ch10_Streams.txt";
StreamWriter text = File.CreateText(textFile);

// enumerate the strings writing each one to the stream
foreach (string item in callsigns)
{
    text.WriteLine(item);
}
text.Dispose(); // release the stream resources

// output all the contents of the file to the Console
WriteLine($"{textFile} contains {new FileInfo(textFile).Length}
bytes.");
WriteLine(File.ReadAllText(textFile));

// define a file to write to using the XML writer helper
string xmlFile = @"C:\Code\Ch10_Streams.xml";
FileStream xmlFileStream = File.Create(xmlFile);
XmlWriter xml = XmlWriter.Create(xmlFileStream, new XmlWriterSettings
{ Indent = true });

// write the XML declaration
xml.WriteStartDocument();

// write a root element
xml.WriteStartElement("callsigns");

// enumerate the strings writing each one to the stream
foreach (string item in callsigns)
{
    xml.WriteElementString("callsign", item);
}
```

```
    // write the close root element
    xml.WriteEndElement();
    xml.Dispose();

    // output all the contents of the file to the Console
    WriteLine($"{xmlFile} contains {new FileInfo(xmlFile).Length}
    bytes.");
    WriteLine(File.ReadAllText(xmlFile));
```

Run the application using *Ctrl* + *F5*:

```
C:\Code\Ch10_Streams.txt contains 68 bytes.

Husker

Starbuck

Apollo

Boomer

Bulldog

Athena

Helo

Racetrack


C:\Code\Ch10_Streams.xml contains 320 bytes.

<?xml version="1.0" encoding="utf-8"?>

<callsigns>

  <callsign>Husker</callsign>

  <callsign>Starbuck</callsign>

  <callsign>Apollo</callsign>

  <callsign>Boomer</callsign>

  <callsign>Bulldog</callsign>

  <callsign>Athena</callsign>

  <callsign>Helo</callsign>

  <callsign>Racetrack</callsign>

</callsigns>
```

# Compressing streams

XML is relatively verbose, so it takes up more space in bytes than plain text. We could squeeze the XML using a common compression algorithm known as **GZIP**.

Import the following namespace:

```
using System.IO.Compression;
```

Add the following code to the end of the `Main` method:

```
// compress the XML output
string gzipFilePath = @"C:\Code\Ch10.gzip";
FileStream gzipFile = File.Create(gzipFilePath);
GZipStream compressor = new GZipStream(gzipFile, CompressionMode.
Compress);
XmlWriter xmlGzip = XmlWriter.Create(compressor);
xmlGzip.WriteStartDocument();
xmlGzip.WriteStartElement("callsigns");
foreach (string item in callsigns)
{
    xmlGzip.WriteElementString("callsign", item);
}
xmlGzip.Dispose();
compressor.Dispose(); // also closes the underlying stream

// output all the contents of the compressed file to the Console
WriteLine($"{gzipFilePath} contains {new FileInfo(gzipFilePath).
Length} bytes.");
WriteLine(File.ReadAllText(gzipFilePath));

// read a compressed file
WriteLine("Reading the compressed XML file:");
gzipFile = File.Open(gzipFilePath, FileMode.Open);
GZipStream decompressor = new GZipStream(gzipFile, CompressionMode.
Decompress);
XmlReader reader = XmlReader.Create(decompressor);
while (reader.Read())
{
    // check if we are currently on an element node named callsign
    if ((reader.NodeType == XmlNodeType.Element) && (reader.Name ==
"callsign"))
    {
        reader.Read(); // move to the Text node inside the element
        WriteLine($"{reader.Value}"); // read its value
```

```
        }
    }
    reader.Dispose();
    decompressor.Dispose();
```

Rerun the application and notice that the compressed XML is less than half the size of the same XML without compression:

```
C:\Code\Ch10.gzip contains 144 bytes.
▼      ♦ {?{??}En?BYjQqf~???????Bj^r~Jf^??RiI??????MrbNNqfz^1?i?QZ??Zd?✿‡@
H♣?$-%?
&gc?t,?????*????H?????t?&?d??%b??H?aUPbrjIQ"?←?◀?♦ ??9→L☺
Reading the compressed XML file:
Husker
Starbuck
Apollo
Boomer
Bulldog
Athena
Helo
Racetrack
```

# Encoding text

Text characters can be represented in different ways. For example, the Western alphabet can be encoded using Morse code, into a series of dots and dashes for transmission over a telegraph line.

In a similar way, text inside a computer is stored as bits; ones and zeros. .NET uses a standard called **Unicode** to encode text internally. Sometimes, you will need to move text outside .NET for use by systems that do not use Unicode or use a variation of Unicode. The following table shows some alternative encodings:

| Encoding | Description |
|---|---|
| ASCII | Encodes a limited range of characters using the lower seven bits of a byte |
| UTF-8 | Represents each Unicode code point as a sequence of one to four bytes |
| UTF-16 | Represents each Unicode code point as a sequence of one or two 16-bit integers |
| ANSI/ISO encodings | Provides support for a variety of code pages that are used to support a specific language or group of languages |

# Encoding strings as byte arrays

Add a new console application project named **Ch10_Encoding**.

Import the System.Text namespace and add the following statement to the Main method. The code encodes a string using the chosen encoding, loops through each byte, and then decodes back into a string and outputs it:

```
WriteLine("Encodings");
WriteLine("[1] ASCII");
WriteLine("[2] UTF-7");
WriteLine("[3] UTF-8");
WriteLine("[4] UTF-16 (Unicode)");
WriteLine("[5] UTF-32");
WriteLine("[any other key] Default");

// choose an encoding
Write("Press a number to choose an encoding: ");
ConsoleKey number = ReadKey(false).Key;
WriteLine();
WriteLine();

Encoding encoder;
switch (number)
{
    case ConsoleKey.D1:
        encoder = Encoding.ASCII;
        break;
    case ConsoleKey.D2:
        encoder = Encoding.UTF7;
        break;
    case ConsoleKey.D3:
        encoder = Encoding.UTF8;
        break;
    case ConsoleKey.D4:
        encoder = Encoding.Unicode;
        break;
    case ConsoleKey.D5:
        encoder = Encoding.UTF32;
        break;
    default:
        encoder = Encoding.GetEncoding(0);
        break;
}
```

```
// define a string to encode
string message = "A pint of milk is £1.99";

// encode the string into a byte array
byte[] encoded = encoder.GetBytes(message);

// check how many bytes the encoding needed
WriteLine($"{encoder.GetType().Name} uses {encoded.Length} bytes.");

// enumerate each byte
WriteLine($"Byte  Hex   Char");
foreach (byte b in encoded)
{
    WriteLine($"{b,4} {b.ToString("X"),4} {(char)b,5}");
}

// decode the byte array back into a string and display it
string decoded = encoder.GetString(encoded);
WriteLine(decoded);
```

Run the application and press 1 to choose ASCII. Notice that when outputting the bytes, the pound sign (£) cannot be represented in ASCII, so it uses a question mark (?) instead:

**Encodings**

**[1] ASCII**

**[2] UTF-7**

**[3] UTF-8**

**[4] UTF-16 (Unicode)**

**[5] UTF-32**

**[any other key] Default**

**Press a number to choose an encoding: 1**

**ASCIIEncoding uses 23 bytes.**

| Byte | Hex | Char |
|------|-----|------|
| 65   | 41  | A    |
| 32   | 20  |      |
| 112  | 70  | p    |
| 105  | 69  | i    |
| 110  | 6E  | n    |
| 116  | 74  | t    |

| 32  | 20 |   |
| --- | -- | - |
| 111 | 6F | o |
| 102 | 66 | f |
| 32  | 20 |   |
| 109 | 6D | m |
| 105 | 69 | i |
| 108 | 6C | l |
| 107 | 6B | k |
| 32  | 20 |   |
| 105 | 69 | i |
| 115 | 73 | s |
| 32  | 20 |   |
| 63  | 3F | ? |
| 49  | 31 | 1 |
| 46  | 2E | . |
| 57  | 39 | 9 |
| 57  | 39 | 9 |

```
A pint of milk is ?1.99
```

Rerun the application and press 3 to choose UTF-8. Notice that UTF-8 requires one extra byte (24 bytes instead of 23 bytes), but it can store the £:

```
UTF8Encoding uses 24 bytes.
```

| Byte | Hex | Char |
| ---- | --- | ---- |
| 65   | 41  | A    |
| 32   | 20  |      |
| 112  | 70  | p    |
| 105  | 69  | i    |
| 110  | 6E  | n    |
| 116  | 74  | t    |
| 32   | 20  |      |
| 111  | 6F  | o    |
| 102  | 66  | f    |
| 32   | 20  |      |
| 109  | 6D  | m    |
| 105  | 69  | i    |
| 108  | 6C  | l    |

| | | |
|---|---|---|
| 107 | 6B | k |
| 32 | 20 | |
| 105 | 69 | i |
| 115 | 73 | s |
| 32 | 20 | |
| 194 | C2 | Â |
| 163 | A3 | £ |
| 49 | 31 | 1 |
| 46 | 2E | . |
| 57 | 39 | 9 |
| 57 | 39 | 9 |

```
A pint of milk is £1.99
```

Rerun the application and press 4 to choose Unicode (UTF-16). Notice that UTF-16 requires two bytes for every character, but it can store the £:

```
UnicodeEncoding uses 46 bytes.
```

# Encoding and decoding text in files

When using stream helper classes such as `StreamReader` and `StreamWriter`, you can specify the encoding you want to use. As you write to the helper, the strings will automatically be encoded, and as you read from the helper, the bytes will be automatically decided. This is how you can specify the encoding:

```
var reader = new StreamReader(stream, Encoding.UTF7);
var writer = new StreamWriter(stream, Encoding.UTF7);
```

 Often, you won't have a choice of encoding to use, because you will be generating a file for use by another system. However, if you do, pick one that uses the least amount of bytes but can store every character you need.

# Serializing object graphs

**Serialization** is the process of converting a live object into a sequence of bytes using a specified format. **Deserialization** is the reverse process.

There are dozens of formats you can choose, but the two most common ones are **eXtensible Markup Language (XML)** and **JavaScript Object Notation (JSON)**.

> JSON is more compact and is best for web and mobile applications. XML is more verbose, but is better supported on older systems.

.NET has multiple classes that will serialize to and from XML and JSON. We will start by looking at `XmlSerializer` and `JavaScriptSerializer`.

# Serializing with XML

Add a new console application project named **Ch10_Serialization**.

> If you are targeting the .NET Core, then you would need to manually add the latest version of the `System.Xml.XmlSerializer` NuGet package.

To show a common example, we will define a custom class to store information about a person and then create an object graph using a list of `Person` instances with nesting.

Add a class named `Person` with the following definition. Notice that the `Salary` property is `protected`, meaning it is only accessible to itself and the derived classes. To populate the salary, the class has a constructor with a single parameter to set the initial salary:

```
public class Person
{
    public Person(decimal initialSalary)
    {
        Salary = initialSalary;
    }
    public string FirstName { get; set; }
    public string LastName { get; set; }
    public DateTime DateOfBirth { get; set; }
    public HashSet<Person> Children { get; set; }
    protected decimal Salary { get; set; }
}
```

Back in `Program.cs`, import the following namespaces:

```
using System;
using System.Collections.Generic;
using System.Xml.Serialization;
using System.IO;
using static System.Console;
```

Add the following statements to the `Main` method:

```
// create an object graph
var people = new List<Person>
{
    new Person(30000M) { FirstName = "Alice", LastName = "Smith",
DateOfBirth = new DateTime(1974, 3, 14) },
    new Person(40000M) { FirstName = "Bob", LastName = "Jones",
DateOfBirth = new DateTime(1969, 11, 23) },
    new Person(20000M) { FirstName = "Charlie", LastName = "Rose",
DateOfBirth = new DateTime(1964, 5, 4), Children = new HashSet<Person>
        { new Person(0M) { FirstName = "Sally", LastName = "Rose",
DateOfBirth = new DateTime(1990, 7, 12) } } }
};

// create a file to write to
string xmlFilepath = @"C:\Code\Ch10_People.xml";
FileStream xmlStream = File.Create(xmlFilepath);

// create an object that will format a List of Persons as XML
var xs = new XmlSerializer(typeof(List<Person>));

// serialize the object graph to the stream
xs.Serialize(xmlStream, people);

// you must dispose the stream to release the file lock
xmlStream.Dispose();

WriteLine($"Written {new FileInfo(xmlFilepath).Length} bytes of XML to
{xmlFilepath}");
WriteLine();

// Display the serialized object graph
WriteLine(File.ReadAllText(xmlFilepath));
```

Run the application with *Ctrl + F5*. Notice that an exception is thrown:

**Unhandled Exception: System.InvalidOperationException: Ch10_
Serialization.Person cannot be serialized because it does not have a
parameterless constructor.**

Back in the `Person.cs` file, add the following statement to define a parameter-less constructor. Notice that the constructor does not need to do anything, but it must exist so that the `XmlSerializer` can call it to instantiate new `Person` instances when deserializing:

```
public Person() { }
```

Rerun the application and see the output. Notice that the object graph is serialized and the `Salary` property is not included:

```
Written 778 bytes of XML to C:\Code\Ch10_People.xml
```

```xml
<?xml version="1.0"?>
<ArrayOfPerson xmlns:xsi="http://www.w3.org/2001/XMLSchema-instance"
xmlns:xsd="http://www.w3.org/2001/XMLSchema">
  <Person>
    <FirstName>Alice</FirstName>
    <LastName>Smith</LastName>
    <DateOfBirth>1974-03-14T00:00:00</DateOfBirth>
  </Person>
  <Person>
    <FirstName>Bob</FirstName>
    <LastName>Jones</LastName>
    <DateOfBirth>1969-11-23T00:00:00</DateOfBirth>
  </Person>
  <Person>
    <FirstName>Charlie</FirstName>
    <LastName>Rose</LastName>
    <DateOfBirth>1964-05-04T00:00:00</DateOfBirth>
    <Children>
      <Person>
        <FirstName>Sally</FirstName>
        <LastName>Rose</LastName>
        <DateOfBirth>1990-07-12T00:00:00</DateOfBirth>
      </Person>
    </Children>
  </Person>
</ArrayOfPerson>
```

We could make the XML more efficient using attributes instead of elements for some fields.

In the `Person.cs` file, import the `System.Xml.Serialization` namespace and modify all the properties, except `Children`, with the `[XmlAttribute]` attribute:

```
[XmlAttribute("fname")]
public string FirstName { get; set; }
[XmlAttribute("lname")]
public string LastName { get; set; }
[XmlAttribute("dob")]
public DateTime DateOfBirth { get; set; }
```

Rerun the application and notice that the XML is now more efficient:

**Written 473 bytes of XML to C:\Code\Ch10_People.xml**

```
<?xml version="1.0"?>
<ArrayOfPerson xmlns:xsi="http://www.w3.org/2001/XMLSchema-instance"
xmlns:xsd="
http://www.w3.org/2001/XMLSchema">
  <Person fname="Alice" lname="Smith" dob="1974-03-14T00:00:00" />
  <Person fname="Bob" lname="Jones" dob="1969-11-23T00:00:00" />
  <Person fname="Charlie" lname="Rose" dob="1964-05-04T00:00:00">
    <Children>
      <Person fname="Sally" lname="Rose" dob="1990-07-12T00:00:00" />
    </Children>
  </Person>
</ArrayOfPerson>
```

# Deserializing with XML

Add the following statements to the end of the `Main` method:

```
FileStream xmlLoad = File.Open(xmlFilepath, FileMode.Open);
// deserialize and cast the object graph into a List of Person
var loadedPeople = (List<Person>)xs.Deserialize(xmlLoad);
foreach (var item in loadedPeople)
{
    WriteLine($"{item.LastName} has {item.Children.Count} children.");
}
xmlLoad.Dispose();
```

Rerun the application and notice that the people are loaded successfully from the XML file:

```
Smith has 0 children.
Jones has 0 children.
Rose has 1 children.
```

# Customizing the XML

There are many other attributes that can be used to control the XML generated. See the references at the end of this chapter for more information.

 When using `XmlSerializer`, remember that only `public` fields and properties are included, and the type must have a parameter-less constructor. You can customize the output with attributes.

# Serializing with JSON

Add a reference to the `System.Web.Extensions` assembly.

 The `System.Web.Extensions` assembly is supported by the .NET Framework only. Use Newtonsoft's JSON.NET if you need to serialize cross platform with the .NET Core, which can be found at `http://www.newtonsoft.com/json`

Import the following namespace at the top of the `Program.cs` file:

```
using System.Web.Script.Serialization;
```

Add the following statements to the end of the `Main` method:

```
// create a file to write to
string jsonFilepath = @"C:\Code\Ch10_People.json";
FileStream jsonStream = File.Create(jsonFilepath);

// create an object that will format as JSON
var jss = new JavaScriptSerializer();

// serialize the object graph into a string
string json = jss.Serialize(people);
```

```
// write the string to a file
var writer = new StreamWriter(jsonStream);
writer.Write(json);

// you must dispose the stream to release the file lock
writer.Dispose();

WriteLine();
WriteLine($"Written {new FileInfo(jsonFilepath).Length} bytes of JSON
to: {jsonFilepath}");

// Display the serialized object graph
WriteLine(File.ReadAllText(jsonFilepath));
```

Rerun the application, and notice that JSON requires less than half the number of bytes compared to XML with elements. It's even smaller than XML that uses attributes:

```
Written 380 bytes of JSON to: C:\Code\Ch10_People.json
```

```
[{"FirstName":"Alice","LastName":"Smith","DateOfBirth":"\/
Date(132451200000)\/", "Children":null},{"FirstName":"Bob","LastName":"Jo
nes","DateOfBirth":"\/Date(-3369600000)\/","Children":null},{"FirstName":
"Charlie","LastName":"Rose","DateOfBirth":"\/Date(-178678800000)\/","Chil
dren":[{"FirstName":"Sally","LastName":"Rose","DateOfBirth":"\/Date(64773
7200000)\/","Children":null}]}]
```

> Use JSON to minimize the size of serialized object graphs. You can also use JSON when sending object graphs to web applications and mobile applications.

# Serializing with other formats

There are many other formats built into .NET that you can use for serialization and even more if you purchase additional libraries.

| Type | Description |
|------|-------------|
| `System.Runtime.Serialization.Formatters.Binary.BinaryFormatter` | This uses a Microsoft proprietary binary format, so it should only be used when a .NET application is both serializing and deserializing the object graph. |

| Type | Description |
|---|---|
| `System.Runtime.Serialization.`<br>`Formatters.Soap.SoapFormatter` | This is used by ASP.NET XML web services to serialize with the SOAP format. To use it yourself, you must add a reference to the `System.Runtime.Serialization.`<br>`Formatters.Soap` assembly and import the `System.Runtime.Serialization.`<br>`Formatters.Soap` namespace. |
| `System.Runtime.Serialization.`<br>`DataContractSerializer` | This is used by **Windows Communication Foundation (WCF)** to serialize with SOAP format (or XML when an endpoint has the `WebHttp` behavior). To use it yourself, you must add a reference to the `System.Runtime.`<br>`Serialization` assembly and import the `System.Runtime.Serialization` namespace. |
| `System.Runtime.Serialization.`<br>`DataContractJsonSerializer` | This is used by WCF to serialize into the JSON format when an endpoint has a `WebHttp` behavior. |
| `System.Runtime.Serialization`<br>`.IFormatter` | This is used to implement your own custom runtime serializers. |

# Serializing with runtime serializers

`BinaryFormatter` type is one of the serializers that can be used only with .NET Framework. These are powerful, but they have the special requirement that the type being serialized must be marked as serializable using an attribute. Like `JavaScriptSerializer`, they are not cross-platform!

| Ch10_Serialization, Version=1.0.0.0, Culture=neutral, PublicKeyToken=null (.NETFramework,Version=v4.6.1) | | | | |
|---|---|---|---|---|
| Target type | .NET Core (Cross platform),Version=v5.0 | .NET Framework,Version=v4.5 | .NET Native,Version=v1.0 | Recommended changes |
| System.Console | ✓ | ✓ | ✗ | |
| WriteLine | ✓ | ✓ | ✗ | |
| WriteLine(System.String) | ✓ | ✓ | ✗ | |
| | | | | |
| System.Runtime.Serialization.Formatters.Binary.BinaryFormatter | ✗ | ✓ | ✗ | |
| #ctor | ✗ | ✓ | ✗ | |
| Serialize(System.IO.Stream,System.Object) | ✗ | ✓ | ✗ | |
| | | | | |
| System.Web.Script.Serialization.JavaScriptSerializer | ✗ | ✓ | ✗ | Use JSON.NET instead |
| #ctor | ✗ | ✓ | ✗ | Use JSON.NET instead |
| Serialize(System.Object) | ✗ | ✓ | ✗ | Use JSON.NET instead |

Import the `System.Runtime.Serialization.Formatters.Binary` namespace:

```
using System.Runtime.Serialization.Formatters.Binary;
```

At the bottom of the `Main` method, add the following statements:

```
string binaryFilepath = @"C:\Code\Ch10_People.bin";";
FileStream binaryStream = File.Create(binaryFilepath);
var bf = new BinaryFormatter();
bf.Serialize(binaryStream, people);
binaryStream.Dispose();
WriteLine($"Written {new FileInfo(binaryFilepath).Length} bytes of
proprietary binary to {binaryFilepath}");}");
WriteLine();
// Display the serialized object graph
WriteLine(File.ReadAllText(binaryFilepath));
```

Rerun the application and notice the exception that is thrown.:

**Unhandled Exception: System.Runtime.Serialization.SerializationException:
Type 'Ch10_Serialization.Person' in Assembly 'Ch10_Serialization,
Version=1.0.0.0, Culture=neutral, PublicKeyToken=null' is not marked as
serializable.**

In the `Person.cs`, add the `[Serializable]` attribute to the `Person` class:

```
[Serializable]
public class Person
```

Rerun the application. Now, the object graph is successfully serialized:

**Written 1573 bytes of proprietary binary to C:\Code\Ch10_People.bin**

```
  ☺  ?????☺        ♀☻  ICh10_Serialization, Version=1.0.0.0,
Culture=neutral, PublicKeyToken=null♦☺  ?☺System.Collections.Generic.
List`1[[Ch10_Serialization.Person, Ch10_Serialization, Version=1.0.0.0,
Culture=neutral, PublicKeyToken=null]] ♥  ♠_items♣_siz_version♦ ←Ch10_
Serialization.Person[] ♥  ♥  ♥  ♥     ☺  ♦ ♦↓Ch10_Serialization.
Person® 　      ♦     ♣     ♠♀  NSystem.Core, Version=4.0.0.0,
Culture=neutral, PublicKeyToken=b77a5c561934e089♣♦  ↓Ch10_
Serialization.Person♣  →<FirstName>k__BackingField↓<LastName>k__
BackingFieldL<DateOfBirth>k__BackingField↓<Children>k__
BackingField‡<Salary>k__Ba?☺System.Collections.Generic.HashSet`1[[Ch10_
Serialization.Person, Ch10_Serialization, Version=1.0.0.0,
Culture=neutral, PublicKeyToken=null]]  ♣☻   ♠Alice♠  ♠Smith @??4?
♣30000☺♣  ♦  ♠  ♥Bob♠♂  ♠Jones @??Pa?  ♦Rose ?rY?& ♪  ♠20000♣♪
?☺System.Collections.Generic.HashSet`1[[Ch10_Serialization.Person, Ch10_
Serialization, Version=1.0.0.0, Culture=neutral, PublicKeyToken=null]]♦
VersioCompareCapacitElements ♥ ?☺System.Collections.Generic.
```

```
ObjectEqualityComparer`1[[Ch10_Serialization.Person, Ch10_Serialization,
Version=1. 0.0.0, Culture=neutral, PublicKeyToken=null]←Ch10_
Serialization.Person[]®      ☺       ☼  ♥           ▶   ♦☼   ?☺System.
Collections.Generic.ObjectEqualityComparer`1[[Ch10_Serialization.
Person, Ch10_Serialization, Version=1.0.0.0, Culture=neutral,
PublicKeyToken=null]]    ▶   ☺   ☺     ♦↓Ch10_Serialization.Person®    @?
♦    ♠‡   ♣Sally!?? ☺0♂
```

Use the BinaryFormatter or any of the other runtime serializers only when you will serialize and deserialize with .NET Framework.

# Practice and explore

Test your knowledge and understanding by answering some questions, getting some hands-on practice, and exploring this chapter's topics with deeper research.

## Exercise 10.1 – test your knowledge

Answer the following questions:

1. What is the difference between using the File class and the FileInfo class?
2. What is the difference between the ReadByte method and the Read method of a stream?
3. When would you use StringReader, TextReader, and StreamReader classes?
4. What does the DeflateStream type do?
5. How many bytes per character does the UTF-8 encoding use?
6. What is an object graph?
7. What is the best serialization format to choose for minimizing space requirements?
8. What is the best serialization format to choose for cross-platform compatibility?
9. Which Microsoft technology uses the DataContractSerializer type by default?
10. Is it possible to create your own custom runtime serializers?

# Exercise 10.2 – practice serializing as XML

Create a console application named **Ch10_Exercise02** that creates a list of shapes, uses serialization to save it to the filesystem using XML, and then deserializes it back:

```
// create a list of Shapes to serialize
var listOfShapes = new List<Shape>
{
    new Circle { Colour = "Red", Radius = 2.5 },
    new Rectangle { Colour = "Blue", Height = 20.0, Width = 10.0 },
    new Circle { Colour = "Green", Radius = 8 },
    new Circle { Colour = "Purple", Radius = 12.3 },
    new Rectangle { Colour = "Blue", Height = 45.0, Width = 18.0 }
};
```

Shapes should have a read-only property named Area so that when you deserialize, you can output a list of shapes, including their areas, as shown here:

```
List<Shape> loadedShapesXml = serializerXml.Deserialize(fileXml) as
List<Shape>;
foreach (Shape item in loadedShapesXml)
{
    WriteLine($"{item.GetType().Name} is {item.Colour} and has an area
of {item.Area}");
}
```

This is what your output should look like when you run the application:

```
Loading shapes from XML:
Circle is Red and has an area of 19.6349540849362
Rectangle is Blue and has an area of 200
Circle is Green and has an area of 201.061929829747
Circle is Purple and has an area of 475.2915525616
Rectangle is Blue and has an area of 810
```

# Exercise 10.3 – explore serialization formats

Create a console application named **Ch10_Exercise03** that queries the Northwind database for all the categories and products, and then serializes the data using all the formats of serialization available in .NET. Which uses the least number of bytes?

# Exercise 10.4 – explore Microsoft's System.IO types

Use ILSpy to explore the Microsoft .NET Framework implementations of the `Stream`, `FileStream`, and `StreamWriter` classes. You will find those classes in the `System.IO` namespace in the `mscorlib.dll` assembly.

In particular, look at the `Dispose` and `Close` methods. My students often ask which to use and whether there is a difference. By viewing the actual implementation, you can find out.

The `Close` method looks like this:

```
// System.IO.Stream
/// <summary>Closes the current
public virtual void Close()
{
    this.Dispose(true);
    GC.SuppressFinalize(this);
}
```

The `Dispose` method looks like this:

```
// System.IO.Stream
/// <summary>Releases all
[__DynamicallyInvokable]
public void Dispose()
{
    this.Close();
}
```

In the .NET Core, Microsoft has removed the `Close` method so you must use the `Dispose` method instead.

# Exercise 10.5 – explore topics

Use the following links to read more on this chapter's topics:

- **File and Stream I/O**: https://msdn.microsoft.com/en-us/library/k3352a4t(v=vs.110).aspx

- **Character encoding in the .NET Framework**: https://msdn.microsoft.com/en-us/library/ms404377(v=vs.110).aspx

- **Serialization**: https://msdn.microsoft.com/en-us/library/7ay27kt9(v=vs.110).aspx

- **Introducing XML serialization**: https://msdn.microsoft.com/en-us/library/182eeyhh(v=vs.110).aspx

- **Serialization and deserialization**: https://msdn.microsoft.com/en-us/library/ms731073(v=vs.110).aspx

# Summary

In this chapter, you learned how to read from and write to text files and XML files, how to compress and decompress files, how to encode and decode text, and how to serialize an object into JSON and XML (and deserialize it back again).

In the next chapter, you will learn how to protect data and applications.

# 11

# Protecting Your Data and Applications

This chapter is about protecting your data from being viewed by malicious users using encryption and from being manipulated or corrupted using hashing and signing. It is also about checking who is running your application and restricting their actions to only those that they are given permission to do.

 Security is tightly bound to the operating system, so this is an area that is not very well supported by the .NET Core (at least for now). To complete the exercises in this chapter, I recommend that you target the .NET Framework on Windows 10. Then, once you have learned the skills, you can try implementing them using the equivalent .NET Core types.

This chapter covers the following topics:

- Understanding the vocabulary of protection
- Encrypting and decrypting data
- Hashing data
- Signing data
- Authenticating and authorizing users

# Understanding the vocabulary of protection

There are many techniques to protect your applications and data, some of them are as follows:

- **Encryption and decryption**: This is a two-way process to convert cleartext into cryptotext and back again

- **Hashes**: This is a one-way process to; generate a hash to securely store passwords, or a hash can be used to detect malicious changes and corruption of data

- **Signatures**: This technique is used to ensure that data has come from someone you trust by validating a signature against someone's public key

- **Authentication**: This technique is used to identify someone by checking their credentials

- **Authorization**: This technique is used to ensure someone has permission to perform an action, or work with some data by checking the roles or groups they belong to

**Best Practice**

If security is important to you, then hire an experienced security expert for guidance rather than relying on advice found online. It is very easy to make small mistakes and leave your applications and data vulnerable without realizing until it is too late!

# Keys and key sizes

Protection algorithms often use a **key**. Keys can be **symmetric** (also known as shared or secret because the same key is used to encrypt and decrypt) or **asymmetric** (a public-private key pair where the public key is used to encrypt and only the private key can be used to decrypt). Keys are represented by byte arrays of varying size.

**Best Practice**

Choose a bigger key size for stronger protection.

# IVs and block sizes

When encrypting large amounts of data, there are likely to be repeating sequences. For example, in an English document the sequence of characters "the" would appear frequently. A good cracker would use this knowledge to make it easier to crack the encryption. Note the becomes hQ2 in the following example:

```
When the wind blew hard the umbrella broke.
5:s4&hQ2aj#D f9d1df8fh"&hQ2s0)an DF8SFd#][1
```

We can avoid repeating sequences by dividing data into **blocks**. After encrypting a block, a byte array value is generated from that block and this value is fed into the next block to adjust the algorithm so that "the" isn't encrypted in the same way. To encrypt the first block, we need a byte array to feed in. This is called the **initialization vector (IV)**.

>  **Best Practice**
> Choose a small block size for stronger encryption.

# Salts

A salt is a random byte array that is used as an additional input to a one-way hash function. If you do not use a salt when generating hashes, then when many of your users register with "**123456**" as their password (about 8% of users still do this!), they all have the same hashed value, and their account will be vulnerable to a dictionary attack.

When a user registers, a salt should be randomly generated and concatenated with their chosen password before being hashed. The output (but not the original password) is stored with the salt in the database.

When the user next logs in and enters their password, you look up their salt, concatenate it with the entered password, regenerate a hash, and then compare its value with the hash stored in the database. If they are the same, you know they entered the correct password.

# Generating keys and IVs

Keys and IVs are byte arrays. You can reliably generate a key or IV using a **password-based key derivation function (PBKDF2)**. A good one is the `Rfc2898DeriveBytes` class, which takes a password, a salt, and an iteration count, and then generates keys and IVs by making calls to its `GetBytes` method.

**Best Practice**

The salt size should be 8 bytes or larger and the iteration count should be greater than zero. The minimum recommended number of iterations is 1000.

# Encrypting and decrypting data

There are multiple encryption algorithms you can choose from in .NET. Some algorithms are implemented by the operating system and their names are suffixed with the text `CryptoServiceProvider`, some are implemented in managed code and their names are suffixed with the text `Managed`, some use symmetric keys, and some use asymmetric keys. The following table summarizes some of the more common encryption algorithms:

| Type | Description |
|---|---|
| RSACryptoServiceProvider | This performs asymmetric encryption and decryption using the implementation of the RSA algorithm. RSA stands for Ron Rivest, Adi Shamir, and Leonard Adleman, who described it in 1978. |
| AesManaged | This provides a managed implementation of the **Advanced Encryption Standard** (**AES**) symmetric algorithm that is based on Rijndael. |
| RijndaelManaged | This provides a managed implementation of the Rijndael symmetric algorithm. |
| RC2CryptoServiceProvider | This defines a wrapper to access the **cryptographic service provider** (**CSP**) implementation of the RC2 symmetric algorithm. |
| DESCryptoServiceProvider | This defines a wrapper to access the CSP version of the **Data Encryption Standard** (**DES**) symmetric algorithm. |

**Best Practice**

Choose AES for symmetric encryption and RSA for asymmetric encryption.

# Encrypting symmetrically with AES

To make it easier to reuse your protection code in the future, we will create a static class named `Protector` in its own class library.

Start Microsoft Visual Studio 2015. In Visual Studio, press *Ctrl* + *Shift* + *N* or navigate to **File** | **New** | **Project**....

In the **New Project** dialog, in the **Installed Templates** list, select **Visual C#**. In the list at the center, select **Class Library**, type the name **Ch11_Cryptography**, change the location to `C:\Code`, type the solution name as **Chapter11**, and then click on **OK**.

Rename `Class1.cs` to `Protector.cs`. Change its contents to look like this:

```
using System;
using System.IO;
using System.Security.Cryptography;
using System.Text;

namespace Ch11_Cryptography
{
    public static class Protector
    {
        // salt size must be at least 8 bytes, we will use 16 bytes
        private static readonly byte[] salt = Encoding.Unicode.
GetBytes("7BANANAS");

        // iterations must be at least 1000, we will use 2000
        private static readonly int iterations = 2000;

        public static string Encrypt(string plainText, string
password)
        {
            byte[] plainBytes = Encoding.Unicode.GetBytes(plainText);
            var aes = Aes.Create();
            var pbkdf2 = new Rfc2898DeriveBytes(password, salt,
iterations);
            aes.Key = pbkdf2.GetBytes(32); // set a 256-bit key
            aes.IV = pbkdf2.GetBytes(16); // set a 128-bit IV
            var ms = new MemoryStream();
            using (var cs = new CryptoStream(ms, aes.
CreateEncryptor(), CryptoStreamMode.Write))
            {
                cs.Write(plainBytes, 0, plainBytes.Length);
            }
            return Convert.ToBase64String(ms.ToArray());
        }

        public static string Decrypt(string cryptoText, string
password)
        {
            byte[] cryptoBytes = Convert.FromBase64String(cryptoText);
            var aes = Aes.Create();
```

```
            var pbkdf2 = new Rfc2898DeriveBytes(password, salt,
iterations);
            aes.Key = pbkdf2.GetBytes(32);
            aes.IV = pbkdf2.GetBytes(16);
            var ms = new MemoryStream();
            using (var cs = new CryptoStream(ms, aes.
CreateDecryptor(), CryptoStreamMode.Write))
            {
                cs.Write(cryptoBytes, 0, cryptoBytes.Length);
            }
            return Encoding.Unicode.GetString(ms.ToArray());
        }
    }
}
```

Note the following about the preceding code:

- We used double the recommended salt size and iteration count
- Although the salt and iteration count can be hardcoded, the password *must* be passed at runtime when calling `Encrypt` and `Decrypt`
- We use a temporary `MemoryStream` variable to store the results of encrypting and decrypting and then call `ToArray` to turn the stream into a byte array
- We convert the encrypted byte arrays to and from the Base64 encoding to make them easier to read

**Best Practice**
Never hardcode a password in your source code because it can be read using ILDASM and other tools.

Add a new Console Application project named **Ch11_Encryption**. Add a reference to the **Ch11_Cryptography** assembly and then import the following namespaces:

```
using Ch11_Cryptography;
using static System.Console;
```

In the `Main` method, add the following statements to prompt the user for a message and a password and then encrypt and decrypt:

```
Write("Enter a message that you want to encrypt: ");
string message = ReadLine();
Write("Enter a password: ");
string password = ReadLine();
string cryptoText = Protector.Encrypt(message, password);
```

```
WriteLine($"Encrypted text: {cryptoText}");
string clearText = Protector.Decrypt(cryptoText, password);
WriteLine($"Decrypted text: {clearText}");
```

Run the application and try entering a message and password, and see the output.

```
Enter a message that you want to encrypt: Hello Bob

Enter a password: secret

Encrypted text: pV5qPDf1CCZmGzUMH2gapFSkn5731g7tMj5ajice3cQ=

Decrypted text: Hello Bob
```

# Hashing data

There are multiple hash algorithms you can choose from in .NET. Some do not use any key, some use symmetric keys, and some use asymmetric keys.

There are two important factors to consider when choosing a hash algorithm:

- **Collision resistance**: How rare is it to find two inputs that share the same hash?

- **Preimage resistance**: For a hash, how difficult would it be to find another input that shares the same hash?

Here are some common hashing algorithms:

| Algorithm | Hash size | Description |
|---|---|---|
| MD5 | 16 bytes | This is commonly used because it is fast, but it is not collision resistant. |
| SHA1, SHA256, SHA384, SHA512 | 20 bytes, 32 bytes, 48 bytes, 64 bytes | These are Secure Hashing Algorithm 2nd generation algorithms (SHA2) with different hash sizes. The use of SHA1 on the Internet has been deprecated since 2011. |

**Best Practice**

Avoid MD5 and SHA1 because they have known weaknesses. Choose a larger hash size to improve collision and preimage resistance.

# Hashing with SHA256

In the Ch11_Cryptography class library project, add a new class named User. This will represent a user stored in memory, a file, or a database.

```
public class User
{
    public string Name { get; set; }
    public string Salt { get; set; }
    public string SaltedHashedPassword { get; set; }
}
```

Add the following code to the Protector class. We will use a dictionary to store multiple users in memory. There are two methods, one to register a new user and one to validate their password when they subsequently log in.

```
public static Dictionary<string, User> Users = new Dictionary<string,
User>();

public static User Register(string username, string password)
{
    // generate a random salt
    var rng = RandomNumberGenerator.Create();
    var saltBytes = new byte[16];
    rng.GetBytes(saltBytes);
    var saltText = Convert.ToBase64String(saltBytes);

    // generate the salted and hashed password
    var sha = SHA256.Create();
    var saltedPassword = password + saltText;
    var saltedhashedPassword = Convert.ToBase64String(sha.
ComputeHash(Encoding.Unicode.GetBytes(saltedPassword)));

    var user = new User
    {
        Name = username,
        Salt = saltText,
        SaltedHashedPassword = saltedhashedPassword
    };
    Users.Add(user.Name, user);

    return user;
}
```

```
public static bool CheckPassword(string username, string password)
{
    if (!Users.ContainsKey(username))
    {
        return false;
    }
    var user = Users[username];

    // re-generate the salted and hashed password
    var sha = SHA256.Create();
    var saltedPassword = password + user.Salt;
    var saltedhashedPassword = Convert.ToBase64String(sha.
ComputeHash(Encoding.Unicode.GetBytes(saltedPassword)));

    return (saltedhashedPassword == user.SaltedHashedPassword);
}
```

Add a new Console Application project named **Ch11_Hashing**. Add a reference to the **Ch11_Cryptography** assembly and then import the following namespaces:

```
using Ch11_Cryptography;
using static System.Console;
```

In the `Main` method, add the following statements to register a user and prompt to register a second user, and then prompt to log in as one of those users and validate the password.

```
WriteLine("A user named Alice has been registered with Pa$$w0rd as her
password.");
var alice = Protector.Register("Alice", "Pa$$w0rd");
WriteLine($"Name: {alice.Name}");
WriteLine($"Salt: {alice.Salt}");
WriteLine($"Salted and hashed password: {alice.
SaltedHashedPassword}");
WriteLine();
Write("Enter a different username to register: ");
string username = ReadLine();
Write("Enter a password to register: ");
string password = ReadLine();
var user = Protector.Register(username, password);
WriteLine($"Name: {user.Name}");
WriteLine($"Salt: {user.Salt}");
WriteLine($"Salted and hashed password: {user.SaltedHashedPassword}");
```

```
bool correctPassword = false;
while (!correctPassword)
{
    Write("Enter a username to log in: ");
    string loginUsername = ReadLine();
    Write("Enter a password to log in: ");
    string loginPassword = ReadLine();
    correctPassword = Protector.CheckPassword(loginUsername,
loginPassword);
    if (correctPassword)
    {
        WriteLine($"Correct! {loginUsername} has been logged in.");
    }
    else
    {
        WriteLine("Invalid username or password. Try again.");
    }
}
```

Run the application by pressing *Ctrl* + *F5* and view the output:

```
A user named Alice has been registered with Pa$$w0rd as her password.
Name: Alice
Salt: tLn3gRn9DXmp2oeuvBSxTg==
Salted and hashed password: w8Ub2aH5NNQ8MJarYsUgm29bbb101V/9dlozjWs2Ipk=


Enter a different username to register: Bob
Enter a password to register: Pa$$w0rd
Name: Bob
Salt: zPU9YyFLaz0idhQkKpzY+g==
Salted and hashed password: 8w14w8WNHoZddEeIx2+UJhpHQqSs4Emyoazqjbmmez0=
Enter a username to log in: Bob
Enter a password to log in: secret
Invalid username or password. Try again.
Enter a username to log in: Alice
Enter a password to log in: secret
Invalid username or password. Try again.
Enter a username to log in: Bob
Enter a password to log in: Pa$$w0rd
Correct! Bob has been logged in.
```

Note that even if two users register with the same password, they have randomly generated salts so that their salted and hashed passwords are different.

# Signing data

To prove that some data has come from someone we trust, it can be signed. Actually, you don't sign the data itself, instead you sign a hash of the data. We will use the RSA algorithm combined with the SHA256 algorithm.

## Signing with SHA256 and RSA

In the **Ch11_Cryptography** class library project, add the following code to the Protector class:

```
public static string PublicKey;

public static string GenerateSignature(string data)
{
    byte[] dataBytes = Encoding.Unicode.GetBytes(data);
    var sha = SHA256.Create();
    var hashedData = sha.ComputeHash(dataBytes);

    var rsa = RSA.Create();
    PublicKey = rsa.ToXmlString(false); // exclude private key

    var signer = new RSAPKCS1SignatureFormatter(rsa);
    signer.SetHashAlgorithm("SHA256");

    return Convert.ToBase64String(signer.CreateSignature(hashedData));
}

public static bool ValidateSignature(string data, string signature)
{
    byte[] dataBytes = Encoding.Unicode.GetBytes(data);
    var sha = SHA256.Create();
    var hashedData = sha.ComputeHash(dataBytes);

    byte[] signatureBytes = Convert.FromBase64String(signature);

    var rsa = RSA.Create();
    rsa.FromXmlString(PublicKey);

    var checker = new RSAPKCS1SignatureDeformatter(rsa);
    checker.SetHashAlgorithm("SHA256");

    return checker.VerifySignature(hashedData, signatureBytes);
}
```

Note the following about the preceding code:

- Only the public part of the public-private key pair needs to be made available to the code that is checking the signature, so we can pass the value `false` when we call the `ToXmlString` method.

- The hash algorithm used to generate the hash from the data must match the hash algorithm set on the signer and checker. In the preceding code, we used SHA256.

Add a new Console Application project named **Ch11_Signing**. Add a reference to the **Ch11_Cryptography** assembly, and then import the following namespaces:

```
using static System.Console;
using Ch11_Cryptography;
```

In the `Main` method, add the following code:

```
Write("Enter some text to sign: ");
string data = ReadLine();
var signature = Protector.GenerateSignature(data);
WriteLine($"Signature: {signature}");
WriteLine("Public key used to check signature:");
WriteLine(Protector.PublicKey);

if (Protector.ValidateSignature(data, signature))
{
    WriteLine("Correct! Signature is valid.");
}
else
{
    WriteLine("Invalid signature.");
}
```

Run the application and enter some text:

```
Enter some text to sign: The cat sat on the mat.

Signature: LSmfgRuRRvYzM1/jg7U7jkKINCU4KKGpFUCvCB87hmWpa3gDVLjLj0Wift+
CktZuPSkc/gAnIzC1bQCOyELsrNWzATnPDFa/B0Gpy0vAJ8VJ9FPs1vFy353mMnGcnQU8
fOummKgEv4r1JpsnkJQ41MGUMNCH9YVod06Bn6o81g0=

Public key used to check signature:

<RSAKeyValue><Modulus>qPnY4UHIqJMuUJ0CQ4F0Xy/fxaugNFFe/QNikGsufdKr
walt+CcQqCmWso4zUDW3NTFCWFGilisJ4SqTBgYee/VT9UGuFng68TrZXNiNJO8dP
8OZHNBirWkhtsNQx9A6rq9bZ/9dsjY1hYsWpGKCw4WhxsHjmGuevQew8C+I2z0=</
Modulus><Exponent>AQAB</Exponent></RSAKeyValue>

Correct! Signature is valid.
```

# Authenticating and authorizing users

Authentication is the process of discovering and verifying the identity of a user by validating their credentials against some authority.

There are multiple authentication mechanisms to choose from. They all implement a pair of interfaces: `IIdentity` and `IPrincipal`. The most common mechanism is Windows authentication.

 You can implement your own authentication mechanism using the `GenericIdentity` and `GenericPrincipal` classes, but that is beyond the scope of this book.

## Managing local accounts

For testing purposes, we will create a new local user account.

In the Windows 10 Start Menu, navigate to **Settings | Accounts | Family and other users**. In the **Other users** section, click on **Add someone else to this PC**, as shown in the following screenshot:

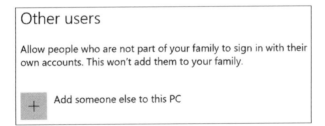

In the **How will this person sign in?** step, click on **The person who I want to add doesn't have an email address**. In the **Let's create an account** step, click on **Add a user without a Microsoft account**.

In the **Create an account for this PC** step, enter AliceJones for the username and Pa$$w0rd for the password, and then click **Next**.

# Authenticating with Windows

Add a new Console Application project named **Ch11_Authentication**. Import the following namespaces:

```
using System;
using System.Security.Permissions;
using System.Security.Principal;
using static System.Console;
```

In the Main method, add the following statements:

```
var user = new WindowsPrincipal(WindowsIdentity.GetCurrent());
WriteLine($"Name: {user.Identity.Name}");
WriteLine($"IsAuthenticated: {user.Identity.IsAuthenticated}");
WriteLine($"AuthenticationType: {user.Identity.AuthenticationType}");
ReadLine(); // keep the application running
```

Run the application. The name of my computer is DARKMATTER, and I am currently logged on to Windows 10 using my linked MSN account, so this is what I see:

```
Name: DARKMATTER\markjprice

IsAuthenticated: True

AuthenticationType: CloudAP
```

In the Windows 10 start menu, click on your username, and then click on **AliceJones**.

Enter **Pa$$w0rd** and wait for the new user to be set up. It should only take a minute or two. Use File Explorer to open the `C:\Code\Chapter11\Ch11_Authentication\bin\Debug` folder and then double-click on the `Ch11_Authentication.exe` file to run it. You will see the following output:

```
Name: DARKMATTER\AliceJones

IsAuthenticated: True

AuthenticationType: NTLM
```

Note that local users are authenticated with **NTLM** (which meant **New Technology LAN Manager** back in the 1990s).

Switch back to your own account by clicking on the username on the start menu.

# Authorizing with Windows

Authorization is usually a check to ensure that the current user belongs to a role or group.

In the `Main` method, add the following statements:

```
// to check if the current user belongs to a specific role
WriteLine($"Is in Administrators group? {user.
IsInRole("Administrators")}");
WriteLine($"Is in Users group? {user.IsInRole("Users")}");
WriteLine($"Is in Sales group? {user.IsInRole("Sales")}");
WriteLine();
WriteLine($"{user.Identity.Name} belongs to these roles/groups:");
foreach (var claim in user.Claims)
{
    if(claim.Type == "http://schemas.microsoft.com/ws/2008/06/
identity/claims/groupsid")
    {
        WriteLine($"{claim.Value}: {(new SecurityIdentifier(claim.
Value)).Translate(typeof(NTAccount)).Value}");
    }
}
```

Note that the roles/groups that a user belongs to are stored in the user's `Claims` collection as security identifier strings (SIDs) using a `Type` of `groupsid`, for example, a Group SID of S-1-5-32-545 means the User's group. To see the group name, we have to translate the SID into an `NTAccount` object.

Run the application by pressing *Ctrl + F5* and view the output:

```
Is in Administrators group? False

Is in Users group? True

Is in Sales group? False


DARKMATTER\markjprice belongs to these roles/groups:

S-1-1-0: Everyone

S-1-5-32-559: BUILTIN\Performance Log Users

S-1-5-32-545: BUILTIN\Users

S-1-5-4: NT AUTHORITY\INTERACTIVE

S-1-2-1: CONSOLE LOGON

S-1-5-11: NT AUTHORITY\Authenticated Users

S-1-5-15: NT AUTHORITY\This Organization
```

S-1-11-96-3623454863-58364-18864-2661722203-1597581903-1800426060-
9997179511-9995030342-2042432011-970967485: MicrosoftAccount\markjprice@
msn.com

S-1-5-113: NT AUTHORITY\Local account

S-1-2-0: LOCAL

S-1-5-64-36: NT AUTHORITY\Cloud Account Authentication

You can use either statements or attributes to prevent the current user from accessing parts of your application.

Add the following method to the Program class. Note that the attribute demands that the current user be in the role named Users. If they are not, then a SecurityException will be thrown.

```
[PrincipalPermission(SecurityAction.Demand, Role = "Users")]
public static void SecureFeature()
{
    WriteLine("This is a secure feature!");
}
```

Add the following statements to the bottom of the Main method. Note that we must set the principal policy to ensure that the current thread knows about the current user in order for the PrincipalPermission attribute to work correctly. This only has to be done once, so it is usually executed as the first statement in a Main method.

```
if(user.IsInRole("Users"))
{
    WriteLine("You are in the role so you are allowed access to this
feature.");
}
else
{
    WriteLine("You are NOT in the role so you are banned from this
feature.");
}
// copy the current user principal to the current thread
AppDomain.CurrentDomain.SetPrincipalPolicy(PrincipalPolicy.
WindowsPrincipal);
try
{
    SecureFeature();
}
catch(Exception ex)
{
    WriteLine($"{ex.GetType()}: {ex.Message}");
}
```

Run the application and view the output:

```
You are in the role so you are allowed access to this feature.
This is a secure feature!
```

Change the role name to `Administrators` in the `if` statement and the attribute, and then rerun the application:

```
You are NOT in the role so you are banned from this feature.
System.Security.SecurityException: Request for principal permission
failed.
```

Unfortunately, the `string` for the `Role` in the `PrincipalPermission` attribute must be a literal value, so it cannot reference a variable.

**Best Practice**
Use the `IsInRole` method to check whether the current user is authorized to access a feature of your application rather than the `PrincipalPermission` attribute.

# Practicing and exploring

Test your knowledge and understanding by answering some questions, get some hands-on practice, and explore the topics covered in this chapter with deeper research.

# Exercise 11.1 – test your knowledge

Answer the following questions:

1. Of the encryption algorithms provided by .NET, which is the best choice for symmetric encryption?

2. Of the encryption algorithms provided by .NET, which is the best choice for asymmetric encryption?

3. For encryption algorithms, is it better to have a larger or smaller block size?

# Exercise 11.2 – practice protecting data with encryption and hashing

Create a console application named **Ch11_Exercise02** that protects an XML file similar to the following code. Note that the customer record credit card number and password are currently stored in clear text. The credit card must be encrypted so that it can be decrypted and used later, and the password must be salted and hashed:

```xml
<?xml version="1.0" encoding="utf-8" ?>
<customers>
  <customer>
    <name>Bob Smith</name>
    <creditcard>1234-5678-9012-3456</creditcard>
    <password>Pa$$w0rd</password>
  </customer>
</customers>
```

# Exercise 11.3 – practice protecting data with decryption

Create a console application named **Ch11_Exercise03** that opens the XML file that you protected in the preceding code and decrypts the credit card number.

# Exercise 11.4 – explore topics

Use the following links to read more about the topics covered in this chapter:

- **Key Security Concepts**: https://msdn.microsoft.com/en-us/library/z164t8hs(v=vs.110).aspx

- **Encrypting Data**: https://msdn.microsoft.com/en-us/library/as0w18af(v=vs.110).aspx

- **Cryptographic Signatures**: https://msdn.microsoft.com/en-us/library/hk8wx38z(v=vs.110).aspx

- **How to: Create GenericPrincipal and GenericIdentity Objects**: https://msdn.microsoft.com/en-us/library/y9dd5fx0(v=vs.110).aspx

# Summary

In this chapter, you learned how to encrypt and decrypt using symmetric encryption, how to generate a salted hash, how to find out who is running the application, and how to check that the user running the application is allowed to access a feature of the application.

In the next chapter, you will use the `Task` type to improve the performance of your applications.

# 12

# Improving Performance and Scalability with Multitasking

This chapter is about allowing multiple actions to occur at the same time to improve performance, scalability, and user productivity.

In this chapter, we will cover the following topics:

- Understanding processes and threads
- Running tasks asynchronously
- The async and await keywords
- Synchronizing access to shared resources

## Understanding processes and threads

A process, like each of the console applications we have created, has resources allocated to it, such as memory and threads. A thread executes your code, statement by statement.

Windows uses pre-emptive multitasking, which simulates the parallel execution of tasks. It divides the processor time among the threads, allocating a "time slice" to each thread, one after another. The current thread is suspended when its time slice finishes. The processor allows another thread to run for a time slice.

When Windows switches from one thread to another, it saves the context of the thread and reloads the previously saved context of the next thread in the thread queue.

Most modern operating systems work the same as Windows, and are known as pre-emptive multitasking OSes.

By default, each process only has one thread, and this can cause problems when we need to do more than one thing at the same time.

# Running tasks asynchronously

First, we will write a simple console application that needs to execute three actions.

## Running multiple actions synchronously

Start Microsoft Visual Studio 2015. In Visual Studio, press *Ctrl* + *Shift* + *N* or go to **File** | **New** | **Project…**.

In the **New Project** dialog, in the **Installed Templates** list, select **Visual C#**. In the center list, select **Console Application**, type the name as **Ch12_Tasks**, change the location to C:\Code, type the solution name as **Chapter12**, and then click on **OK**.

Ensure that the following namespaces have been imported:

```
using System;
using System.Threading;
using System.Threading.Tasks;
using System.Diagnostics;
using static System.Console;
```

In the Program class, add the following code. There are three methods that need to be executed: the first takes three seconds, the second takes two seconds, and the third takes one second. To simulate work, we can use the Thread class to tell the current thread to go to sleep for a specified number of milliseconds:

```
static void MethodA()
{
    WriteLine("Starting Method A...");
    Thread.Sleep(3000); // simulate three seconds of work
    WriteLine("Finished Method A.");
}
static void MethodB()
{
    WriteLine("Starting Method B...");
    Thread.Sleep(2000); // simulate two seconds of work
    WriteLine("Finished Method B.");
}
```

```
static void MethodC()
{
    WriteLine("Starting Method C...");
    Thread.Sleep(1000); // simulate one second of work
    WriteLine("Finished Method C.");
}
```

In the `Main` method, add the following statements:

```
static void Main(string[] args)
{
    var timer = Stopwatch.StartNew();
    WriteLine("Running methods synchronously on one thread.");
    MethodA();
    MethodB();
    MethodC();
    WriteLine($"{timer.ElapsedMilliseconds:#,##0}ms elapsed.");
    WriteLine("Press ENTER to end.");
    ReadLine();
}
```

Run the application by pressing *Ctrl + F5* and view the output. Since there is only one thread, the total time required is just over six seconds.

```
Running methods synchronously on one thread.
Starting Method A...
Finished Method A.
Starting Method B...
Finished Method B.
Starting Method C...
Finished Method C.
6,047ms elapsed.
Press ENTER to end.
```

# Running multiple actions asynchronously using tasks

The `Thread` class has been available since the first version of C#, but it can be tricky to work with directly. C# 4 introduced the `Task` class, which is a wrapper around a thread that enables easier management. Creating multiple threads wrapped in tasks will allow our code to execute asynchronously (at the same time).

We will look at three ways to start the methods using `Task` instances. Each has a slightly different syntax, but they all define a task and start it. Comment out the calls to the three methods and the associated console message, and then add the highlighted statements in the following code:

```
static void Main(string[] args)
{
    var timer = Stopwatch.StartNew();
    //WriteLine("Running methods synchronously on one thread.");
    //MethodA();
    //MethodB();
    //MethodC();
    WriteLine("Running methods asynchronously on multiple threads.");
    var taskA = new Task(MethodA);
    taskA.Start();
    var taskB = Task.Factory.StartNew(MethodB);
    var taskC = Task.Run(new Action(MethodC));
    WriteLine($"{timer.ElapsedMilliseconds:#,##0}ms elapsed.");
    WriteLine("Press ENTER to end.");
    ReadLine();
}
```

Rerun the application by pressing *Ctrl + F5* and view the output.

The actual elapsed milliseconds will depend on the performance of your CPU, so you are likely to see a different value than shown in the following example output:

```
Running methods asynchronously on multiple threads.
10 milliseconds elapsed.
Press ENTER to end.
Starting Method C...
Starting Method A...
Starting Method B...
Finished Method C.
Finished Method B.
Finished Method A.
```

Notice that the stopwatch displays the elapsed time almost immediately, because each of the three methods are now being executed by three new threads. The original thread continues executing until it reaches the `ReadLine` call at the end of the `Main` method.

Meanwhile, the three new threads execute their code in parallel, and they start in any order. MethodC will usually finish first, because it takes only one second, then MethodB, and finally MethodA, because it takes three seconds.

However, the actual CPU used has a big effect on the results. It is the CPU that allocates time slices to each process to allow them to execute their threads. You have little control over when the methods run.

# Waiting for tasks

Sometimes you need to wait for a task to complete before continuing. To do this, you can use the Wait method on a Task instance, or the WaitAll or WaitAny method on an array of Task instances, as shown in the following table:

| Method | Description |
|---|---|
| Wait | Waits for this instance of the task to complete execution |
| WaitAny | Waits for any of the provided task objects to complete execution |
| WaitAll | Waits for all of the provided task objects to complete execution |

Add the following statements to the Main method immediately after creating the three tasks. This will combine references to the three tasks into an array and pass them to the WaitAll method. Now, the original thread will pause on that statement, waiting for all three tasks to finish before outputting the elapsed time:

```
Task[] tasks = { taskA, taskB, taskC };
Task.WaitAll(tasks);
```

Rerun the application by pressing *Ctrl* + *F5* and view the output:

```
Running methods asynchronously on multiple threads.

Starting Method B...

Starting Method C...

Starting Method A...

Finished Method C.

Finished Method B.

Finished Method A.

3,024 milliseconds elapsed.

Press ENTER to end.
```

Note that the total time is now slightly more than the time to run the longest method. If all three tasks can be performed at the same time, then this would be all we need to do.

However, often, a task is dependent on the output from another task. To handle this scenario, we need to define **continuation tasks**.

# Continuing with another task

Add the following methods to the `Program` class:

```
static decimal CallWebService()
{
    WriteLine("Starting call to web service...");
    Thread.Sleep((new Random()).Next(2000, 4000));
    WriteLine("Finished call to web service.");
    return 89.99M;
}
static string CallStoredProcedure(decimal amount)
{
    WriteLine("Starting call to stored procedure...");
    Thread.Sleep((new Random()).Next(2000, 4000));
    WriteLine("Finished call to stored procedure.");
    return $"12 products cost more than {amount:C}.";
}
```

These methods simulate a call to a web service, that returns a monetary amount that then needs to be used to retrieve how many products cost more than that amount in a database. The result returned from the first method needs to be fed into the input of the second method.

 I have used the `Random` class to wait for a random interval of between two and four seconds for each method.

Inside the `Main` method, comment out the previous tasks by highlighting the statements and pressing *Ctrl + K, C*. Then, add the following statements before the existing statement that outputs the total time elapsed and then calls `ReadLine` to wait for the user to press *Enter*:

```
WriteLine("Passing the result of one task as an input into another.");
var taskCallWebServiceAndThenStoredProcedure =
Task.Factory.StartNew(CallWebService)
    .ContinueWith(previousTask =>
CallStoredProcedure(previousTask.Result));
WriteLine($"{taskCallWebServiceAndThenStoredProcedure.Result}");
```

Run the application by pressing *Ctrl + F5* and view the output:

```
Passing the result of one task as an input into another.
Starting call to web service...
Finished call to web service.
Starting call to stored procedure...
Finished call to stored procedure.
12 products cost more than £89.99.
5,971 milliseconds elapsed.
Press ENTER to end.
```

# Nested and child tasks

Add a new console application project named **Ch12_NestedAndChildTasks**. In the solution's **Properties**, remember to change the **Startup Project** to **Current selection**.

Ensure the following namespaces have been imported:

```
using System;
using System.Threading;
using System.Threading.Tasks;
using System.Diagnostics;
using static System.Console;
```

Inside the Main method, add the following statements:

```
var outer = Task.Factory.StartNew(() =>
{
    WriteLine("Outer task starting...");
    var inner = Task.Factory.StartNew(() =>
    {
        WriteLine("Inner task starting...");
        Thread.Sleep(2000);
        WriteLine("Inner task finished.");
    });
});
outer.Wait();
WriteLine("Outer task finished.");
ReadLine();
```

Run the application by pressing *Ctrl + F5* and view the output:

```
Outer task starting...
Outer task finished.
Inner task starting...
Inner task finished.
```

Notice that although we wait for the outer task to finish, its inner task does not have to finish as well. To link the two tasks, we must use a special option.

Modify the code that defines the inner task to add `TaskCreationOption` of `AttachedToParent`:

```
var inner = Task.Factory.StartNew(() =>
{
    WriteLine("Inner task starting...");
    Thread.Sleep(2000);
    WriteLine("Inner task finished.");
}, TaskCreationOptions.AttachedToParent);
```

Rerun the application by pressing *Ctrl + F5*. Notice that the inner task must finish before the outer task is allowed to:

```
Outer task starting...
Inner task starting...
Inner task finished.
Outer task finished.
```

# The async and await keywords

C# 5 introduced two new keywords to simplify working with the `Task` type. They are especially useful when multitasking with graphical user interfaces.

## Creating a GUI that blocks

In Visual Studio, go to **File** | **Add** | **New Project....** In the **Add New Project** dialog, in the **Installed Templates** list, select **Visual C#**. In the center list, select **WPF Application**, type the name as **Ch12_GUITasks**, and then click on **OK**.

We will use a WPF application because these can be created on versions of Windows older than 10. In *Chapter 13, Building Universal Windows Platform Apps Using XAML*, you will learn about modern Windows apps. However, these can only be created on Windows 10. Obviously, Windows applications of *any* sort are not cross-platform, so they cannot be executed by the .NET Core!

You will learn more about XAML in the next chapter, but for now, just enter the following code in the XAML view inside the `<Grid>` element:

```
<StackPanel>
    <Button Name="GetProductsButton">Get Products</Button>
    <TextBox>Type in here while the products load...</TextBox>
    <ListBox Name="ProductsListBox"></ListBox>
</StackPanel>
```

Your main editor window should now look like this:

Inside the `Button` element, after setting the `Name`, enter an attribute named `Click`, as shown in the following screenshot, and when the IntelliSense appears, press *Enter* to insert a new event handler:

```
<Grid>
    <StackPanel>                              [≡] <New Event Handler>
        <Button Name="GetProductsButton" Click="">Get Products</Button>
        <TextBox>Type in here while the products load...</TextBox>
```

Choose the **View** | **Code** menu or press *F7*. Add the following code to the top of the code file:

```
using System.Data.SqlClient;
```

Add the following code inside the `GetProductsButton_Click` method.

Note the following:

- The database connection string uses Microsoft SQL Server LocalDb and connects to the Northwind sample database
- The SQL statement waits for five seconds before returning four columns from the `Products` table

```
var connection = new SqlConnection(@"Data Source=(localdb)\
mssqllocaldb;Initial Catalog=Northwind;Integrated Security=true;");
connection.Open();
var getProducts = new SqlCommand("WAITFOR DELAY '00:00:05';SELECT
ProductID, ProductName, UnitPrice FROM Products", connection);
SqlDataReader reader = getProducts.ExecuteReader();
int indexOfID = reader.GetOrdinal("ProductID");
int indexOfName = reader.GetOrdinal("ProductName");
int indexOfPrice = reader.GetOrdinal("UnitPrice");
while (reader.Read())
{
    ProductsListBox.Items.Add($"{reader.GetInt32(indexOfID)}: {reader.
GetString(indexOfName)} costs {reader.GetDecimal(indexOfPrice):C}");
}
reader.Dispose();
connection.Dispose();
```

Run the application by pressing *Ctrl + F5*.

Click inside the text box and enter some text. The user interface is responsive. Click on the **Get Products** button and then try to enter some text in the text box. The user interface is blocked because the thread is busy running the SQL command:

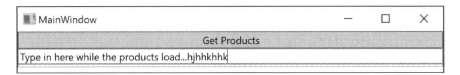

# Creating a GUI that doesn't block

The types in the `SqlClient` namespace have been improved in .NET Framework 4.5 and later by giving any method that might take a long time an asynchronous equivalent that returns a `Task`.

For example, the `SqlConnection` class has both an `Open` method, that returns void, and an `OpenAsync` method, that returns `Task`. `SqlCommand` has both an `ExecuteReader` method, that returns `SqlDataReader`, and an `ExecuteReaderAsync` method, that returns `Task<SqlDataReader>`.

We can use these `Task` objects as we did earlier, but that would still block the user interface when we call any of the `Wait` methods.

Instead we can use `await` keyword for any `Task`. This means that the main thread will not be blocked while we wait, but will remember its current position within the statements so that once the `Task` has completed, the main thread continues executing from that same point. This allows us to write code that looks as simple as synchronous, but underneath, it is actually much more complex.

 Internally, `await` creates a state machine to manage the complexity of passing state between any worker threads and the user interface thread.

Modify the code like this. Notice that to use the `await` keyword, we must mark any method that contains `await` with the `async` keyword. They always work as a pair:

```
private async void GetProductsButton_Click(object sender,
RoutedEventArgs e)
{
    var connection = new SqlConnection(@"Data Source=(localdb)\
mssqllocaldb;Initial Catalog=Northwind;Integrated Security=true;");
    await connection.OpenAsync();
```

```
    var getProducts = new SqlCommand("WAITFOR DELAY '00:00:05';SELECT
ProductID, ProductName, UnitPrice FROM Products", connection);
    SqlDataReader reader = await getProducts.ExecuteReaderAsync();
    int indexOfID = reader.GetOrdinal("ProductID");
    int indexOfName = reader.GetOrdinal("ProductName");
    int indexOfPrice = reader.GetOrdinal("UnitPrice");
    while (await reader.ReadAsync())
    {
        ProductsListBox.Items.Add($"{await reader.GetFieldValueAsync
<int>(indexOfID)}: {await reader.GetFieldValueAsync<string>(indexOf
Name)} costs {await reader.GetFieldValueAsync<decimal>(indexOfPrice)
:C}");
    }
    reader.Dispose();
    connection.Dispose();
}
```

Run the application by pressing *Ctrl* + *F5*.

This time, after clicking on the **Get Products** button, you will be able to enter text in the text box while the command executes:

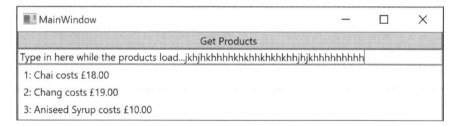

## Other types with Async methods

Here are some of the other types that have asynchronous method support:

| Class | Methods |
|-------|---------|
| HttpClient | GetAsync, PostAsync, PutAsync, DeleteAsync, SendAsync |
| StreamReader | ReadAsync, ReadLineAsync, ReadToEndAsync |
| StreamWriter | WriteAsync, WriteLineAsync, FlushAsync. |
| SOAP service clients | When you generate a proxy to a SOAP service using Visual Studio's Add Service Reference dialog or the svcutil.exe command-line tool, the class created can include Async methods for the service operations |

Any time you see a method that ends in the suffix `Async`, check to see whether it returns `Task` or `Task<T>`. If it does, then you can call it using `await` if you mark your method using `async`.

## await in catch blocks

In C# 5, it was only possible to use the `await` keyword in a `try` exception handling block, but not in a `catch` block.

In C# 6, it is now possible to use `await` in both `try` and `catch` blocks.

# Improving scalability for client-server applications

In the previous example, we saw how using the `async` and `await` keywords can improve the performance of a client-side graphical application by preventing the blocking of the user interface thread.

The same keywords can be applied on the server-side when building web applications and services. From the client application's point of view, nothing changes (or they might even notice a small increase in the time for a request to return). So, from a single client's point of view, the use of `async` on the server side makes their experience worse!

On the server-side, additional, cheaper worker threads are created to wait for long-running tasks to finish so that expensive I/O threads can handle other clients' requests instead of being blocked. This improves the overall scalability of a web application or service. More clients can be supported simultaneously.

You will create asynchronous operations on the server-side in *Chapter 14, Building Web Applications and Services Using ASP.NET Core*.

# Synchronizing access to shared resources

When you have multiple threads executing at the same time, there is a possibility that two or more threads may access the same variable or other resource at the same time and cause a problem.

For this reason, you should carefully consider how to make your code "thread safe".

The simplest mechanism for implementing thread safety is to use an object variable as a "flag" or "traffic light" to indicate when a shared resource has an exclusive lock applied.

 In William Golding's *Lord of the Flies*, Piggy and Ralph spot a conch shell and use it to call a meeting. The boys impose a "rule of the conch" on themselves, deciding that no one can speak unless he's holding the conch. I like to name the object variable I use the "conch". When a thread has the conch, no other thread can access the shared resource(s) represented by that conch.

# Accessing a resource from multiple threads

In Visual Studio, go to **File | Add | New Project...**. In the **Add New Project** dialog, in the **Installed Templates** list, select **Visual C#**. In the center list, select **Console Application**, type the name as **Ch12_LockAndMonitor**, and then click on **OK**.

Modify the Program class to:

- Declare and instantiate an object to generate random wait times

- Declare a string variable to store a message (this will be the shared resource)

- Declare two methods that add a letter, A or B, to the shared string five times in a loop, and wait for a random interval of up to two seconds for each iteration

- A Main method that starts both methods on separate threads using a pair of tasks and waits for them to complete before outputting the elapsed milliseconds they took:

```
using static System.Console;
using System.Threading;
using System.Threading.Tasks;
using System;
using System.Diagnostics;

namespace Ch12_LockAndMonitor
{
    class Program
    {
        static Random r = new Random();
        static string Message; // a shared resource
```

```
static void MethodA()
{
    for (int i = 0; i < 5; i++)
    {
        Thread.Sleep(r.Next(2000));
        Message += "A";
        Write(".");
    }
}

static void MethodB()
{
    for (int i = 0; i < 5; i++)
    {
        Thread.Sleep(r.Next(2000));
        Message += "B";
        Write(".");
    }
}

static void Main(string[] args)
{
    WriteLine("Please wait for the tasks to complete.");
    Stopwatch watch = Stopwatch.StartNew();

    Task a = Task.Factory.StartNew(MethodA);
    Task b = Task.Factory.StartNew(MethodB);

    Task.WaitAll(new Task[] { a, b });
    WriteLine();
    WriteLine($"Results: {Message}.");
    WriteLine($"{watch.ElapsedMilliseconds:#,##0} elapsed
milliseconds.");
    }
        }
    }
```

Press *Ctrl + F5* to run the application and view the output:

```
Please wait for the tasks to complete.
..........
Results: BABBABBAAA.
6,099 elapsed milliseconds.
```

Notice that the results show that both threads were modifying the message concurrently. In an actual application, this could be a problem. We could prevent concurrent access by using a mutually exclusive lock or conch.

# Applying a mutually exclusive lock to a resource

In the `Program` class, define an object variable for the conch:

```
static object conch = new object();
```

In both the methods, add a `lock` statement around the `for` statement:

```
lock (conch)
{
    for (int i = 0; i < 5; i++)
    {
        Thread.Sleep(r.Next(2000));
        Message += "A";
        Write(".");
    }
}
```

Press *Ctrl* + *F5* and view the output:

**Please wait for the tasks to complete.**

**. . . . . . . . . .**

**Results: AAAAABBBBB.**

**9,751 elapsed milliseconds.**

Notice that although the time elapsed was longer, only one method at a time could access the shared resource.

# Understanding the lock statement

The compiler changes this:

```
lock (conch)
{
    // access shared resource
}
```

Into this:

```
try
{
    Monitor.Enter(conch);
    // access shared resource
}
finally
{
    Monitor.Exit(conch);
}
```

Knowing how the `lock` statement works internally is important because using the `lock` statement can cause a deadlock.

Deadlocks occur when there are two or more shared resources (and therefore conches), and the following sequence of events happens:

- Thread X locks conch A
- Thread Y locks conch B
- Thread X attempts to lock conch B, but is blocked because thread Y already has it
- Thread Y attempts to lock conch A, but is blocked because thread X already has it

A proven way to prevent deadlocks is to specify a timeout when attempting to get a lock. To do this, you must manually use the `Monitor` class instead of using the `lock` statement.

Modify your code to replace the `lock` statements with code that tries to enter the conch with a timeout like this:

```
try
{
    Monitor.TryEnter(conch, TimeSpan.FromSeconds(15));
    for (int i = 0; i < 5; i++)
    {
        Thread.Sleep(r.Next(2000));
        Message += "A";
        Write(".");
    }
}
finally
{
    Monitor.Exit(conch);
}
```

Press *Ctrl* + *F5* and view the output. It should be the same as before.

# Making operations atomic

Look at the following increment operation:

```
int x = 3;
x++;
```

It is not atomic! Incrementing an integer requires three CPU operations:

- Load a value from an instance variable into a register
- Increment the value
- Store the value back into the instance variable

A thread could be pre-empted after executing the first two steps. A second thread could then execute all three steps. When the first thread resumes execution, it would overwrite the value in the variable, and the effect of the increment or decrement performed by the second thread would be lost!

Declare another shared resource that will count how many operations have occurred:

```
static int Counter; // another shared resource
```

In both methods, add the following statement to safely increment the counter:

```
Interlocked.Increment(ref Counter);
```

After outputting the elapsed time, output the counter:

```
WriteLine($"{Counter} string modifications.");
```

Press *Ctrl* + *F5* and view the output:

```
10 string modications.
```

# Applying other types of synchronization

The `Monitor` and `Interlocked` mutually exclusive locks are simple and effective, but sometimes, you need more advanced options to synchronize access to shared resources, as shown in the following table:

| Type | Description |
|---|---|
| ReaderWriterLock and ReaderWriterLockSlim (recommended) | Allows multiple threads to be in the shared read mode, allows one thread to be in the write mode with exclusive ownership of the lock, and allows one thread that has read access to be in the upgradeable read mode, from which the thread can upgrade to the write mode without having to relinquish its read access to the resource |

| Type | Description |
|------|-------------|
| `Mutex` | Similar to Monitor in that it provides exclusive access to a shared resource, except when it is used for inter-process synchronization |
| `Semaphore` and `SemaphoreSlim` | Limits the number of threads that can access a resource or pool of resources concurrently |
| `AutoResetEvent` and `ManualResetEvent` | Event wait handles allow threads to synchronize activities by signaling each other and by waiting for each other's signals |

# Practicing and exploring

Test your knowledge and understanding by answering some questions, get some hands-on practice, and explore this chapter's topics with deeper research.

## Exercise 12.1 – test your knowledge

Answer the following questions:

1. By convention, what suffix should be applied to a method that returns `Task` or `Task<T>`?

2. To use the `await` keyword inside a method, what keyword must be applied to the method declaration?

3. How do you create a child task?

4. Why should you avoid the `lock` keyword?

5. When should you use the `Interlocked` class?

## Exercise 12.2 – explore topics

Use the following links to read more about this chapter's topics:

- **Threads and threading**: `https://msdn.microsoft.com/en-us/library/6kac2kdh(v=vs.110).aspx`

- **Task parallelism (task parallel library)**: `https://msdn.microsoft.com/en-us/library/dd537609(v=vs.110).aspx`

- **await (C# reference)**: `https://msdn.microsoft.com/en-GB/library/hh156528.aspx`

- **Asynchronous Programming with Async and Await (C# and Visual Basic)**: `https://msdn.microsoft.com/en-us/library/vstudio/hh191443.aspx`

- **Interlocked Operations**: https://msdn.microsoft.com/en-us/library/sbhbke0y(v=vs.110).aspx

- **EventWaitHandle, AutoResetEvent, CountdownEvent, ManualResetEvent**: https://msdn.microsoft.com/en-us/library/ksb7zs2x(v=vs.110).aspx

# Summary

In this chapter, you learned how to define and start a task, how to wait for one or more tasks to finish, and how to control task completion order. You also learned how to use `async` and `await` to prevent the user interface thread from being blocked, and how to synchronize access to shared resources.

In the next chapter, you will learn how to create apps for the Universal Windows Platform.

# 13
# Building Universal Windows Platform Apps Using XAML

This chapter is about seeing what can be achieved with XAML when defining the user interface for a graphical app, in particular, for the **Universal Windows Platform** (**UWP**).

In a single chapter, we will only be able to scratch the surface of everything that can be done with UWP. However, I hope to excite you into wanting to learn more about this cool technology and platform.

Think of this chapter as a whistle-stop tour of the coolest parts of UWP and XAML, including template-able controls, data binding, and animation!

 UWP apps are not cross-platform, but they are cross-device, if those devices run a modern flavor of Windows. You will need Windows 10 to create the examples in this chapter.

In this chapter, we will cover the following topics:

- Understanding the UWP
- Understanding XAML
- Creating a Windows Desktop Application using WPF
- Creating an app for the UWP
- Using resources and templates
- Data binding
- Animating with storyboards
- Testing in emulators

# Understanding the UWP

The UWP is Microsoft's latest technology solution to build applications for its Windows suite of operating systems.

UWP provides a guaranteed API layer across multiple device types. You can create a single app package that can be uploaded to a single Windows Store to be distributed to reach all the device types your app can run on. These devices include Windows 10, Windows 10 Mobile, Xbox One, and Microsoft HoloLens.

# Adapting your app's layout

XAML and UWP provide layout panels that adapt how they display their child controls to make the most of the device they are currently running on. It is the Windows app equivalent of web page responsive design.

XAML and UWP provide visual state triggers to alter the layout, based on dynamic changes such as the horizontal or vertical orientation of a tablet.

# Taking advantage of unique device capabilities

UWP provides standard mechanisms to detect the capabilities of the current device and then activate additional features of your app to fully take advantage of them.

# Understanding XAML

**XAML** can be used to create:

- UWP apps for Windows 10
- Windows Store apps for Windows 8 and 8.1
- **Windows Presentation Foundation** (**WPF**) applications for the Windows desktop, including Windows 7 and later
- Silverlight applications for web browsers, Windows Phone, and desktop

 Although Silverlight is still supported by Microsoft, it is not being actively developed, so it should be avoided.

# Simplifying code using XAML

XAML simplifies C# code, especially when building a user interface.

Imagine that you need two or more buttons laid out horizontally to create a toolbar. In C#, you would write this code:

```
var toolbar = new StackPanel();
toolbar.Orientation = Orientation.Horizontal;
var newButton = new Button();
newButton.Content = "New";
newButton.Background = new SolidColorBrush(Colors.Pink);
toolbar.Children.Add(newButton);
var openButton = new Button();
openButton.Content = "Open";
openButton.Background = new SolidColorBrush(Colors.Pink);
toolbar.Children.Add(openButton);
```

In XAML, it would be simplified to the following lines of code. When this XAML is processed, the equivalent properties are set and methods are called, to achieve the same goal as the preceding C# code:

```
<StackPanel Name="toolbar" Orientation="Horizontal">
    <Button Name="newButton" Background="Pink">New</Button>
    <Button Name="openButton" Background="Pink">Open</Button>
</StackPanel>
```

XAML is an alternative (better) way of declaring and instantiating .NET types.

# Creating a Windows desktop application using WPF

In 2006, Microsoft released WPF, which was the first technology to use XAML. It is is still used today to create desktop applications.

 Microsoft Visual Studio 2015 and Microsoft Blend are WPF applications.

Start Microsoft Visual Studio 2015. In Visual Studio, press *Ctrl + Shift + N*, or choose **File** | **New** | **Project...**.

In the **New Project** dialog, in the **Installed Templates** list, select **Visual C#**. In the center list, select **WPF Application**, type the name as **Ch13_WPF**, change the location to C:\Code, type the solution name as **Chapter13**, and then click on **OK**.

You will see the XAML design window showing a graphical view and an XAML view of the MainWindow.xaml file. You will be able to make the following observations:

- The XAML designer is split horizontally, but you can toggle to vertical split and collapse one side by clicking the buttons on the right edge of the divider
- You can swap the views by clicking the double-arrow button in the divider
- You can scroll and zoom both views:

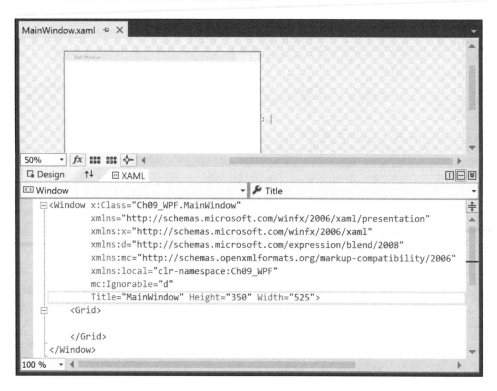

On the **View** menu, choose **Toolbox,** or press *Ctrl + W, X.* Notice that the toolbox has sections for **Common WPF Controls** and **All WPF Controls**:

Drag and drop the **Button** control from the toolbox onto the graphical view. Notice that the button is given a fixed width and margin to position it inside the grid:

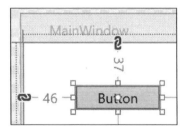

Although you can drag and drop controls, it is better to use the XAML view for layout.

In the XAML view, find the Button element and delete it.

In the XAML view, inside the Grid element, type the following line of code, and notice that the button stretches to take up the whole grid:

```
<Button Margin="6" Padding="6" Name="clickMeButton">Click Me</Button>
```

Modify the XAML to put the `Button` element inside a `StackPanel`, and notice the change in its layout:

```
<StackPanel Orientation="Horizontal" VerticalAlignment="Top">
    <Button Margin="6" Padding="6" Name="clickMeButton">Click Me</
Button>
</StackPanel>
```

Modify the `Button` element to give it a new event handler for its `Click` event:

```
<Button Margin="6" Padding="6" Name="clickMeButton"
Click="clickMeButton_Click">Click Me</Button>
```

In the `MainWindows.xaml.cs` file, add the following statement to the event handler:

```
clickMeButton.Content = DateTime.Now.ToLongTimeString();
```

Run the application by pressing *Ctrl + F5* and view the window:

Click on the **Click Me** button. Every time you click the button, the button's content changes to show the current time:

# Choosing common controls

There are lots of predefined controls that you can choose from for common user interface scenarios. Almost all versions of XAML support the controls in the following table:

| Control(s) | Description |
|---|---|
| Button, Menu, Toolbar | Executing actions |
| CheckBox, RadioButton | Choosing options |
| Calendar, DatePicker | Choosing dates |
| ComboBox, ListBox, ListView, TreeView | Choosing items from lists and hierarchical trees |

| Control(s) | Description |
|---|---|
| `Canvas, DockPanel, Grid, StackPanel, WrapPanel` | Layout containers that affect their children in different ways |
| `Label, TextBlock` | Displaying read-only text |
| `RichTextBox, TextBox` | Editing text |
| `Image, MediaElement` | Embedding images, videos, and audio files |
| `DataGrid` | Viewing and editing bound data |
| `Scrollbar, Slider, StatusBar` | Miscellaneous. user interface elements |

 You can learn more about the controls available at `https://msdn.microsoft.com/en-us/library/windows/apps/mt185405.aspx`.

# Creating an app for the Universal Windows Platform

To be able to create apps for the UWP, you must enable the developer mode in Windows 10.

Go to the **Start Menu | Settings | Update & Security**, and then click on **Developer mode**. Close the **Settings** app:

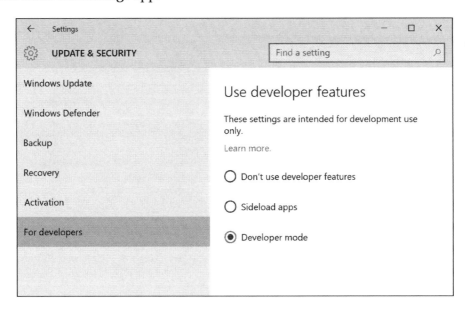

Start Microsoft Visual Studio 2015. In Visual Studio, click on **File | Add | New Project…**. In the **Add New Project** dialog, in the **Installed Templates** list, select **Visual C#**. In the center list, select **Blank App (Universal Windows)**, type the name as **Ch13_UWP**, and then click on **OK**.

Set the solution's startup project to be the current selection.

In the **Solution Explorer** window, double-click on the `MainPage.xaml` file to open it for editing.

Modify the XAML to put a `Button` element inside a `StackPanel`. Add the event handler by choosing **New Event Handler**, so that a method is created in the code-behind file:

```
<StackPanel VerticalAlignment="Top">
    <StackPanel Orientation="Horizontal">
        <Button Margin="6" Padding="6" Name="clickMeButton"
Click="clickMeButton_Click">Click Me</Button>
    </StackPanel>
</StackPanel>
```

Right-click and chose **View Code** or press *F7*.

In the `clickMeButton_Click` method, add the following statement:

```
clickMeButton.Content = DateTime.Now.ToLongTimeString();
```

Run the application by pressing *Ctrl + F5*, and notice the warning:

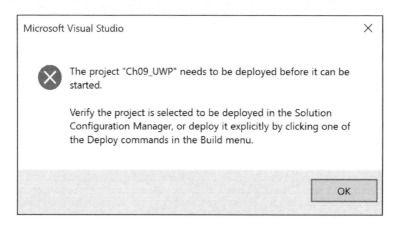

UWP apps have extra requirements compared to console and WPF applications. They must be deployed before being run.

On the **Build** menu, choose **Deploy Ch13_UWP**.

You will see a compile error. This is because UWP apps have a more limited version of the base-class libraries, and the `ToLongTimeString` method has not been implemented for instances of `DateTime`:

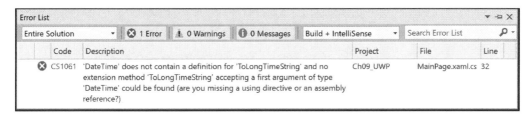

 UWP apps cannot use the full features of .NET. because they use a custom implementation of .NET Core.

Modify your code to make it look like this:

```
clickMeButton.Content = DateTime.Now.ToString("hh:mm:ss");
```

Redeploy the application and then run it by pressing *Ctrl + F5*.

This time, it works just as our WPF application did earlier, except that this app will also run on Windows 10 Mobile phones, Xbox One, and even HoloLens:

## Analyzing UWP portability

If you run the .NET Portability Analyzer on this project, you will see the following report:

| Ch13_UWP, Version=1.0.0.0, Culture=neutral, PublicKeyToken=null (.NETCore,Version=v5.0) | | | |
|---|---|---|---|
| Target type | .NET Core (Cross-platform),Version=v5.0 | .NET Framework,Version=v4.5 | .NET Native,Version=v1.0 |
| System.Runtime.InteropServices.WindowsRuntime.EventRegistrationToken | ✗ | ✓ | ✓ |
| System.Runtime.InteropServices.WindowsRuntime.WindowsRuntimeMarshal | ✗ | ✓ | ✓ |
| AddEventHandler`1(System.Func{`0,System.Runtime.InteropServices.WindowsRuntime.EventRegistrationToken},System.Action{System.Runtime.InteropServices.WindowsRuntime.EventRegistrationToken},`0) | ✗ | ✓ | ✓ |

Note that UWP apps do not support cross-platform .NET Core because they use a custom implementation of .NET Core. However, they are cross-device if that device runs a modern flavor of Windows. Also, they support .NET Native. This means that the .NET code is compiled to native CPU instructions for a smaller memory footprint and faster execution.

# Using resources and templates

When building graphical user interfaces, you will often want to use a resource such as a brush to paint the background of controls. These resources can be defined in a single place and shared throughout the app.

## Sharing resources

In the **Solution Explorer** window, double-click on the **App.xaml** file. Add the following statement to it:

```xml
<Application.Resources>
    <LinearGradientBrush x:Key="rainbow">
        <GradientStop Color="Red" Offset="0" />
        <GradientStop Color="Orange" Offset="0.1" />
        <GradientStop Color="Yellow" Offset="0.3" />
        <GradientStop Color="Green" Offset="0.5" />
        <GradientStop Color="Blue" Offset="0.7" />
        <GradientStop Color="Indigo" Offset="0.9" />
        <GradientStop Color="Violet" Offset="1" />
    </LinearGradientBrush>
</Application.Resources>
```

In the `MainPage.xaml` file, modify the `Grid` element to make it look like this:

```
<Grid Background="{StaticResource rainbow}">
```

Redeploy and run the application:

 A resource can be an instance of any object. To share it within an application, define it in the `App.xaml` file and give it a unique Key. To set an element's property to apply the resource, use `StaticResource` with the Key.

# Replacing a control template

You can redefine how a control looks by replacing its default template.

One of the most common resources is a `Style` that can set multiple properties at once. If a style has a unique Key, then it must be explicitly set, like we did earlier with the linear gradient. If it doesn't have a Key, then it will be automatically applied based on the `TargetType`. For example, if the `TargetType` is Button then all Buttons will have the style applied.

In `App.xaml` file, add the following statements:

```
<ControlTemplate x:Key="DarkGlassButton" TargetType="Button">
    <Border BorderBrush="#FFFFFFFF" BorderThickness="1,1,1,1"
CornerRadius="4,4,4,4">
        <Border x:Name="border" Background="#7F000000"
BorderBrush="#FF000000" BorderThickness="1,1,1,1"
CornerRadius="4,4,4,4">
            <Grid>
                <Grid.RowDefinitions>
                    <RowDefinition Height="*"/>
                    <RowDefinition Height="*"/>
                </Grid.RowDefinitions>
                <Border Opacity="0" HorizontalAlignment="Stretch"
x:Name="glow" Width="Auto" Grid.RowSpan="2" CornerRadius="4,4,4,4">
                </Border>
                <ContentPresenter HorizontalAlignment="Center"
VerticalAlignment="Center" Width="Auto" Grid.RowSpan="2" Padding="4"/>
                <Border HorizontalAlignment="Stretch" Margin="0,0,0,0"
x:Name="shine" Width="Auto" CornerRadius="4,4,0,0">
```

```
                    <Border.Background>
                        <LinearGradientBrush EndPoint="0.5,0.9"
    StartPoint="0.5,0.03">
                            <GradientStop Color="#99FFFFFF"
    Offset="0"/>
                            <GradientStop Color="#33FFFFFF"
    Offset="1"/>
                        </LinearGradientBrush>
                    </Border.Background>
                </Border>
            </Grid>
        </Border>
    </Border>
</ControlTemplate>
<Style TargetType="Button">
    <Setter Property="Template" Value="{StaticResource
DarkGlassButton}" />
    <Setter Property="Foreground" Value="White" />
</Style>
```

Redeploy and run the application:

# Data binding

When building graphical user interfaces, you will often want to bind a property of one control to another or to some data.

## Binding to elements

In the `MainWindow.xaml` file, add the following elements after the `Button` element, inside the horizontal `StackPanel`:

```
<Slider Value="50" Maximum="100" Minimum="0" Width="200"
Name="slider"/>
<TextBlock Text="{Binding ElementName=slider, Path=Value}"
VerticalAlignment="Center" Margin="10"/>
```

Redeploy and then run the app. Click and drag the slider, and notice that the text block always shows the current value of the slider:

Under the horizontal stack panel, add these statements:

```
<Rectangle Height="100" Width="100" Fill="Red">
    <Rectangle.RenderTransform>
        <RotateTransform Angle="{Binding ElementName=sliderRotation,
Path=Value}" />
    </Rectangle.RenderTransform>
</Rectangle>
<TextBlock>Use the slider to rotate the square:</TextBlock>
<Slider Value="0" Minimum="0" Maximum="360" Name="sliderRotation"/>
```

Redeploy and run the app:

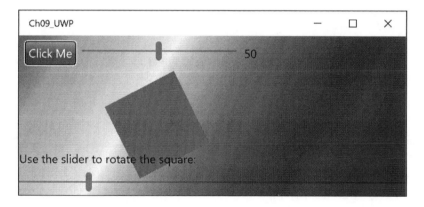

# Binding to data

Add a new **Blank App (Universal Windows)** project named **Ch13_DataBinding**.

In the **Solution Explorer** window, right-click on the new project and add a new folder named **Models**.

Right-click on the **Models** folder and add a new class named `Employee`. Add the following statements to it:

```
public class Employee
{
    public int EmployeeID { get; set; }
    public string FirstName { get; set; }
    public string LastName { get; set; }
    public DateTime DOB { get; set; }
    public decimal Salary { get; set; }
}
```

Add another class named `EmployeesViewModel`:

```
public class EmployeesViewModel
{
    public HashSet<Employee> Employees { get; set; }
    public EmployeesViewModel()
    {
        Employees = new HashSet<Employee>();
        Employees.Add(new Employee { EmployeeID = 1, FirstName =
"Alice", LastName = "Smith", DOB = new DateTime(1972, 1, 27), Salary =
34000M });
        Employees.Add(new Employee { EmployeeID = 2, FirstName =
"Bob", LastName = "Jones", DOB = new DateTime(1965, 4, 13), Salary =
64000M });
    }
}
```

Open `MainPage.xaml`. Add the following `ListBox` element, whose items are bound to each employee instance in the `Employees` hash set of the view model:

```xml
<ListBox ItemsSource="{Binding Employees}">
    <ListBox.ItemTemplate>
        <DataTemplate>
            <StackPanel Orientation="Horizontal">
                <TextBox Text="{Binding EmployeeID}" />
                <TextBox Text="{Binding FirstName}" />
                <TextBox Text="{Binding LastName}" />
                <DatePicker Date="{Binding DOB}" />
                <TextBox Text="{Binding Salary}" />
            </StackPanel>
        </DataTemplate>
    </ListBox.ItemTemplate>
</ListBox>
```

Since the data won't be loaded until runtime, you won't see a preview of the layout in the design window. You can configure a UWP project with sample data for use at design time, but that is beyond the scope of this book.

In the XAML for the `Page` element, insert a new event handler for the `Load` event:

```
Loading="Page_Loading"
```

Press *F7* to view the code.

Add the following statement to the event handler for `Page_Loading`. The `DataContext` method is inherited by all controls, so the instance of the view model can be easily bound to by everything on the page:

```
DataContext = new Models.EmployeesViewModel();
```

Deploy and run the application.

The user can click inside each box to modify the data values. Notice the date picker. This looks different and is optimized for input on different devices:

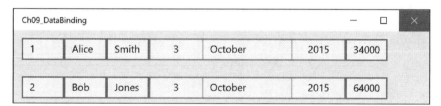

In the real world, you would load the data from a file or service. You will learn how to build services in *Chapter 14, Building Web Applications and Services Using ASP.NET Core*.

# Animating with storyboards

You can make your application feel more natural and organic (and fun) using storyboard animations.

Add a new **Blank App (Universal Windows)** project named **Ch13_BouncingBall**.

Open the `MainPage.xaml` file, change `Grid` into `Canvas` and add an ellipse to make a red ball. Save your changes:

```xaml
<Canvas Background="{ThemeResource
ApplicationPageBackgroundThemeBrush}">
    <Ellipse Fill="Red" Height="100" Width="100"/>
</Canvas>
```

In the **Solution Explorer** window, right-click on the **Ch13_BouncingBall** project and choose **Design in Blend...**.

The project will open in the **Microsoft Blend for Visual Studio** tool that is used by designers, because it has better support for graphical effects and animation than Visual Studio does.

On the drawing surface, click on the ellipse to select it.

In the **Objects and Timeline** window, click on the small green + button to create a new storyboard resource:

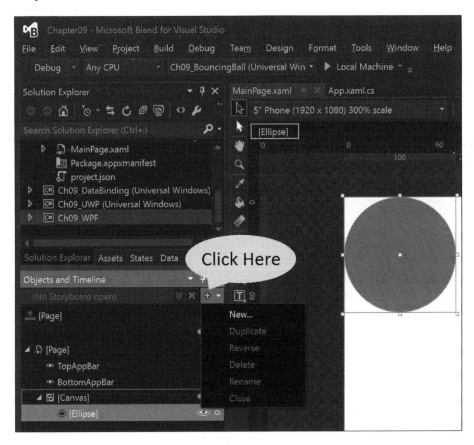

Change the name of the storyboard resource to **BounceBall** and click on **OK**:

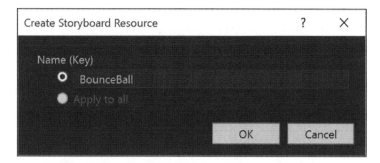

A red box appears around the drawing surface, and you will see in the top-right corner that the timeline recording is on. Later, you will click on the red dot to stop recording:

BounceBall timeline recording is on.

In the **Objects and Timeline** window, click on the **Record Keyframe** button (it looks like a green **+** symbol combined with a small diamond, and it is to the left of the current time indicator). This will record the current properties of the ball at time 0:00.000:

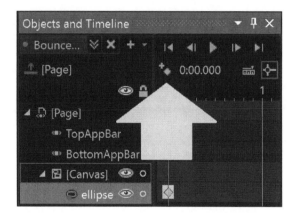

On the timeline, drag the down-pointing orange triangle and its vertical orange line to time position 0:00.800. This means 0.8 seconds later:

On the drawing surface, drag the ball down and a little to the right. This change will be recorded automatically:

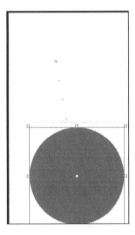

Drag the orange triangle to time position 0:01.000. Click and drag the resize handle at the top of the ball to squash it down a little.

Drag the orange triangle to time position 0:01.200. Resize the ball to stretch it back to its original height.

Drag the orange triangle to time position 0:02.000. Click in the middle of the ball and drag it back up to near the top of the window and a little to the right.

Click the red dot to stop recording:

● BounceBall timeline recording is off.

In the **Objects and Timeline** window, click on the small green triangle **Play** button.

You should see the red ball smoothly drop down. When it hits the bottom, it squashes slightly as a rubber ball would in real life, before bouncing back up to the top.

Exit from Blend. When you return to Visual Studio, it should warn you that the file has changes and prompt you to reload it. Click on **Yes**.

Notice that Blend created some XAML elements to define a storyboard named `BounceBall` that animates properties of the `Ellipse` object.

In the toolbox, choose **Button** and draw one on the canvas named **BounceBallButton**. Change its contents to **Bounce Ball**. Give it a `Click` event handler. Add the following statement to the event handler method:

```
BounceBall.Begin();
```

Deploy and run the application. Click on the **Bounce Ball** button to run the animation:

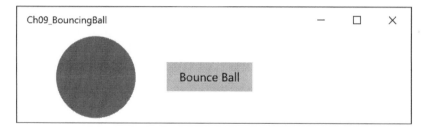

# Testing in emulators

While developing a UWP app, you can quickly see what it would look like on various devices in the XAML design window. The following screenshot is showing the 23" Desktop (1920 x 1080) 100% scale emulator:

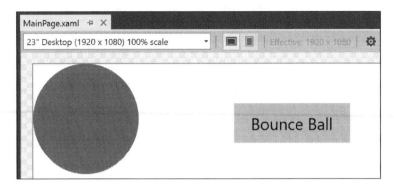

Switch to a phone option with a vertical layout. The following screenshot is showing the 5" Phone (1920 x 1080) 300% scale emulator. You can see that the right-hand edge is visible:

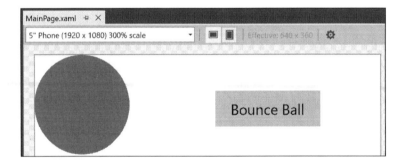

You can also run the app in a **Simulator** rather than on **Local Machine**. You can also choose **Remote Machine** or **Device**:

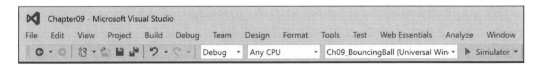

The Simulator can rotate, and change input modes and screen resolution, using the buttons in the toolbar, on the right-hand edge of the Simulator window:

 Test your apps with the Simulator, and then test on all of the actual devices that your users will deploy your app to.

# Practicing and exploring

Test your knowledge and understanding by answering some questions, get some hands-on practice, and explore this chapter's topics with deeper research.

## Exercise 13.1 – test your knowledge

Answer the following questions:

1. Which control would you choose to allow the user to easily choose their date of birth on many different types of devices?
2. Which XAML element would you use to adapt the layout of your app to handle different device families?
3. How can you set multiple properties on an XAML element as a single group?
4. What is the difference between a control template and a data template?
5. Can XAML bindings be two way or just one way?

## Exercise 13.2 – practice building a universal tip calculator

Create an app for UWP that calculates a tip for common percentages.

## Exercise 13.3 – explore topics

Use the following links to read more about this chapter's topics.

- **Enable your device for development**: https://msdn.microsoft.com/en-us/library/windows/apps/dn706236.aspx
- **Guide to UWP apps**: https://msdn.microsoft.com/library/windows/apps/hh465424.aspx
- **How-to guides for Windows 10 apps**: https://msdn.microsoft.com/library/windows/apps/xaml/mt244352.aspx

# Summary

In this chapter, you learned how to build a graphical user interface using XAML, how to share resources in a central location, how to replace a control's template, how to bind to data and controls, and how to animate properties.

In the next chapter, you will learn how to build web applications and services.

# 14

# Building Web Applications and Services Using ASP.NET Core

This chapter is about building web applications and services using a modern HTTP architecture on the server-side using Microsoft ASP.NET Core 1.0. You will learn about the startup configuration, routes, models, views, and controllers that make up ASP.NET Core.

This chapter will cover the following topics:

- Understanding ASP.NET Core
- ASP.NET Core startup
- ASP.NET Core controllers
- ASP.NET Core models
- ASP.NET Core views
- Taking ASP.NET Core further
- ASP.NET Core Web API

# Understanding ASP.NET Core

Microsoft ASP.NET Core 1.0 is part of a suite of Microsoft technologies to build web applications and services that have evolved over the years as shown in the following bullet points:

- ASP.NET Web Forms was released in 2002 and is designed to enable non-web developers, such as those familiar with Visual Basic, to quickly create web applications. Web Forms can only be hosted on Windows, but are used in products such as Microsoft SharePoint. It should be avoided for new projects in favor of ASP.NET Core.

- ASP.NET XML Web Services was released in 2002 and enables developers to build SOAP services. It should be avoided for new projects in favor of WCF or ASP.NET Web API.

- Windows Communication Foundation (WCF) was released in 2006 and enables developers to build SOAP and REST services. SOAP is powerful but complex, so it should be avoided unless you need advanced features, such as distributed transactions and complex messaging topologies.

- ASP.NET MVC was released in 2009 and is designed to cleanly separate the concerns of web developers between the models that represent the data, the views that present that data, and the controllers that fetch the model and pass it to a view. This separation enables improved scalability and unit testing.

- ASP.NET Web API was released in 2012 and enables developers to create HTTP services that are simpler and more scalable than SOAP services.

- ASP.NET Core was released in 2016, and combines MVC and Web API running on the .NET Core. Therefore, it is cross-platform.

**Best Practice**

Choose ASP.NET Core to develop web applications and services, because it includes MVC and Web API, which are modern and cross-platform.

# Classic ASP.NET versus modern ASP.NET Core

ASP.NET is almost 15 years old. Until now, it has been built on top of a major part of the .NET Framework, the System.Web.dll assembly. Over the years, it has accumulated a lot of features, many of which are not suitable for modern, cross-platform development.

ASP.NET Core is a major redesign of ASP.NET. It removes the dependency on the System.Web.dll assembly, and is composed of modular lightweight components.

You can develop and run ASP.NET Core applications cross-platform on Windows, Mac OS X, and Linux. The entire stack is open source, and it is designed to integrate with a variety of client-side frameworks, including AngularJS, KnockoutJS, and Bootstrap.

# Client-side web development

When building web applications, a developer needs to know more than just C# and .NET. On the client (that is, in the web browser), you will use a combination of the following components of a web page:

- **HTML5**: This is used for the content and semantics of elements
- **CSS3**: This is used for the format and layout applied to elements
- **JavaScript**: This is used for the behavior of elements

This book is about C#, so we will cover some of the basics. For more information on web browser technologies, I recommend that you refer to the book *HTML5 Web Application Development By Example* by *Packt Publishing* at https://www.packtpub.com/web-development/html5-web-application-development-example-beginners-guide.

To make it easier to work with HTML5, CSS3, and JavaScript, I recommend that developers install the free Web Essentials extension for Visual Studio.

# Install Web Essentials 2015

Start Microsoft Visual Studio 2015. On the **Tools** menu, choose **Extensions and Updates**. In the left-hand list, select **Online**. In the search box, enter **web essentials**, select **Web Essentials 2015.1**, click on the **Download** button, and then follow the instructions:

# The HyperText Transfer Protocol (HTTP)

To communicate with a server, the client makes calls over the network using a protocol known as HTTP. HTTP is the technical underpinning of the "web". So when we talk about "web" applications or "web" services, we mean they use HTTP to communicate between a client (often a web browser) and a server.

A client makes an HTTP request for a resource, such as a page identified by a URL (Uniform Resource Locator), and the server sends back an HTTP response. You can use Microsoft Edge and other browsers to record requests and responses.

Start Microsoft Edge. Press *F12* to show developer tools. Click on the **Network** tab. If the **Start profiling session** button has not been pressed, click on it to start recording, or press *Ctrl + E*:

In Microsoft Edge's address box, enter `http://www.asp.net/mvc`.

In the **F12 Developer Tools** window, in the list of recorded requests, click on the first entry:

| | | | | |
|---|---|---|---|---|
| mvc<br>http://www.asp.net/ | HTTP | GET | 200<br>OK | text/html |

On the right-hand side, you will see details about the request and the response:

Note the following aspects:

- The request method is GET. Other methods that HTTP defines include POST, PUT, DELETE, HEAD, and PATCH.

- The response status code is 200 OK. This means the server found the resource the browser requested. Other status codes include 404 Missing.

- The request headers include what formats the browser will accept. In this case, the browser is saying it understands HTML, XHTML, and others.

- The browser has told the server that it understands the GZIP and DEFLATE compressions algorithms.

- The browser has told the server which human languages it would prefer: US English, British English, and then any other dialect of English.

- I have been to this site before, so a cookie that was defined by the site is being sent to the server so that it can track me. Microsoft has named it omniID. Does that sound ominous to you?

- The server has sent back the response, compressed using the GZIP algorithm, because it knows that the client can decompress that format.

- The server is running **Internet Information Services (IIS)** 8.0.

# Create a web application project

In Visual Studio, press *Ctrl + Shift + N* or choose **File | New | Project...**.

In the **New Project** dialog, in the **Installed Templates** list, select **Visual C#**. In the center list, select **ASP.NET Web Application**, type the name as **Ch14_WebApp**, type the solution name as **Chapter14**, and then click on **OK**:

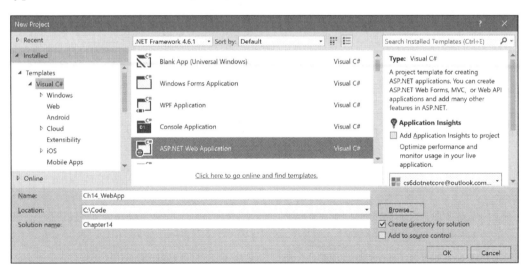

In the **New ASP.NET Project** dialog box, in the **ASP.NET Core 1.0 Templates** section, select the **Web Application** template.

At the time of writing this book, the final version of ASP.NET Core 1.0 and its Visual Studio project templates have not been released. So, the screenshots in this book show the old branding, ASP.NET 5!

Click on the **Change Authentication** button and choose **No Authentication**. Then, click on **OK**. This tells Visual Studio to allow all users access to the application. We can change this later to secure our web application.

Uncheck the **Host in the cloud** box, because we want to run this locally. We can always deploy to the Microsoft Azure cloud later.

Click on **OK**:

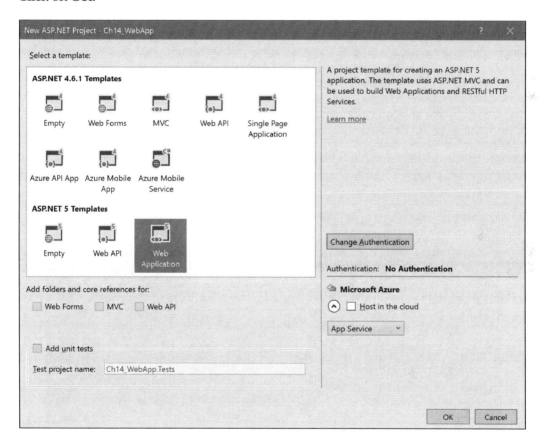

After a few seconds, your **Solution Explorer** window will look like this:

Run the application by pressing *F5*. The web application is hosted in the free version of IIS Express using a random port number for local testing.

Notice that the home page has a black navigation bar with links to an **About** page and a **Contact** page. The home page has a carousel with four rotating items and four columns of links underneath:

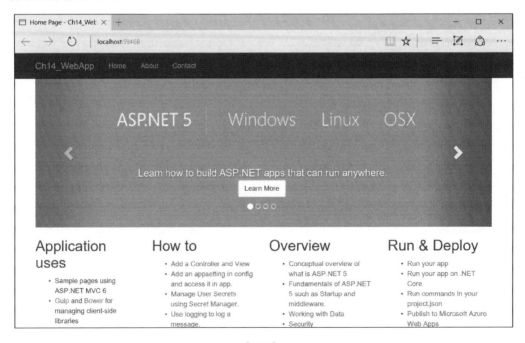

Click on the links to the **About** page and the **Contact** page, and notice the URLs that are used. To get to the **About** page, the user could enter /Home/About in the browser address box:

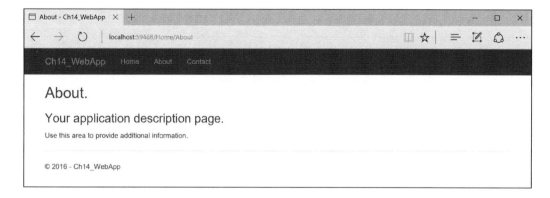

Resize the width of the browser window and notice that the navigation bar becomes a clickable "hamburger" menu (three horizontal lines):

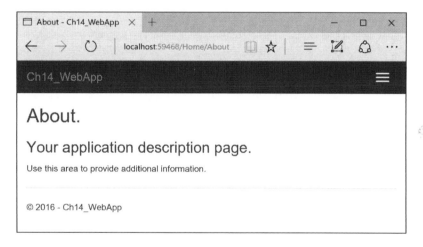

This is an example of responsive web design. The page looks good on both desktop and mobile devices, by automatically adapting based on the current width of the window:

# Exploring the parts of an ASP.NET Core web application

Let's walk through the parts that make up a modern ASP.NET Core application.

In Visual Studio, look at **Solution Explorer** for the **Ch14_WebApp** project and note the following points:

- wwwroot: This folder contains static content, such as stylesheets, images, scripts, and common libraries, that combine resources such as jQuery and Bootstrap
- Dependencies: This folder contains Bower and npm for modern package management
- Controllers: This folder contains C# classes that have methods (known as actions) that fetch a model and pass it to a view
- Models: This (optional) folder contains C# classes that represent all the data required for a request
- Views: This folder contains .cshtml files that combine HTML and C# code to enable the dynamic generation of an HTML response
- project.json: This file contains a list of NuGet packages (such as the Entity Framework Core) that your project requires and other project configuration

- `Startup.cs`: This file contains the `Main` entry point for your application and configures the services, pipeline, and routes for your application

The following screenshot shows the parts of a typical ASP.NET Core project:

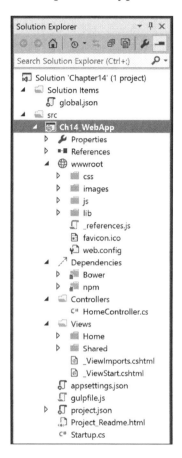

# ASP.NET Core startup

In the **Solution Explorer** window, double-click on the `Startup.cs` file.

Notice the `ConfigureServices` method that adds support for MVC. Later, we will add statements here to add support for the Entity Framework Core:

```
public void ConfigureServices(IServiceCollection services)
{
    // Add framework services.
    services.AddMvc();
}
```

Next, we have the `Configure` method.

The most important statement here is the one that calls `UseMvc` and maps a default route. This route is very flexible, because it would match almost any incoming URL:

```
public void Configure(IApplicationBuilder app, IHostingEnvironment
env, ILoggerFactory loggerFactory)
{
    loggerFactory.AddConsole(Configuration.GetSection("Logging"));
    loggerFactory.AddDebug();
    if (env.IsDevelopment())
    {
        app.UseBrowserLink();
        app.UseDeveloperExceptionPage();
    }
    else
    {
        app.UseExceptionHandler("/Home/Error");
    }
    app.UseIISPlatformHandler();
    app.UseStaticFiles();
    app.UseMvc(routes =>
    {
        routes.MapRoute(
            name: "default",
            template: "{controller=Home}/{action=Index}/{id?}");
    });
}
```

# Understanding the default route

The default route looks at any URL entered by the user in the address bar and matches it to extract the name of a controller, the name of an action, and an optional `id` value (the `?` symbol makes it optional). If the user hasn't entered these names, it uses defaults of Home for the controller, and Index for the action (the `=` assignment sets a default for a named segment).

Contents in curly brackets {} are called **segments**, and they are like a named parameter of a method. The value of these segments can be any string.

The responsibility of a route is to discover the name of a controller and an action.

Here's a table of example URLs and how MVC would work out the names. Notice that if the user does not supply a name, then the defaults **Home** and **Index** are used, as specified when the route was registered. You could change these defaults if you wanted:

| URL | Controller | Action | ID |
|---|---|---|---|
| / | Home | Index | |
| /Muppet | Muppet | Index | |
| /Muppet/Kermit | Muppet | Kermit | |
| /Muppet/Kermit/Green | Muppet | Kermit | Green |
| /Products | Products | Index | |
| /Products/Detail | Products | Detail | |
| /Products/Detail/3 | Products | Detail | 3 |

# ASP.NET Core controllers

Now that MVC knows the names of the controller and action, it will look for a class that implements an interface named `IController`. To simplify the requirements, Microsoft supplies a class named `Controller` that your classes can inherit from.

The responsibilities of a controller are as follows:

- To extract parameters from the HTTP request
- To use the parameters to fetch the correct model and pass it to the correct view
- To return the results from the view to the client as an HTTP response

# Defining the Home controller's actions

In the **Solution Explorer** window, expand the **Controllers** folder and double-click on the file named `HomeController.cs`:

```
public class HomeController : Controller
{
    public IActionResult Index()
    {
        return View();
    }
    public IActionResult About()
    {
        ViewData["Message"] = "Your application description page.";
```

```
            return View();
        }
        public IActionResult Contact()
        {
            ViewData["Message"] = "Your contact page.";
            return View();
        }
        public IActionResult Error()
        {
            return View();
        }
    }
```

 If the user enters /, or /Home, then it is the equivalent of /Home/Index because those were the defaults.

Note the following aspects:

- None of the action methods currently use a model
- Two of the action methods use a dictionary named ViewData to store a string message that can then be read inside a view
- All action methods execute a method named View and return the results to the client

# ASP.NET Core models

In MVC, the model represents the data required for a request. For example, an HTTP GET request for http://www.example.com/products/details/3 would mean you are asking for the details of product number 3.

The controller would need to use the ID value 3 to retrieve the record for that product and pass it to a view that can then turn the model into HTML for display in the browser.

For this initial example, we will create an Entity Data Model (EDM) to access data in the Northwind database.

 **Best Practice**
Use a data repository (typically implemented as a service) to manage your data.

# Create Entity models for Northwind

If you have not already installed the Northwind database, then follow the instructions at the beginning of *Chapter 8, Working with Relational Data Using the Entity Framework*.

On the **Tools** menu, choose **NuGet Package Manager** and then **Package Manager Console**.

In the PM> prompt, enter the following commands:

```
Install-Package EntityFramework.MicrosoftSqlServer
```

```
Install-Package EntityFramework.Commands
```

```
Install-Package EntityFramework.MicrosoftSqlServer.Design :
```

 If the preceding commands give errors, then add -pre to the end of each command to install the pre-release version as shown in the following screenshot.

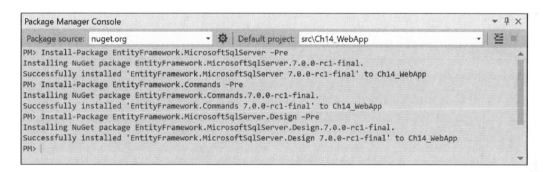

In the **Solution Explorer** window, double-click on **project.json**. Notice that three dependencies have been added for the Entity Framework Core:

```
{
  "version": "1.0.0-*",
  "compilationOptions": {
    "emitEntryPoint": true
  },

  "dependencies": {
    "EntityFramework.Commands": "7.0.0-rc1-final",
    "EntityFramework.MicrosoftSqlServer": "7.0.0-rc1-final",
    "EntityFramework.MicrosoftSqlServer.Design": "7.0.0-rc1-final",
    "Microsoft.AspNet.Diagnostics": "1.0.0-rc1-final",
```

In the **commands** section, add a new command for ef, as follows:

```
"commands": {
  "web": "Microsoft.AspNet.Server.Kestrel",
  "ef": "EntityFramework.Commands"
},
```

Save project.json file.

In the **Solution Explorer** window, right-click on the project and choose **Add, New Folder...**, and then enter the name of the model.

Right-click on the **Ch14_WebApp** project and choose **Open Folder in File Explorer**. Click in the address box and copy the path to the clipboard by pressing *Ctrl + C*.

Click the Windows Start button and start Command Prompt. In Command Prompt window, enter cd, and then right-click to paste the path to your project. Press *Enter* to change to that directory:

**cd C:\Code\Chapter14\src\Ch14_WebApp**

Enter the following command to tell the .NET Version Manager to use the latest version of .NET Core:

**dnvm use 1.0.0-rc1-update1**

 At the time of writing this book, .NET Core was a release candidate. By the time you follow these instructions, the final version should be available, and use the new .NET CLI so the commands dnvm and dnx will be replaced by the command dotnet.

Enter the following command to generate classes that represent entities for all the tables in the Northwind database in the Models subfolder:

**dnx ef dbcontext scaffold "Server=(localdb)\mssqllocaldb;Database=No rthwind;Trusted_Connection=True;" EntityFramework.MicrosoftSqlServer --outputDir Models**

In the **Solution Explorer** window, expand the Models folder. You will see that a class has been created for each entity, and a class named NorthwindContext has been created to represent the whole database:

# Configure Entity Framework Core as a service

Dependency injection is central to ASP.NET Core. Services, such as the Entity Framework Core that are needed by MVC controllers, must be registered as a service during startup.

In the **Solution Explorer** window, open the `Startup.cs` file. Import the following namespaces:

```
using Ch14_WebApp.Models;
using Microsoft.Data.Entity;
```

Add the following statements to the `ConfigureServices` method:

```
var connection = @"Server=(localdb)\mssqllocaldb;Database=Northwind;Tr
usted_Connection=True;";
services.AddEntityFramework()
    .AddSqlServer()
    .AddDbContext<NorthwindContext>(options => options.
UseSqlServer(connection));
```

Since we are setting the database connection string in the ASP.NET Core startup, it does not need to be done in the `NorthwindContext` class.

In the **Solution Explorer** window, in the `Models` folder, open the `NorthwindContext.cs` file and delete the following method:

```
protected override void OnConfiguring(DbContextOptionsBuilder options)
{
    options.UseSqlServer(@"Server=(localdb)\mssqllocaldb;Database=Nort
hwind;Trusted_Connection=True;");
}
```

# Create view models for requests

Imagine that when a user comes to our website, we want to show them a list of products and a count of the number of visitors we have had this month. All the data that we want to show in response to a request is the MVC model, sometimes called a **view model** because it is a *model* that is passed to a *view*.

In the **Solution Explorer** window, select the **Models** folder. On the **Project** menu, choose **Add Class...**, and in the dialog box, choose **Class** and name it **HomeIndexViewModel**.

Modify the class definition to make it look like this:

```
public class HomeIndexViewModel
{
    public int VisitorCount;
    public ICollection<Products> Products { get; set; }
}
```

# Fetch the model in the controller

Open the `HomeController` class. Import the `Ch14_WebApp.Models` namespace.

Add a field to store a reference to a `NorthwindContext` instance and initialize it in a constructor:

```
private NorthwindContext db;

public HomeController(NorthwindContext injectedContext)
{
    db = injectedContext;
}
```

Modify the contents of the `Index` action method to make it look like this:

```
var model = new HomeIndexViewModel
```

```
{
    VisitorCount = (new Random()).Next(1, 1001),
    Products = db.Products.ToArray()
};
return View(model); // pass model to view
```

Note that we will simulate a visitor count using the `Random` class to generate a number between 1 and 1000.

 If you build the project now, you might get "CS0833 An anonymous type cannot have multiple properties with the same name" errors due to bugs in the scaffolding feature. To fix the errors, simply delete the duplicate members.

# ASP.NET Core views

The responsibility of a view is to transform a model into HTML or other formats. There are multiple **view engines** that can be used to do this. The default view engine for ASP.NET MVC 3 and later is called **Razor**, and it uses the @ symbol to indicate server-side code execution.

# Rendering the Home controller's views

In the **Solution Explorer** window, expand the **Views** folder. Expand the **Home** folder. Note the three files with the `.cshtml` file extension.

 The `.cshtml` file extension means this is a file that mixes C# and HTML.

When the `View` method is executed in a controller action, MVC looks in the **Views** folder for a subfolder with the same name as the current controller, that is, Home. It then looks for a file with the same name as the current action, that is, Index, About, or Contact.

In the `Index.cshtml` file, notice the block of code wrapped in @{ }. This will execute first and can be used to store data that needs to be passed into a shared layout file:

```
@{
    ViewData["Title"] = "Home Page";
}
```

Note the static HTML content in several DIV elements that uses Bootstrap for styling.

**Best Practice**
Instead of defining your own styles, use a library, such as Bootstrap, that implements responsive design using standard CSS3 principles.

# Sharing layouts between views

There is a file, named _ViewStart.cshtml, that gets executed by the View method. It is used to set defaults that apply to all views.

For example, it sets the Layout property of all views to a shared layout file:

```
@{
    Layout = "_Layout";
}
```

In the Shared folder, open the _Layout.cshtml file. Notice that the title is being read from the ViewData dictionary that was set earlier in the Index.cshtml view:

```
<title>@ViewData["Title"] - Ch14_WebApp</title>
```

Note the rendering of common styles to support Bootstrap and the two sections. During development, the fully-commented and nicely formatted versions of CSS files will be used. For staging and production, the minified versions will be used:

```
<environment names="Development">
    <link rel="stylesheet" href="~/lib/bootstrap/dist/css/bootstrap.
css" />
    <link rel="stylesheet" href="~/css/site.css" />
</environment>
<environment names="Staging,Production">
    <link rel="stylesheet" href="https://ajax.aspnetcdn.com/ajax/
bootstrap/3.3.5/css/bootstrap.min.css"
            asp-fallback-href="~/lib/bootstrap/dist/css/bootstrap.min.
css"
            asp-fallback-test-class="sr-only" asp-fallback-test-
property="position" asp-fallback-test-value="absolute" />
    <link rel="stylesheet" href="~/css/site.min.css" asp-append-
version="true" />
</environment>
```

Note the rendering of hyperlinks to allow users to click between pages using the navigation bar at the top of every page. The <a> elements use "tag helper" attributes to specify the controller name and action name that will execute when the link is clicked:

```
<div class="navbar-collapse collapse">
    <ul class="nav navbar-nav">
        <li><a asp-controller="Home" asp-action="Index">Home</a></li>
        <li><a asp-controller="Home" asp-action="About">About</a></li>
        <li><a asp-controller="Home" asp-action="Contact">Contact</
a></li>
    </ul>
</div>
```

Note the rendering of the body:

```
@RenderBody()
```

Note the rendering of script blocks at the bottom of the page (so that it doesn't slow down the display of the page):

```
<environment names="Development">
    <script src="~/lib/jquery/dist/jquery.js"></script>
    <script src="~/lib/bootstrap/dist/js/bootstrap.js"></script>
    <script src="~/js/site.js" asp-append-version="true"></script>
</environment>
<environment names="Staging,Production">
    <script src="https://ajax.aspnetcdn.com/ajax/jquery/jquery-
2.1.4.min.js"
            asp-fallback-src="~/lib/jquery/dist/jquery.min.js"
            asp-fallback-test="window.jQuery">
    </script>
    <script src="https://ajax.aspnetcdn.com/ajax/bootstrap/3.3.5/
bootstrap.min.js"
            asp-fallback-src="~/lib/bootstrap/dist/js/bootstrap.min.
js"
            asp-fallback-test="window.jQuery && window.jQuery.fn &&
window.jQuery.fn.modal">
    </script>
    <script src="~/js/site.min.js" asp-append-version="true"></script>
</environment>
```

You can add you own script blocks into an optional defined section named **scripts**:

```
@RenderSection("scripts", required: false)
```

# Defining custom styles

In the wwwroot\css folder, open the site.css file.

Add a new style that will apply to an element with the newspaper ID, like this:

```
#newspaper {
    column-count: 3;
}
```

Notice that the `column-count` property has a purple squiggle under it. When you hover over it, you will see that only Internet Explorer 10 (or later) and Opera 11.6 (or later) currently implement this standard. Luckily, Web Essentials can fix this for us.

Click on the `column-count` property, hover your mouse over the small blue bar, click on the button to pop open a menu, and then click on **Add missing vendor specifics**.

You will see that Web Essentials has added two extra statements. They are faded out to indicate that they will automatically change when you change the value for the original `column-count` property:

```
#newspaper {
    -moz-column-count: 3;
    -webkit-column-count: 3;
    column-count: 3;
}
```

> To learn more about CSS3 and responsive design, read the book *Responsive Web Design with HTML5 and CSS3 - Second Edition* by *Packt Publishing* at `https://www.packtpub.com/web-development/responsive-web-design-html5-and-css3-second-edition`.

# Defining a typed view

To improve the IntelliSense when writing a view, you can define the type the view can expect using a `@model` directive at the top.

Back in the `Index.cshtml` view, enter the following code as the first line of the file:

```
@model Ch14_WebApp.Models.HomeIndexViewModel
```

Now whenever we enter `@Model`, Visual Studio's code editor will know the correct type and will provide IntelliSense.

> To declare the type of the model, use `@model` (with lowercase m).
> To read the model, use `@Model` (with uppercase M).

In `Index.cshtml`, delete all the `<div>` elements and replace them with this code:

```
<div class="row">
    <div class="col-md-12">
        <h1>Northwind</h1>
```

```
        <p class="lead">We have had @Model.VisitorCount visitors this
month.</p>
        <h2>Products</h2>
        <div id="newspaper">
            <ul>
            @foreach (var item in @Model.Products)
            {
                <li><a asp-controller="Home" asp-
action="ProductDetail" asp-route-id="@item.ProductID">@item.
ProductName costs @item.UnitPrice.Value.ToString("C")</a></li>
            }
            </ul>
        </div>
    </div>
</div>
```

Note how easy it is to mix static HTML elements, such as `<ul>` and `<li>`, with C# code to output the list of product names.

Note the `<div>` element with the `id` attribute of `newspaper`. This will use the custom style that we defined earlier, so all the content in that element will display in three columns.

To test the web application, press *F5*. The results in Microsoft Edge will look something like this:

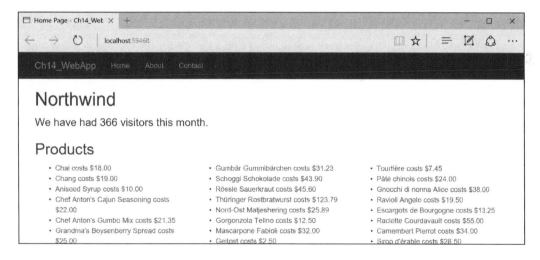

# Taking ASP.NET Core further

Now that you've seen the basics of how models, views, and controllers work together to provide a web application, let's look at some common scenarios, such as passing parameters and annotating models.

## Passing parameters using a route value

Back in the `HomeController` class, add the following action method. It uses something called the **default model binder** to automatically match the id passed in the route to the parameter named `id` in the method.

> Model binders are very powerful, and the default one does a lot for you. For advanced scenarios, you can create your own by implementing the `IModelBinder` interface, but that is beyond the scope of this book.

Inside the method, we check to see whether the `id` is null, and if so, it returns a 404 status code and message. Otherwise, we can connect to the database and try to retrieve a product using the `id` variable. If we find a product, we pass it to a view; otherwise, we return a different 404 status code and message:

```
public IActionResult ProductDetail(int? id)
{
    if (!id.HasValue)
    {
        return HttpNotFound("You must pass a product ID in the route,
for example, /Home/ProductDetail/21");
    }
    var model = db.Products.SingleOrDefault(p => p.ProductID == id);
    if (model == null)
    {
        return HttpNotFound($"A product with the ID of {id} was not
found.");
    }
    return View(model); // pass model to view
}
```

Now we need to create a view for this request.

Inside the **Views** folder, right-click on **Home** and choose **Add | New Item...**.

Choose **MVC View Page** and name it **ProductDetail.cshtml**:

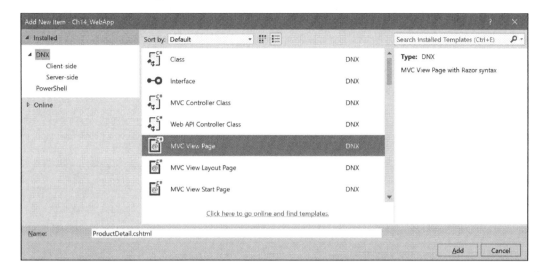

Modify the contents as shown here:

```
@model Ch14_WebApp.Models.Products
@{
    ViewData["Title"] = "Product Detail - " + Model.ProductName;
}
<h2>Product Detail</h2>
<hr />
<div>
    <dl class="dl-horizontal">
        <dt>Product ID</dt>
        <dd>@Model.ProductID</dd>
        <dt>Product Name</dt>
        <dd>@Model.ProductName</dd>
        <dt>Category ID</dt>
        <dd>@Model.CategoryID</dd>
        <dt>Unit Price</dt>
        <dd>@Model.UnitPrice.Value.ToString("C")</dd>
        <dt>Units In Stock</dt>
        <dd>@Model.UnitsInStock</dd>
    </dl>
</div>
```

Test the new action and view by pressing *F5*.

When the home page appears with the list of products, click one of them, for example, product 26. The result should look something like this:

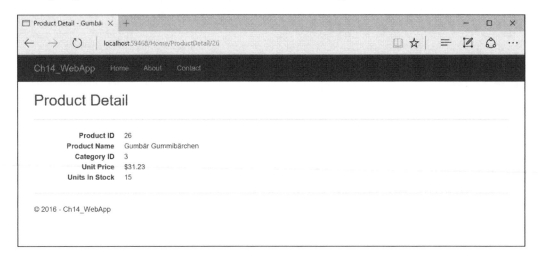

# Passing parameters using a query string

In the `HomeController` class, import the `Microsoft.Data.Entity` namespace.

Add a new action method like this:

```
public IActionResult ProductsThatCostMoreThan(decimal? price)
{
    if (!price.HasValue)
    {
        return HttpNotFound("You must pass a product price in the
query string, for example, /Home/ProductsThatCostMoreThan?price=50");
    }
    var model = db.Products.Include(p => p.Category).Include(p =>
p.Supplier).Where(p => p.UnitPrice > price).ToArray();
    if (model.Count() == 0)
    {
        return HttpNotFound($"No products cost more than {price:C}.");
    }
    ViewData["MaxPrice"] = price.Value.ToString("C");
    return View(model); // pass model to view
}
```

Inside the **Views** folder, right-click on **Home** and choose **Add | New Item...**.

Choose **MVC View Page** and name it **ProductsThatCostMoreThan.cshtml**.

Modify the contents like this:

```
@model IEnumerable<Ch14_WebApp.Models.Products>
@{
    ViewData["Title"] = "Products That Cost More Than " +
ViewData["MaxPrice"];
}
<h2>Products That Cost More Than @ViewData["MaxPrice"]</h2>
<table class="table">
    <tr>
        <th>
            @Html.DisplayNameFor(model => model.Category.CategoryName)
        </th>
        <th>
            @Html.DisplayNameFor(model => model.Supplier.CompanyName)
        </th>
        <th>
            @Html.DisplayNameFor(model => model.ProductName)
        </th>
        <th>
            @Html.DisplayNameFor(model => model.UnitPrice)
        </th>
        <th>
            @Html.DisplayNameFor(model => model.UnitsInStock)
        </th>
    </tr>
    @foreach (var item in Model)
    {
        <tr>
            <td>
                @Html.DisplayFor(modelItem => item.Category.
CategoryName)
            </td>
            <td>
                @Html.DisplayFor(modelItem => item.Supplier.
CompanyName)
            </td>
            <td>
                @Html.DisplayFor(modelItem => item.ProductName)
            </td>
            <td>
                @Html.DisplayFor(modelItem => item.UnitPrice)
            </td>
```

```
            <td>
                @Html.DisplayFor(modelItem => item.UnitsInStock)
            </td>
        </tr>
    }
</table>
```

In the **Views** folder, in the **Home** folder, open `Index.cshtml` file and add the following `div` element at the bottom of the file. This will provide a form for the user to enter a price. The user can then click on a submit button to call the action method that shows only products that cost more than the entered price:

```
<div class="row">
    <form asp-action="ProductsThatCostMoreThan" method="get">
        <input name="price" placeholder="Enter a product price" />
        <input type="submit" />
    </form>
</div>
```

Run the web application by pressing *F5*. On the home page, scroll down and enter a price in the form. Then, click on **Submit Query**:

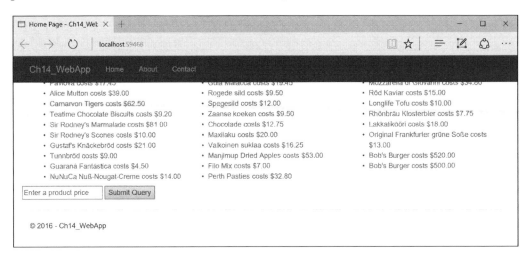

You will see a table of the products that cost more than the price you entered:

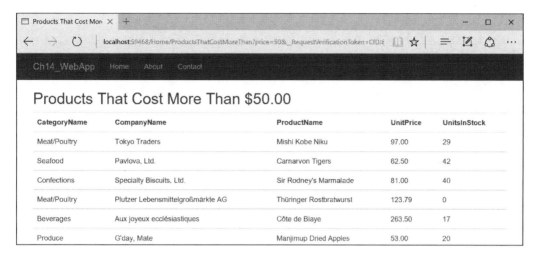

# Annotating models

You might have noticed that the column headings in the table used the names of the properties by default. This means that if the property is multiple words, it won't have spaces. We can use data annotations to improve this.

In the `Models` folder, open the `Products` class. Import the `System.ComponentModel.DataAnnotations` namespace.

Add `[Display]` attributes before each property if you want to have a different label, for example, Product Name, Unit Price, Units In Stock, and so on:

```
[Display(Name = "Product Name")]
public string ProductName { get; set; }
```

Apply the `[Display]` attribute to the properties of three other classes: Category's Category Name, Customer's Company Name, and Supplier's Company Name.

Start the web application by pressing *F5*.

Enter a product price and click on **Submit Query**. Notice that the column headings now reflect the display attributes and not the actual property names:

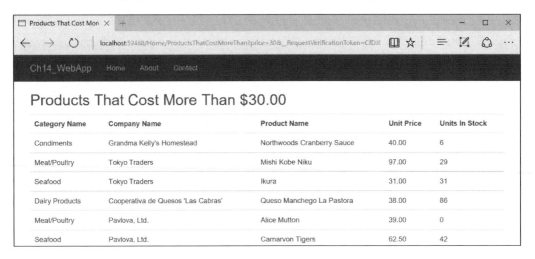

# ASP.NET Core Web API

Although HTTP was originally designed to request and respond with HTML and other resources for us to look at, it is also good for building services. Roy Fielding stated, in his doctoral dissertation describing the **Representational State Transfer (REST)** architectural style, that the HTTP standard defines:

- URLs to uniquely identify resources
- Methods to perform common tasks, such as GET and DELETE
- The ability to negotiate media formats such as XML and JSON

To allow the easy creation of services, ASP.NET Core has combined what used to be two types of controller.

In earlier versions of ASP.NET, you would derive from ApiController to create a Web API service, and then register API routes in the same route table that MVC uses.

With ASP.NET Core, you use exactly the same Controller base class used with MVC, except the routes are usually configured on the controller itself, using attributes, rather than in the route table.

# Scaffolding an API controller

In the **Solution Explorer** window, right-click on the **Controllers** folder and choose **Add | New Item...**. Choose **Web API Controller Class**, enter the name as **ShippersController**, and then click on **Add**:

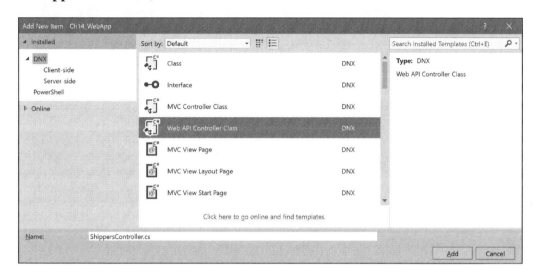

API controllers do not have views. Instead, they use automatic content negotiation with the client to return XML, JSON, or X-WWW-FORMURLENCODED data formats.

In `ShippersController` class, add the following code:

```
[Route("api/[controller]")]
public class ShippersController : Controller
{
    private NorthwindContext db;
    public ShippersController(NorthwindContext injectedContext)
    {
        db = injectedContext;
    }
    // GET: api/shippers
    [HttpGet]
    public IEnumerable<Shippers> Get()
    {
        return db.Shippers.ToArray();
    }
```

If you have used older versions of ASP.NET Web API, then you know that in that technology, you could create C# methods that begin with any HTTP method (GET, POST, PUT, and so on), and the controller will automatically execute the correct one. In ASP.NET Core, this doesn't happen anymore, because we are not inheriting from ApiController. So you must apply an attribute such as [HttpGet] to explicitly map HTTP methods to C# methods.

Press *F5* to run the application.

In the address bar, enter **api/shippers** at the end of the URL and press *Enter*. You will see this JSON response:

 If you test with Chrome rather than Microsoft Edge, then you will get an XML response because Chrome prefers XML over JSON.

# Calling a Web API service from a UWP app

Now that we have a service that allows HTTP requests to be used to manage the Shippers table, we can create a client application to call it. The client will often be an HTML page that uses JavaScript to make the calls. However, since this book is about modern C# and .NET, we will build a UWP app.

In Visual Studio, click on **File | Add | New Project...**. In the **Add New Project** dialog, in the **Installed Templates** list, select **Visual C#**. In the center list, select **Blank App (Universal Windows)**, type the name as **Ch14_WinApp**, and then click on **OK**.

In **Solution Explorer** window, right-click on the new project and choose **Manage NuGet Packages…**. In the search box, enter **web api client** and press *Enter*. Click on **Install**:

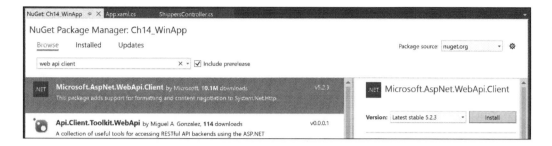

On the **Project** menu, choose **Add Class** and name it **Shipper**:

```
public class Shipper
{
    public int ShipperID { get; set; }
    public string CompanyName { get; set; }
    public string Phone { get; set; }
}
```

Open `MainPage.xaml` file and add the following XAML inside the existing `Grid` element:

```
<StackPanel Padding="6">
    <TextBlock FontSize="24">Shippers</TextBlock>
    <GridView ItemsSource="{Binding}">
        <GridView.ItemTemplate>
            <DataTemplate>
                <Border Margin="6" Padding="10" CornerRadius="10"
Background="LightCyan">
                    <Grid>
                        <Grid.ColumnDefinitions>
                            <ColumnDefinition Width="Auto" />
                            <ColumnDefinition Width="Auto" />
                        </Grid.ColumnDefinitions>
                        <Grid.RowDefinitions>
                            <RowDefinition />
                            <RowDefinition />
                            <RowDefinition />
                        </Grid.RowDefinitions>
                        <TextBlock Text="Shipper ID" />
                        <TextBlock Text="{Binding ShipperID}" Grid.
Column="1" />
```

```
                        <TextBlock Text="Company Name" Grid.Row="1" />
                        <TextBlock Text="{Binding CompanyName}" Grid.
   Row="1" Grid.Column="1" />
                        <TextBlock Text="Phone" Grid.Row="2" />
                        <TextBlock Text="{Binding Phone}" Grid.Row="2"
   Grid.Column="1" />
                   </Grid>
                </Border>
            </DataTemplate>
        </GridView.ItemTemplate>
    </GridView>
</StackPanel>
```

This defines a `GridView` control bound to the `DataContext` class that we will set when the page loads to the response coming back from the service.

In the `Page` element, add an event handler for `Loading` function:

```
Loading="Page_Loading"
```

In the `MainPage.xaml.cs` file, import the following namespace:

```
using System.Net.Http;
```

Add the following statements to the `Page_Loading` method, and add the `async` keyword to the method's declaration:

```
var client = new HttpClient();
client.BaseAddress = new Uri("http://localhost:59468/");
HttpResponseMessage response = await client.GetAsync("api/shippers");
DataContext = await response.Content.ReadAsAsync<Shipper[]>();
```

> Make sure you use the same random port number that Visual Studio allocated to your ASP.NET Core application. It is unlikely to be 59468!

On the **Build** menu, choose **Deploy Ch14_WinApp**. In the **Solution Explorer** window, right-click on the solution and choose **Properties**.

Select **Multiple startup projects**. Set the action for **Ch14_WebApp** to **Start without debugging**. Set the action for **Ch14_WinApp** to **Start**:

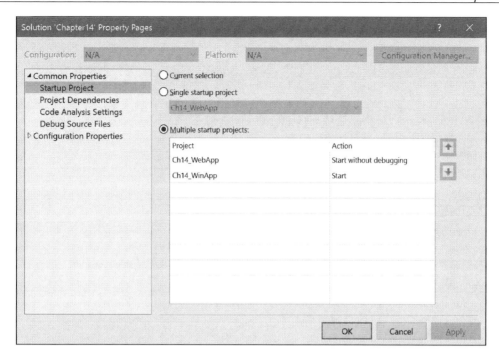

On the **Debug** menu, choose **Start Debugging** or press *F5*. You will see that the UWP app called the service, deserialized the JSON data, and bound it to the list box:

# Practicing and exploring

Test your knowledge and understanding by answering some questions, get some hands-on practice, and explore this chapter's topics with deeper research.

## Exercise 14.1 – test your knowledge

Answer the following questions:

1. What is the difference between a web browser and a web server?
2. What is the difference between a URI, a URL, and a URN?
3. What are the four most common HTTP methods?
4. What does it mean when a web server responds with status code 302?
5. What are the responsibilities of a route?
6. What are the responsibilities of a controller?
7. What are the responsibilities of a model?
8. What are the responsibilities of a view?
9. How does ASP.NET distinguish a request for MVC from a request for Web API?
10. What data formats does Web API support by default?

## Exercise 14.2 – practice building a data-driven web application

Create an ASP.NET Core web application that connects to the Northwind sample database and enables the user to see a list of customers grouped by country. When the user clicks on a customer record, they then see a page showing the full contact details of that customer and a list of their orders.

## Exercise 14.3 – explore topics

Use the following links to read more details about this chapter's topics:

- **Learn about ASP.NET Web Forms**: http://www.asp.net/web-forms
- **What is Windows Communication Foundation**: https://msdn.microsoft.com/en-us/library/ms731082(v=vs.110).aspx
- **Learn about ASP.NET MVC**: http://www.asp.net/mvc
- **Learn about ASP.NET Web API**: http://www.asp.net/web-api

# Summary

In this chapter, you learned how to build an ASP.NET Core MVC web application, and an ASP.NET Core Web API service that manages data using Entity Framework Core. You also learned how to consume a REST/HTTP service using `HttpClient`.

In the next chapter, you will learn how to build an ASP.NET Core web application that can be hosted cross-platform on Windows, Linux, or Mac OS X.

# 15
# Taking C# Cross-Platform

This chapter is about how you can take C# cross-platform using .NET Core 1.0, ASP.NET Core 1.0, Entity Framework Core 1.0, and Visual Studio Code.

 You will need a computer running Mac OS X to complete this chapter if you want to follow the directions as written. You could choose to use a Linux variant such as Ubuntu 14.04 or a Docker container instead of Mac OS X, but the installation steps and some of the command-line tools will be different from what I have described in this chapter. You can read more about using .NET Core on Ubuntu 14.04 or Docker at http://dotnet.github.io/getting-started/.

In this chapter, we will cover the following topics:

- Understanding cross-platform development
- Installing Visual Studio Code and ASP.NET Core
- Building cross-platform web applications using ASP.NET Core
- Understanding .NET Core command-line tools

# Understanding cross-platform development

Cross-platform development means being able to both write code and run the results on operating systems other than Windows.

## Visual Studio Code

Visual Studio Code is an open source, cross-platform, extensible, code-focused editor with some basic IDE features based on Google's Chromium project. Microsoft and Google have worked closely together to ensure that Visual Studio Code is a decent choice for cross-platform development.

However, it has significant limitations compared to Visual Studio 2015. Luckily, you can use Visual Studio 2015 on Windows for your initial development and then open the same files in Visual Studio Code when you need to work with your code on other platforms.

## .NET Core 1.0

.NET Core 1.0 is a forked open source and cross-platform implementation of .NET that is designed for modern development. It is a subset of the Windows-only .NET Framework, but it has the advantage of running cross-platform across Windows, Mac OS X, Linux operating systems, and Docker containers.

Microsoft has informally announced that .NET development is now happening first on .NET Core, with changes backported to the Windows-only .NET Framework.

## ASP.NET Core 1.0

ASP.NET Core 1.0 (which includes the latest versions of MVC and Web API) can be used to develop web applications and services that run on the .NET Core for cross-platform hosts, or on the .NET Framework for hosting on Windows.

## Entity Framework Core 1.0

Entity Framework Core 1.0 (EF Core) can be used cross-platform to manage relational data (stored in Microsoft SQL Server on Windows today and natively on Linux starting in 2017, MySQL, and others) and non-relational data (stored in Microsoft Azure Table storage, Redis, and others).

# .NET Native

.NET Native is a runtime that compiles .NET applications to native code. You can use it to create console applications, and ASP.NET Core applications and services, all running natively on Windows, Linux, and Mac OS X.

# Xamarin

Xamarin enables developers to build apps for Apple iOS and Google Android using C#. It is based on a third-party open source implementation of .NET known as Mono.

Applications built with Xamarin draw the user interface using native platform widgets, so the app looks natural on the target mobile platform.

Developers can code in either Visual Studio 2015 (which requires a paid license from Xamarin for their extensions) or using the free **Xamarin Studio**, which runs on Windows and Mac.

> If you would like to learn more about Xamarin, then I recommend *Xamarin Cross-platform Application Development (Second Edition)* by *Jonathan Peppers*, and *Mastering Cross-Platform Development with Xamarin* by *Can Bilgin*, by *Packt Publishing*.

# Cross-device Universal Windows Platform (UWP)

UWP apps are compiled using .NET Native for efficient resource usage and faster performance, but they are only supported on the Windows 10 platform. This means Windows 10 desktops, laptops, and tablets; Windows 10 Mobile phones; Xbox One; and HoloLens.

> Think of UWP as being cross-device rather than cross-platform.

# Installing Visual Studio Code and ASP.NET Core

First, we will install Visual Studio Code on Mac OS X.

 If you are using Linux, you can read the directions at
`https://code.visualstudio.com/Docs/?dv=linux64.`

## Installing Visual Studio Code

To install Visual Studio Code, you need to perform the following steps:

1.  Start Safari or Chrome, go to `https://code.visualstudio.com/Docs/editor/setup`, and then click on **Download Visual Studio Code for Mac OS X**.

2.  After downloading the ZIP file, double-click on it to extract the `Visual Studio Code.app` file. Drag the file to your `Applications` folder:

3.  When you first run Visual Studio Code, you will see that it is a very simple editor:

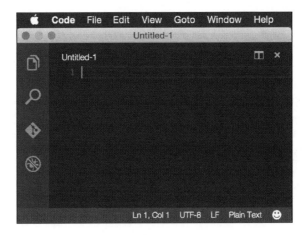

If you want to add Visual Studio Code to your dock for easy access, then right-click on its icon and go to **Options | Keep in Dock**.

# Managing development from the terminal

You will use the command line (the **Terminal** app) a lot during development on the Mac.

Start Mac OS X's **Terminal** app. Get a list of all files in your current directory by entering the following command:

```
ls -a
```

The **Terminal** output should look something like this:

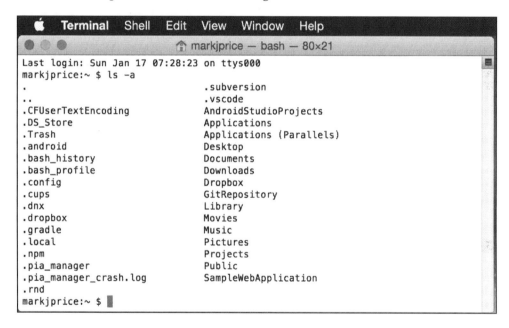

If you do not already have a file named `.bash_profile`, then enter the following command:

```
touch .bash_profile
```

Enter the following command to edit the file with the nano text editor:

```
nano .bash_profile
```

In the editor, add the following statements:

```
code () {
    if [[ $# = 0 ]]
    then
        open -a "Visual Studio Code"
    else
        [[ $1 = /* ]] && F="$1" || F="$PWD/${1#./}"
        open -a "Visual Studio Code" --args "$F"
    fi
}
```

Press *Ctrl + O* to save changes, press *Enter* to accept the filename, and then press *Ctrl + X* to exit and return to the prompt.

> You could also use TextEdit to modify the `.bash_profile` file using the following command:
>
> **open -e .bash_profile**

Restart the **Terminal** app or enter `source .bash_profile` to force it to be reprocessed.

From now on, you will be able to change to a directory containing any project and enter `code .` to open Visual Studio Code and start editing that project.

# Installing Homebrew

The next step is to install Homebrew if you don't already have it.

> Homebrew installs the stuff you need that Apple didn't already install.

Enter the following in the **Terminal** prompt:

```
ruby -e "$(curl -fsSL https://raw.githubusercontent.com/Homebrew/install/
master/install)"
```

Now, we will use Homebrew to install ASP.NET Core and its .NET Version Manager (dnvm).

At the time of writing this book, Microsoft is in the middle of changing the command-line tools for .NET Core. When the final version is released, they plan to use a similar tool named dotnet instead of dnvm. Most of the commands will be similar to what I will show you in this chapter. You can keep yourself updated by visiting http://cs6dotnetcore.azurewebsites.net/.

# Installing ASP.NET Core and the .NET Version Manager

Enter the following commands in Command Prompt:

brew tap aspnet/dnx

brew install dnvm

dnvm upgrade

source dnvm.sh

dnvm

The last command displays an overview of what you can do with dnvm:

# Listing the installed versions of .NET

One of the most important commands is getting a detailed list of the installed versions. Enter the following command in the prompt:

```
dnvm list -detailed
```

You will see output like the following screenshot:

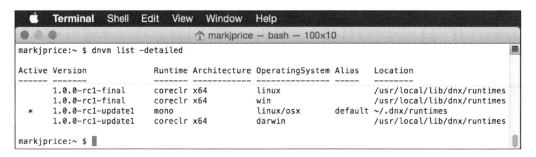

 At the time of writing this book, the final version of .NET Core has not been released. All screenshots in this chapter show a release candidate version.

# Switching from Mono to .NET Core

You may have noticed that the default runtime is Mono, not .NET Core. We can use the dnvm use command to switch the runtime to .NET Core, as you can see in this screenshot of the dnvm use command's parameters:

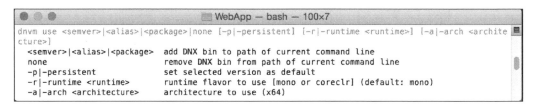

In the **Terminal** app, enter the following commands:

```
dnvm use 1.0.0-rc1-update1 -runtime coreclr -arch x64 -persistent
dnvm list -detailed
```

You will see that the active (and default) version has now switched to .NET Core:

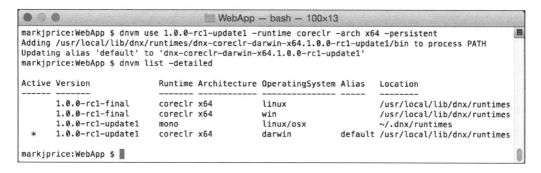

# Building a console application

To test the installation, let's make a simple console application that outputs `Hello C# running cross-platform!`.

# Creating the source files

We need to enter some commands in the **Terminal** prompt to:

- Create a new directory named `ConsoleApp` and change to it
- Create two files named `program.cs` and `project.json`
- Start Visual Studio Code so that we can edit the files in an IDE

Here are the commands to enter:

```
mkdir ConsoleApp
cd ConsoleApp
touch program.cs
touch project.json
code .
```

# Editing the code

In Visual Studio Code, click on the `program.cs` file on the left-hand side and then enter these statements:

```csharp
using static System.Console;

public class Program
{
    public static void Main()
    {
        WriteLine("Hello C#, running cross-platform!");
    }
}
```

When targeting the .NET Framework, a developer can rely on the fact that if the .NET Framework has been installed, then all the base class libraries would be available to them. This means the developer could compile the previous code and know it will execute, just as we did in *Chapter 1, Hello, C#! Welcome, .NET Core!*

When targeting .NET Core, the developer would need to specify the dependencies that their code has so that only those NuGet packages are deployed along with the developer's assembly.

You specify options such as which versions of .NET you would like to target and what dependencies your code has, in a file named `project.json`.

 You can read the documentation for the `project.json` file at https://github.com/aspnet/Home/wiki/Project.json-file.

Click on the `project.json` file on the left-hand side and then enter these statements:

```json
{
    "dependencies": {
    },
    "commands": {
        "ConsoleApp": "ConsoleApp"
    },
    "frameworks": {
        "dnx451": { },
        "dnxcore50": {
            "dependencies": {
                "System.Console": "4.0.0-beta-*"
            }
        }
    }
}
```

**dnx451** means .NET Framework 4.5.1, which has no dependencies, because the entire base class library would be available. **dnxcore50** means .NET Core 1.0, which must have any dependencies explicitly listed. Both these names are likely to change in the future when Microsoft switches to the .NET Platform Standard, which is described at `https://github.com/dotnet/corefx/blob/master/Documentation/architecture/net-platform-standard.md`.

Visual Studio Code should look like the following screenshot:

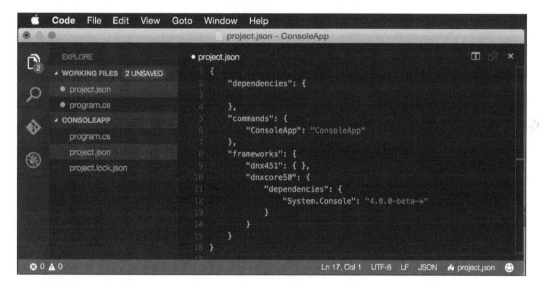

Go to **File** | **Save All** to save the changes to both files and then quit Visual Studio Code.

 Visual Studio Code will notice that you need to download some dependency packages. Although it can issue the command for you, we will do it manually.

# Downloading dependency packages and compiling

In the prompt, enter the following commands to download dependency packages and run the application:

```
dnu restore

dnx ConsoleApp run
```

You will see the following output:

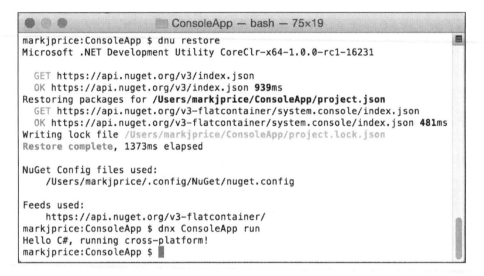

# Building cross-platform web applications using ASP.NET Core

Now, let's make a simple ASP.NET Core web application.

# Creating the simplest ASP.NET Core web application

You will enter some commands in the **Terminal** prompt to:

- Create a new directory named HelloWeb and move into it
- Create two files named startup.cs and project.json
- Start Visual Studio Code so that we can edit the files in an IDE

Here are the commands to enter:

```
cd ~
mkdir HelloWeb
cd HelloWeb
touch startup.cs
touch project.json
code .
```

In Visual Studio Code, click on the startup.cs file on the left-hand side and then enter these statements:

```
using Microsoft.AspNet.Builder;
using Microsoft.Extensions.Logging;

namespace HelloWeb
{
    public class Startup
    {
        public void Configure(IApplicationBuilder app, ILoggerFactory
loggerFactory)
        {
            loggerFactory.AddConsole();
            app.UseIISPlatformHandler();
            app.UseStaticFiles();
            app.UseWelcomePage();
        }
    }
}
```

Click on the project.json file on the left-hand side and then enter the following statements to:

- Specify a version for our code
- Specify a directory name for the root of our website that will be used to store static content such as HTML, CSS, JavaScript libraries, and assets such as images and videos
- Exclude any files in the root of our website from the compilation process
- Exclude design-time files such as .kproj files from the deployment package
- Define a list of dependency packages for our code

- Target both the .NET Framework 4.5.1 (dnx451) and the .NET Core 1.0 (dnxcore50)

- Define a dnx command named web that will start the web application hosted in the Kestrel cross-platform web server listening on port 5004

Here are the statements:

```
{
    "version": "1.0.0-*",
    "webroot": "wwwroot",
    "exclude": [
        "wwwroot"
    ],
    "packExclude": [
        "**.kproj",
        "**.user",
        "**.vspscc"
    ],
    "dependencies": {
        "Microsoft.AspNet.Server.Kestrel": "1.0.0-*",
        "Microsoft.AspNet.IISPlatformHandler": "1.0.0-*",
        "Microsoft.AspNet.Diagnostics": "1.0.0-*",
        "Microsoft.AspNet.Hosting": "1.0.0-*",
        "Microsoft.AspNet.StaticFiles": "1.0.0-*",
        "Microsoft.Extensions.Logging.Console": "1.0.0-*"
    },
    "commands": {
        "web": "Microsoft.AspNet.Server.Kestrel --server.urls http://
localhost:5004"
    },
    "frameworks": {
        "dnx451": { },
        "dnxcore50": { }
    }
}
```

Save all the changes. Visual Studio Code should look something like the following screenshot. Note the warning about unresolved dependencies. This time we will use Visual Studio Code to restore the dependency packages.

Click on **Restore**:

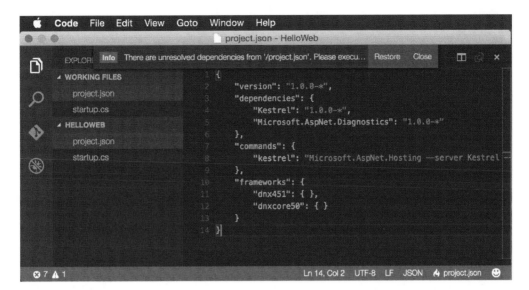

 You can also restore the dependency packages in the **Terminal** prompt by entering the `dnu restore` command, as we did earlier.

It might take a few minutes to download all the packages, so be patient!

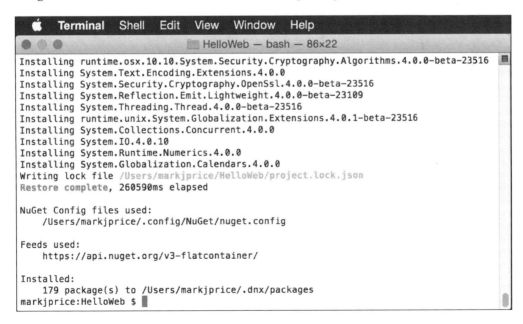

In the prompt, enter the following command to run the application:

`dnx web`

You will see the following output:

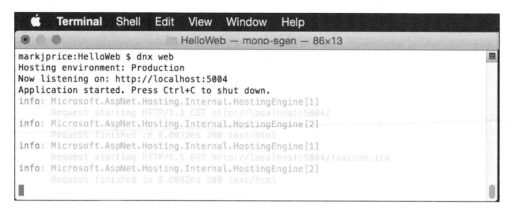

Run your favorite Mac OS X web browser and enter this URL in the address bar and press **Enter**:

`http://localhost:5004/`

You should see the following page:

# Installing Yeoman and related tools

As you have seen earlier in this book, Visual Studio 2015 has many project templates that make it easy to get started with projects, from console applications to web applications and services.

A command-line tool named **Yeoman** can be used to provide a similar scaffolding feature. To use Yeoman, we first need to install the **Node Package Manager** (**npm**) from `http://nodejs.org/`, and you will see the following home page:

In the **Terminal** prompt, enter the following commands to install Yeoman, Bower, Grunt, Gulp, and the ASP.NET Core generator:

```
npm install -g yo bower grunt-cli gulp
npm install -g generator-aspnet
```

 If you get a permission error, then prefix the commands with `sudo` to execute them using the super user account. The `-g` flag installs the tools globally, so you can run them from any directory.

# Scaffolding projects using Yeoman

Enter the following commands in the **Terminal** prompt to create a new directory for a project and create a scaffolded project template inside it:

```
cd ~
```

```
yo aspnet
```

When Yeoman runs, you will see the the output as shown in the following screenshot.

Choose **Web Application Basic [without Membership and Authorization]** and press *Enter*. Then, enter the name WebApp. Yeoman will now create a set of files for a basic web application project:

In the **Terminal** prompt, enter the following commands to change to the new directory that Yeoman created for you. Then, see a listing of all the files, restore dependent packages, and finally execute the Kestrel web server and start it listening on port 5000.

```
cd WebApp
ls -a
dnu restore
dnx web
```

As you enter the preceding commands, you will see output as shown in the following screenshot:

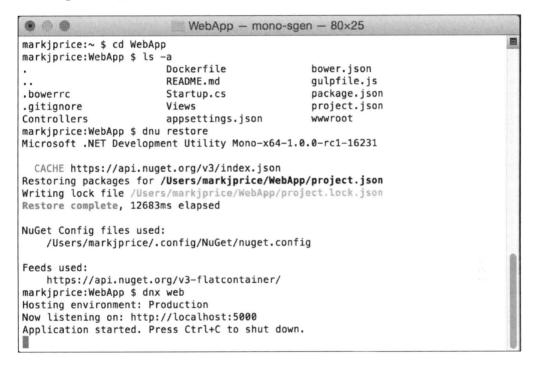

 If you get an error message about being unable to resolve project that is most likely because you have executed the dnu restore command in a directory without a project.json file.

Start a web browser and go to `http://localhost:5000/`:

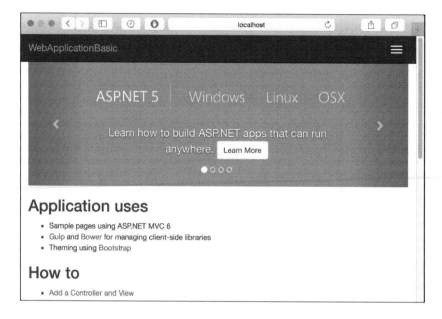

By default, every request from the browser is logged to the **Terminal** window.

Note that the first request is to `http://localhost:5000/`, which caused the `Index` action method of `HomeController` to return the results of a view named `/Views/Home/Index.cshtml`:

Close the web browser, and in **Terminal**, press *Ctrl + C* to stop the Kestrel web server.

# Editing projects using Visual Studio Code

You could open this project using Visual Studio 2015 if you have Windows, which provides a better developer experience, but we will use Visual Studio Code.

In **Terminal**, enter `code .` to start Visual Studio Code and load this project. Browse the files to see how it all fits together, as shown in the following screenshot. The same C# code that you learned in *Chapter 14, Building Web Applications and Services Using ASP. NET Core*, applies here.

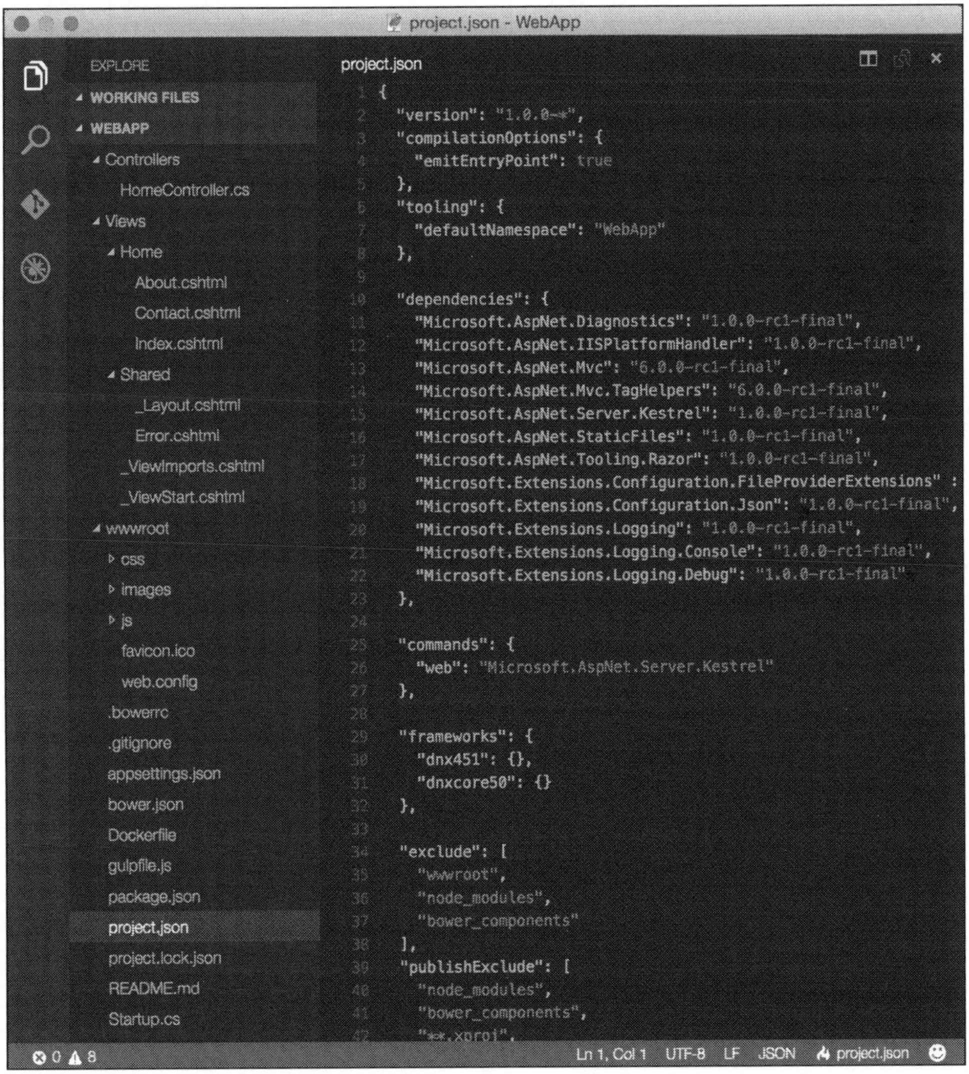

Instead of having to run **Terminal**, you can execute commands directly inside Visual Studio Code.

Press *Command + Shift + P*. Then, in the > prompt, type dnx, and you will see that a drop-down command list filters to show two commands related to dnx:

Press *Enter* to see the actual command (dnu restore), and then press *Enter* again to execute it in the directory shown:

The **Terminal** prompt will become active, and you will see the results of running the command.

 In 2016, Microsoft SQL Server only runs on Windows, but in 2017, it will be available for Linux. If you need a RDBMS that is completely cross-platform today, then you should use SQLite. For more information, visit https://github.com/aspnet/Microsoft.Data.Sqlite.

# Understanding the .NET Core command-line tools

There are two sets of command-line interface tools that you can use to manage .NET Core.

## Understanding the DNX tools

The .NET Version Manager, .NET Execution Environment, and .NET Development Utilities (dnvm, dnx, and dnu) were used by Microsoft during the initial development of the .NET Core between 2013 and 2015. They are installed as part of Visual Studio 2015.

The .NET Version Manager (dnvm) is used to install various versions of the .NET Execution Environment (dnx).

A dnx is a software development kit (SDK) and runtime environment that has everything you need to build and run .NET applications, including a host process, CLR, and managed entry-point discovery. There are three common dnxes: the .NET Framework, the .NET Core, and Mono.

The .NET Development Utilities (dnu) tool provides functions to help with ASP.NET Core development. The most common function is to use dnu to install and manage library packages in our application by using its restore feature.

## Understanding the CLI tools

The .NET CLI (dotnet) is a "driver" that will be used by the final release of the .NET Core. It provides a simplified layer on top of other underlying tools. The .NET CLI must be installed separately.

## Common DNX commands

To install the latest version of the .NET Execution Environment and make it temporarily active, use the following command:

```
dnvm install latest
```

To install a specific version of a dnx and make it temporarily active, use the following command:

```
dnvm install latest -runtime coreclr -arch x64
```

To install a version and make it permanently active by modifying the PATH variable use upgrade instead of `install`:

```
dnvm upgrade latest -runtime coreclr -arch x64
```

To switch to a different version, use the following command:

```
dnvm use 1.0.0-rc1-update1 -runtime coreclr -arch x64
```

# Common CLI commands

First, we must install the .NET CLI.

Start Safari or Chrome and go to `https://github.com/dotnet/cli`.

Scroll down the page to find **Installers** and click on the link to download the **PKG** file for Mac OS X. Open the package and install it.

In the **Terminal** prompt, enter the following command:

```
dotnet
```

You should see the following output:

```
markjprice:~ $ dotnet
.NET Command Line Tools (1.0.0)
Usage: dotnet [common-options] [command] [arguments]

Arguments:
  [command]     The command to execute
  [arguments]   Arguments to pass to the command

Common Options (passed before the command):
  -v|--verbose  Enable verbose output
  --version     Display .NET CLI Version Info

Common Commands:
  new       Initialize a basic .NET project
  restore   Restore dependencies specified in the .NET project
  compile   Compiles a .NET project
  publish   Publishes a .NET project for deployment (including the runtime)
  run       Compiles and immediately executes a .NET project
  repl      Launch an interactive session (read, eval, print, loop)
  pack      Creates a NuGet package
markjprice:~ $
```

Enter the following commands in the **Terminal** prompt to create a new directory, change to it, create a new console application in the directory, and then list the files it created:

```
mkdir ConsoleApp2
cd ConsoleApp2
dotnet new
ls
```

You should see that the dotnet tool has created three new files for you: NuGet.Config, Program.cs, and project.json.

In the **Terminal** prompt, enter the following command to start Visual Studio Code:

```
code .
```

In Visual Studio Code, click on Program.cs on the left-hand side and modify the WriteLine statement like this:

```
Console.WriteLine("Hello C#, Welcome .NET Core!");
```

Save changes and quit Visual Studio Code.

In the **Terminal** prompt, enter the following commands:

```
dotnet restore
dotnet run
```

After a few seconds, all the dependency packages will be downloaded, and your application will run, showing the following output:

To compile the source code into an assembly containing IL code, enter the following command, as shown in the following screenshot:

```
dotnet build
```

If you navigate into the subdirectories, you will note that a \bin\Debug\dnxcore50\ directory has been created with a Unix executable named ConsoleApp2 in it.

 Debug is the configuration name. The framework name is dnxcore50. This will change in the release version of the .NET Core.

# Practicing and exploring

Test your knowledge and understanding by answering some questions, get some hands-on practice, and explore this chapter's topics with deeper research.

## Exercise 15.1 – test your knowledge

Answer the following questions:

1. What platforms are supported by .NET Core and ASP.NET Core?
2. What command downloads dependent packages for a project?
3. What file does project directory require in order to restore packages?
4. What command will show the currently installed versions of .NET?
5. What command will switch to a different version of .NET?

## Exercise 15.2 – practice transferring an existing ASP.NET application

Take the ASP.NET Core application that we created in *Chapter 14, Building Web Applications and Services Using ASP.NET Core*, restore its packages, and host it in the Kestrel web server.

What happens? Why?

> The project uses a database connection string that attempts to connect to a Microsoft SQL Server LocalDb instance, but Mac OS X does not support this. So, an unhandled exception is thrown causing the **Terminal** window to crash! We would need to change the database connection string to point to a Windows Server or Linux running the full (or Express) version of Microsoft SQL Server instead. Alternatively, we could use the Microsoft Azure SQL Database instead.

# Exercise 15.3 – explore topics

Use the following links to read more about this chapter's topics:

- **Requirements for Visual Studio Code**: `https://code.visualstudio.com/Docs/supporting/requirements`

- **Visual Studio Code for Mac developers**: `https://channel9.msdn.com/Series/Visual-Studio-Code-for-Mac-Developers`

- **.NET Core Roadmap**: `https://github.com/dotnet/core/blob/master/roadmap.md`

- **Project.json file**: `https://github.com/aspnet/Home/wiki/Project.json-file`

- **Microsoft .NET Native**: `https://msdn.microsoft.com/en-us/vstudio/dotnetnative.aspx`

- **Compiling Apps with .NET Native**: `https://msdn.microsoft.com/en-us/library/dn584397.aspx`

- **ASP.NET Core Documentation**: `http://docs.asp.net/en/latest/`

# Summary

In this chapter, you learned how to build an ASP.NET Core application that can be hosted cross-platform on Windows, Linux, a Docker container, and Mac OS X.

> If this chapter stoked your interest and you want more details, then check out Packt Publishing's web site at `http://www.packtpub.com/` because the most likely book I write next will be a deeper dive into ASP.NET Core and Entity Framework Core using Visual Studio Code.

In the next chapter, you will learn how to build a complete web application and service for a Quiz app.

# 16
# Building a Quiz

This chapter is about designing and building a quiz application that helps students learn the C# language, .NET Core, and related topics.

This chapter covers the following topics:

- Designing the quiz application
- Building the quiz solution
- Running the quiz
- Hosting ASP.NET Core web apps in Microsoft Azure

# Designing the quiz application

The first decision for designing the quiz that we need to make is on which platform to implement the quiz. We want this quiz to be usable for as many students as possible, wherever and whenever.

## Choosing the platform

A web application that uses responsive design to support mobile devices as well as desktops would be a good choice. To provide maximum scalability and flexibility for the choice of host, we want a platform that will run on Windows or Linux, either the full operating system, or a Docker container.

The application will therefore use the following:

- ASP.NET Core 1.0 for its server-side processing
- Entity Framework Core 1.0 for data storage
- HTML5 and CSS3 for a user experience that adapts to different devices

> Since this is only a sample project and will have a small amount of data, we will use an in-memory database to remove data storage costs. In the real world, you will have to pay for storage of quizzes and their questions.

# Deciding the functional requirements

The application will maintain multiple quizzes about various topics. To simplify the design, the questions will always be multiple choices, where the quiz taker picks one answer from four possibilities.

At the end, the quiz taker will be told how many questions they got right out of the total, and they will be given a list of their answers to compare against the correct answers.

# Separating concerns

We will follow best practice and create a solution with multiple projects, each of which has responsibilities as described in the following bullets:

- **Ch16_QuizModels**: This is a **Class Library (Package)** for the entity classes, that represents a quiz and a question with no dependency on a data access library.

- **Ch16_QuizRepository**: This is a **Class Library (Package)** with a dependency on the Entity Framework Core 1.0, to enable data access and storage of the entities. We will use the new in-memory database, but we will design the repository to support easy swapping of alternatives such as Microsoft SQL Server and Microsoft Azure DocumentDB.

- **Ch16_QuizWebApp**: This is a **ASP.NET Core 1.0 Web Application**, with view models that represent a user's current answers, and a list of questions stored in the session state.

# Building the quiz solution

Start Microsoft Visual Studio 2015. In Visual Studio, press *Ctrl + Shift + N*, or navigate to **File | New | Project...**.

In the **New Project** dialog, in the **Installed Templates** list, select **Visual C#**. In the list at the center, select **Class Library (Package)** and enter the name **Ch16_QuizModels**. Change the location to C:\Code, enter the solution name **Chapter16**, and then click on **OK**.

# Defining the entity models

Right-click on **Class1.cs** file and choose **Rename**, and enter a name for the quiz.
Open the file and modify the code to look like this:

```
using System.Collections.Generic;

namespace Packt.QuizWebApp
{
    public class Quiz
    {
        public string QuizID { get; set; } // e.g. CSHARP
        public string Title { get; set; } // e.g. C# and OOP
        public string Description { get; set; }

        // one-to-many relationship with a collection of Questions
        public virtual ICollection<Question> Questions { get; set; }

        // constructor to instantiate an empty collection
        public Quiz()
        {
            Questions = new HashSet<Question>();
        }
    }
}
```

 We have not defined the Question class yet, so you will not see it appear in IntelliSense and you will not be able to compile the project.

On the **Project** menu, choose **Add Class...** and name it **Question**. Modify the code to look like this:

```
namespace Packt.QuizWebApp
{
    public class Question
    {
        public int QuestionID { get; set; } // identity
        public string QuestionText { get; set; }
        public string AnswerA { get; set; }
        public string AnswerB { get; set; }
        public string AnswerC { get; set; }
        public string AnswerD { get; set; }
        public string CorrectAnswer { get; set; } // e.g. B
```

```
            // the other side of the one-to-many relationship
            public virtual Quiz Quiz { get; set; }
        }
    }
```

You should now be able to build this project with no errors, by pressing F6.

# Creating the data repository

Add a new **Class Library (Package)** project named **Ch16_QuizRepository**. Add a reference to the **Ch16_QuizModels** project.

From the **Tools** menu, choose **NuGet Package Manager**, and then choose **Package Manager Console**.

In the **Package Manager Console**, ensure that the package source is set to **nuget.org** and the default project is set to **Ch16_QuizRepository**, and then enter the following command at the prompt:

**install-package entityframework.inmemory**

 By the time you read this book, the final release version should be available, so the preceding command will work. If you get an error with the preceding line of code, add the –pre flag at its end to install the pre-release version.

Right-click on **Class1.cs** and choose **Rename**. Enter the name **QuizContext**. Modify the code to look like this:

```
    using Microsoft.Data.Entity;
    using Microsoft.Data.Entity.Infrastructure;

    namespace Packt.QuizWebApp
    {
        public class QuizContext : DbContext
        {
            public DbSet<Quiz> Quizzes { get; set; }
            public DbSet<Question> Questions { get; set; }

            // Best practice is to allow the options to be
            // passed into a constructor so that we remove any
            // assumptions about where the data is stored: in-memory,
            // SQL Server, and so on.
            public QuizContext(DbContextOptions options) : base(options) {
    }
```

```
        protected override void OnModelCreating(ModelBuilder
modelBuilder)
        {
            modelBuilder.Entity<Quiz>().HasMany<Question>().WithOne(q
=> q.Quiz);
            base.OnModelCreating(modelBuilder);
        }
    }
}
```

You should now be able to build this project with no errors, by pressing F6.

# Creating the web application

Add a new **ASP.NET Web Application** project named **Ch16_QuizWebApp**.
Choose the **ASP.NET Core 1.0 Templates – Web Application** template, leave the
authentication as **Individual User Accounts**, clear the **Host in the cloud** checkbox,
and click on **OK**:

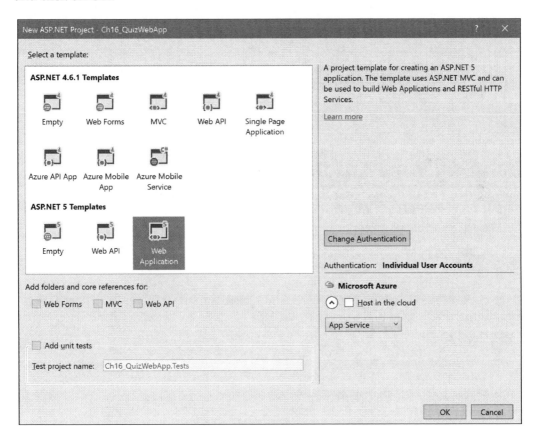

At the time of writing, the final version of ASP.NET Core 1.0 had not been released, so the screenshots in this book show the old branding: ASP.NET 5.

In the **Solution Explorer** window, right-click on the **Ch16_QuizWebApp** project and choose **Set as StartUp Project**.

Add references to the **Ch16_QuizModels** and **Ch16_QuizRepository** projects.

From the **Tools** menu, choose **NuGet Package Manager**, and then choose **Package Manager Console**. In the **Package Manager Console** window, ensure that the package source is set to **nuget.org** and the default project is set to **Ch16_QuizWebApp**. Next, enter the following commands at the prompt:

```
install-package microsoft.netcore.portable.compatibility
install-package newtonsoft.json
install-package microsoft.aspnet.session
install-package microsoft.extensions.caching.memory
install-package entityframework.inmemory
```

By the time you read this book, the final release versions of the ASP.NET Core NuGet packages should be available, so the preceding commands will work. If you get an error with any of the preceding lines, add the -pre flag to the end to install the pre-release version.

# Defining view models

View models are all the data required by a view. We need to define two view models—one for the view that displays a question, and another for the view that displays the list of answers at the end of a quiz.

In the **Solution Explorer** window, in the **ViewModels** folder, add a folder named **Home**.

Right-click on the **Home** folder, choose **Add Class...**, name it **QuestionViewModel**, and modify the code to define a class that represents all the data required when viewing a question:

```
using Packt.QuizWebApp;

namespace Ch16_QuizWebApp.ViewModels.Home
{
```

```
public class QuestionViewModel
{
    public Question Question { get; set; }
    public string Answer { get; set; }
    public int Number { get; set; }
    public int Total { get; set; }
}
}
```

Right-click on the **Home** folder, choose **Add Class...**, name it **FinishViewModel**, and modify the code to define a class that represents all the data required when viewing the results of a quiz:

```
using Packt.QuizWebApp;
using System.Collections.Generic;

namespace Ch16_QuizWebApp.ViewModels.Home
{
    public class FinishViewModel
    {
        public Quiz Quiz { get; set; }
        public Dictionary<int, string> Answers { get; set; }
        public int CorrectAnswers { get; set; }
    }
}
```

# Adding sample quiz questions

We need some sample quiz questions. We will store them in a JSON file and deserialize them into the in-memory database provided by the Entity Framework Core.

Right-click on the **wwwroot** directory of the **Ch16_QuizWebApp** project and navigate to **Add | New Item...** or press *Ctrl + Shift + A*.

Choose a **JSON File**, name it **samplequestions.json**, and click on **OK**.

Modify the file as shown in the following block of code. Note that any string can be used as a `$id` and `$ref` in order to define references between objects. I chose to use Q1, Q2, and so on, to identify quizzes, and Q1.1, Q1.2, and so on, to identify questions that belong to quizzes:

```
{
  "$values": [
    {
      "$id": "Q1",
```

```
      "QuizID": "CSHARP",
      "Title": "C# and OOP",
      "Description": "Questions about the C# language and object-
oriented programming.",
      "Questions": {
        "$values": [
          {
            "$id": "Q1.1",
            "QuestionID": 0,
            "QuestionText": "Which modifier would you apply to a
type's member to allow only code within that type access to it?",
            "AnswerA": "internal",
            "AnswerB": "protected",
            "AnswerC": "private",
            "AnswerD": "public",
            "CorrectAnswer": "C",
            "Quiz": {
              "$ref": "Q1"
            }
          },
          {
            "$id": "Q1.2",
            "QuestionID": 0,
            "QuestionText": "Which keyword would you apply to a type's
field to prevent its value from changing after an instance of the type
has been created?",
            "AnswerA": "const",
            "AnswerB": "readonly",
            "AnswerC": "static",
            "AnswerD": "protected",
            "CorrectAnswer": "B",
            "Quiz": {
              "$ref": "Q1"
            }
          }

        ]
      }
    },
    {
      "$id": "Q2",
      "QuizID": "FILEIO",
      "Title": "File I/O",
```

```
      "Description": "Questions about the file input/output features
of the .NET Framework including serialization.",
        "Questions": {
          "$values": [
            {
              "$id": "Q2.1",
              "QuestionID": 0,
              "QuestionText": "What are the requirements for a type to
be serialized by using the BinaryFormatter?",
              "AnswerA": "Apply [Serializable] to the type.",
              "AnswerB": "Apply [Serializable] to the type and make all
fields public.",
              "AnswerC": "Ensure the type is public with a parameterless
contructor.",
              "AnswerD": "Ensure the type is public with a parameterless
contructor and make any fields you want to include public.",
              "CorrectAnswer": "A",
              "Quiz": {
                "$ref": "Q2"
              }
            }
          ]
        }
      }
    ]
}
```

 Add at least five questions for each quiz. The preceding code is trimmed to save space.

Right-click on the **Models** folder and choose **Add Class...**, name it **QuizConfig**, and modify the code to enable the Entity Framework Core in-memory database. Populate it with the deserialized sample quiz questions, as follows:

```
using Packt.QuizWebApp;
using Microsoft.AspNet.Builder;
using Microsoft.Data.Entity;
using Newtonsoft.Json;
using System.IO;
using System.Collections.Generic;

namespace Ch16_QuizWebApp.Models
{
```

```
    public static class QuizConfig
    {
        public static void UseSampleQuestions(this IApplicationBuilder
app, string path)
        {
            // load a sample JSON file of questions
            string json = File.ReadAllText(Path.Combine(path,
"samplequestions.json"));

            var settings = new JsonSerializerSettings
                { PreserveReferencesHandling =
PreserveReferencesHandling.All };

            List<Quiz> quizzes = JsonConvert.DeserializeObject<List<Qu
iz>>(json, settings);

            // Configure the in-memory database option
            var optionsBuilder = new DbContextOptionsBuilder<QuizCont
ext>();
            optionsBuilder.UseInMemoryDatabase();

            using (var context = new QuizContext(optionsBuilder.
Options))
            {
                foreach (Quiz quiz in quizzes)
                {
                    // mark each quiz and its question entities as
Added
                    context.Add(quiz, GraphBehavior.
IncludeDependents);
                }
                // Save the entities to the data store
                context.SaveChanges();
            }
        }
    }
}
```

# Configuring session state

Open the `Startup.cs` file and add the following statements to the end of the `ConfigureServices` method, after the call to the `AddMvc` method:

```
services.AddCaching();
services.AddSession(options =>
    {
        options.CookieName = ".Packt.QuizWebApp";
        options.IdleTimeout = TimeSpan.FromMinutes(10);
    });
```

Add the following statements to the end of the `Configure` method, before and after the call to the `UseMvc` method, to use the session state and to populate the sample questions:

```
app.UseSession(); // must be added before MVC

app.UseMvc(routes =>
{
    routes.MapRoute(
        name: "default",
        template: "{controller=Home}/{action=Index}/{id?}");
});

app.UseSampleQuestions(env.MapPath("")); // pass the path to the
wwwroot directory
```

# Adding custom controller actions

Open the **Controllers** folder and the `HomeController` class, and modify the code as follows:

- Define a custom `JsonSerializerSettings` class that handles circular references correctly for the quiz-questions relationship
- Define pairs of methods to set and get the current user's quiz and the user's questions from their user session stored as JSON
- A constructor that sets the database context to use an in-memory database
- Index action that passes all the quizzes to a home page view
- The `TakeQuiz` action that shows a summary of the chosen quiz ready, for the user to start it

- The Question GET action that shows a specified question
- The Question POST action that stores the user's selected answer and then redirects to the next question
- The Finish action that shows the results
- The Error action that shows the default error page

Here is the code:

```
using Packt.QuizWebApp;
using Microsoft.Data.Entity;
using System.Collections.Generic;
using System.Linq;
using System.Threading.Tasks;
using Microsoft.AspNet.Mvc;
using Microsoft.AspNet.Http;
using Newtonsoft.Json;

namespace Ch16_QuizWebApp.Controllers
{
    public class HomeController : Controller
    {
        private QuizContext db;

        public JsonSerializerSettings settings = new
JsonSerializerSettings
            { PreserveReferencesHandling = PreserveReferencesHandling.
All };

#region Helper methods to store state in Session
        public void SetQuiz(Quiz input)
        {
            string json = JsonConvert.SerializeObject(input,
Formatting.None, settings);
            HttpContext.Session.SetString("usersquiz", json);
        }

        public Quiz GetQuiz()
        {
            string json = HttpContext.Session.GetString("usersquiz");
            return JsonConvert.DeserializeObject<Quiz>(json,
settings);
        }
```

```
        public void SetAnswers(Dictionary<int, string> input)
        {
            string json = JsonConvert.SerializeObject(input,
settings);
            HttpContext.Session.SetString("usersanswers", json);
        }

        public Dictionary<int, string> GetAnswers()
        {
            string json = HttpContext.Session.
GetString("usersanswers");
            return JsonConvert.DeserializeObject<Dictionary<int,
string>>(json, settings);
        }
#endregion

        public HomeController()
        {
            var optionsBuilder = new DbContextOptionsBuilder<QuizCont
ext>();
            optionsBuilder.UseInMemoryDatabase();
            db = new QuizContext(optionsBuilder.Options);
        }

        // make the method asynchronous to improve scalability
        public async Task<IActionResult> Index()
        {
            var model = await db.Quizzes.ToListAsync();
            ViewData["Title"] = "Home";
            return View(model);
        }

        public IActionResult TakeQuiz(string id)
        {
            Quiz model = db.Quizzes.Where(q => q.QuizID == id).
Include(q => q.Questions).FirstOrDefault();
            if (model == null)
            {
                return HttpNotFound($"A quiz with the ID of {id} was
not found.");
            }
            SetQuiz(model);
            SetAnswers(new Dictionary<int, string>());
            ViewData["Title"] = "Take Quiz";
```

```
                    return View(model);
            }

        public IActionResult Question(int? id)
        {
            if (!id.HasValue)
            {
                return HttpNotFound("You must pass an id of a
question.");
            }
            var quiz = GetQuiz();
            var answers = GetAnswers();
            var model = new ViewModels.Home.QuestionViewModel
            {
                Question = quiz.Questions.Skip(id.Value - 1).Take(1).
FirstOrDefault(),
                Answer = answers.ContainsKey(id.Value - 1) ?
answers[id.Value - 1] : string.Empty,
                Number = id.Value,
                Total = quiz.Questions.Count()
            };
            ViewData["Title"] = $"Question {model.Number} of {model.
Total}";
            return View(model);
        }

        [HttpPost]
        public IActionResult Question(int? id, string submit, string
answer)
        {
            if (!id.HasValue)
            {
                return HttpNotFound("You must pass an id of a
question.");
            }
            var answers = GetAnswers();
            answers[id.Value - 1] = answer;
            SetAnswers(answers);
            if (submit == "Previous")
            {
                id--;
            }
```

```
        else if (submit == "Next")
        {
            id++;
        }
        else if (submit == "Finish")
        {
            return RedirectToAction("Finish");
        }
        else
        {
            return RedirectToAction("Index");
        }
        return RedirectToAction("Question", new { id = id });
    }

    public IActionResult Finish()
    {
        var quiz = GetQuiz();
        var model = new ViewModels.Home.FinishViewModel
        {
            Quiz = quiz,
            Answers = GetAnswers()
        };
        for (int i = 0; i < model.Quiz.Questions.Count; i++)
        {
            if (model.Quiz.Questions.ToList()[i].CorrectAnswer ==
model.Answers[i]) model.CorrectAnswers++;
        }
        ViewData["Title"] = "End of Quiz";
        return View(model);
    }

    public IActionResult Error()
    {
        return View();
    }
}
}
```

# Adding custom views

In the **Views** folder, in the **Home** folder, rename the **About.cshtml** file to **TakeQuiz.cshtml**, and then modify the view as follows:

```
@model Packt.QuizWebApp.Quiz
@{
    ViewBag.Title = $"{Model.Title} Quiz";
}
<div class="jumbotron">
    <h2>@Model.Title Quiz</h2>
    <p>@Model.Description</p>
    <p>This quiz has @Model.Questions.Count questions.</p>
    <p>
        <a class="btn btn-success" href="@Url.Action("Question", new {
id = 1 })">Start &raquo;</a>
    </p>
</div>
```

In the **Views** folder, go in the **Home** folder, rename the **Contact.cshtml** file to **Question.cshtml**, and then modify the view as follows:

```
@model Ch16_QuizWebApp.ViewModels.Home.QuestionViewModel
@{
    ViewBag.Title = "Question " + Model.Number;
}
<div class="jumbotron">
    <h2>Question @Model.Number</h2>
    <p>
        @Model.Question.QuestionText
    </p>
    <form action="@Url.Action("Question", new { id = Model.Number })"
method="post" class="form-inline">
        <div class="row">
            <div class="col-md-5 alert alert-info">
                <input type="radio" class="radio radio-inline"
name="answer" id="ARadio" value="A"
                       @if (Model.Answer == "A") { @:
checked="checked"
                                                     } />
                <label for="ARadio">@Model.Question.AnswerA</label>
            </div>
            <div class="col-md-1"></div>
            <div class="col-md-5 alert alert-info">
                <input type="radio" class="radio" name="answer"
id="BRadio" value="B"
```

```
                                @if (Model.Answer == "B") { @:
checked="checked"
                                                    } />
                <label for="BRadio">@Model.Question.AnswerB</label>
            </div>
        </div>
        <div class="row">
            <div class="col-md-5 alert alert-info">
                <input type="radio" class="radio" name="answer"
id="CRadio" value="C"
                        @if (Model.Answer == "C") { @:
checked="checked"
                                                        } />
                <label for="CRadio">@Model.Question.AnswerC</label>
            </div>
            <div class="col-md-1"></div>
            <div class="col-md-5 alert alert-info">
                <input type="radio" class="radio" name="answer"
id="DRadio" value="D"
                        @if (Model.Answer == "D") { @:
checked="checked"

} />
                <label for="DRadio">@Model.Question.AnswerD</label>
            </div>
        </div>
        <div class="row">
            <div class="col-md-4">
                <input name="submit" type="submit" value="End Quiz"
class="btn btn-warning" />
            </div>
            <div class="col-md-4">
                @if (Model.Number > 1)
                {
                    @:<input name="submit" type="submit"
value="Previous" class="btn btn-default" />
                }
            </div>
            <div class="col-md-4">
                @if (Model.Number == Model.Total)
                {
                    @:<input name="submit" type="submit"
value="Finish" class="btn btn-default" />
                }
                else
```

```
            {
                @:<input name="submit" type="submit" value="Next"
class="btn btn-success" />
            }
        </div>
    </div>
</form>
</div>
```

In the **Views** folder, go in the **Home** folder, copy and paste the **Index.cshtml** file, rename the copy to **Finish.cshtml**, and then modify the view as follows:

```
@model Ch16_QuizWebApp.ViewModels.Home.FinishViewModel
@{
    ViewBag.Title = "Finish";
}
<div class="jumbotron">
    <h2>Finish</h2>
    <p>
        You scored @Model.CorrectAnswers out of @Model.Quiz.Questions.
Count
    </p>
</div>
<div class="row">
    <table class="table">
        <tr>
            <th>Question</th>
            <th>Correct Answer</th>
            <th>Your Answer</th>
        </tr>
        @for (int i = 0; i < Model.Quiz.Questions.Count; i++)
        {
            <tr>
                <td>
                    @Html.DisplayFor(modelItem => Model.Quiz.
Questions.ToList()[i].QuestionText)
                </td>
                <td>
                    @Html.DisplayFor(modelItem => Model.Quiz.
Questions.ToList()[i].CorrectAnswer)
                </td>
```

```
        <td>
            @Html.DisplayFor(modelItem => Model.Answers[i])
        </td>
    </tr>
    }
    </table>
</div>
```

In the **Views** folder, go in the **Home** folder, open the **Index.cshtml** file, and modify the view as follows:

```
@model IEnumerable<Packt.QuizWebApp.Quiz>
<div class="jumbotron">
    <h1>Quiz Web App</h1>
    <p class="lead">Quiz Web App is a web application built using C#
and ASP.NET Core as an example for the Packt Publishing book "C# 6 and
.NET Core 1.0".</p>
    <p><a href="http://packtpub.com/" class="btn btn-primary btn-
lg">Learn more about the C# 6 and .NET Core 1.0 book &raquo;</a></p>
</div>
@{
    var x = 0;
}
<div class="row">
    @foreach (var item in Model)
    {
        x++;
        <div class="col-md-6 col-sm-12">
            <h2>@item.Title</h2>
            <p>@item.Description</p>
            <p>
                <a class="btn btn-default" href="@Url.
Action("TakeQuiz", new { id = item.QuizID })">Take the @item.Title
quiz &raquo;</a>
            </p>
        </div>
        if (x % 2 == 0)
        {
            @:</div><div class="row">
        }
    }
</div>
```

# Running the quiz

Before we can run the quiz, we need to configure it to use the cross-platform Kestrel web server, and host it on .NET Core.

## Configuring the project to use Kestrel and .NET Core

In the **Solution Explorer** window, in the **Ch16_QuizWebApp** project, double-click on **Properties**, click on the **Debug** tab, and set the following options:

- Set the profile to **web** (the Kestrel cross-platform web server)
- Check the box for **Use Specific Runtime** and choose the latest version
- Set the platform to **.NET Core**
- Set the architecture to **x64**, as shown in the following screenshot:

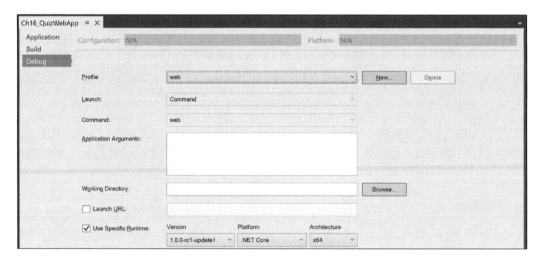

Save your changes, and then in the Visual Studio toolbar, choose the **web** profile:

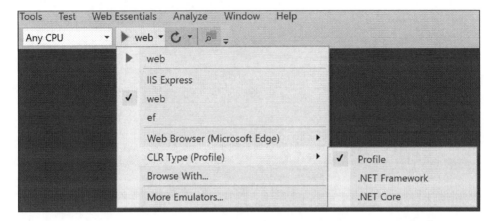

Start the application by pressing *F5*. Note that the Kestrel web server has started and is hosted on the CoreCLR for 64-bit CPUs:

```
C:\Users\markjprice\.dnx\runtimes\dnx-coreclr-win-x64.1.0.0-rc1-update1\...      —      □      ✕
info: Microsoft.Extensions.DependencyInjection.DataProtectionServices[0]
      User profile is available. Using 'C:\Users\markjprice\AppData\Local\ASP.NET\DataProtection-Key
s' as key repository and Windows DPAPI to encrypt keys at rest.
Hosting environment: Development
Now listening on: http://localhost:5000
Application started. Press Ctrl+C to shut down.
```

Start Microsoft Edge and enter the following into the address box:

```
http://localhost:5000/
```

Note that when the browser's width is too small, the list of quizzes on the home page uses a vertical layout instead of two quizzes side by side, as you can see from the following screenshot:

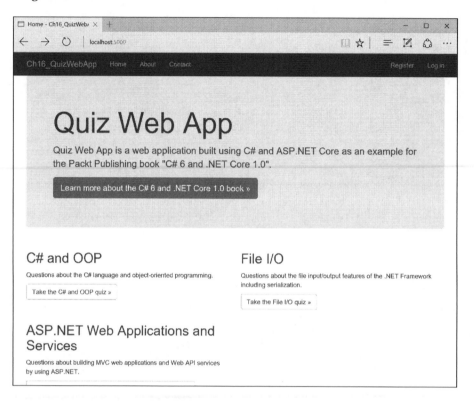

Click on the **Take the C# and OOP quiz** button:

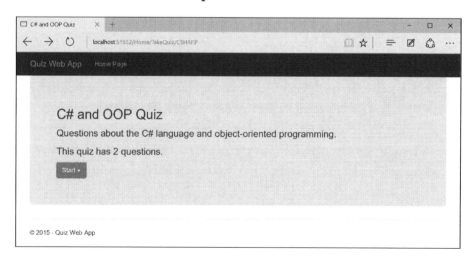

Click on **Start**, answer the first question, and then click on **Next**:

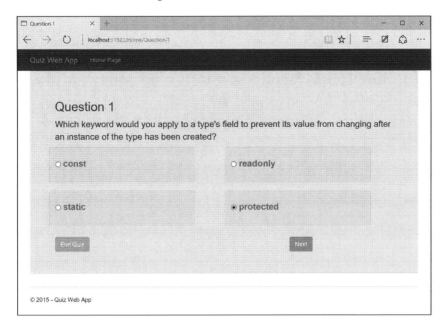

Answer the second question and click on the **Previous** button. Note that it remembers your answer to the first question. Click on **Next**, answer all the questions, and then click on **Finish**:

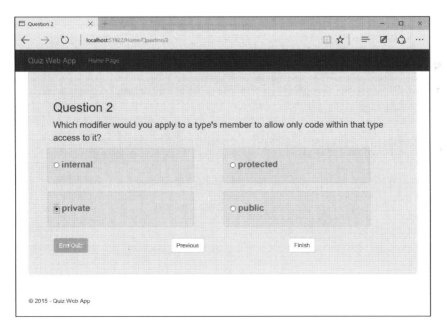

On the **Finish** page, click on **Home Page** in the navigation bar:

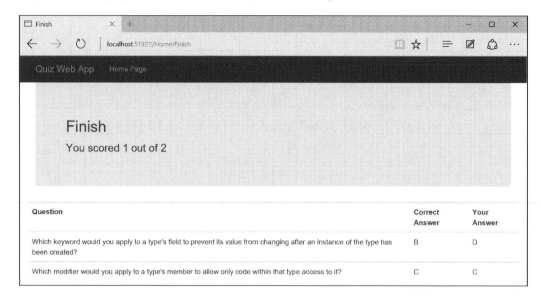

# Hosting ASP.NET Core web apps in Microsoft Azure

First, you need to register an account with Microsoft Azure.

## Register an Azure account

Go to `http://portal.azure.com/` and register an account to get a free trial. You will be able to continue after the end of the free trial because we will only use the free features of Azure.

You can use any Microsoft account, for example, Hotmail, MSN, or Live account. For this book, I registered a new account named `cs6dotnetcore@outlook.com`.

# Create an Azure web app

Go to the Azure portal (`https://portal.azure.com/`), where you will see the Azure dashboard:

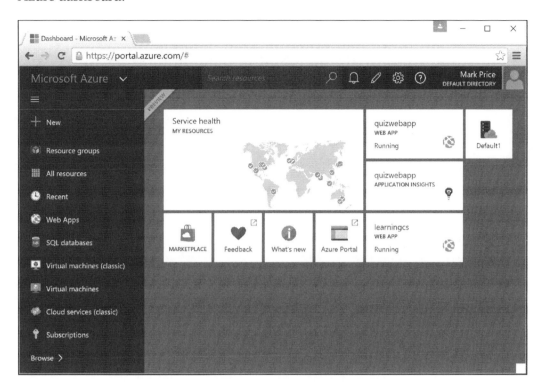

Click on **All resources** and then click on the **+ Add** button:

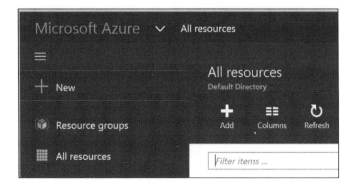

In the **Search Everything** box, enter **web app** and press *Enter*. Click on **Web App** and then click on **Create**:

In the **Web App** blade, enter a globally unique name for your web app:

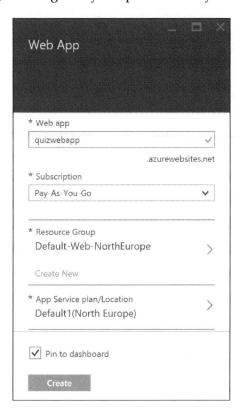

I entered `quizwebapp`, so this name is now taken. No one else will be able to have a Web App with that name. You will need to choose something different.

Leave the other options as their defaults and click on **Create**. You will be taken back to the Azure dashboard where you will see a new tile telling you that your Web App is being deployed. This process normally takes a few minutes. Once it is running, click on it:

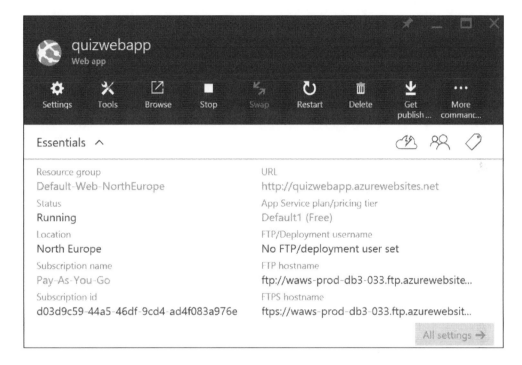

Click on the **URL** to open a browser and show the example web page. You are now ready to deploy any ASP.NET web application project (both ASP.NET 4.6 and ASP.NET Core) to your Web App in Azure.

# Publishing an ASP.NET web application to the Web App

In the **Solution Explorer** window, right-click on the **Ch16_QuizWebApp** project and choose **Publish...**.

Select **Microsoft Azure Web Apps** as the publish target:

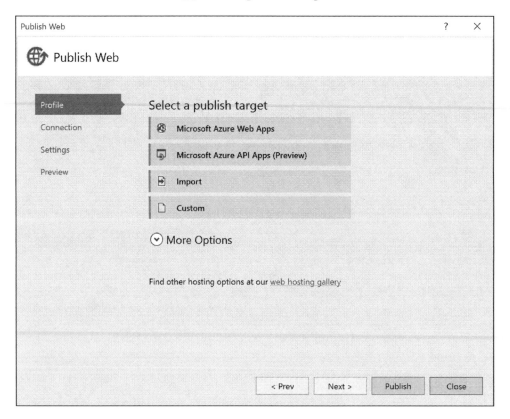

In the **App Service** dialog, choose the account that you previously registered, and choose the web app name that you created earlier:

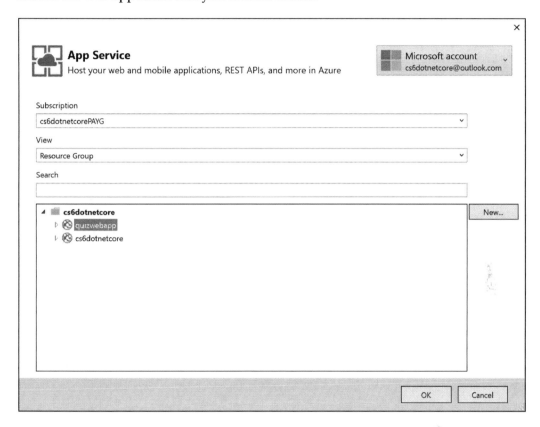

Visual Studio will download a **publishing profile** that you can use to easily deploy the web application to Azure. Click on **Validate Connection** and wait for the green tick mark, and then click on **Publish**:

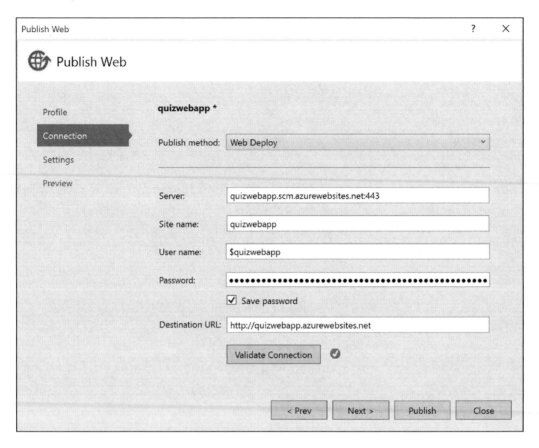

Visual Studio will rebuild and deploy your application, and then start a browser to show that it has succeeded:

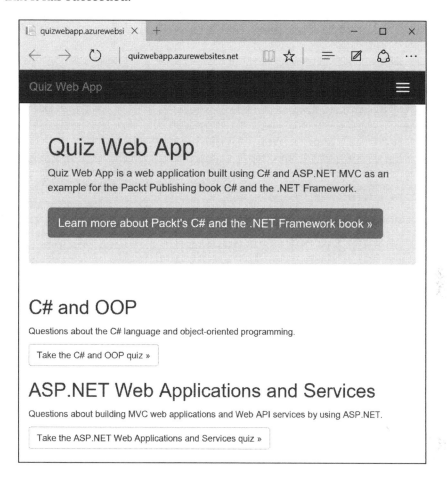

# Practicing and exploring

Test your knowledge and understanding by answering some questions, get some hands-on practice, and explore with deeper research into the topics covered in this chapter.

## Exercise 16.1 – test your knowledge

Answer the following questions:

1. How many web apps can you host in Microsoft Azure for free?
2. Does Microsoft Azure only support Windows as a host operating system?
3. What options does Microsoft Azure offer for data storage?

## Exercise 16.2 – practice by extending the quiz web app

How would you improve this quiz app? Here are some suggestions:

- Use Visual Studio's scaffolding feature to allow an administrator to add, edit, and delete quizzes and questions
- Allow more complex types of questions, for example, multiple correct answers to a question
- Create an Ubuntu or Docker virtual machine in Microsoft Azure and deploy the quiz application to that platform

## Exercise 16.3 – explore topics

Use the following links to read more about the topics covered in this chapter:

- **Installing ASP.NET Core 1.0 on Linux**: https://docs.asp.net/en/latest/getting-started/installing-on-linux.html
- **Microsoft Azure: Cloud and Computing Services**: https://azure.microsoft.com/en-us/

# Summary

In this chapter, we created a quiz app using ASP.NET Core and Entity Framework Core hosted in Microsoft Azure. It could easily be deployed to a Microsoft Windows Nano Server, Microsoft Azure Service Fabric, a Linux virtual machine, or a Docker container, to minimize costs and maximize scalability. It can be deployed to alternative cloud hosts or on-premise servers.

Hopefully this book, and the C# language and .NET features we've covered, will inspire you to think about how you can use C# and .NET to build well-architected and modern applications that run cross-platform on Windows, Mac OS X, Docker, and Linux.

With C# and .NET in your arsenal of tools and technologies, you can conquer the universe of cross-platform development and build any type of application that you need.

# A
# Answers to the Test Your Knowledge Questions

This appendix has the answers to the questions in the *Test Your Knowledge* section at the end of each chapter.

## Chapter 1 – Hello, C#! Welcome, .NET Core!

1. Why can a programmer use different languages to write applications that run on .NET?

   Multiple languages are supported on .NET because each one has a compiler that translates the source code into IL (intermediate language) code. This IL code is then compiled to native CPU instructions at runtime by the CLR.

2. What do you type at the Command Prompt to compile C#?

   ° For .NET Framework, we type `csc sourcecode.cs`

   ° For .NET Core using .NET CLI in a folder with a `project.json` file, we type `dotnet build`

3. What is the Visual Studio 2015 keyboard shortcut to save, compile, and run an application without attaching the debugger?

   *Ctrl + F5*

4. What is the Visual Studio 2015 keyboard shortcut to view the **Error List**?

   *Ctrl + W, E*

5. What does `ildasm.exe` do?

   The IL Disassembler (`ildasm.exe`) tool reveals the manifest, metadata, embedded resources, and IL code inside a compiled .NET assembly.

6. Is the .NET Core better than the .NET Framework?

   It depends on what you need. The .NET Core is a slimmed down, cross-platform version of the more full-featured, mature .NET Framework.

7. How is .NET Native different from .NET Core?

   .NET Native is an ahead-of-time compiler that can produce native code assemblies that have better performance and reduced memory footprint, and it has its .NET assemblies statically linked, which removes its dependency on CoreCLR.

8. What does the .NET Portability Analyzer do?

   It scans an assembly and produces a report that lists any features the assembly uses that are not supported on your chosen target platform. For any missing features, it can make a recommendation to use an alternative.

9. What is the difference between Git and GitHub?

   Git is a source code management platform. GitHub is a popular web service that implements Git.

10. What is the name of the entry point method of a .NET application and how should it be declared?

    ```
    public static void Main()
    ```

    Its name is Main and the preceding code is how it is declared. An optional string array for command-line arguments and a return type of int are recommended, but they are not required.

# Chapter 2 – Speaking C#

What type would you choose for the following "numbers"?

1. A person's telephone number

   `string`

2. A person's height

   `float` or `double`

3. A person's age

   `int` for performance or `byte` (0 to 255) for size

4. A person's salary

   `decimal`

5. A book's ISBN

   `string`

6. A book's price

   `decimal`

7. A book's shipping weight

   `float` or `double`

8. A country's population

   `uint` (0 to about 4 billion)

9. The number of stars in the universe

   `ulong` (0 to about 18 quadrillion) or `System.Numerics.BigInteger` (allows an arbitrarily large integer)

10. The number of employees in each of the small or medium businesses in the UK (up to about 50,000 employees per business)

    Since there are hundreds of thousands of small or medium businesses, we need to take memory size as the determining factor so choose `ushort` because it only takes 2 bytes compared to an `int`, which takes 4 bytes.

# Chapter 3 – Controlling the Flow, Converting Types, and Handling Exceptions

1. What happens when you divide an `int` value by 0?

   A `DivideByZeroException` is thrown when dividing an integer or decimal.

2. What happens when you divide a `double` value by 0?

   The `double` contains a special value of `Infinity`. Instances of floating-point numbers can have special values: `NaN` (not a number), `PositiveInfinity`, and `NegativeInfinity`.

3. What happens when you overflow an `int` value that is set to a value beyond its range?

   It will loop unless you wrap the statement in a `checked` block in which case an `OverflowException` will be thrown.

4. What is the difference between `x = y++;` and `x = ++y;`?

   In `x = y++;`, `y` will be assigned to `x` and then `y` will be incremented, and in `x = ++y;`, `y` will be incremented and then the result will be assigned to `x`.

5. What is the difference between `break`, `continue`, and `return` when used inside a loop statement?

   The `break` statement will end the whole loop and continue executing after the loop, the `continue` statement will end the current iteration of the loop and continue executing at the start of the loop block for the next iteration, and the `return` statement will end the current method call and continue executing after the method call.

6. What are the three parts of a `for` statement and which of them are required?

   The three parts of a `for` statement are the initializer, condition, and incrementer. The condition is required to be an expression that returns `true` or `false`, but the other two are optional.

7. What is the difference between the `=` and `==` operators?

   The `=` operator is the assignment operator for assigning values to variables, and the `==` operator is the equality check operator that returns `true` or `false`.

# Exercise 3.2

What will happen if this code executes?

```
int max = 500;
for (byte i = 0; i < max; i++)
{
    WriteLine(i);
}
```

The code will loop nonstop because the value of `i` can only be between `0` and `255`, so once it gets incremented beyond `255`, it goes back to `0` and therefore will always be less than `max` (`500`).

To prevent it from looping nonstop, you can add a checked statement around the code. This would cause an exception to be thrown after 255, like this:

```
254
```

```
255
```

```
System.OverflowException says Arithmetic operation resulted in an
overflow.
```

# Chapter 4 – Using Common .NET Types

1.  Does every assembly that you create have a reference to the `mscorlib.dll` assembly?

    No. Although by default every assembly will have an automatic reference to the `mscorlib.dll` assembly, there is a compiler flag that can prevent this. For details, visit:

    https://msdn.microsoft.com/en-us/library/fa13yay7.aspx

2.  What is the maximum number of characters that can be stored in a `string` variable?

    The maximum size of a `string` variable is 2 GB or about 1 billion characters because each `char` variable uses 2 bytes due to the internal use of Unicode (UTF-16) encoding for characters.

3.  When and why should you use the `SecureString` type?

    The `string` type leaves text data in memory for too long and it's too visible. The `SecureString` type encrypts the text and ensures that the memory is released immediately. WPF's `PasswordBox` control stores the password as a `SecureString` variable, and when starting a new process, the `Password` parameter must be a `SecureString` variable. For more discussion, visit:

    http://stackoverflow.com/questions/141203/when-would-i-need-a-securestring-in-net

4.  When should you use a `LinkedList<T>` variable?

    Each item in a linked list has a reference to its previous and next siblings as well as the list itself so should be used when items need to be inserted and removed from positions in the list without actually moving the items in memory.

5. When should you use a `SortedDictionary` variable rather than a `SortedList` variable?

   The `SortedList` class uses less memory than `SortedDictionary`, `SortedDictionary` has faster insertion and removal operations for unsorted data. If the list is populated all at once from sorted data, `SortedList` is faster than `SortedDictionary`. For more discussion, visit:

   `http://stackoverflow.com/questions/935621/whats-the-difference-between-sortedlist-and-sorteddictionary`

6. Why should you *not* use the official standard for e-mail addresses to create a regular expression to validate a user's e-mail address?

   The effort is not worth the pain for you or your users. Validating an e-mail address using official specification doesn't check whether that address actually exists or whether the person entering the address is its owner. For more discussion, visit:

   `http://davidcel.is/posts/stop-validating-email-addresses-with-regex/`

   `http://stackoverflow.com/questions/201323/using-a-regular-expression-to-validate-an-email-address`

# Chapter 5 – Using Specialized .NET Types

1. What is the difference between pressing *F5*, *Ctrl + F5*, *Shift + F5*, and *Ctrl + Shift + F5*?

   *F5* saves, compiles, runs, and attaches the debugger, *Ctrl + F5* saves, compiles, and runs the debugger, *Shift + F5* stops the debugger, and *Ctrl + Shift + F5* restarts the debugger.

2. What is the ISO culture code for Welsh?

   `cy-GB`

   For a complete list of culture codes, visit:

   `http://timtrott.co.uk/culture-codes/`

3. What information can you find out about a `Process` variable?

   The `Process` class has many properties including: `ExitCode`, `ExitTime`, `Id`, `MachineName`, `PagedMemorySize64`, `ProcessorAffinity`, `StandardInput`, `StandardOutput`, `StartTime`, `Threads`, `TotalProcessorTime`, and so on. You can find more information about **Process Properties** at `https://msdn.microsoft.com/en-us/library/System.Diagnostics.Process_properties(v=vs.110).aspx`.

4. Can your applications write to the security event log in Windows?

   No. The security event log is for use only by the operating system. You can find more information about the security event log at `https://msdn.microsoft.com/en-us/library/windows/desktop/aa363658(v=vs.85).aspx`.

5. How accurate is the `Stopwatch` class?

   The `Stopwatch` class can be accurate to within a nanosecond (a billionth of a second) but you shouldn't rely on that. You can improve accuracy by setting processor affinity as shown in the article at `http://www.codeproject.com/Articles/61964/Performance-Tests-Precise-Run-Time-Measurements-wi`.

6. What is the difference between localization, globalization, and internationalization?

   Localization is about changing the user interface to a specific language, for example, French; whereas globalization is about writing code so that the language and region are taken into account when formatting numbers and dates and when sorting text. Finally, internationalization is a combination of both.

# Chapter 6 – Building Your Own Types with Object-Oriented Programming

1. What are the four access modifiers and what do they do?

   ° `private`: This modifier makes a member only visible inside the class

   ° `internal`: This modifier makes a member only visible inside the class or within the same assembly

   ° `protected`: This modifier makes a member only visible inside the class or derived classes

   ° `public`: This modifier makes a member visible everywhere

2. What is the difference between the `static`, `const`, and `readonly` keywords?

   ○ `static`: This keyword makes the member shared by all instances and accessed through the type

   ○ `const`: This keyword makes a field a fixed literal value that should never change

   ○ `readonly`: This keyword makes a field that can only be assigned at runtime using a constructor

3. How many parameters can a method have?

   A method with 16383 parameters can be compiled, ran, and called. Any more than that and an unstated exception is thrown at runtime. IL has predefined opcodes to load up to four parameters and a special opcode to load up to 16-bits (65,536) parameters. A best practice is to limit your methods to three or four parameters. You can combine multiple parameters into a new class to encapsulate them into a single parameter. You can find more information on this at `http://stackoverflow.com/questions/12658883/what-is-the-maximum-number-of-parameters-that-a-c-sharp-method-can-be-defined-as`.

4. What does a constructor do?

   A constructor allocates memory and initializes field values.

5. Why do you need to apply the `[Flags]` attribute to an `enum` type when you want to store combined values?

   If you don't apply the `[Flags]` attribute to an `enum` type when you want to store combined values, then a stored `enum` value that is a combination will return as the stored integer value instead of a comma-separated list of text values.

6. What is a delegate?

   A delegate is a type-safe method reference. It can be used to execute any method with a matching signature.

7. What is an event?

   An event is a field that is a delegate having the `event` keyword applied. The keyword ensures that only `+=` and `-=` are used; this safely combines multiple delegates without replacing any existing event handlers.

8. Why is the `partial` keyword useful?

   You can use the `partial` keyword to split the definition of a type over multiple files.

# Chapter 7 – Implementing Interfaces and Inheriting Classes

1.  How is a base class and a derived class related?

    A derived class (or subclass) is a class that inherits from a base class (or superclass).

2.  What is the difference between the `is` and `as` operators?

    The `is` operator returns `true` if an object can be cast to the type. The `as` operator returns a reference if an object can be cast to the type; otherwise, it returns `null`.

3.  Which keyword is used to prevent a class from being derived from, or a method from being overridden?

    `sealed`

    Find more information on the `sealed` keyword at `https://msdn.microsoft.com/en-us/library/88c54tsw.aspx`.

4.  Which keyword is used to prevent a class from being instantiated with the `new` keyword or force a method to be overridden?

    `abstract`

    Find more information on the `abstract` keyword at `https://msdn.microsoft.com/en-us/library/sf985hc5.aspx`.

5.  Which keyword is used to allow a member to be overridden?

    `virtual`

    Find more information on the `virtual` keyword at `https://msdn.microsoft.com/en-us/library/9fkccyh4.aspx`.

6.  What's the deal with polymorphism?

    Polymorphism is a fancy academic OOP concept that rarely has an impact on real-world code.

7. What are the signatures of the constructors that all exceptions should have?

The following are the signatures of the constructors that all exceptions should have:

- ° A constructor with no parameters
- ° A constructor with a `string` parameter usually named `message`
- ° A constructor with a `string` parameter, usually named `message`, and an `Exception` parameter usually named `innerException`

8. What is an extension method and how do you define one?

An extension method is a compiler trick that makes a static method of a static class appear to be one of the members of a type. You define which type you want to extend by prefixing the type with `this`.

# Chapter 8 – Working with Relational Data Using the Entity Framework

1. Which .NET data provider would you use to work with Microsoft Access .MDB database files?

.NET Framework Data Provider for OLE DB.

2. Which .NET data provider would you use to work with Microsoft SQL Server 2012 Express Edition?

.NET Framework Data Provider for SQL Server.

3. What must you do with a `DbConnection` variable before executing a `DbCommand`?

Ensure that its state is open by calling the `Open()` method.

4. When would you use the `CommandBehavior.SequentialAccess` property?

This option provides a way for a `DbDataReader` class to handle rows that contain columns with BLOBs (binary large objects), such as videos and images, by not loading the entire row at once and instead loading one column at a time, allowing skipping of columns, and reading the BLOB data as a stream.

5. ADO.NET instead of Entity Framework?

You would use classic ADO.NET instead of Entity Framework when you need the best performance, when most data access must use stored procedures, and when maintaining legacy code written using classic ADO.NET.

6. When defining a `DbContext` class, what type would you use for the property that represents a table, for example, the `Products` property of a Northwind context?

   `DbSet<T>`, where `T` is the entity type, for example, `Product`.

7. What are the EF conventions for primary keys?

   The property named `ID` or `ClassNameID` is assumed to be the primary key. If the type of that property is any of the following, then the property is also marked as being an `IDENTITY` column: `tinyint`, `smallint`, `int`, `bigint`, `guid`.

8. When would you use an annotation attribute in an entity class?

   You would use an annotation attribute in an entity class when the conventions cannot work out the correct mapping between the classes and tables. For example, if a class name does not match a table name or a property name does not match a column name.

9. Why might you choose fluent API in preference to annotation attributes?

   You might choose fluent API in preference to annotation attributes when the conventions cannot work out the correct mapping between the classes and tables, and you do not want to use annotation attributes because you want to keep your entity classes clean and free from extraneous code.

10. What is the difference between Database-First and Code-First in EF6?

    Database-First creates a design-time file with the EDMX that contains XML files that define the conceptual, storage, and mappings between the two. These XML files must be kept synchronized with future changes to the classes and tables. Code-First does not need a design-time EDMX file. Instead, a combination of conventions, annotation attributes, and fluent API is used to define the conceptual storage and mappings between the two. Code-First is more difficult to learn in the short term but it is more manageable in the long term which is why Entity Framework Core 1.0 drops support for design-time EDMX files.

# Chapter 9 – Querying and Manipulating Data with LINQ

1. What are the two requirements to use LINQ?

   You must import the `System.Linq` namespace to make the LINQ extension methods available and reference a LINQ provider assembly for the type of data that you want to work with.

2. Which LINQ extension method would you use to return a subset of properties from a type?

   The `Select` method allows projection (selection) of properties.

3. Which LINQ extension method would you use to filter results?

   The `Where` method allows filtering by supplying a delegate (or lambda expression) that returns a Boolean to indicate whether the value should be included in the results.

4. List five LINQ extension methods that perform aggregation.

   `Max`, `Min`, `Count`, `Average`, `Sum`, and `Aggregate`.

5. What is the difference between the `Select` and `SelectMany` extension methods?

   `Select` returns exactly what you specify to return. `SelectMany` checks that the items you have selected are themselves `IEnumerable<T>` and then breaks them down into smaller parts. For example, if the type you select is a `string` value (which is `IEnumerable<char>`), `SelectMany` will break each `string` value returned into their individual `char` values.

# Chapter 10 – Working with Files, Streams, and Serialization

1. What is the difference between using the `File` class and the `FileInfo` class?

   The `File` class has static methods so it cannot be instantiated. It is best used for one-off tasks such as copying a file. The `FileInfo` class requires the instantiation of an object that represents a file. It is best used when you need to perform multiple operations on the same file.

2. What is the difference between the `ReadByte` method and the `Read` method of a stream?

   The `ReadByte` method returns a single byte each time it is called and the `Read` method fills a temporary array with bytes up to a specified length. It is generally best to use `Read` to process blocks of bytes at once.

3. When would you use the StringReader, the TextReader, and the StreamReader classes?

   ○ StringReader is used for efficiently reading from a string stored in memory

   ○ TextReader is an abstract class that StringReader and StreamReader both inherit from for their shared functionality

   ○ StreamReader is used for reading strings from a stream that can be any type of text file, including XML and JSON

4. What does the DeflateStream type do?

   DeflateStream implements the same compression algorithm as GZIP but without a cyclical redundancy check, so although it produces smaller compressed files, it cannot perform integrity checks when decompressing.

5. How many bytes per character does the UTF-8 encoding use?

   It depends on the character. Most Western alphabet characters are stored using a single byte. Other characters may need two or more bytes.

6. What is an object graph?

   An object graph is any instance of classes in memory that reference each other, thereby forming a set of related objects. For example, a Customer object may have a property that references a set of Order instances.

7. What is the best serialization format to choose for minimizing space requirements?

   JavaScript Object Notation (JSON).

8. What is the best serialization format to choose for cross-platform compatibility?

   eXtensible Markup Language (XML), although JSON is almost as good these days.

9. Which Microsoft technology uses the DataContractSerializer class by default?

   Windows Communication Foundation (WCF) for creating SOAP services.

10. Is it possible to create your own custom runtime serializers?

    Yes. Create a class that implements the interface System.Runtime.Serialization.IFormatter. For details, visit:

    https://msdn.microsoft.com/en-us/library/system.runtime.serialization.iformatter(v=vs.110).aspx

# Chapter 11 – Protecting Your Data and Applications

1.  Of the encryption algorithms provided by the .NET Framework, which is the best choice for symmetric encryption?

    The AES algorithm is the best choice for symmetric encryption.

2.  Of the encryption algorithms provided by the .NET Framework, which is the best choice for asymmetric encryption?

    The RSA algorithm is the best choice for asymmetric encryption.

3.  For encryption algorithms, is it better to have a larger or smaller block size?

    For encryption algorithms, it is better to have a smaller block size.

# Chapter 12 – Improving Performance and Scalability with Multitasking

1.  By convention, what suffix should be applied to a method that returns a `Task` or a `Task<T>`?

    Async, for example, `OpenAsync` for a method named `Open`.

2.  To use the `await` keyword inside a method, which keyword must be applied to the method declaration?

    The `async` keyword must be applied to the method declaration.

3.  How do you create a child task?

    Call the `Task.Factory.StartNew` method with the `TaskCreationOptions.AttachToParent` option to create a child task.

4.  Why should you avoid the `lock` keyword?

    The `lock` keyword does not allow you to specify a timeout; this can cause deadlocks. Use `Monitor.Enter` with a `TimeSpan` and `Monitor.Exit` instead.

5.  When should you use the `Interlocked` class?

    If you have integers and floats that are shared between multiple threads, you should use the `Interlocked` class.

# Chapter 13 – Building Universal Windows Platform Apps Using XAML

1. Which control would you choose to allow the user to easily choose their date of birth on many different types of device?

   The `DatePicker` control will allow the user to easily choose their date of birth on many different types of device.

2. Which XAML element would you use to adapt the layout of your app to handle different device families?

   The `VisualStateManager` element is used to adapt the layout of your app to handle different device families.

3. How can you set multiple properties on an XAML element as a single group?

   We can set multiple properties on an XAML element as a single group by defining a style with setters.

4. What is the difference between a control template and a data template?

   Control templates are used to define the look and feel of the external parts of a control, such as a button or list box. Data templates are used to define the look and feel of the internal content of a button or the items with a list box.

5. Can XAML bindings be two-way bindings or just one-way bindings?

   XAML bindings can be two-way, one-way, or one-time.

# Chapter 14 – Building Web Applications and Services Using ASP.NET Core

1. What is the difference between a web browser and a web server?

   A web browser makes HTTP requests for resources and a web server sends HTTP responses back containing a mix of HTML, CSS, JavaScript, and other media formats, which the browser then displays to the end user.

2. What is the difference between a URI, a URL, and a URN?

   Uniform Resource Identifier (URI) is the more general term instead of URL or URN. A Uniform Resource Locator (URL) is a type of URI that species a location of a resource. A Uniform Resource Name (URN) is intended to serve as persistent, location-independent identifier.

3.  What are the four most common HTTP methods?

    The GET, POST, PUT, and DELETE are the most common HTTP methods.

4.  What does it mean when a web server responds with status code 302?

    The web server is indicating a temporary redirect. This means that the web server found the resource but it is at a different location. A response header is used to tell the web browser about the new location. Note that status code 301 is similar but represents a permanent redirect.

5.  What are the responsibilities of a route?

    At the minimum, a route must provide the name of a controller and an action. It can also provide additional parameter values defined in segments.

6.  What are the responsibilities of a controller?

    A controller (and one of its actions) must examine the request and decide which model needs to be passed to which view and then return the response to the client.

7.  What are the responsibilities of a model?

    A model represents all the data required for a particular request.

8.  What are the responsibilities of a view?

    A view converts a model into another format, typically HTML, but it could be any media type, for example, JPEG, DOCX, JSON, XML, and so on.

9.  How does ASP.NET distinguish a request for MVC from a request for Web API?

    Multiple entries are added to the route table. By convention, Web API controllers should use attributes to register routes that look for URLs that begin with api/. If a URL doesn't begin with api/ then it should match other routes registered by MVC.

10. What data formats does Web API support by default?

    x-www-formurlencoded, JSON, and XML.

# Chapter 15 – Taking C# Cross-Platform

1. Which platforms are supported by .NET Core and ASP.NET Core?

   Windows, Mac OS X, Docker, and Linux are the platforms supported by .NET Core and ASP.NET Core.

2. What command downloads dependent packages for a project?

   The `dnu restore` or `dotnet restore` commands downloads dependent packages for a project.

3. What file does project directory require in order to restore packages?

   The `project.json` file is required in project directory in order to restore packages.

4. What command will show the currently installed versions of .NET?

   The `dnvm list -detailed` command will show the currently installed versions of .NET.

5. What command will switch to a different version of .NET?

   The `dnvm use [parameters]` command will switch to a different version of .NET.

# Chapter 16 – Building a Quiz

1. How many web apps can you host in Microsoft Azure for free?

   10

2. Does Microsoft Azure only support Windows as a host operating system?

   No. You can create Virtual Machines to host Linux, Docker, and other operating systems.

3. What options does Microsoft Azure offer for data storage?

   The following options are what Microsoft Azure offers for data storage:

   - Azure Storage:  For schema-less entities, blobs, and files
   - Azure Redis for distributed caching and general entity storage
   - Azure DocumentDb for schema-less JSON entities
   - Azure SQL Database for relational data
   - Azure Data Lake for hybrid storage and analysis

# B

# Creating a Virtual Machine for Your Development Environment

This appendix shows you how to set up a virtual machine hosted in Microsoft Azure to use as a development environment.

The most popular, client, non-Microsoft operating system is Apple's Mac OS X, so that's what I will use in these instructions.

You can use any operating system, such as Ubuntu 14.04, that has the ability to make a connection to a virtual machine using Microsoft's Remote Desktop Protocol (RDP).

This chapter covers the following topics:

- Signing up for a Microsoft account
- Creating a Microsoft Azure subscription
- Creating a virtual machine
- Connecting a virtual machine using remote desktop
- Supporting other platforms

## Signing up for a Microsoft account

If you already have a Microsoft account, for example, a Hotmail, MSN, Live, or Passport account, then you can choose to use that. Even if you do, you might choose to create a new account just for experimenting with Microsoft Azure.

You can sign up for a Microsoft account at `https://signup.live.com/`.

# Creating a Microsoft Azure subscription

You can sign in to a Microsoft Azure account at `https://azure.microsoft.com/en-us/account/`, you will see the the Manage your Azure account page as shown in the following screenshot:

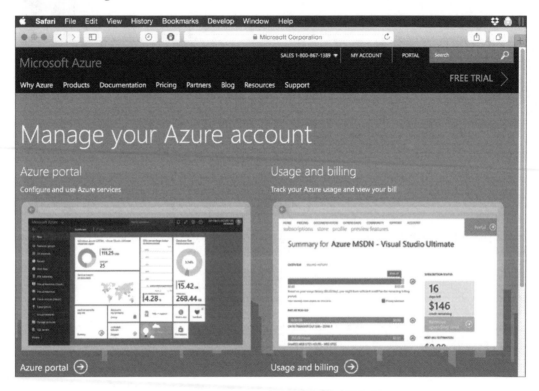

Click on **Usage and billing** and then sign in with your Microsoft account.

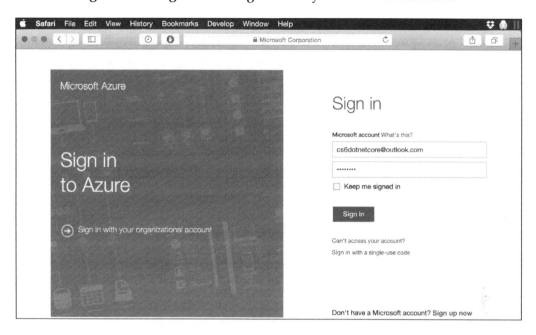

Once you have signed in, you need to create an Azure subscription. Click on **Sign up for a free trial** at the bottom of this page.

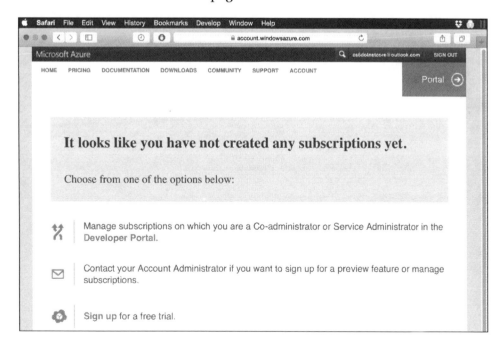

Enter your details in the **About you** section and complete the **Verification by phone** section.

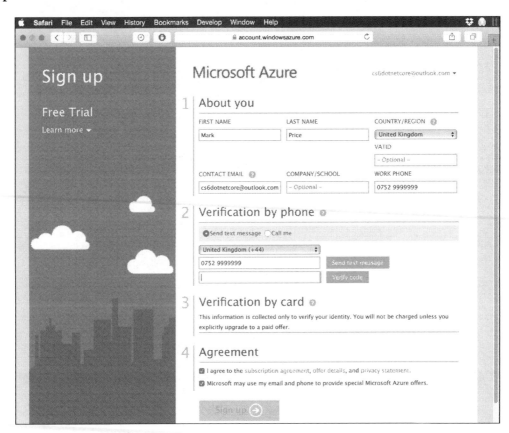

You will also need to verify your identity using your credit or debit card.

You can then click on the **Sign up** button.

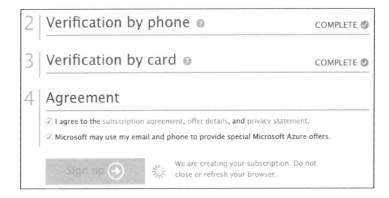

It will take a few minutes to get things ready for you.

Finally, your subscription will be ready for you to use, as shown in the following screenshot:

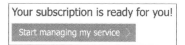

# Managing your Microsoft Azure account

Click on **Start managing my service** or use your browser to navigate to `https://portal.azure.com/`.

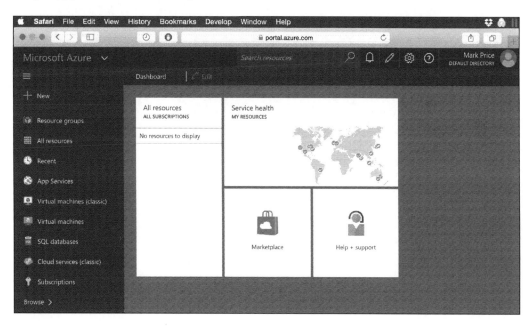

This is the modern Microsoft Azure portal with a customizable dashboard that allows you to manage all your resources that are hosted in Azure. Tiles can be added to the dashboard, resized and rearranged, and can be removed by clicking on the **Edit** button.

# Creating a virtual machine

On the left-hand side of the Azure Portal's **Dashboard,** click on the **+ New** option and then click on **Compute** to see a list of common operating systems that you can choose to hosted on a virtual machine in Azure.

Click inside the **Search the marketplace** box to search for, and select, the **Visual Studio Community 2015 with Update 1 on Microsoft Windows Server 2012 R2** option, as shown in the following screenshot.

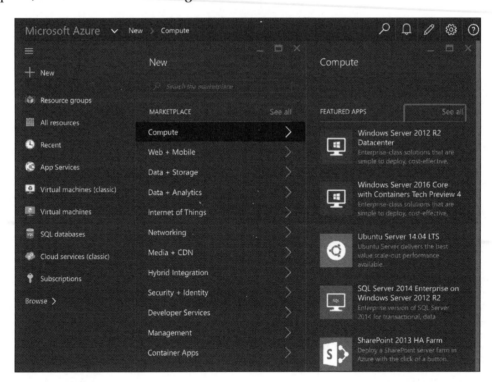

 Microsoft does not offer Windows 10 as an operating system for hosting in Microsoft Azure unless you are an MSDN subscriber. Unfortunately, that means you will not be able to complete the hands-on practical exercises in *Chapter 13, Building Universal Windows Platform Apps Using XAML,* but you will be able to complete all the other chapters.

Ensure that **Resource Manager** is selected as the deployment model and then click on the **Create** button.

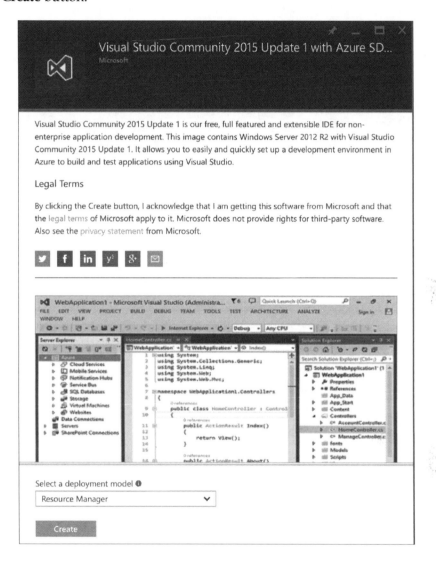

Microsoft Azure has two deployment models—the old **Azure Service Management (ASM)** and the new **Azure Resource Manager (ARM)**. You can read more about the differences at https://azure.microsoft. com/en-gb/documentation/articles/resource-manager-deployment-model/.

Complete the **Basics** blade. You will need to choose the following:

- A machine name (make a note because you will need this later)
- A username and password to log in with (you will need this later)
- A resource group (to manage the virtual machine and other resources)
- A data center location

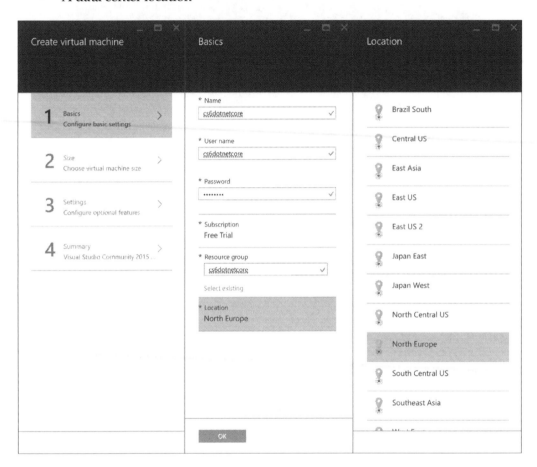

Click on **OK** on the **Basics** blade.

Complete the **Size** blade by choosing the capabilities of your virtual machine and then click on **Select**.

The prices shown are estimates of monthly cost, including license fees for the software such as the Windows operating system. You will only be charged per minute of compute time. An average month has 43,200 minutes, so for a virtual machine and its software costing £117.26 per month, you would be charged about five pence for twenty minutes' use once your free trial has expired.

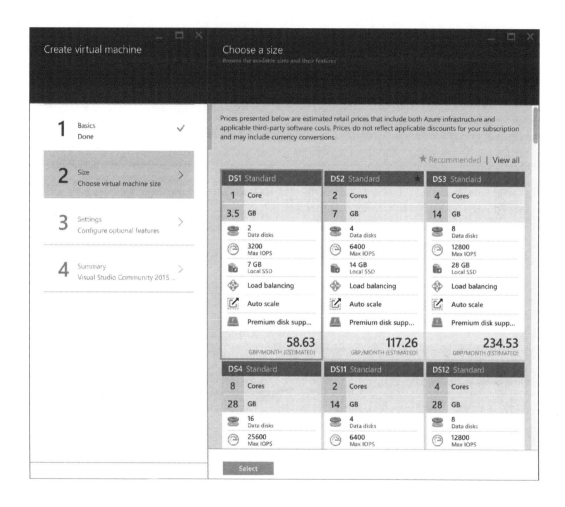

In the **Settings** blade, you can choose storage, network, and monitoring options. The defaults are usually sufficient.

On the **Summary** blade, select **Create** to start deployment.

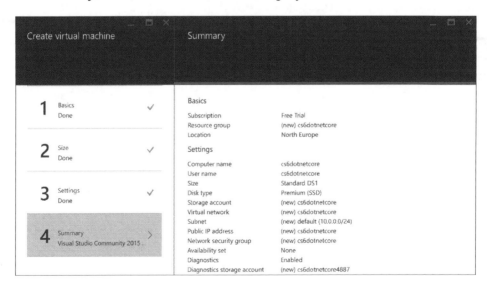

After a few minutes, your **Dashboard** will show the new virtual machine.

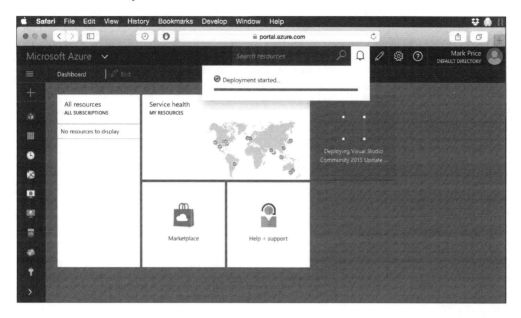

# Connecting to your virtual machine using remote desktop

To connect to a Microsoft Azure virtual machine, you can install Microsoft Remote Desktop from the Apple Mac OS X App Store.

Any remote desktop software that supports Microsoft's RDP will work from any operating system.

On the **Dashboard** window, click on **All resources**, and then click on the virtual machine you created earlier.

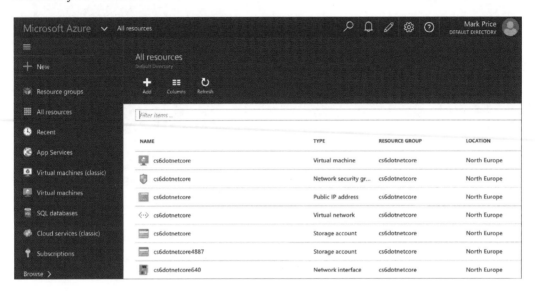

If your virtual machine does not have **Running** as the status, then click on **Start**.

Wait for the virtual machine to start. Click on **Connect** to download an RDP file.

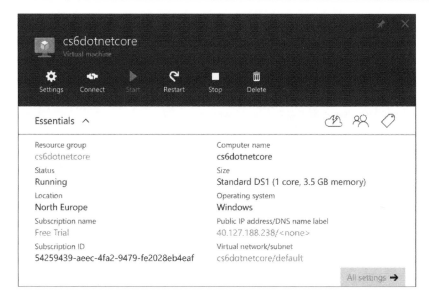

Double-click on the RDP file to connect to the virtual machine.

Click on **Continue** to accept the certificate.

Log in by entering the user name `machinename\username` and the password, which you chose when creating the virtual machine earlier, and then click on **OK**.

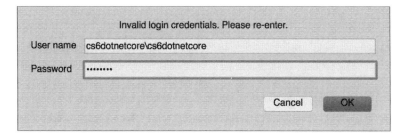

After logging in, you will have a window into the virtual machine. Click on the Windows Start button and start typing `vis` to find and run Visual Studio 2015.

When you are finished, the start screen will display a power button that allows the remote desktop window to disconnect or shut down.

Click on the power button and then click on **Shut down**.

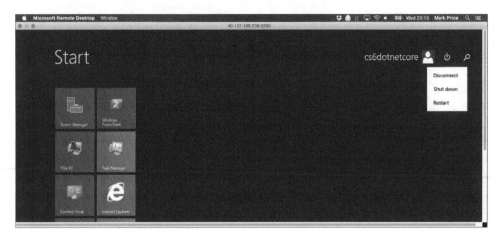

After the remote desktop window closes, return to the Azure portal. Note the orange warning that states that even though the virtual machine is shut down, it is still incurring charges because it is still using some resources.

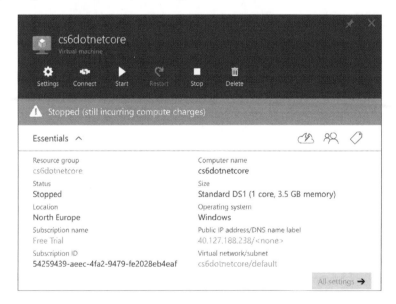

Click on **Stop** and then click on **Yes** to stop the virtual machine fully.

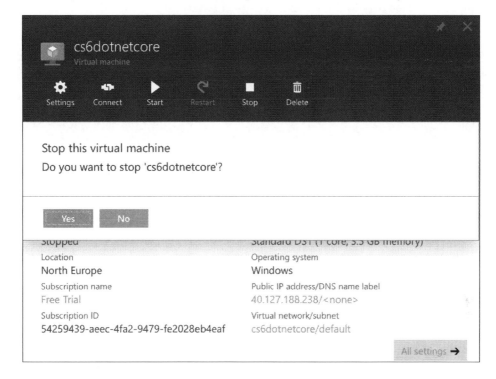

Wait for the virtual machine to stop.

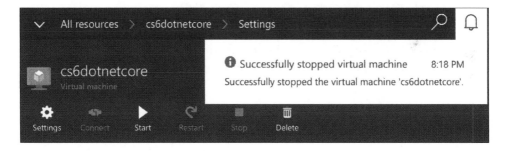

Once the virtual machine is stopped, it will have **Stopped (deallocated)** as the status. This means that you are not being charged for this virtual machine.

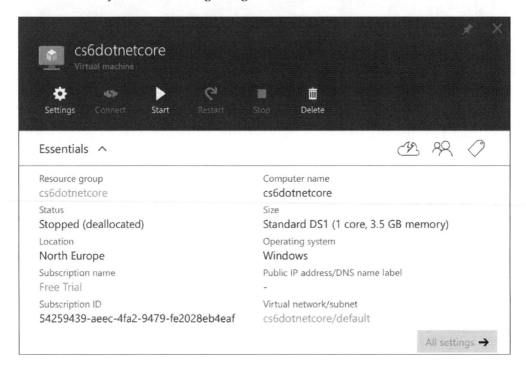

# Supporting other platforms

There are Microsoft RDP clients for multiple operating systems, including iOS for iPad. It's pretty cool being able to run the full version of Visual Studio 2015 on an iPad mini!

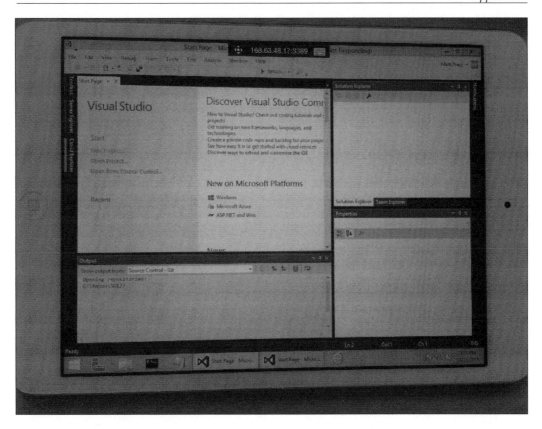

# Summary

In this appendix, you learned how to use remote software on almost any operating system to connect to a virtual machine running Windows Server and Visual Studio 2015 hosted in Microsoft Azure.

# Index

Microsoft Visual Studio 2015
custom installation, selecting  4, 5
default installation, selecting  4
installation, completing  6
installing  3
Microsoft Visual Studio Code
about  2
URL  2
modern ASP.NET Core
versus classic ASP.NET  373
MonoDevelop
about  2
URL  2
Mono project
about  10
reference link  10
Mono, to .NET Core
switching from  416
multiple actions
running, asynchronously  330, 331
multiple threads
resource, accessing from  342-344
using, with parallel LINQ (PLINQ)  274, 275
multiple values
storing, collections used  175
storing, in array  62, 63
mutually exclusive lock
applying, to resource  344

# N

named and optional arguments
    (C# programming guide)
reference link  193
named arguments  181, 183
named method
targeting  263
Namespace Keywords (C# Reference)
reference link  104
namespaces
about  20, 108
browsing  113-115
for collections  122
importing  64, 111, 112
using  107
native  226

nested tasks  335, 336
New Technology LAN Manager
    (NTLM)  323
Northwind sample database  222-225
Northwind.sql file
download link  222
nouns  52
Nullable Types (C# Programming Guide)
reference link  75
numbers
rounding  86
storing  55

# O

Object Browser  113
object graphs
deserializing, with XML  299
serializing  295
serializing, with JSON  300, 301
serializing, with other formats  301, 302
serializing, with runtime
    serializers  302, 304
serializing, with XML  296-299
object-relational mapping (ORM)  232
objects
about  165
comparing, when sorting  196, 197
object type  60
old collections
avoiding  128
OOP  165
operations
atomic, making  346
operators
about  70, 168
arithmetic operators  72
Boolean operators  73
comparison operators  73
methods, simplifying with  188
unary operators  71, 72
optional parameters  181, 183
OrderBy
entities, sorting with  264
output
displaying, to user  63, 64

**overflow**
checking for 94
**overloading 51**
**overriding**
preventing 207

## P

**parallel LINQ (PLINQ)**
about 274
multiple threads, using with 274, 275
**partial**
used, for splitting classes 183
**password-based key derivation function
(PBKDF2) 311**
**paths**
managing 285, 286
**pattern matching**
with regular expressions 120, 121
**patterns & practices group, Microsoft**
about 102
reference link 104
**performance**
monitoring 139-142
**Platform Invoke (P/Invoke)**
about 159
Win32 API, accessing with 161, 162
**platforms**
supporting 504
**POCO (Plain Old CLR Object) 236**
**polymorphism 166, 208**
**processes 329**
**processing strings**
efficiency, measuring of 142-144
**Process type, members**
VirtualMemorySize64 142
WorkingSet64 142
**projection 267**
**project.json file**
reference link, for documentation 418
**projects**
configuring, to use Kestrel 456-460
configuring, to use .NET Core 456-460
creating, .NET Core used 29
editing, Visual Studio Code used 429, 430
scaffolding, Yeoman used 426-429

**properties**
about 168
access, controlling with 184

## Q

**queues 124**
**Queue<T> Class**
reference link 130
**quiz**
running 456
**quiz application, designing**
about 437
functional requirements, deciding 438
platform, selecting 437, 438
separating concerns 438
**quiz solution**
building 438
custom controller actions, adding 447, 448
custom views, adding 452-455
data repository, creating 440, 441
entity models, defining 439, 440
sample quiz questions. adding 443-445
session state, configuring 447
view models, defining 442
web application, creating 441, 442

## R

**Razor 389**
**RC2CryptoServiceProvider 312**
**read-eval-print loop (REPL) 23**
**read-only fields 167**
**read-only properties**
defining 184, 185
**real numbers**
about 55
storing 56
**reference type**
memory, managing with 199
**reflection 52**
**Regex Class**
reference link 130
**Regular Expression Language**
reference link 130

converting, to string 86
counting 52, 53
documenting 211, 213
efficiency, evaluating of 139
extending 215
inferring, of local variable 61
with Async methods 340

# U

unary operators 71, 72
unchecked statement 96
Unicode 291
union 266
unit of code
  creating 152
unit test
  project, creating 152-154
  running 154
Universal Windows Platform. *See* UWP
unmanaged code
  interoperating with 159
unmanaged resources
  about 92
  releasing 201-203
users
  authenticating 321
  authenticating, with Windows 322, 323
  authorizing 321
  authorizing, with Windows 324-326
  input, obtaining from 64
  output, displaying to 63, 64
using statement
  disposal, simplifying with 93
UWP
  about 349, 350
  advantage, taking of unique device
    capabilities 350
  app, creating for 355-357
  app's layout, adapting 350
  portability, analyzing 358

# V

value
  storing, enum keyword used 173-175
value type
  memory, managing with 199

nullable, making 62
**var (C# Reference)**
  reference link 75
**variables**
  declaring 54
  naming 54
**verbs 51**
**view engines 389**
**view model 388**
**virtual machine**
  connecting, remote desktop used 499-503
  creating 494-499
**Visual Studio**
  development settings, selecting 7, 8
  extensions, updating 8, 9
  older versions, using 10
  products, updating 8, 9
  registration link 7
  signing in to 6
**Visual Studio 2015**
  used, for creating .NET Core
    application 33-35
  using, on Windows 10 3
**Visual Studio Code**
  about 410
  installing 412, 413
  reference link, for installation
    instructions 412
  used, for editing projects 429, 430
**Visual Studio Code, for Mac OS X**
  development, managing from
    terminal 413, 414
  download link 412
**Visual Studio Dev Essentials 3**
**Visual Studio Team Services 36**

# W

web application
  ASP.NET web application, publishing
    to 464-467
  project, creating 376-379
**Web Essentials 2015**
  installing 374
**Where extension method**
  entities, filtering with 262, 263
**while statement 81**

Made in the USA
San Bernardino, CA
21 April 2017